My Canadian Journal

Locket presented by Her Majesty to her Godchild
the infant daughter of Their Excellencies
the Earl and Countess of Dufferin

Lady Dufferin

My Canadian Journal
1872 - 1878

EDITED AND ANNOTATED

BY

GLADYS CHANTLER WALKER

Longmans Canada Limited

Longmans Canada Limited
55 Barber Greene Road
Don Mills, Ontario

Set 10/12 Baskerville
Paper: 60 lb. Library Book
Printed in Canada by The Alger Press Limited

To My Canadian Friends
This Little Book
Is Affectionately Inscribed

HARIOT DUFFERIN AND AVA

Contents

ILLUSTRATIONS

Introduction

Lord Dufferin lived most of his life with two women who were authors. His association with the first, his mother, lasted for forty years; that with the second, his wife, was of the same duration. The two periods overlapped by only five years, from the time of his marriage to Hariot Hamilton, in 1862, to the death of his mother, Helen Selina Sheridan Blackwood, in 1867.

Through long years of companionship with his mother, Frederick Temple Blackwood, Lord Dufferin, became aware of the great cloud of literary glory that was his inheritance. It had been accumulating among her Irish ancestors since the days when one of them, the Reverend Denis Sheridan, translated the Bible into the Irish language, shortly after the King James Version appeared in English. However, his work was not printed until some forty years later, when another native of Ireland, Robert Boyle the chemist, financed and guided Sheridan's labour of love through the press.

A grandson of Denis, Dr. Thomas Sheridan, a Dublin schoolmaster, not only translated Latin texts, but served as an underpaid literary assistant to Dean Swift. His son, also Thomas, published Swift's works. He was married to a playwright, Frances Chamberlaine, with whom he was associated in the management of the Royal Dublin Theatre. Going to London, they both played at Covent Garden and at Drury Lane. Sheridan became acquainted with Garrick and Dr. Samuel Johnson, and, like the latter, published an English dictionary. Garrick staged some of Mrs. Sheridan's plays in the seventeen-sixties.

Richard Brinsley Sheridan was a son of this talented couple. After six years' formal education at Harrow, young Richard wrote and published some poetry and translations. However, his serious work began in 1773, after he married Elizabeth Linley, a gifted singer. Two years later he had his first play, *The Rivals*, staged at Covent Garden. Garrick was then at the height of his career, and was not to be outdrawn at the box office. He revived a play, *The Discovery*, which had been written by Sheridan's mother, then deceased, and staged it simultaneously at Drury Lane, to the disadvantage of *The Rivals* at Covent Garden, round the corner. In 1777 another of Sheridan's classic comedies, *The School for Scandal*, packed Drury Lane.

Sheridan's talented wife died of tuberculosis in 1792, as did their son Tom twenty-five years later. He, like his grandfather, after whom he was named, married an author, Caroline Callander. When Tom Sheridan, a government official at the Cape of Good Hope, died, his wife was left with seven children and her ability to provide for their needs as a working novelist. In 1825 the eldest daughter, Helen Selina, became the wife of Commander Price Blackwood of Clandeboye, County Down, in Ireland. Their son, the future Governor-General of Canada, was born the following year. He remembered his mother's twenty-first birthday, and for nearly forty years she was his companion and confidant, since before inheriting the family title his father spent much time at sea. In 1841 the father died suddenly while crossing from England to his estate in Ireland, leaving a young widow and his son, then fifteen.

Helen Selina Blackwood, Lady Dufferin, then took up her pen, following the example of her own mother when left a widow; but this time it was not a matter of necessity. With her it was a natural urge and a family tradition. Her poems were written with such transparent meaning that the reader's mind was left free to enjoy the music of the lines, while imbibing the sentiment. Her *Lament of the Irish Emigrant*, included in the Ontario Fourth Reader in 1885, is there described as "one of the most tenderly beautiful idylls in the language." The emigrant is saying farewell to familiar scenes and to the grave of his wife and infant daughter.

> I'm sitting on the stile, Mary,
>   Where we sat side by side
> On a bright May morning, long ago,
>   When first you were my bride.
>
> . . . .
>
> I'm bidding you a long farewell,
>   My Mary, kind and true!
> But I'll not forget you, darling,
>   In the land I'm going to;
> They say there's bread and work for all,
>   And the sun shines always there, –
> But I'll not forget old Ireland,
>   Were it fifty times as fair!

This sympathy for Ireland's people was handed down to her son, who made a lasting name for himself by his efforts to relieve and comfort the famine-striken Irish during the tragic eighteen-forties.

The year of his marriage, 1862, brought an honour to Lord Dufferin that placed him as a worthy descendant of the great Richard Brinsley Sheridan. On the death of Albert, the Prince Consort, Queen Victoria's husband, he was asked to deliver in the House of Lords the address expressing the nation's sorrow and sympathy.

Dufferin's administration in Canada has frequently been compared with that of Lord Elgin. Both were during difficult periods, but the problems were not the same. The discontent with which the Dufferins were confronted was definitely one of separate provinces against the central Government. The Governor-General, in his own way, was a powerful force in resolving many of these differences and promoting harmony, where formerly hostility had existed. In these accomplishments his wife was a potent factor, and the day-to-day record which she unfolds in *My Canadian Journal* is most revealing. Lord Dufferin could have been describing their conjoined efforts when he once said, "Two charming people in the midst of a numerous company can spread good-will throughout the whole assembly. A factor in this charm is the non-critical attitude." These sentiments sound like the precepts of Helen Selina Sheridan – precepts not neglected by her son while facing the problems which responsibility had cast upon his shoulders.

Toronto   *Frank Norman Walker*
June 5, 1969

Foreword

It is now seventy-eight years since *My Canadian Journal* first appeared in book form. In it Lady Dufferin has recorded in a charming and witty manner affairs of family interest, with many shrewd and perceptive comments about people whom they met while Lord Dufferin was Governor-General of Canada from 1872 to 1878.

In this present edition only a few items that seemed repetitive have been omitted. Inserted are short notes intended to bring the public activities and personalities of that day into sharper focus. Also included are excerpts from some of Lord Dufferin's eloquent and timely speeches, which modesty forbade his wife's recording.

This *Journal*, written first as letters to her mother, was begun when she was twenty-nine years of age. It reveals a warm-hearted, sympathetic, vivacious woman, ready to engage in any new and unusual activity which life in Canada involved. Figure-skating, tobogganing, curling, fishing, picnics, as well as the most exacting social duties, all receive her attention. She was charitable, kindly, interested in both old and young, whether wealthy aristocrats or the humbler folk she and Lord Dufferin met on their many travels. Stage plays for children became a feature at Rideau Hall, and her enthusiasm inspired the youthful actors. For some of these plays she, or Lord Dufferin, wrote the scripts; at times she arranged the music. As we read the *Journal* we recognize the names of many men and women who played important parts in making Canadian history. To all she gave a gracious welcome and a kindly thought.

One source of inspiration granted this woman, whose grace, ingenuity and gentleness won all Canadian hearts, was a childhood spent in beautiful and historic surroundings. Hariot Rowan Hamilton's birthplace and girlhood home was the Norman castle of Killyleagh, founded about 1177. Still one of the finest inhabited castles in the

British Isles, it had been acquired by the Hamilton family in the reign of James I. It has the qualities of a dream castle. The chivalry and romance of the Crusades lurk within its walls, turrets and courtyard. There trumpets have summoned knights to tournaments, pageants and feasts.

Hariot's father, Archibald Rowan Hamilton, was a close friend and relative of Lord Dufferin. Both were descended from James Hamilton, Viscount Clandeboye, whose death came in 1643. When Hariot was seventeen her father died at the age of forty-two, leaving four sons and three daughters, the youngest only two weeks old. To Killyleagh came Lord Dufferin to advise and assist her mother in the management of the estate. The shy, reserved, beautiful girl won the heart of the thirty-five-year-old administrator and orator. Two years later they were married and, dressed in their wedding garments, drove north to Clandeboye, greeted all along the way by friends, neighbours and tenants. As they neared the end of their twelve-mile journey children strewed flowers before them and strong, capable hands unhitched the horses and pulled the carriage with ropes.

During his occupancy of Clandeboye Lord Dufferin made many changes. Trees were swept away and hillsides rounded, a new lake reflected the spacious home, and a two-mile avenue cut through the trees revealed views down to the pounding surf of the Irish Sea. Acutely conscious of the sufferings endured by his countrymen during the distressing years of the Irish famine, Lord Dufferin had this work done to provide assistance for his starving tenants. As well, on a high hill Helen's Tower was built. This tribute to his mother has some of her poems inscribed on oak panels in its walls.

In this comfortable home, Clandeboye, during the next ten years were born five children. Two more were to join the family circle while they lived at Rideau Hall in Ottawa. In 1872 Queen Victoria appointed Lord Dufferin Governor-General of Canada. At a farewell dinner tendered the Dufferins in Belfast on June 12, 1872, were eight hundred guests, many of them tenants, gathered with friends and officials from County Down. Speaking of Canada, and reflecting his lofty approach to the task he had assumed, Lord Dufferin said:

Ladies and gentlemen, it may be doubted whether the inhabitants of the Dominion themselves are as yet fully awake to the magnificent destiny in store for them – [hear, hear] – or have altogether realized the promise of their young and virile nationality. Like a virgin goddess in a primaeval world, Canada still walks in unconscious beauty

Preface

This Journal was sent as weekly letters to my mother, and the first pages were written nearly twenty years ago. Places I mention as villages have become towns; Ottawa has quite out-grown my memories of it; and the contemplated improvements, designed to keep Quebec the most beautiful city in the world, have been accomplished. My Journal, therefore, is a record of the past. In it I find the names of many who have passed away, some leaving never-to-be-filled blanks in their own homes, others mourned by a whole nation.

The Prime Ministers, who, with their wives, were constantly associated with all we did, are only occasionally mentioned, though the warm affection we felt for Sir John and Lady Macdonald, and for Mr. and Mrs. Mackenzie, are amongst the pleasantest recollections of our Canadian life.

I have been sorry to pass lightly over the cordiality and friendliness invariably shown us whenever we crossed our borders into the United States. For whether we were travelling officially through Chicago or Detroit, or went as ordinary visitors to New York or Boston, we were always received with a kindness and hospitality which we can never forget.

I must also say one word as to the silence on all political matters maintained in this Journal. I have not attempted to record in it any part of the business of the Governor-General; and it is only as they affected our movements, or our social arrangements, that I have, even distantly, alluded to public events, and then, I fear, in a somewhat light and irresponsible spirit.

The Governor-General and his wife belong to no party; and we met with such universal kindness from all, that I never wanted to remember that people differed from each other in their political views, and was only too glad to leave politics to those whom they necessarily concerned.

Hariot Dufferin and Ava

Clandeboye: August 18, 1891

CHAPTER 1

Arrival in Canada
JUNE - AUGUST 1872

S.S 'PRUSSIAN': FRIDAY, JUNE 14TH, 1872. – Ugh! Ugh! horrid! Very rough; everybody ill except the wretched baby, Basil, who is perfectly well, but can get no one to dress him, and is handed about, unwashed, to engineers, waiters, to anyone who can stand.

MONDAY, 17TH. – The ship rolling from side to side till one's back aches. Such a noise of splashing and dashing and falling about, and such fears lest my infants should follow the example of my tooth-brush, and come flying across the room! To add to my fears, two steerage passengers came to D. in the night, to inquire whether he thought there was any danger, and if the captain might not be asked to put into port until it became calmer. In the morning these men were found sleeping with life-belts on.

WEDNESDAY, 19TH. – We are much better now, and quite enjoy our meals, which D. and I have in a cabin by ourselves.

We are also able to look about, and find that there are 107 'street Arabs' on board, brought out by a saint of a woman, who, although very sick and miserable herself, sings to them, reads out loud, goes down into the steerage, sees them to bed, and performs many other trying offices in the most unselfish manner. Miss Macpherson pays her own passage and expenses. Each child costs 10£ to bring out, and will eventually be adopted into a Canadian family, where it will have a happy home. This seems to be an excellent charity.

SUNDAY, 23RD. – A beautiful day – a hot sun and a perfectly calm sea. Our parasols and shady hats have come out for the first time, and Hermie and Basil are being made very much of by the convalescent passengers. Preparations are making for our arrival at Quebec; and, as it has been discovered that there is no Canadian flag on board, my

1

maid, Mrs. Dent, is busily engaged in trying to manufacture one. No-body is quite sure what it is, but all suppose that there must be a beaver and a maple-leaf in it. I sincerely hope that no great herald will be waiting to receive us.

We have attended a meeting in the steerage, where some of the Canadian passengers talked to the emigrants about the country they are going to. D. also spoke, and told them that in Canada they need never complain, as he had heard one of them do, 'that he had too many children,' for that there the more they had the better. An en-thusiastic young man on hearing this slapped D. on the back and said, 'That is just what I have been telling Emily.'

QUEBEC: TUESDAY, 25TH. – A lovely morning. We anchored early, but did not land till ten, when the Ministers, Lieutenant-Governor, and several other officials, came on board, and with them we went ashore. A salute was fired from the citadel as D. stepped on land, and we walked through lines of troops to a carriage-and-four, in which we drove to Spencer Wood, the Lieutenant-Governor's residence. We passed through Quebec, up a very steep hill. The road was rough, and it was extremely hot and dusty. I could not see the view as we were driving away from the river, and also, I was much occupied in looking at the people who filled the streets; but when we got to Spen-cer Wood we were charmed with it, and it looks right down upon the St. Lawrence.

At three o'clock D. was sworn in as Governor-General of Canada, and received some addresses of welcome, – but, as I remained quiet in my country retreat, I can tell you nothing of the ceremony. Our host is Sir Narcisse Belleau; his wife is a nice quiet little French-woman, and he is pleasant and kind. There was a dinner in the evening, – but I don't feel that I have seen enough of any of the guests to tell you about them to-day, except that the Prime Minister, Sir John Mac-donald, is the image of Dizzy.

By *Dizzy* Lady Dufferin meant of course Benjamin Disraeli, the first Earl of Beaconsfield, 1804-1881. He became a Member of Parliament in 1837, rose to be Chancellor of the Exchequer, and for a few months in 1868 was Prime Minister. He again occupied that high position from 1874 to 1880.

Spencer Wood was beautifully located on part of an estate acquired by Louis d'Ailleboust de Coulonge, who from 1648 to 1651 was the

third Governor of New France. In 1657 he gave it the name of
Castellany of Coulonge.

After his death, three years later, the property was acquired by the
Quebec Seminary, which kept it intact until 1766. Then financial difficulties forced the seminary to dispose of some of its holdings, and in
1780 Brigadier-General H. W. Powell purchased the part south of the
Saint Louis Road, and changed the name to Powell Place. Here Sir
James Craig spent several summers, and the garden parties he gave
were fabulously extravagant.

In 1815, Hon. H. M. Perceval gave the property the name of
Spencer Wood, in honour of his uncle, Spencer Perceval, a former
Prime Minister of England, who had been assassinated in the lobby
of the House of Commons on May 11, 1812.

In the eighteen-thirties, a new owner, Henry Atkinson, a merchant
of Quebec, further beautified the grounds and gardens. In 1852, the
Province of Canada purchased Spencer Wood to use as the official
residence of the Governor-General. The house was destroyed by fire in
1860, but under Lord Monck's supervision a new and larger residence
was built.

After Confederation, in 1867, Spencer Wood was given to the Province
of Quebec, as a home for its Lieutenant-Governor. In 1950, paying
tribute to one of the founders of Canada, the Legislative Assembly of
Quebec gave it back its first name, Coulonge. It became known as
Le Bois de Coulonge. The disastrous fire on the night of February 21,
1966, which destroyed this beautiful and historic building, unfortunately
took the life of the Honourable Paul Comtois, Lieutenant-Governor of
Quebec.

Narcisse (later Sir Narcisse) Fortunat Belleau, 1808-1894, was called
to the bar of Lower Canada in 1832, and made a Q.C. in 1854. He was
appointed to the Legislative Council of Canada in 1852 and five years
later became Speaker of that body. At a special levee during the visit
of the Prince of Wales to Canada in 1860, he was knighted by the
Prince with all the traditional pomp and ceremony. When Sir Etienne
Taché, who had been head of the coalition government formed to
bring in Confederation, retired in 1865, Belleau became Prime Minister
of Canada (the united provinces of Canada East and Canada West).
After Confederation had been consummated, Sir Narcisse was appointed
the first Lieutenant-Governor of Quebec.

WEDNESDAY, 26TH. – The papers give a most amusing description of D.,

stating his apparent weight and height. I am very flatteringly described, though the ignorant male writer speaks slightingly of my dress
as being a 'plain blue silk,' whereas it was in reality excessively smart,
and had caused me infinite trouble and anxiety! However, I had the
satisfaction of hearing from Lady Harriet Fletcher that the ladies knew
better, and had appreciated it.

Lady Harriet and I had a drive about the old town, and I was quite
delighted with it. The views are perfectly lovely, and it would be such
a charming place to live in, – if only we had a house here!

In the afternoon we started for Ottawa in a magnificent river-
steamer with four storeys and streets of cabins, and a grand *table
d'hôte* on board. We sat on deck and enjoyed ourselves immensely as
we went up the St. Lawrence. I cannot tell you what a lovely voyage
this was! – so lovely that I cannot believe we did it of necessity, and
not for pleasure only.

THURSDAY, 27TH. – We arrived at Ottawa, the first view of which is
magnificent; but once landed there was no time to look at anything!
There were nine addresses to be listened to, and after that we drove
off to our new home!

We have been so very enthusiastic about everything hitherto that
the first sight of Rideau Hall did lower our spirits just a little! The
road to it is rough and ugly, the house appears to me to be at the
land's end, and there is no view whatever from it, though it is near
the river – and we have come through hundreds of miles of splendid
scenery to get to it! Then I have never lived in a Government House
before, and the inevitable bare tables and ornamentless rooms have
a depressing effect: for the first time I realise that I have left my own
home for many years, – and this is its substitute!

One of the most competent contractors in charge of stonemasonry
during the building of the Rideau Canal was Thomas McKay, who had
emigrated from Scotland in 1817. With some of his profits he bought
a large tract of land on the eastern outskirts of where Ottawa now
stands. In this district of New Edinburgh he built in 1838 a magnificent
stone house, which he named Rideau Hall. Here he lived with his wife
and some of their sixteen children, and here gracious hospitality was
dispensed. He died in 1855.

Bytown was incorporated as the City of Ottawa in 1854, and three
years later Queen Victoria selected it as the capital of Canada. This
choice was finally ratified by the Canadian Parliament in 1859;

construction then began on the new Parliament Buildings. The corner-stone was laid in 1860 by Edward, Prince of Wales. Despite the unfinished state of the buildings, the government began moving from Quebec in 1865.

In that same year Rideau Hall was leased as a residence for Lord Monck. It was later purchased by the Government and became the official residence of Canada's Governor-General. The original structure still remains, but there have been many additions made since.

When Lord Monck returned home, Lord and Lady Lisgar took up residence there. The third Governor-General to occupy Rideau Hall was Lord Dufferin.

FRIDAY, 28TH. – Please forget the above growl. The morning has brought more cheerful reflections. We are not intended to live here at midsummer, and I dare say that in winter this place looks lovely! Our house is, they say, very warm and comfortable, and the Houses of Parliament – which, after all, I do see from my windows – are very beautiful. And I can cover up the tables and supply the homey look which at present is wanting – so why did I grumble?

We have driven in state through the town, and have visited the Government buildings. I was delighted with the Senate, and with the Library – a large, circular room. When the House is sitting I may come and listen to debates, but the Governor-General may not!

The weather is extremely hot, and we are not going to remain here. D. goes to-morrow to inspect militia at Prescott, and I meet him there two days later.

MONDAY, JULY 1ST. – We went for a row on the river in the evening, which was delicious. It was very pretty; and we had a breath of fresh air, and got out of a perspiration for the first time for a week!

We have been busy making a number of household arrangements. I have chosen my nurseries; and it has been decided to add a storey to the little house in the garden in which the Fletchers will live, – for they have a number of children too. The non-arrival of all our heavy luggage has been an anxiety; so far our Viceregal establishment pos-sesses about six plates and as many cracked tea-cups; and our own supply of china, plate, and linen seems to be trying to see the country, and to travel for pleasure, instead of coming and settling down here as it should.

Perhaps you may wonder where my children are all this time. The three elder ones are still in Europe, trying to learn a little French, and Hermione and Basil, who came out with us, are now at Rivière du Loup, where we have taken a house for the summer. There, also, are the Fletcher children. Colonel and Lady Harriet Fletcher came out to Canada the mail before we did, and made all arrangements for us and for themselves.

We have two very nice A.D.C.s at present. One of them was with Lord Lisgar, and has kindly volunteered to stay and help us for a time. The other is Mr. Coulson, who is regularly appointed, and who will remain even after Fred comes out. Please tell the latter that I find an A.D.C. is a charming institution. These two ask me 'if I will drive,' 'or walk,' 'or boat,' or 'if I want anything from the town'; and if I turn my head, they find out what I am looking for, and get it for me. So Fred need not hope to get off any of his duties through my ignorance of them!

> It had been arranged that her brother Fred, Lieutenant (later Lieutenant-Colonel) Frederick Rowan Hamilton, who had been appointed an aide-de-camp, should come out later. He arrived in Canada in October, 1872, bringing with him the Dufferins' three eldest children: Archie, aged nine, Helen (Nelly), aged seven, and Terence, who was six years old.

> Colonel Fletcher, of the Scots Fusilier Guards, was Lord Dufferin's Military Secretary. His wife, Lady Harriet, was a daughter of the Earl of Romney.

D. is very happy, and is much taken with the country and the people; and all here seem pleased with him. I think I am getting on pretty well too, – though I say it that should be silent in the matter; and the papers, who talk about us a good deal, lay great stress on my not being affected – a negative virtue which I may mention without appearing too conceited!

My attentive A.D.C.s have taken me to see the Chaudière Fall. It is close to Ottawa, and very beautiful. There is a mass of water which appears to fall in three different directions into the same pool, and a great smoke of foam rises from the splash; it looks just like a big cauldron. Close to it is a saw-mill. The trunks of forest-trees are carried by the stream to the door of the mill, where they are caught by chains and slowly dragged into the teeth of a bundle of saws. After passing through these, the trees fall in planks, which are quickly taken up by another machine to have their sides neatly trimmed. As they pass a man marks them with a pencil according to their quality.

After this we 'ran the slide,' which was very exciting. The 'slide' is a long incline of water, divided into a series of small waterfalls, and is the artificial road by which the timber from the higher levels is brought down into the St. Lawrence. The wood is made up into rafts, and you sit upon these while they slip down the incline. It looks rather alarming to see one of these great monsters go headlong into the water at the foot of each fall; but, although I got on board with my heart in my mouth, I liked it extremely, and when I found myself safe on the calm level of the Ottawa, I would gladly have recommenced the journey had it been possible: but when one has slid down this steep hill of water to the river, one is miles away from the starting-point, and has to go home another way. The rafts and the quantities of wood lying about in all directions are the most curious sights here, but I see no really fine timber growing in this neighborhood.

WEDNESDAY, 3RD. – I left Ottawa early, and met D. at Prescott. He had been inspecting volunteer camps at Kingston and Prescott, and is to see another at Laprairie to-morrow.

We shot the rapids. The rapids are places where there is a tremendous stream rushing over a rocky descent. When the steamer comes to them the engine is stopped, and the current carries the vessel over the broken water at a great rate. If the pilot were to make a mistake, or lose command of the ship, she would be wrecked. The rapids look like a stormy sea, but you do not go up and down in them, and rather feel as though the vessel were being buffeted about, and as if it were striking some hard substance. The worst rapid is called the 'Lachine,' and that does look rather alarming. The rapids are all down hill, and going at such a great pace the pilot appears to be steering straight upon some fearful rock, peeping above water, when just as you expect the crash, the stream takes the vessel and carries her clear of the danger. The pilot on this occasion was 'Old Baptiste,' who took us down a channel he had himself first found in 1842.

We were met at Montreal by the Mayor [Charles Joseph Coursol] and a guard of honour.

QUEBEC: FRIDAY, 5TH. – I saw a little of Montreal yesterday, but not enough to warrant a description. We went to a little country place, where we had strawberries and cream under the trees, and when I returned to the hotel I received visitors. I find Canadian society very easy to get on with: the people talk, and they are very simple and natural, and willing to be pleased, so that receiving seventy or eighty total strangers is made pleasant instead of an arduous task, – as it might be.

D. was occupied all day inspecting a camp, and in receiving addresses.

We dined early, and went on board the steamer for Quebec. There were 800 passengers, most of them lying about on the floors; but we had comfortable cabins, and slept well all night. The only new things we saw on this journey were the fire-flies; they were so numerous on the wooded banks of the river that their lights looked like those of a distant town.

SATURDAY, 6TH. – The Governor-General has some of the privileges of the old kings of France, and one of them is that he has the right to enter the cloistered convents. In his train, therefore, we have been to the Ursulines and to the Hotel-Dieu. The Vicar-General went with us, and at each convent, after inspecting the ordinary arrangements of the house, we went into a room where the nuns were arranged in rows, and where we sat on thrones on a dais. In a clever, easy way the Vicar inaugurated a kind of general conversation about the convent, and the nuns laughed at his little jokes, and answered any questions put to them. We were greatly struck by their manners, so pleasant and cheerful, without the slightest affectation or shyness.

MONDAY, 8TH. – We made an expedition to the Montmorency Falls. D. went in the *Dauntless*, a thirty-six ton yacht which he has bought, and we rowed in a big boat. The fall is six miles from Quebec. The day was very fine, and as we saw them from the river the shining tin roofs of the town looked beautiful in the sunshine.

The first view of the fall is spoilt by the quantity of timber at its base. The bay is crammed with stacks of boards and wood, piled up in every way, and there are saw-mills hard at work; but when you get close enough to see it, the Montmorency is really beautiful. It is 170 feet high and it falls perfectly straight down to the earth, clouds of spray rising up in front of it. The water does not appear to rush on as in most waterfalls, and it is supposed that it dives into the ground, and comes out elsewhere.

We had brought provisions with us, so we lighted a fire, cooked an excellent lunch, and afterwards made tea. In the cool of the evening we rowed back to Quebec, and got on board the steamer for Rivière du Loup. This is the fashionable time for going to the seaside, so the boats are very full.

RIVIÈRE DU LOUP: TUESDAY, 9TH. – Our house here is a nice little cottage, but it is a long way from the sea, and I don't think that we shall care to shut ourselves up in it for long. We are impatient to see more of the country and the people, and if only we can find a house at Quebec we shall go there; for the more we see of that place, the more we like it.

WEDNESDAY, 10TH. – After getting my letters ready for the mail we set out for the yacht. H.E. [His Excellency] was delighted with the *Dauntless*. His sailors are not very smart, but he is looking forward to the arrival of Hammond, an English sailor, who will soon give it the air of an English yacht. The *Dauntless* has a well to sit in, and a large but rather low cabin. She is one of the *flat* yachts with a sliding keel. D. steered back into the harbour before an admiring crowd just arrived by the steamer. An American on the shore called out, 'Well, Governor, you seem to be used to this kind of work.'

THURSDAY, 11TH. – Dr. Campbell, of Montreal, came here to offer D. some salmon-fishing. He has accepted for two days, and goes next Wednesday, the 17th – Colonel Fletcher with him. They will live in a camp, and be eaten by black flies and mosquitoes. The former have a sharp lance, which they insert under the skin. You do not feel the bite at the time, but it bleeds freely and inflames next day. While fishing, you keep your face and neck covered with a preparation which the flies dislike. Dr. Campbell gave an exciting account of the fishing, and how the fisherman runs along the banks as fast as he can, while the salmon rushes down the rapids. I think *I* should like to go too – but ladies are not invited.

SATURDAY, 20TH. – H.E. returned in the evening. He enjoyed his trip very much, though the salmon were scarce, and he only caught five trout. Dr. Campbell, Mr. Urquhart, Colonel Fletcher, and himself, were the party. Mr. Urquhart attended to the dinner, and was 'most anxious' about it, – it consisted of salmon and cold beef, and was very good; still, it does not sound as if it required immense thought and preparation.

MONDAY, 22ND. – Colonel Fletcher has gone off to see houses at Quebec. In the afternoon we drove to Cacouna, a more fashionable watering-place than this, where there is a large hotel frequented by

Americans, who amuse themselves by dressing four times a day.

WEDNESDAY, 24TH. – D. and I started in the afternoon for Tadousac. It was quite dark when we got there, after two hours in the steamer, and we could only see that we drove up a most dangerous road. It was a wooden ramp, just wide enough for the carriage, and with a little precipice on each side. It led to the hotel, which we found extremely clean and comfortable. I think they manage these things very well in Canada. There is a complete absence of pretence. The furniture is very plain: just a strip of carpet in one's bedroom, common-looking French beds, washing-stand and chest of drawers – no curtains anywhere – the only luxury being extreme cleanliness. There is a *table d'hôte* where all dine – servants at the same table as the other guests – and the food is very good. We had private rooms and private meals, but no one else would think of such a thing. The same simplicity strikes me as characteristic of the people. They do not *pretend* to be fine or smart, or anything but what they are; they believe every word you say, and take all polite exaggerations *au pied de la lettre*. They are exceedingly friendly and kind-hearted, so that their saying what they think does not lead to any uncomfortable speeches.

Tadousac is the oldest, but I should think the smallest, place in the Dominion. Not only as tourists, but as sailors, we are delighted with it. The hotel is situated in the curve of a lovely bay, with a nice sandy beach all round it. There are rocky walks of the most amusing description for the walker, a good anchorage for the yachtsman, and as all the fishing is up the Saguenay, and this place is at its mouth, there is sport for the sportsman. There are white porpoises and seals, and occasional whales to be seen rolling and jumping about, – and altogether we thought the place most attractive, and have some idea of building a house here for the summer.

THURSDAY, 25TH. – We got up at six to go out fishing, and drove down to the pier, where we found Mr. Radford, a resident here, who had promised to chaperon us to the fishing-ground. It was rather too stormy, but we started nevertheless in the yacht, followed by two row-boats. We had a charming sail, a beautiful coast to look at, and white porpoises and seals appearing in the water to amuse us. When we reached the Bergeron we anchored, and went on shore to prepare our fishing-rods. I was just being instructed in the art of throwing the fly, and was standing up in the row-boat, lashing the water with my line, when H.E. called out from the other boat, 'Put up your rod, and come and save the ship.' The yacht had dragged her anchor, and was fast going on the rocks. We got on board as quickly as we could, fastened tow-ropes to the two row-boats, and with great difficulty got her out of the current; her sails filled, and off we went. 'Home,' said His Excellency – and in fact it had come on to blow too hard for fishing, as the trout go into deep water when the waves are too much for them. We had a very rough sail back to Tadousac, but rather enjoyed it. We reached the hotel in time for lunch, and settled with our friend to get up at five next day and try again.

In the afternoon we took a walk, and were quite charmed with Tadousac. It is at the mouth of the Saguenay river, and the hotel is built close to the water, above a beautiful bay. Our walk was a climb, and yet it was not too fatiguing; the rocks are smooth, with no sharp points, and tufts and shrubs grow in the interstices, so that there is always something to catch hold of if you slip. When we got home, Mr. Radford brought two Rice Lake canoes, and D. tried paddling in one, while I went out in the other.

FRIDAY, 26TH. – Called at 5 a.m., with the information that the day was very favourable for fishing. We were at the wharf at six – a beautiful morning. There were two row-boats ready for us, and we set off, up the Saguenay.

The river is like a rift in a rocky mountain, great cliffs on each side, the river every now and then spreading out into a bay, and looking like a lake, the entrance quite hidden by projecting rocks. We had a three-hours' row, and arrived at St. Etienne, a feeding-ground of the trout. I again began to throw my fly, and soon became quite expert at it. I caught sixteen, and D. nineteen, and after my arm ached Mr. Radford took my rod and caught four; so our bag was a pretty good one.

We lunched on the rocks, sailed nearly the whole way home, and got back in time for dinner. Our long day was not over yet. The young ladies of Tadousac had got up a charity concert, which we attended: it was in the hotel, and between the songs there were some pretty *tableaux*. When all was over I was glad to return to my dear bed which I had left so early in the morning.

SATURDAY, 27TH. – We like Tadousac so much that we have actually chosen a site, and are going to build a wooden house here for next year. The air is delicious, and we feel so well and cheerful!

After breakfast we walked to an Indian hut to see a young bear they had found on the hills. He was very little and very unamiablelooking. The Indian women are very dark and ugly, and have their hair tied up in little bags on each side of their faces. At two we got on board the steamer, and returned to Rivière du Loup.

Colonel and Lady Harriet Fletcher came down to meet us, and we hear from him that the artillery quarters at Quebec are more likely to suit us than any other house we can get this year. D. will go and see them.

MONDAY, 29TH. – Directly after breakfast Lady H. and her governess and children came in to help me prepare for my first Canadian entertainment! Unfortunately, D. will not be at it, as he has gone off to Quebec. Of course we have small means here of doing anything grand – no ornaments at all; thick, white earthenware cups, lodging-house furniture, etc., and only wild flowers to be had. With them we determined to do a great deal. We got moss and ferns, wild roses and red berries, called in soup-plates, finger-glasses, and bark canoes, and had in the drawing-room fourteen bouquets – eight on brackets round the walls, and one on each table. Then we put moss on the chimney-piece and filled it with bright flowers, and covered the board in front of the fireplace with fir-branches, etc. Opposite the drawing-room is the best bedroom. We carried out the bed, arranged the fireplace in the same way, and had tables with tea, coffee, iced milk, champagne cup and cakes there. On one side of our house we had croquet, and on the other chairs, and I received my company at four o'clock in the chair department.

The arrangements took us the whole morning, and amused us very much; the only drawback was that we had no man, not even an aide-de-camp! Luckily, the day was splendid. We sat ourselves upon the lawn, and soon the first people came. The second carriage contained three priests with French names! They had no cards, and Nowell, our English servant, whom I had told to be very particular about announcing the names clearly, remembering my instructions, and unable to pronounce them, stopped my guests outside and made them write their names on a piece of paper. One of them, a very jolly Irishman, asked, 'Are you His Excellency's aide-de-camp?'

When all had arrived a good game of croquet was got up, and the people who did not play sat on the lawn and talked. I had over thirty, and they admired our decorations very much.

The moment my party broke up, and in sight of many of the visitors, my neighbours' servants came to fetch the things they had lent me; and it was funny to see cups and soup-plates and chairs being carried off to their lawful owners. I had asked people from four to six, and, like Cinderella, they rushed off when the hour struck.

WEDNESDAY, 31ST. – We arrived at Tadousac late last night, bringing the children with us. I took them this morning to a sandy place, where they soon improvised spades and began to 'make a dirt,' as Hermie said.

In the afternoon Lady H. and I went a drive. We got a pretty peep of the Saguenay, while heretofore we had been looking upon the St. Lawrence. D. and the Colonel went out boating.

SUNDAY, AUGUST 4TH. – We walked to the little church, which D. admires, and where, he says, we see 'the first principles of architecture.' It is the first church ever built in Canada, and is made of wood, just as you would make one with a child's box of bricks; the walls are long and short bars of wood, piled one upon the other. It is very quaint and simple.

MONDAY, 5TH. – We were suddenly struck with the idea of going salmon-fishing; so we ordered a hamper of provisions to be ready in twenty minutes, took a comb and brush and a pocket-handkerchief in a bag, and set off, D. and I in the *Imogene,* which is a small yawl, Hammond following in the *Dauntless.*

We had a lovely sail up the Saguenay to the mouth of the Marguerite river, where we arrived about four o'clock, and sent ashore for the fisherman. Then we each got into a canoe, and began to ascend the rapids! A man stands at each end of the canoe, with a long pole in his hand; the passenger sits in the middle, on the floor. The men *pole* the boat along, first giving a shove on one side and then on the other, *shaving* rocks, and conducting her safely with wonderful skill. It is very hard work going *up* the rapids; coming down the rush is with you. We landed about eight o'clock at the edge of a wood, groped our way up a narrow path, and found three small wooden huts. The first was a dining-room and pantry, the second two bed-rooms, the third a place for the men. Opposite the dining-room was an open shed, which I found to be the kitchen; and as I sat at the head of the table I saw Imps dancing about the fire cooking our dinner.

Opposite our encampment there is a curious geological – or clayolog-ical – formation; it looks as if half a high hill had been cut clean away with a knife – in fact, a perfect section of a hill is exposed to view. It is as flat as the side of a cheese, with nothing growing upon it, but the top is crowned with trees. The side is grey clay, and it is *six hundred* feet high.

We were very glad to retire soon to our little iron beds, and to creep under our mosquito-curtains; but I confess I felt a certain emotion at the idea of sleeping in such a lonely place, with no one between us and the North Pole!

TUESDAY, 6TH. – I slept and was ready to get up at five. We performed a hasty 'toilette,' swallowed a cup of tea, and took to the canoes for fishing. We were both most industrious, and flogged the water with our flies, but had no bites. Then 'Peter,' the fisherman, took my rod and hooked a salmon. My rod is small and the salmon ran off with the line. Quick as possible he jumped into a canoe, and we saw a most exciting chase; the salmon flying off with yards of line, – being wound up again, – giving an occasional jump into the air, and battling courageously for life. When he was getting worn out Peter landed and insisted upon my holding the rod. I found it almost too heavy for me, and I had a great deal of help in finishing the poor victim, who still made dashes to release himself. At last we got him near the shore, when a cruel gaff was stuck into him, and a cry of triumph from the men announced his death to us, and to the listening woods. The salmon weighed fifteen pounds.

At nine we went home to our breakfast. After it we sat at the kitchen fire and burnt holes in the only boots we had with us! At four o'clock, fishing recommenced. We were oiled all over, face and neck and hands, with a strong-smelling stuff, to keep off the mosquitoes.

Again D. and I began to work, and soon *he* hooked a salmon, and I laid down my rod to see the fight. It lasted a long time, and the fish led the fisherman a good dance. He weighed fourteen and a quarter pounds, and was His Lordship's first salmon!

WEDNESDAY, 7TH. – At eight o'clock we left the huts and went down the rapids, the men singing some of their wild and curious boat-songs as they paddled us along. We had arranged to fish for trout at the place where we had anchored the yachts, and then be picked up by the steamer, to go on to Rivière du Loup. However, the steamer had been detained by fog. There was nothing for it but to sail back to Tadousac, and await the steamer there. We finally arrived at our destination in a fog, a thunderstorm, and a heavy shower. We merely lay down upon our beds, and waited till five o'clock in the morning, when the steamer at last arrived; D. and I and our two sleepy children got on board. D. went straight on to Quebec, so he retired to bed. But as we were to reach Rivière du Loup in two hours, we remained up, and got there at last very hungry and tired.

CHAPTER 2

Quebec
AUGUST - SEPTEMBER 1872

THE CITADEL: FRIDAY, AUGUST 9TH. – Lady Harriet and I have joined D. at Quebec, and I am much pleased with my barrack home. All books about Canada will tell you how splendid is the situation of the Citadel; very high, and commanding a magnificent view of that great river the St. Lawrence. Our house – 'quarters,' I should say – is not yet quite ready, and workmen are still busy papering and making alterations. The old mess-room is our dining-room, and the drawing-room is above it. It is a long room, with windows at either end: those facing the river open on to an immense platform, the outer wall of which forms a balustrade. There I sit and look down hundreds of feet upon the town lying below me; or into the ships, on to whose decks I fancy I could almost throw a stone; or at the St. Lawrence itself, and at the blue hills far away – in fact, at one of the most celebrated views of the world! There are great black cannon also looking out from the Citadel, and the Union Jack and the Dominion Flag are flying beside me. I assure you it is very romantic!

I am rather afraid that with your little English ideas you will not understand the size of my 'platform,' but it is big enough to give a ball on, or a garden party, or a charity bazaar, or any other sort of gathering you like!

D. and Colonel Fletcher rode, and I went for a charming drive, and was more pleased than ever with the country round Quebec. Everything is growing so luxuriantly now. The hedges are full of flowers and large wild maidenhair fern, and quantities of berries which all seem to be eatable; and the crops, which, before they were fully developed, looked miserable, have suddenly swelled out and filled up all the bare places one deplored a month ago.

MONDAY, 12TH. – The weather is very hot, but not oppressive. People

16

here live behind green blinds, and shut the sun out of their houses; they cannot understand our liking to see it shine in, and they complain of the heat much more than we do.

TUESDAY, 13TH. – In the afternoon we went out to do some shopping. The most important part of it was choosing furniture for a little room. It was difficult to get what we wanted. They have no plain stuffed sofas or chairs – everything is surrounded by elaborate carvings in wood, and the men are astonished that their Excellencies 'n'aiment pas la sculpture.'

We are miserable over our heavy luggage, which will not arrive. We have nine dessert-plates, and no other china, no silver plate at all, no harness, and it is impossible to 'set up' or to give dinners until these things arrive. No one travelling here should lose sight of his box for an instant. Things are never lost, but they may be months getting to their owner.

I have been looking for a scullery-maid, and find women-servants are very scarce. I have only seen one young lady in search of the place: she spoke with a real Irish brogue, and appeared in a smart hat and feathers. She was extremely surprised at my wishing to have a character. She had one, but had left it at home: of course she could fetch it. Next morning she brought me three lines, on very common paper, which, in very bad writing, certified her to be honest and 'oblidgeing.' In spite of the brogue she was Canadian.

FRIDAY, 16TH. – Having got my eleven letters shut up all ready for the mail, I took a complete holiday from writing. We look upon our epistles as seed sown, and are always egging each other on to write to new people, that our harvest of news may be plentiful.

Colonel Strange (in command of B Battery, Canadian Artillery) has lent us some arms, and at the top of our crimson-clothed staircase we have a magnificent arrangement of swords and spears and flags; opposite it is a star of bayonets. Our drawing-room is not yet finished, but we hope it will be ready by Monday, when we have a dinner of twenty-four people; 'and yet I am not happy,' for glass, plate, and china are still on their travels. Eleven of our twenty-four are cricketers, who are expected to arrive to-morrow from England.

Mr. Pattisson, D.'s Private Secretary, arrived from Ottawa.

MONDAY, 19TH. – We were busy the whole morning arranging the drawing-room; then we drove to the town to get table-covers and some finishing touches. Our efforts were crowned with success, and the room looked extremely pretty.

Nearly everything had to be hired for the dining-room; but about an hour before dinner a few cases arrived, and two or three salvers were got out to ornament the sideboard.

We had thirty people – eleven of them cricketers. The dinner was supposed to be at 7.30, and the Canadians arrived punctually, but the English guests were somewhat London-like in their hours. In the evening the officers of the B Battery, quartered in the Citadel, came in. Everyone admired our new platform very much, and as a most splendid moon shone down upon the St. Lawrence for the occasion, it was really very nice. The attractions of the platform almost emptied the drawing-room.

TUESDAY, 20TH. – In the afternoon we drove out, Lady Harriet, Mr. Coulson, and I. First we went over an asylum, part of which is for old men and old women. The first old gentleman I saw said, 'I was just coming up to see you. I come from Killyleagh.' [Killyleagh was her old home in County Down.]

At each side of the buildings are orphan asylums. We went over everything thoroughly, going up to the attics and down to the kitchens, and examining both the summer and winter clothing of the boys and girls.

THURSDAY, 22ND. – The morning looked damp and uncertain, but we started on a picnic. A tandem led the way. Our 'guide' is quite a character and of a most sanguine disposition: he declared the distance to the lake was only twenty miles, that there we should catch fish of enormous weights, that moose and bear and cariboo would be shot by us in the bush, and, although it poured as we drove along, that the weather would be lovely 'in half an hour.'

D. thought of turning back, but things soon looked much better. When we reached the 'twenty miles' we found we were about half way, and stopped at a cottage to change carriages. The rest of the road was too rough for our barouche, so we got into the wagon with the tandem, while the cook set out in a cart. We gave the horses an hour to rest, while we sat in the garden and talked to the man and his wife. She was Scotch, and he a very good specimen of an Irishman. He had bought eighty acres for 100£., but thinks a tenant in Ireland better off, in spite of his 'rent.' They both dread the long winters, and the heat of the summer.

When we reached our destination, we found our three tents pitched on the borders of Lake St. Joseph, which is ten miles long, and surrounded by hills covered with woods. At sunset it was lovely, the hills becoming purple and blue, and the water looking like molten brass. Close to our encampment was a farm-house, and a nice Irish family, all with charming manners – the father a magistrate.

Our guide was radiant now that the weather looked better, had shown us the tea-plant, the saffron-plant, etc., and told us a good deal about the country and the people. He sent us out to fish; with us went a Mr. White, one of the afore-mentioned Irish family. We were just throwing out our first line, when Mr. White said, 'There is a great storm coming: we must get under the trees.' We jumped out of the boats, got under some bushes, and pulled a waterproof over us: a terrific storm, with *tropical* rain came on, and we got quite wet.

When it was over, we set off for our encampment. Our guide met us on the shore. His spirits were not damped, and when Colonel Fletcher inquired anxiously if the tents had let in any water, he replied, 'Not a drop, Colonel; not a drop.' On reaching them, however, we found every bed and blanket wet through! They had looked so nice and comfortable when we went out, and now all our possessions were soaking.

We lighted a fire, – for which the Whites sacrificed all their nice palings, – and surrounded it with the wet shawls, and beds, and bedding; then we pulled our table close to the warm blaze, and our cook sent us soup and *entrées,* and roasts and pudding, and we were quite happy. As soon as the things were dry we went to bed.

FRIDAY, 23RD. – The fire was crackling outside my tent when I awoke. The day was lovely, and we were all full of anticipation. Our guide appeared so radiant and so exactly the image of the celebrated 'Mr. Briggs' in 'Punch,' that he now goes by that name amongst us. There he was, with his short coat, and a great wide-awake hat, on each side of which drooped an enormous long white cock's feather; the living picture of Mr. Briggs when he stated that 'his heart was in the Highlands.'

The gentlemen were to go into the bush with him, while we ladies were to fish. We had a very pleasant day, and caught fifty bass – a very good fresh-water fish, and an amusing one to catch. We came home to lunch, sat two hours in the sunshine, and went out on the lake again in the afternoon.

Our cook had shot us some snipe and squirrels, and gave us an excellent dinner; we tasted the squirrels, but they were strong of turpentine and were very nasty.

When something was said to Hammond about Mr. Briggs, he said,

'He turned out all hands this morning after the roosters to get those two feathers for his hat.'

SATURDAY, 24TH. – We had breakfast down on the edge of the lake, and sat a long time enjoying the sun; then we rowed over to the other side to see the pitcher-plant growing wild. We also saw a turtle found in the lake. At noon we started on our journey home. The views the whole way were lovely, and we stopped to lunch on the borders of the Jacques Cartier River, lighted a fire, and had broiled fish, etc. At the half-way house we were well received, and the lady had baked us some fine plum-cakes, which she begged us to take home.

MONDAY, 26TH. – D. held a levée, and was fully occupied till seven o'clock.

TUESDAY, 27TH. – In the evening we had a dinner of twenty-five people. Mr. Russell Gurney and Mr. W. H. Smith, M.P. for Westminster, and Colonel and Mrs. Fessenden, Americans, were our strangers: the rest were all Canadians.

> Russell Gurney, a son of Sir John Gurney, was then sixty-eight years of age. A Member of Parliament, he had become a Privy Councillor in 1866, and had served on many royal commissions.
>
> William Henry Smith, 1825-1891, entered his father's news-agency business in the Strand when but sixteen, becoming a junior partner at age twenty-one. He secured a bookstall monopoly at railway stations, thereby enormously expanding the firm's activities.
>   Interested in educational matters, he became in 1871 a member of the first London School Board. He joined Disraeli's Cabinet as First Lord of the Admiralty in 1877. *My Canadian Journal*, 1891 edition records in a footnote: 'Right Honourable W. H. Smith, First Lord of the Admiralty, 1891.'

WEDNESDAY, 28TH. – Mr. R. Gurney and Mr. Smith breakfasted with us, and went over the University with D. We had another dinner; twenty people. At nine 'Her Excellency' had a reception, to which all the people who had called were asked. Our platform was hung with Chinese lanterns.

Society is at present my business in life, and this is how my week is laid out: Monday, I remain at home to receive visitors. Tuesday, Wednesday, Thursday, we have large dinners. Friday we keep for sight-seeing, and Saturday we have small dinners. On the big nights we have a 'drum.'

There is a delightful old French lady here, Madame Duval, who thoroughly enjoys society and 'drums.' Unfortunately she is in mourning at present, and cannot come unless I diplomatically suggest that the invitation is a 'command.' Mourning is kept here in the strictest manner, and I believe there is a time fixed for keeping down a thick veil – a time for paying mourning visits, etc., etc.

> The use of the word 'drum' to describe an afternoon tea or an evening party originated in India where officers on the alert had their tea and refreshments served on a drum-head.

After dinner we had a drum, at which nearly the whole of Quebec appeared. I tried to have some singing, but there was too much talk. The band played, and unluckily, finished its performance with 'God save the Queen': the instant the familiar bars were heard, half-finished ices were thrown down and everyone rushed away.

THURSDAY, SEPTEMBER 5TH. – Lady Harriet and I called at the Ursuline Convent. We took the babies, and I was more struck with the peculiarities of convent life than when we went through the establishment before; for, not having D. with us, we were not admitted, but had to talk to the nuns through iron bars. It was quite funny to hear them all buzzing inside their cage, laughing and talking, and handing sugar to the babies and admiring them! Luckily they (the babies) behaved well, and both examined the curious scene with the utmost gravity.

FRIDAY, 6TH. – I was writing this morning when D. called me to see eight bishops, archbishops, and *grand vicaires* who had particularly asked for me. I went into the drawing-room and found all these ecclesiastics in full dress. *Our* Grand Vicar as usual put everyone at his ease, and initiated a lively conversation.

Immediately after lunch we started off in a small steamer to the other side of the river. We were met by Mr. and Mrs. Roberts, who came out with us in the *Prussian,* and they took us to the Chaudière Falls. There is a great body of water, of a deep brown colour, which tumbles down from a good height, and the waterfall is very wide; the cloud of white spray looks so pretty against the dark water.

SATURDAY, 7TH. – In the evening we had a small dinner, and as soon as the gentlemen came up we had singing and playing. Mrs. Pemberton sang Irish melodies, and Madame Sericole French songs, and M. LaRue sang a little of everything. Then we had a number of Canadian boat-songs, the music wild and plaintive.

The versatile Dr. Hubert LaRue, 1833-1881, a professor of medicine at Laval University, had published a collection of the songs of early Canada. He was also the author of books on history and agriculture.

The Chaudière Falls on the south side of the St. Lawrence River, not far from Quebec City, are not to be confused with those of the same name on the Ottawa River, just above Ottawa.

Our old friend, Madame Duval, was in great force, and she and her daughter dictated a song to M. LaRue, which was amusing. Madame Sericole sang, 'I will be an eel in a pond to escape from you;' then he, 'Si vous vous faites anguille, je me ferai pêcheur pour vous prendre en pêchant;' then she, 'Si vous vous faites pêcheur pour me prendre en pêchant, je deviendrai alouette,' etc. This kind of conversation goes on to any length, till finally she says she will become a nun, when he makes himself 'prêcheur pour vous prendre en prêchant.' This fidelity she is unable to resist, and, 'Puisque tu m'aimes tant pour te faire prêcheur pour me prendre en prêchant, I will marry you.'

MONDAY, 9TH. – Mr. and Mrs. T. Brassey and Miss Robinson dined with us. He has just come from England in his yacht, a twenty-eight days' voyage; Mrs. Brassey came out in the steamer.

Thomas Brassey (later Lord Brassey), the eldest son of the eminent railway contractor, who helped build the Grand Trunk Railway of Canada, was an ardent yachtsman. In 1878 an account of their trip around the world, 1876-77, written by Lady Brassey, appeared under the title *Voyage of the Sunbeam*.

WEDNESDAY, 11TH. – The Bishop of Quebec and Judge Stuart came to breakfast, and at eleven we started on an educational tour. At the first school separate addresses were made to each of us, and I was asked for a holiday. I think we went to six schools; at each an address was read, and at each we gave a holiday.

We also went to see the Houses of Parliament – that is, the *local* Parliament. Before the seat of Government was moved it was the imperial one. It is in good taste; the outside quite plain.

The Legislative Buildings in Quebec were burned in 1854 and the Government moved temporarily into a building originally designed for a post office. It was there the famous Quebec Conference of 1864 was held. The corner-stone of the present beautiful Parliament Buildings was not laid until June 17, 1884.

Judge Andrew (later Sir Andrew) Stuart became Chief Justice of the Superior Court of Quebec in 1885.

After we went to see some Egyptian curiosities, I hurried home to rest for twenty minutes before my dinner. We had twenty-two people, the Brasseys among the number.

THURSDAY, 12TH. – At two we went down to the Convent of St. Roch, where our reception was most charming. The nuns received us at the door and led us into a very large room, the walls of which were lined from floor to ceiling with little children: they each wore either a blue or a red ribbon, and they were all from three to eight years old – five hundred in number.

About twenty stood in the middle of the room and sang a song of welcome, and whenever they came to the word 'Excellence,' or 'Milor,' they all curtseyed together. Then one came forward and made a little address, adding that this great occasion was worthy of 'a double holiday.' In his reply D. said that although he had never heard of that phenomenon in nature 'a double holiday,' he was happy to grant it. Then we went upstairs to see the older pupils. I cannot tell you what a pretty ceremony it was, and how gracefully they all made their révérences together.

MONDAY, 16TH. – We went to the Ursuline Convent, looked at pictures and at Montcalm's skull, until all was ready. Then we went to the great door and knocked. Some nuns opened to us, and conducted us to a large room, where we found all the pupils dressed in white and with wreaths of flowers on their heads. They sang a song of welcome as we came in; then two came forward and one gave a little address in English and one in French. All the time we were there waves of curtseys kept sweeping along in the line every time our names were mentioned, and as we passed down the room. We heard the pupils play a piece on five pianos and a harmonium at once.

In the evening we went to a ball given in our honour by the Lieutenant-Governor, Sir Narcisse Belleau. It was held in the music-hall, a very fine room. D. danced everything, and I danced the square dances.

TUESDAY, 17TH. – In spite of our fatigues, we had to start early to visit another convent, 'Jésus Marie,' at Sillery. Here our reception was too lovely. The convent has only been built three years, and is a splendid house, with all the new improvements, and with fine grounds surrounding it. In one hall there are twelve glass boxes, each containing a piano, so that the pupils can practise simultaneously; whilst in another glass house sits the mistress, overlooking, but, happily for her, not overhearing.

We were met at the door by the Lady Superior, and first paid our respects to the nuns – little black ladies with white, large-bordered caps. They conducted us through passages ornamented with maple-leaves, and placed us on thrones in presence of the pupils. The children were in white, and a circle of twelve of them began a dramatic conversation, in which they consulted each other as to the best way of doing us honour. One suggested that the 'Genius of Canada' should be asked her opinion on the subject, and, like a good fairy, she immediately appeared upon the scene, and settled the question by giving me a large bunch of artificial roses made in the convent, singing meanwhile a song the refrain of which was –

> 'Ce sont des roses sans épines,
> Que l'on vous offre au Canada.'

After this the nuns gave us cake and sweet wine, and we hurried off to another convent. On our way we went to look at a church, and called on Lady Belleau, and then rushed back to be 'at home' all the afternoon.

I had my room full of people from three till six, so I was pretty tired when the hour for rest came. D. and I dined alone, which is much more of an event now than a dinner-party would be.

WEDNESDAY, 18TH. – The day of our first ball. We were excessively busy making decorations. Nevertheless, we had to go out to pay a state visit to the Université Laval. There we were received by the Archbishop, etc., and, after seeing the young boys, D. went through the building, museum, and library, and finally into the great room, where we were received by the University proper. The hall was filled with students, priests and guests; the Rector and the Professors, in robes, walked in and read an address, and listened to D.'s reply. Then we went up on the roof, looked at the magnificent view, and peeped at the sun through a telescope. After this, home, where we partly rested and partly looked after the ball.

Our room has light-coloured walls and a high arched roof, and we ornamented it with festoons of blue and white, fastened with great bunches of pink and white roses – the ceiling the same. We had a military band outside, where there was a very good floor, and a string band in the room; so people danced both outside and in, and they kept it up till three with great spirit. They really did enjoy themselves, which is encouraging, as we have another on Friday.

THURSDAY, 19TH. – Gay people that we are! to-day we had a paper hunt. We started at eleven, D. riding, and I taking two Frenchmen who are staying here – le Comte de Montebello and le Baron Brun – in the carriage.

> Comte de Montebello, 1804-75, son of a distinguished French soldier
> in the Napoleonic Wars, had been an aide-de-camp to Napoleon III.

It poured at first, but cleared soon. We crossed the river in a ferry, carriage and all, and were told where to place ourselves; so we were much amused, as we saw the jumping perfectly. When the paper was 'killed,' we met at some country barracks, had lunch, and formed a 'club,' 'the Stadacona Hunt' with D. as president.

FRIDAY, 20TH. – We inspected an indiarubber manufactory, and saw the material from the time it comes out of the tree till it leaves the place as goloshes. Then we proceeded to a wood-mill, where all carpentering is done by machinery, and where we saw our Tadousac house laid out. It will be made there, and transported in barges to its site.

We had a second ball in the evening, and this time we had an awning on the platform, which was hung with Chinese lanterns. It looked very pretty, and it entirely prevented any crowd in the ballroom; in fact, it was almost the more popular place of the two.

SATURDAY, 21ST. – H. E. had suggested some athletic sports, so we went down to see them and to lunch with the Mayor. There was a very good place for the games – a smooth field, surrounded by high grass banks on two sides, and with houses on the third. People sat on the banks and in the houses, and, as the day was lovely, there was an immense concourse of spectators.

The hills all round, as seen from our celebrated platform, are of the most lovely autumn colours, and, covered as they are with red and orange trees, they really look like flames in the distance, or like gigantic flower-gardens; for our *trees* are quite as brilliant as your best *flowers,* and if you can imagine your conservatory magnified a million times, and spread over miles and miles of hill and dale, you will begin to understand how we do things in this Canada of ours.

MONDAY, 23RD. – We left Quebec to-day, and received quite an ovation at our departure. The weather was lovely, and we started from the Citadel at three, escorted by a guard of honour. The streets, hung with flags, were full of people. At one corner, the boys of the Université Laval met us, and about fifty of them each presented me with a bouquet, so that I was half buried with flowers. When we arrived at the wharf, we found almost the whole of the society waiting to say good-bye to us. The Mayor read an address, and invited us to a ball, and D. replied. Then we shook hands with everyone, and went on board. Every part of the town, right up to the Citadel, was crowded, and six steamers full of people accompanied us for ten miles. When we got to Cap Rouge, the steamers turned back, the people on board cheering and waving their handkerchiefs. On the coast, too, at each little wharf, people were collected, and at the houses far up on the shore we saw waving flags and tablecloths. As we passed the Sillery Convent, all the children came out with flags. No wonder we like Quebec!

Replying to the Mayor's address, Lord Dufferin said:

When we first arrived here we were unknown to you all, and strangers in the land. When we next come to Quebec we feel we shall be returning to a circle of warm friends.

Encamped as we have been upon the rock above us, and confined within the narrow casemates of the Citadel, it was impossible for us to open our doors as widely as we could have wished. But though in one sense the space at our disposal for your accommodation has been restricted, in another way we can make ample provision for you all. In the chambers of our hearts there is room and verge for many friends. Their avenues are guarded by no state, nor ceremonial; no introduction is needed to gain admission there, and those who once enter need never take their leave. [Cheers.]

Shortly after, with a final salute from a hundred cannon, the *Montreal* slowly pulled away from the wharf.

CHAPTER 3

Ontario
SEPTEMBER - OCTOBER 1872

TUESDAY, SEPTEMBER 24TH. – The train left Montreal at 8 a.m., and we were in it till 11.30 at night – a very long journey. However, we had a most comfortable car, with armchairs and sofas, and managed to sleep a good deal. In spite of the lateness of the hour we were met at Toronto by crowds of people and a torchlight procession. The Lieutenant-Governor, Mr. Howland, took us to his house, which was magnificently illuminated.

> Government House, set in spacious grounds on the south-west corner of King and Simcoe Streets, had been erected on the site of Elmsley House, the residence occupied by previous governors. On this occasion the large building was artistically outlined with flickering gas-lights.

> William (later Sir William) Pearce Howland, the owner of large mills at Lambton, west of Toronto, had been one of the ministers to go to London in 1866 to discuss the terms of the British North America Act. Two years later he had become Lieutenant-Governor of Ontario.

> Frederick William Cumberland, the capable A.D.C., met their Excellencies and did not arrive home till 2 a.m. The next evening he and Mrs. Cumberland dined at Government House, and their daughters attended the ball which followed.

WEDNESDAY, 25TH. – A large dinner-party and a very pretty ball, the house and grounds being illuminated.

THURSDAY, 26TH. – At eleven o'clock, we started by special train for Hamilton. It is a very prettily situated town on Lake Ontario, which looks more like the sea than a lake. All the streets are planted with trees, and there is a high hill behind the town, from which the view is magnificent. We were received at the station by the Mayor and Corporation, who presented an address, and drove to the Cattle Show yard, where there was another, and D. and I walked round the grounds and looked at the animals, while the people looked at us. We examined prize horses, cows, and pigs, but found the crowd so great that we resolved to return in the morning to see everything more quietly. We are staying with Mr. McInnes, who makes us very comfortable.

FRIDAY, 27TH. – We were at the exhibition early, and went round sewing-machines, pictures, refrigerators, stoves, vegetables, fruit, etc.

After this we drove to the City Hall and received a deputation from the Six Nations. The chief 'Chief' was finely dressed, and wore feathers in a hat, and many medals on his breast. He carried the silver pipe of peace, but also had on a scalping-knife, a tomahawk, and a dagger; and he was enchanted when, in allusion to these weapons, D. told him that he would rather have him for a friend than an enemy.

He was a fine-looking man, and had the best of manners. He read the address in English, the other Chiefs standing by in plain clothes, and when D. replied, the Chief translated into Indian each sentence of his speech. As soon as the Indians left we had a general reception, and afterwards drove out to a lovely country place belonging to Mr. McInnes. There we lunched, and then hurried off to the train.

In an hour and a half we reached Toronto, and the grand, official reception took place. A guard of honour and the Mayor met us at the station, and we drove to the Town Hall. All the streets were crowded with people, the windows full, and the houses ornamented with flags. There were some splendid triumphal arches, and the whole way along we were cheered. We made quite a procession, fire-engines and carriages leading the way for us. Another guard of honour met us at the hall, and we went in and had two more addresses. D. did not find his written replies at the station as he expected, so he had to speak extempore, and I think that pleased his audience more.

After this, we again got into the carriages and drove to the hotel through crowds, where we remained as the guests of the city. In the evening twenty of the Corporation dined with us. I sat by the Mayor, Mr. Sheard – a very nice man. After dinner we drove out to see the illuminations: there were some very pretty ones, and the arches looked beautiful.

The Civic reception tendered their Excellencies was at the City Hall, located on Front Street, between Jarvis and Market Streets. They were the guests of the city at the Queen's Hotel, situated on the site of the present Royal York Hotel. It was there the luncheon took place the following day.

The levee on the 28th was held in the Parliament Buildings, also on Front Street, but farther west, just south of Government House. Mr. Cumberland presented the guests.

SATURDAY, 28TH. – The weather is quite splendid, and the Corporation took us for a drive. This town is one of those wonderful quick-growing places: the streets are very wide, and trees are planted on each side of them. There are some very handsome buildings and numbers of the most charming villas. On our return, we had lunch. Our health and the Mayor's health were drunk; and as the latter made frequent mention of me as D.'s 'kind lady,' I am in hopes I made an impression.

At three, D. had a levée, and after this we returned to Government House. Another dinner of twenty to-night.

We are thinking of spending a week at Niagara, and wrote to the hotel-keeper there to ask price of rooms, etc. He replied first to the business part, and then added, 'I should like to know how many guests His Excellency will bring with him, as I wish to give a little hop while he is here, and I have to write for the music', etc.

P.S. 'The hop and the music will not be charged extra'!

We declined the 'hop.'

MONDAY, 30TH. – We have arrived at Niagara, and I am not in the least disappointed, but I don't think the first view is so overpowering grand as I expected. The Fall is so wide that it rather takes from the height. Sir Hastings Doyle is staying with us.

General Sir Charles Hastings Doyle, 1805-83, had been appointed commander of the troops in Nova Scotia in 1861, and after Confederation became that province's first Lieutenant-Governor.

The Clifton House, facing Niagara Falls, where the vice-regal party stayed, had been built in the eighteen-forties by Samuel Zimmerman, a wealthy railway contractor and bridge-builder. Its gardens, fountains and statuary had made it the show place of the Niagara Peninsula.

TUESDAY, OCTOBER 1ST. – We went to a convent; after lunch we crossed the bridge and went into the States.

From that side we prepared to visit the 'Cave of the Winds.' I was surprised to find we were expected to array ourselves in yellow oil-cloth trousers, with jackets and hoods of the same material. Thus accoutred we descended a flight of stairs, and found ourselves at the foot of a waterfall. On our feet we had soft cloth shoes, which enabled us to climb down the steepest and most slippery rocks. The spray beat in our faces, and we could only occasionally open our eyes to see the splendid rainbow in the water, and the great height above us from which the water was rushing down. We climbed over rocks and small wooden bridges until we came to the Fall, and walked behind it, in a complete shower-bath, – but I enjoyed it immensely. We did look a funny yellow party, dripping with water.

THURSDAY, 3RD. – We were joined by Sir Edward Thornton, our Minister at Washington, and walked to the foot of the Horseshoe Fall.

We went by train to see a great engineering work undertaken by Mr. Gzowski. He is making a bridge over the Niagara, close to Buffalo; the piers have to be built in water eighty feet deep, where the stream is rushing along twenty miles an hour. Colonel Fletcher put on a diver's dress and went down the eighty feet, bringing us some stones from the bottom. Mr. and Mrs. Gzowski took us for a drive through Buffalo.

> Casimir (later Sir Casimir) Stanislaus Gzowski was born in Russia in 1813, but had arrived in Canada in 1841 and undertaken large engineering projects. The bridge under construction at that time was the International Bridge linking Fort Erie to Buffalo. In 1879 he was appointed honorary A.D.C. to the Queen with the rank of Colonel.

FRIDAY, 4TH. – Sir Hastings Doyle left us to-day. We were very sorry to part from him; he was always so cheerful and such an amusing companion.

TORONTO: SATURDAY, 5TH. – We have hired a house at Toronto, and are settling ourselves in it to-day. There is a very bad epidemic among the horses here, and ours are suffering from it too, which is inconvenient.

> During their stay in Toronto, the Dufferins occupied Holland House. This turreted, castle-like mansion stood amid trees and shrubbery a little west of Bay Street, between Wellington and Piper Streets. It had

been built in 1831 by the Honourable Henry John Boulton, who named it after the famous Holland House in Kensington in which he had been born in 1790.

TUESDAY, 8TH. – We had our first Drawing-room. There were about 1,500 people present, and, as I had to curtsey all the time, I had plenty of exercise. The room looked very handsome when thus filled with smart people. This was quite a new experiment in Canada, drawing-rooms not having been held before, and it seems to be approved.

WEDNESDAY, 9TH. – Having recovered the fatigues of the Drawing-room, I drove in the afternoon to see a lacrosse match. It is almost the national game here, very pretty and amusing to watch. The game was whites *versus* Indians. The latter showed us their war-dance before we left.

LONDON: THURSDAY, 10TH. – Our train left Toronto at 9 a.m., and on our way we stopped at Woodstock to receive addresses. The station at London was prettily arranged. Immense numbers of people gave us a warm reception. We drove to the Cattle Show yard, where there were more addresses.

After lunch at the Member's house, Lady Harriet and I returned to the hotel, where the City entertained us, and D. went on to Hellmuth College and to some oil-refineries. We dined alone, and just as we had finished a torchlight procession passed, throwing up Roman candles and rockets. Being dressed for the ball, I was requested to show myself to the guests in the hotel, and the American mistress of the place said to me, 'Well, missis, I must compliment you very highly.'

The ballroom was fine and His Excellency danced every dance.

FRIDAY, 11TH. – We started at eleven, with a large party 'on board the cars,' to visit the oil-wells of 'Petrolia,' where we saw the oil as it comes up through the pump – thick, black, and mixed with water. We also saw the process of looking for a well, 'sinking a shaft,' and all the machinery used. The oil leaves Petrolia free from water, but black and thick; the refining is done at London. The oil district is, of course, ugly, the ground black and swampy. Stumps of trees and wooden erections – some like enormous barrels – cover the whole place; but it was very interesting to see.

On our way back we were shown into a 'drawing-room' car, where we found about twenty tables laid, each one for two people. We had an excellent hot lunch cooked on board, and got back to London at three o'clock. Here the party left us, and we returned to Toronto.

SATURDAY, 12TH. – Lady Harriet and I inspected an orphan home. A dinner party closed the day.

TUESDAY, 15TH. – D. and I drove to see a fine Wesleyan church. Then we went on to Bishop Strachan's Church of England Ladies' School. The girls played and sang and read to us. As they had decorated their bedrooms we had to go into each one.

WEDNESDAY, 16TH. – At eleven our duties began again, and we visited the Normal and Model Schools. These are the *National* Schools of Canada, and members of all denominations met us, the English clergyman introducing the R. C. Bishop. This afternoon I have been to two orphan asylums, this evening to a charity concert.

THURSDAY, 17TH. – My children and my brother Fred sail for Canada to-day. H. E. and I went out at the usual hour of eleven and paid a visit to Trinity College, one of the first-fruits of disestablishment here. It is especially a Church of England University. Then we drove to the lunatic asylum. One new feature in this asylum is a paying department, which is of course cheap, but has all the comforts of a private asylum.

> Trinity College stood then in spacious grounds on the north side of Queen Street opposite Strachan Avenue. Its ornate entrance gates still mark the site.

> Everywhere Lord Dufferin sought intimate personal acquaintance with the Canadian educational system. Particularly was he pleased when he visited the Normal School and met the aging Reverend Dr. Egerton Ryerson and his deputy, Dr. J. G. Hodgins. They were the ones who had introduced into Ontario the school readers used in Ireland.

> Lord Dufferin's trip to the western part of the province brought forth the remark that Ontario had two gifts that reminded him of Biblical times: it was endowed to an unlimited extent with *corn* and *oil*. The Cattle Show in London recalled experiences on his own farm at Clandeboye. The farm had not been profitable and he had taken considerable interest in the breeding of stock. Among his herd was a somewhat famous bull, which had secured a number of silver medals, of the value of about five pounds, which represented

about a thousand pounds that had been expended in efforts to acquire them.

We had a dinner-party of twenty-four; one M.P. and his wife, two legal gentlemen, two R.C. Bishops, a Volunteer colonel. the editor of a newspaper with his pretty little wife, who sang for us, some members of the Government, and some of the Board of Trade.

FRIDAY, 18TH. – D. and I drove to the City Hall to receive an address from the 'York Pioneers' – Toronto used to be called 'York,' and these are the first settlers here.

> This society had been organized just three years previously in 1869 for the purpose of 'more intimately uniting in friendly relations those who are natives of or who have immigrated to the original County of York.' Incorporated in 1891 as 'The York Pioneer and Historical Society,' its ever widening activities now include museums, historic buildings, and the collecting and preserving of documents, pictures and artifacts of pioneer days.

> A dinner commemorating the centenary of the Society was held on April 15, 1969, in the beautifully restored St. Lawrence Hall. It had been the scene of "The First Grand Dinner," held in 1870, "to celebrate the formation of the Society, April 17, 1869."

After lunch we went to the University, where D. gave away the prizes, and made a speech. The hall was filled with all the beauty and fashion of Toronto: they complimented me, and D. complimented them, and the proceedings went off very well.

This is a great place for presents – a very friendly custom. I have fruit, flowers, butter, fancy bread, fish, and game sent me constantly. Nearly every day brings some offering. The Show sent me apples and pears – a few of each kind, arranged so as to have some every day of the year.

SATURDAY, 19TH. – In the afternoon I went for a sail with D., and in the evening we had a large party of about 150 people.

MONDAY, 21ST. – This morning we inspected some Roman Catholic Schools. The first place we went to was the Convent of the 'Precious Blood.' I think I told you about this order of praying nuns – it is very strict, and they use corporal self-punishments. The dress of the nuns is beautiful – a white dress, with a broad piece of blood-red coloured cashmere hanging straight down both the back and the front of it, and a black veil on the head. Their beds are boards, and they get up twice in the night to pray. They looked quite merry.

There happened a great *contretemps* this afternoon. I was to be at home to receive visitors; so Lady Harriet and I sat in state, and nobody came! At five D. returned home, and I said to him, 'Not a single soul has come to see us.' Tea came in, and he asked, 'Has nobody called?' 'Oh, yes,' said the servant, 'but I said, "Not at home."' We sent for the book, and found 104 people had been, so we had to sit down and write 104 notes to explain. I had a dinner-party in the evening, and, luckily, no one seems to have been offended, though our conduct did look rude this afternoon. We had a great deal of music after dinner. All the young ladies sing and play without their music, and are very good-natured about it.

WEDNESDAY, 23RD. – D. visited the National Schools, and after lunch I went with him to finish the Roman Catholic institutions. We drove to the Loretto Abbey Convent, where we were laden with bouquets. The next place was a 'House of Providence,' where old, incurable, orphans, and sick are cared for. The third visit was to a boys' school under the Christian Brothers.

THURSDAY, 24TH. – I went over the Toronto Hospital this morning – a fine building and well managed, but badly off for funds. To-night we have an enormous ball.

FRIDAY, 25TH. – Our ball last night was a great success. The Parliament Buildings, in which it took place, were arranged for us by the Ontario Government. We had two ballrooms, both ornamented with a good deal of crimson drapery, arms and shields, which lighted up very well. The supper-room was upstairs. I suppose we had about 1,200 guests. There was not a hitch in the arrangements, and people looked nice and fresh. I danced all the square dances, and D. every dance, with a selection of celebrities. When the programme was over, 'God save the Queen' was played, and we stood on the dais while the people passed out before us.

D. had to be off to a college at eleven this morning, but I was lazy, and reserved myself till one, when we went to the Law Courts to lunch. The building, 'Osgoode Hall,' is fine, and the Courts much better than any I have seen – lofty and comfortable rooms. We had our healths drunk, and D. told them the one blot he had discovered in Canadian affairs was the lowness of the judges' salaries; this, of course, the company present were very glad to hear.

Osgoode Hall, Lord Dufferin was to learn, was another of the many beautiful buildings designed by his genial aide-de-camp, Colonel Cumberland. The latter, at the age of twenty-six, had arrived in Canada in 1847. The experience gained as engineer on the London-to-Birmingham Railway, on the naval docks at Portsmouth, and on the Parliament Buildings at Westminster, had soon been called into service. Before five years had passed he had designed the Normal School, the Mechanics' Institute with its charming music hall, and St. James Cathedral. Surveying for the Northern Railway, linking Lakes Ontario and Huron, had followed. Further architectural achievements occupied the next few years. In 1859 his masterpiece, University College, was opened. On his visit there Lord Dufferin had said:

Until I reached Toronto I confess I was not aware that so magnificent a specimen of architecture existed upon the American continent. [Applause] I can only say that the citizens of Toronto, as well as the students of this University, have to be congratulated that, amongst the inhabitants of their own Province, there should have been found a gentleman so complete a master of his art, as to have been enabled to decorate this town with such a magnificent specimen of his skill.

SATURDAY, 26TH. – There were to have been athletic sports to-day, special trains, etc., but there is a steady downpour and they have been put off till Monday. I received a good many farewell visits, and in the evening we went to a performance at the theatre for the Protestant orphans. The theatre is small, but very pretty, and 'London Assurance' was well given – especially the part of Lady Gay Spanker, by Mrs. Morrison. She presented me with a splendid bouquet in which my monogram was made in shamrocks.

For many years John Nickinson was manager of the Royal Lyceum Theatre, located between Bay and York Streets and approached by Theatre Lane which ran south from King Street. His actress daughter, Charlotte, married Daniel Morrison, the editor of the *Examiner*. After her husband's death in 1872 she resumed her profession and became manager of the theatre.

SUNDAY, 27TH. – This morning, at ten, we visited a Sunday-school. Very great attention is paid to Sunday-schools in Canada, and the children of all classes attend them. There was a separate room for infants, and the man teaching them gave his instruction orally and with

a blackboard, upon which he wrote; the children answered all together, and seemed bright and intelligent. They also sang hymns.

The larger children were downstairs. D. made them a little address,
and we heard them sing too. This was the [St. James] cathedral
school, and the average attendance every Sunday is 500. There is a
class every week for the teachers, and the same lesson is given all over
the school.

MONDAY, 28TH. – We left Toronto at nine, and a number of people
came to see us off, and cheered our departing train. We had a twelve
hours' journey, and were glad to reach Ottawa.

OTTAWA: TUESDAY, 29TH. – My poor children have had a very long
journey: they arrived at Quebec on Monday, after a rough passage
from Liverpool, and did not get here till this evening, when I devoted
myself to giving them tea, putting them to bed, and hearing them
chatter.

WEDNESDAY, 30TH. – The children are well and enjoying the fine day.
Mr. Coulson goes on leave, so Fred at once begins his duties as
A.D.C., but he comes in for a time of rest.

CHAPTER 4

Ottawa
NOVEMBER 1872 - JANUARY 1873

SATURDAY, NOVEMBER 2ND. – The journal here will grow very dull, I fear. We are 'settling down,' and do very little that is interesting.

Ottawa is a small town, with incongruously beautiful buildings crowning its insignificance. A very bad road leads to Rideau, which is a long, two-storeyed villa, with a small garden on one side of it and a hedge which bounds our property on the other – so that at this time of the year there is really no place to walk. When the 'road-maker,' as they call the frost, comes, and when the ground is covered with snow, we shall be independent of roads; and the knowledge of this makes the inhabitants careless of the state they may be in at other times of the year.

The gentlemen try to ride every day, and come back covered with mud. I walked into the town one day with D., and the following paragraph appeared in the evening paper: –

Lady Dufferin. – It would astonish some of our fine ladies to see Lady Dufferin walking about the town. She dresses plainly and sensibly, wears thick boots, and does not shrink from the muddiest of our crossings.

This comes of my Irish training!

MONDAY, 4TH. – Directly after lunch, Fred and I began our duties. I was 'at home,' and he announced the visitors and helped me to talk to them. We had 108. I was pleased with the society, and Ottawa it-self improves on acquaintance, especially as I have discovered a nice common and wood behind the house, where the children will be hap-py. Mr. Archibald, Lieutenant-Governor of Manitoba, and the Pattis-sons dined with us.

In addition to his social duties, Fred has to look after all the stable matters, expenditure included, after the invitations, the amusements, such as skating-rink, etc., so he is not idle.

TUESDAY, 5TH. – The little ones, Basil and Hermie, arrived from Quebec, looking well and merry. It is nice to be all together again.

SATURDAY, 9TH. – The weather is lovely, and I generally walk in and out of town. After lunch, games of football, stilts, hoops, etc., go on. We have five-o'clock tea, and family gatherings, the babies first, and then the *old* children.

The house gets on very slowly: the hall door is still boarded up, the schoolroom full of workmen who do not work, the gas-pipes still innocent of gas. I suppose we shall be settled by January. The Fletcher's house will, I hope, be ready for them in a few days, and when they get into it we shall feel more settled ourselves. At present they are staying with us.

SUNDAY, 10TH. – We went to our very small parish church at New Edinburgh. It is very primitive, but we like the service, and it is so much nearer to us than the cathedral.

MONDAY, 11TH. – We took a walk to prepare for the labours of the afternoon. Between three and five I received 144 visitors; Fred, Lady Harriet, and Mrs. Pattisson helping me.

THURSDAY, 14TH. – This is Thanksgiving Day, so we went to church at the cathedral, but (as the papers tell us) we did it in an 'unostentatious manner.' The first snow fell.

FRIDAY, 15TH. – A telegram arrived from Australia, the first which has been sent direct: it arrived at 9.10 this morning, having been sent at 10 – to-night. Rather puzzling to think of. D. replied, 'Canada re-echoes Australia's toast – our Queen and a United Empire.'

SUNDAY, 17TH. – A beautiful, ideal winter day: the ground and trees white with snow, blue sky, and bright sun. We went to church, and the children were unable to resist some of the pleasures of a first day of snow, and tumbled about in it as though it were sand.

You should see them, all five in blanket coats, which are made of thick blue cloth, with red epaulets and sashes, and pointed hoods lined and piped with red. The coats are very long and straight, and the little figures in them look both funny and picturesque. They have sealskin turbans, and pull up the hoods if necessary. We all wear moccasins on our feet; they are of cloth, with indiarubber soles, and

generally a flower embroidered in colours on the toes. The only drawback to going out here is the amount of dressing one has to do to
prepare for it. There are over-stockings, over-boots, over-etcs. of all
descriptions to be put on; there are fur caps with woollen clouds tied
over them as becomingly as possible, fur coats, fur gloves, muffs, etc.,
etc. But once out it is delightful, and most exhilarating.

We have been tobogganing, though the snow is not deep yet, and
our present efforts are very amateurish. We sit, stand, or lie on a
straight board which is curled at one end, and slide down snow-covered hills. The children enjoy it immensely, and have splendid exercise pulling their sleighs, or toboggans, up the hill again.

The 'Black Rod,' Mr. Kimber, was one of our guests at dinner
to-night. He sang us one of Figaro's songs, acting it with great spirit,
and amusing us very much. He also sang some pretty Canadian boat-
songs. Another guest was Miss Griffin, a lady who acted in a play with
Dickens at Montreal twenty years ago.

WEDNESDAY, 20TH. – D., Colonel Fletcher, Fred, and Mr. Campbell
(D.'s shorthand writer, and a favourite member of the Staff), went
to Montreal.

SATURDAY, 23RD. – I had a long letter from D., giving me an account of
his doings. After a long journey on Wednesday, they reached Montreal in the evening, and were conducted by the Mayor and Sir Hugh
Allan to the latter's house.

> Sir Hugh Allan, founder of the Allan Line of steamships, had a large
> home, Ravenscrag, part way up the mountain in Montreal.

On Thursday D. unveiled the Queen's statue, and in the evening
he danced all night at a ball, never flagging till four in the morning,
and being pronounced 'a brick' by the young ladies of Montreal. He
had a dinner at a club on Friday, and returned here to-day, fatigued
but pleased. We are both going to Montreal in January for a 'season.'

WEDNESDAY, 27TH. – We are gradually settling down in our house, and
are dragging from obscure packing-cases the few ornaments that have
emigrated with us. I have set up a boudoir, and in it put all my
favourite things, so as to have one home-like sanctum. The state-
rooms continue, I fear, to have a hopelessly company look.

We had a dinner-party of twenty-six, a great number of Ministers
among them. There is no clock (going) in the drawing-room, so my

guests fidgeted off before ten, and had to wait in the cloak-room for their carriages. When one person moves, they all go, and it is useless to say, 'Do stay.'

There was snow in the afternoon, and we are getting up the double windows. Most people have not only the extra windows, but stuff cotton wool into every crevice. Their houses are very hot.

TUESDAY, DECEMBER 3RD. – Yesterday I went for my first drive in a sleigh. I think I shall like it very much when there is a little more snow.

I will tell you how we pass an ordinary day. We breakfast at nine, then separate to our various offices and places of business. Fred goes to the stables, and afterwards helps to write invitations, though Mr. Coulson manages the society at present. At eleven they all go into town. We lunch at one – the children and I generally alone, the gentlemen returning when they like. After lunch we go out: in this weather it is a duty, but later, I think, we shall have great fun out of doors. On our return we have tea, and books and children; dinner at 7.30. The Fletchers come often, and we have one or two large dinners every week.

WEDNESDAY, 4TH. – I put on snow-shoes for the first time. One's foot looks like a dot in the centre of a large racket, and I expected to trip up on my own shoes; but I found it quite easy to walk with them, and very amusing.

FRIDAY, 6TH. – Sir John and Lady Macdonald are staying with us for two nights. In the morning I took Lady Macdonald and Lady Harriet for a sleigh-drive, and in the afternoon we all rested for the coming dinner-party. We had twenty-eight guests.

One of them, a senator and mill-owner employing 500 labourers all the year round at high wages, told me that when he came here himself he earned ten shillings a month. Mr. Todd, the librarian here, was another guest. He is the author of the best book on the British Constitution. Then there was a railway celebrity, who got out of a sick bed to come; he brought with him a pleasant sister-in-law and a very pretty daughter. Sir Hugh Allan also dined with us, and Sir Francis Hincks.

Sir Francis Hincks, born in Ireland in 1807, was at that time Member of Parliament for Vancouver and Minister of Finance in Sir John A. Macdonald's Cabinet.

SATURDAY, 7TH. – Lady Macdonald left, and I went out to see some tobogganing. The high hill is sufficiently covered with snow, and the children are very brave about going down it. To-day they looked so odd, all covered with snow, while the gentlemen's beards, eyelashes and hair, had the snow frozen into them. The thermometer was 10° below zero, but the day was bright, and we did not feel the cold.

MONDAY, 9TH. – One of my exhausting 'at home' days. My labours began at 1.30, for I had the managers of a concert I am getting up to lunch, and went on till six – a steady flow of visitors. It was a very cold day, – luckily for the conversation required of me, – and ninety-three varieties of 'How cold you must have found your drive!' did I invent. On these occasions D. comes in when all is over and asks 'what news we have heard,' and we always have to say we have heard nothing. I generally keep Monday evening sacred to repose, but to-day we were obliged to invite travellers, and two Torontonians, the Pattissons and Fletchers making up twelve. Our tourists came to America for ten months, but have found travelling so expensive they have to hurry home at the end of four. Their bill for ten days at a New York hotel was 150£.

TUESDAY, 10TH. – D. has invited these young men to come and to-boggan, and it made me freeze to look at their costumes: knicker-bockers, no gloves, thin boots, English hats! – when flannel and cloth trousers, boots of cloth with indiarubber soles, fur gloves, and fur hats are necessary. I only hope they won't be laid up with 'pains.' One foolish footman of ours who came out in the carriage with cotton socks and leather boots has had a fearful attack of acute inflammatory rheumatism, and two Sisters of Mercy are now nursing him. Yesterday, Terence, having a hole in one of his gloves, came home with his finger frost-bitten, and Nelly had two suspicious white spots in her face: they were rubbed with snow, and are all right.

WEDNESDAY, 11TH. – I had half an hour's skating: the first time we have been able to use the rink. I did not do much, as we had a dinner in the evening.

SATURDAY, 14TH. – This has been one of our regular Ottawa weeks. After the Wednesday's dinner a quiet night; then a visit from a Minister and his wife, Dr. and Mrs. Tupper, who remained the night, and a visit the next night from two Ministers, and one wife, – Monsieur Langevin, and Mr. and Mrs. Howe. These latter preferred returning home to sleep, either because they liked their own stove side, or because the next day was Mr. Howe's seventieth birthday. He was a violent politician, but is less active now, and is talked of as a probable Lieutenant-Governor for Nova Scotia.

> Dr. Charles (later Sir Charles) Tupper, a physician from Nova Scotia, was at that time Minister of Inland Revenue. For three months, in 1896, he was to occupy the position of Prime Minister of Canada.
>
> Hector (later Sir Hector) Louis Langevin was Minister of Public Works.
>
> The Honourable Joseph Howe, Secretary of State for the Provinces, was appointed Lieutenant-Governor of Nova Scotia in May, 1873. He died a few weeks later.

We are working at our outdoor rink, and find it rather troublesome to manage. An Englishman exclaims, 'Flood it!' But this is just the difficulty, for the water freezes as it touches the ice, and will not 'flood it.' And if, by having a circle of barrels round the space and upsetting them all at the same time, we do succeed in covering it with water, and go happy to bed dreaming of beautiful ice and a capital skate, we wake in the morning to find either that it has snowed, or that the wind has blown old snow over the rink, which a ray of sunshine having partially melted, has stuck hard to our lovely ice; and there we are longing to skate and obliged to begin '*au déluge*' again.

WEDNESDAY, 18TH. – We had a ball. The room was well lighted; the supper (by the new cook) was very good, and I hope everyone was happy. Sir Hugh and Miss Allan arrived for it, and remain till Saturday! Colonel Fletcher was told that 'Mr. Hamilton will be spoilt here, people like him so much.'

FRIDAY, 20TH. – A great snowstorm. I was to have gone to a mission service, but could not face the weather.

MONDAY, 23RD. – This morning we visited the Grey Sisters. Then I came home and arranged my concert-room with stage, etc.

The Belgian Minister at Washington arrived in time for an early dinner, and is staying with us. At eight the singers arrived, and began to dress, and at 8.30 the listeners came pouring in, were cordially greeted by His Ex. and Her Ex. at the door, and were seated by obliging A.D.C.s and secretaries.

The music began at nine – it really was very good, and the acting admirable! The costumes were perfect, and everyone was delighted with the two hours' amusement.

I allowed the three children to be present, and they enjoyed it immensely. Terence was in fits over 'Figaro,' and in great anxiety the whole time to understand everything. We had supper at eleven, and the whole entertainment was considered a great success.

TUESDAY, 24TH. – Oh! this really is cold; two ears, two faces, two knees, and one finger frozen in our family. We are 22° below zero, and are devoted to our clouds [scarves], in which we wallow. In spite of this we skate, but are thankful to think we are feeling the worst cold we need expect here.

CHRISTMAS DAY. – Thermometer 20° below zero. Proprieties out of the question – must go to church in sealskin turbans, and must undress when we get there, as we sit near the stove. When we leave, the amount of things to be put on is frightful. There is my cloak, and my cloud, fur gauntlets, and woollen cuffs; there is Archie's coat, and his cloud, and turban, and gloves. Then Fred and D. have to be clothed; happily, everyone in the church is equally busy muffling up. D., you will be surprised to hear, wears less than he used to do in May at home, and scarcely seems to feel the cold at all. Fred, too, bears it well, with the exception of his ears, about which he is decidedly nervous. He is always feeling them and inquiring from passers-by whether they are frozen. The children play in the snow as if it were hay, and enjoy themselves immensely. Their nurse, Mrs. Hall, dislikes the wrapping up, but has been consoled by a present of a pair of skates. Their governess is learning too; she won't wrap up, and I really fear some accident for her. Nothing but a frost-bite will make her careful.

We have arranged a Christmas-tree, and this evening all the children of the family assembled for it. They came at five, and the nine of them, with their governesses and nurses, were ushered into the room with great ceremony. Hermie rushed at a doll. 'There is my doll,' and kissed it most fervently. They all got various presents, and the big ones dined with us, and afterwards played blind man's bluff, snapdragon, etc., etc.

The pictures have arrived, and are a great improvement to the house. In my room I have drawings of Killyleagh and Clandeboye, and there are a few oil-portraits in the dining-room, which make it look home-like. We shall be quite sorry to go away next week, to undertake a long journey in the snow, and to be a month in hotels.

FRIDAY, 27TH. – We continue to practise our skating. I get on very well with ordinary skating. D. can go backwards and do the figure

of eight. Fred is beginning the outside edge, and is studying the art
with great care. The children are not industrious; they find making
snow houses and tobogganing much more amusing than lamely shuf-
fling over the ice.

SATURDAY, 28TH. – This morning we visited the 'Congregation de
Notre Dame,' where Nelly was shown a Christmas-tree, and told to
choose what she liked best on it. In spite of my nudges, truth would
out, and she took a pretty doll instead of the insignificant present I
was trying to suggest to her.

Directly after lunch I went down to the rink to receive my skating-
party. It went off extremely well. Some of the young people skated
beautifully, Miss Patrick and Miss Kingsford, two pretty girls, being
the best performers. Skating is very graceful when well done, and the
scene on the rink so gay. I had on my skates, but did not feel equal
to skating before such experts.

When it became cold, we came into the house, drank tea and
mulled claret, and danced for an hour. We intend to repeat these
parties once a week. The dancing was quite a surprise this time, but
it will be expected now, and parcels of shoes and various decorations
will be brought next Saturday.

MONDAY, 30TH. – I think the pleasures of sleighing are exaggerated;
it appears to me much the same as driving in a cart. You have no
springs, and the snow gets into hard, rough ruts. This is treason! One
ought to be enthusiastic over its delights. The bells and the red
plumes on the horses' backs are the best of it.

WEDNESDAY, JANUARY 1ST. 1873. – New Year's Day is kept here as a
visiting day. All the ladies stay at home, and all the gentlemen visit.
D. and I were 'at home' from three to five and received 293 men. It
was a most lovely day, warm and bright, with only ten degrees of
frost.

CHAPTER 5

Montreal
JANUARY-FEBRUARY 1873

ST. LAWRENCE HALL: SUNDAY, JANUARY 5TH. – We left Rideau yesterday, had dinner at Prescott, and reached Montreal at night. The Mayor met us, and we drove to this hotel, where we have taken rooms for a month. Our own cooks and servants arrive early in the week and arrange everything, while we go down to Quebec for a ball.

MONDAY, 6TH. – We went early to the Rink, which we were curious to see. It is a great place, 250 feet long, of smooth, dull-looking ice. Most of the skaters were children of four years old and upwards, going backwards and forwards, Dutch rolling, making eights – looking as if they had been born on skates.

Skating is particularly pretty for ladies, as the dress hides the machinery which is visible when men skate. An indoor rink is dull, however, I think, compared to skating out of doors.

We went down to the station at 11 p.m. D. and I had two good bed-rooms, and the others had beds in a Pullman car. Mrs. Dent had a sofa in the sitting-room, and His Ex.'s shorthand writer, finding he was expected to occupy a couch opposite to my fair maid, shyly jumped into it with his hat on, which I suppose he considered gave an air of respectability to the proceeding. Dent was giggling at him under her rug, and was still more amused when, later, the hat of propriety rolled off, and the little man pulled his clothes right over his head.

TUESDAY, 7TH. – We awoke in time to have a cup of tea at a passing station, and arrived at Quebec at twelve.

The morning was lovely, and the Citadel, the river, and Quebec looked so picturesque, with the sun shining on the snow. We crossed in the steamer, cutting through ice, and were accompanied by the Mayor. We drove up to the hotel over the most bumpy roads – the snow in great mounds, and the jump from one hill to another quite amusing. The warm reception we met with was very pleasant.

WEDNESDAY, 8TH. – This morning we went to the Rink, where D. is practising hard, aided by all the young ladies of Quebec, who give him lessons in turn. In the afternoon we opened a poultry show, and I examined each scrubby fowl, and made the most of my home experience. This place in winter is not suited to poultry, and their plumage shows that they are shut up in stables.

The Citizens' Ball took place to-night. It is one given for us by the city, and for which we were invited to return when we left in the autumn. It was a splendid entertainment. The room was decorated with our colours, and with wreaths of roses, and there was a large reception committee, who took great care of me all the evening.

THURSDAY, 9TH. – An excursion to Montmorency was arranged for to-day, but I did not go. At noon, forty-two sleighs, each driving a tandem, came to the door, and D. got into the first in a snowstorm. The weather cleared later, and they drove twelve miles, had lunch, visited the Fall, and were back by dusk. They enjoyed it, though they came in very cold.

D. and I dined alone, and then went off to a skating ball. The Rink was lighted up, hung with flags and lanterns, and there were regular dancing programmes. It was a very pretty sight. I can't conceive anything more graceful than the lancers skated; waltzing also is pretty, but few people, even here, can do it. I had a very comfortable seat, and sat there with a never-ceasing stream of figures passing before me.

D. skated a good deal at the ball, and Fred took some turns with the young ladies hand-in-hand round the place, but they did not dance. I went round twice, but am not a good enough skater for these public demonstrations.

FRIDAY, 10TH. – I proceeded to the grating at the Ursuline Convent to thank the nuns for some lovely specimens of their work, which they sent me as a New Year's gift. Then I 'received' farewell visits. All at Quebec are so nice to us – they are very home-like.

We left the hotel in the evening, crossed the river, and had our special car, in which we first had tea and whist, and then went to bed, while Fred and Mr. Coulson attended 'a party' in the next carriage.

SATURDAY, 11TH. – We arrived at Montreal in time for breakfast, skated, and had interviews with the Mayor and various officials; but our work only begins on Monday.

MONDAY, 13TH. – D. visited a hospital, the Law Courts, and some churches after lunch. In the evening we had a Drawing-room. There were about 1,000 people at it.

TUESDAY, 14TH. – We skated and visited a school in the morning, and at night had our first dinner here – twenty-eight people: Bishop Oxenden and his wife, the Mayor and his wife, and others. Our drawing-room is small for so many, but they left early, as we were going to a ball at Mons. Papineau's – the first private entertainment I have been to in Canada. His wife must have been handsome, with brown eyes, and white hair powdered. They have a pretty house, and the ball was pleasant.

L. J. Amédée Papineau, a lawyer and notary, was a son of Hon. Louis Joseph Papineau, the French-Canadian reformer. His wife, Eleanor Westcott Papineau, was from Saratoga in New York State.

WEDNESDAY, 15TH. – This evening we attended a snow-shoe torchlight procession given in our honour. At eight o'clock the president of the society came for us, and we drove out till we met the 'snowshoes.' They wore white blanket coats, tight leggings, and red caps, and the sight really was picturesque and very Canadian: the bright night, the snow-covered ground, hundreds of sleighs and thousands of tinkling bells, the torches, and the gaiety of the whole scene, were delightful. The procession walked up the mountain, and we drove round it, watching the fiery serpent winding among the trees. The roads were excellent, and it was the first sleigh-drive I have really enjoyed. In about an hour we arrived at a house where supper was prepared, and where we had a very amusing evening. There was a long list of toasts, and a song with a chorus was sung after each. There was the usual amount of compliments to the country, to us, to the Mayor, to everybody. Canada was the finest country, the Canadians the finest people, His Excellency worthy to be a Canadian, Her Excellency most excellent, the Mayor admirable, the Mayoress most hospitable, our hosts . . . words failed! When the Mayor got up to return thanks, he said that 'As Canadians, we have one fault – we are too fond of praising ourselves; but in this case it is sincere.' When all was over, we got into our sleigh again, and the fresh air was delightful! The snowshoers were by this time 'jolly good fellows,' and I found them rather alarming to our horses and to me; so we begged them not to accompany us home, and I think they were not sorry to return to the supper-room.

THURSDAY, 16TH. – I may tell you, once for all, that we spend the morning in the Rink.

We had a large dinner in the evening; Sir Francis and Miss Hincks were of the party. I fear it was not lively, but what can one do in a small room with thirty strangers?

SATURDAY, 18TH. – We had tea with the Bishop and Mrs. Oxenden. They have a nice house and had collected a little party to meet us; but we had to hurry away, as it was snowing hard, and we had to dress for a dinner-party. It was to have been a small one, but stretched out to twenty-four, and was, I thought, the pleasantest we have had here.

MONDAY, 20TH. – This was rather a hard day. Sir Hugh Allan and M. Delfosse came to breakfast at nine, and D. went off to be photographed for a paper dollar immediately after. At eleven we proceeded to the Rink, and only returned for His Ex. to receive an address from the Board of Trade.

When that deputation was dismissed, we drove to a Protestant deaf-and-dumb institution, which was a very good one; but it was the wrong one as far as I was concerned, as that I wished to see was the Catholic establishment, where the deaf-mutes are taught to *speak*.

A refuge for old people was the next institution on our list, and we only got home for a short rest before a big dinner. I enjoyed the evening, and some nice people dined with us.

TUESDAY, 21ST. – Miss Allan came to lunch with me, and D. and I drove in state to M'Gill College. Here our horses were taken out by the students, and we were dragged up to the door. Speeches were made and we were shown everything of interest; but while D. was taken to the dissecting-room, I went to have tea with the ladies.

Commenting on the action of the students in pulling their sleigh by long ropes to the college doors, Lord Dufferin said:

Only upon one other occasion, and that the most important in the lives of each of us, have Lady Dufferin and myself been treated to similar honour, and that was upon our marriage day. I can only say that if the "coaches" of this college are as good as the "horses" [applause and laughter] the students cannot fail to take very high and creditable degrees.

We dined with the Mayor. He has a nice house, and there was a splendid display of flowers on his table; in fact, I believe he had bought every flower in Montreal for the occasion.

WEDNESDAY, 22ND. – We had (of course) a dinner-party. D. took in a bride, and I had a senator and a judge on either side of me.

THURSDAY, 23RD. – At ten D. went to a military school, and had the rest of the day for amusing himself with skating and curling. We had another large dinner: 130 people will have dined with us this week, most of whom are new acquaintances.

FRIDAY, 24TH. – There was a tremendous snowstorm to-day, but we had an appointment to visit 'Monklands.' It used to be the Governor-General's house when the Government was at Montreal. I believe the situation is fine, but it must have been too far from the town for a Government House. It has been enlarged, and now contains 22 nuns and 150 pupils.

> Monklands was built in the eighteenth century, probably by Hon. James (later Sir James) Monk, 1745-1826. In the seventeen-nineties it was his country home. At that time the official residence of the governors was the Château de Ramezay in Montreal. But in 1844 Montreal replaced Kingston as the capital of the Province of Canada, and the Government rented Monklands as the Governor's residence. It was occupied in turn by Baron Metcalfe, Earl Cathcart and Lord Elgin.
>
> After the burning of the Parliament Building in 1849, Montreal no longer remained the capital. Five years later Monklands was purchased by the Congregation of Notre Dame, and since that time has served as a central building for a girls' school—the Villa Maria Convent.

We had a small dinner and were tolerably merry. One of our young ladies turned out to be a 'blue-stocking,' and amused us much by laying down the law to the company.

SATURDAY, 25TH. – I took a drive along the river to prepare for the labours of the afternoon, being 'at home.' We began to receive at three, and had a constant stream of visitors till 5.30. My conversation was 'How do you do?' 'How cold you must be!' 'Good-bye!'

MONDAY, 27TH. – After skating, I brought Miss Allan back to lunch, and we went to a chemical lecture. It was given to ladies, and I am patroness of the association. D. visited the Montreal Waterworks.

We had a dinner of thirty-six – our last here. The children arrived at midnight, looking extremely well.

TUESDAY, 28TH. – We all went to visit a large convent called Hochelaga. It is a fine building, and contains a beautiful chapel copied from one in Rome. We heard the organ played and the novices sing.

In the evening there was a 'citizens' ' ball given in our honour. There was an excellent ballroom, with an enormous supper-room off it. An arrangement was made at one end, like the canons' stalls in a cathedral; these were lined with green, and decorated with the antelope and heart, our motto, etc., etc.; in each a chair, but only one stall was used all the night, and that by me. The whole room was ornamented with flags and 'V.R.s' and 'D.s', and was very pretty. There was a state quadrille first, of enormous length, reaching the whole way down the room, and with us and the Mayor alone at the ends. I enjoyed my share of the evening, and danced all the squares before supper, leaving soon after. An official list of partners was made out for D., and he remained dancing with dowagers until four o'clock in the morning.

WEDNESDAY, 29TH. – D. had some relaxation to-day, skating and curling. I went over the R.C. Deaf-and-dumb Institutions; there the poor creatures are being taught to speak, and very successfully too. There are separate establishments for the boys and girls.

This is a bright, cold day, 20° below zero. I spent the evening with the children, D. and staff having gone to a night-tobogganing party and dance. The former returned at twelve, and the young ones not till nearly three. They enjoyed it, but thought it a dangerous amusement in the dark, and Mr. Coulson had the sleeves completely cut out of his coat by a toboggan coming down on top of him.

THURSDAY, 30TH. – The fancy-dress skating ball took place in the evening, and was a most beautiful sight, besides being great fun.

We drove to the Rink wearing morning dress, and went out on a balcony to look down upon the scene. It was like a fairy pantomime of gigantic size, and most striking. The building was hung with flags and Chinese lanterns, and from one end to the other there were gaily dressed figures of every sort and variety moving about with that easy, graceful swing which belongs to skating. When we went downstairs we were conducted to the further end of the rink, where a platform and chairs at the edge of the ice were prepared for us.

Here we stood, while the two sets of 'state' lancers were danced in front of us. One was a *poudré* set: each couple skated in, bowed to us as they passed, and took their places. I think I have already told you how beautiful the lancers are when skated, and you can imagine how the addition of costume increases their beauty: I never saw anything half so pretty. When they were over D. and Fred put on dominoes, and skated off too. I collected a few friends under my canopy, the children sat on the edge of it, and we were amused the whole evening watching the different characters as they came before us. There was one delightful old gentleman who passed us every round in some different way, acting capitally the whole time. There was an excellent and large monkey, who performed for the children. There were Indians and Chinamen, cavaliers, etc., etc. The ladies' costumes had of necessity short petticoats, so there was every variety of peasant – Dolly Vardens, Watteaus, etc. – and very pretty they were! In fact, to an ordinary fancy ball you have to add perpetual motion, – for no one ever stands still on the ice. The spectators lined the walls. We were torn away to have some supper, and after it I sat on the upper balcony to see the general effect. They danced another set of lancers, and 'Sir Roger de Coverley.' I am sure that if they had not turned the Governor-General out, by playing 'God save the Queen,' I never should have been able to get him away, he enjoyed it so much.

FRIDAY, 31ST. – D. visited the blind schools, and, from his account of them, I was quite sorry not to have gone with him. He was so touched by a little blind child feeling his face all over with her tiny fingers to feel what he was like.

SATURDAY, FEBRUARY 1ST. – We went this afternoon to see some snow-shoe races, and, for the first time since we have been in Canada, we were all thoroughly cold, and were glad when it was over.

In the evening some games at the Rink were very amusing. One sport looked dangerous: it was a hurdle-race, and the skaters had to jump over stiff barriers placed in their way. Numbers of them caught their feet on the top bar, and came down; it was wonderful that they escaped being seriously hurt. The funniest race to watch was the barrel race: a number of flour-barrels without ends were placed at intervals along the course. The first row had the same number of barrels as boys; the second, and the third sets had fewer, for the competitors got separated and did not all reach the barrels at the same time. Each boy dived down when he reached the barrel, crept through it, and skated on, as fast as possible, to the next. Of course the barrels rolled and tumbled about on the ice, and some boys were much quicker at getting through them than others. There were also backward races, and girls' races, and boys' races, etc., all on skates. I gave the prizes at the end.

MONDAY, 3RD. – In the morning we went to the Rink, and a small band of music having been obtained, there were lancers danced, and waltzes, and everyone worked hard, some because they skate for the prizes to-morrow, and some because it was to be our last day there.

We went to an Irish concert after dinner. All the songs were Irish, and there was a little speechifying between times.

TUESDAY, 4TH. – It thaws to-day, and is consequently horrid, but we are all full of excitement about the skating-matches this afternoon. Quebec has sent a champion lady, and has told her she need not return to her ancient city if she does not win the locket D. has offered as a prize.

Later. – The ladies' match was very interesting, but the day was spoilt by two *contretemps*. The judges said there were ties, and awarded the prize to two, which ended in D.'s having to duplicate the locket he had chosen. Then, at the very last moment, the gentlemen found fault with some arrangement, and refused to skate, so one walked over the course by himself!

The little girls' skating was beautiful. When the matches were over, there was dancing till eleven o'clock.

CHAPTER 6

Our First Parliamentary Session
FEBRUARY-MAY 1873

OTTAWA: FRIDAY, FEBRUARY 14TH. – The curling-rink, outside our windows, was ready to-day, and the gentlemen had a game in the morning and skated in the afternoon. We played 'puss in the corner,' and 'friar's ground' on skates with the children, who were delighted with this idea – mine, I beg to say.

SATURDAY, 15TH. – Curling and skating are our exercises every day. We have had a great consultation over our arrangements for the 'season.' During Lent there can be no balls, but we shall have some plays. Two pieces, 'The First Night' and 'To Oblige Benson,' are already in hand, and we are to have one play each week, and each play twice. This will give us four entertainments. After Easter we shall give a big ball in the new room.

For the opening of Parliament we have invited Mr. and Mrs. Howland, with whom we stayed in Toronto, to come to us. The meeting is on the 5th, and we have a Cabinet dinner the night before, a dinner the day after, an ice-party on Friday, and a small dinner on Saturday.

I suppose the House will 'sit' all through April, so that we can ask the 280 members to dinner before they leave Ottawa.

The children's dreadful colds are all better, but the doctor tells me he has had over 200 cases of the same. At one o'clock in the night the thermometer was 20° below zero, and at one in the day 50° above – a difference of seventy degrees – so it is not extraordinary that people catch colds!

D. continues to feel quite warm and comfortable, and not to wear a fur coat: his turn will come in the summer, when he will begin to wrap up.

MONDAY, 17TH. – Fred, Nelly and I took a drive this morning, as the day was so splendid. In the afternoon I received 133 visitors, and if the weather has ears they must have been extremely hot when we had finished discussing it on every side.

The 'Witness' publishes an account of 'Hamilton Rowan,' mentioning me as his grand-daughter, which, they are pleased to say, 'accounts for the good drop in me.' This is the paper which came to ask Fred for details of our engagements at Montreal, and said, 'Oh! we will miss the ball, if you please; we are a religious paper.'

WEDNESDAY, 19TH. – Such a thaw to-day; our ice was all under water, and we are quite afraid the winter is going. We shall have a very *mauvais quart d'heure* between this and summer – a time when skating is impossible, and walking and driving nearly so, everything dripping around us.

Some of Lady Harriet's 'imported' servants are beginning to marry; happily, mine are still fancy free.

SATURDAY, 22ND. – The actors in 'To Oblige Benson' arrived at twelve this morning to rehearse the piece. They none of them knew it in the least. 'They' are Fred and Mr. Coulson, Colonel and Mrs. Stuart, and a nice-looking Miss Himsworth.

Sir John and Lady Macdonald, and M. Langevin, arrived, to stay till Monday. Sir John is the Prime Minister, and M. Langevin the Public Works, who has built our ball-room and does all our improvements.

MONDAY, MARCH 3RD. – To-morrow the Session, with its duties, commences.

TUESDAY, 4TH. – As the dancing is over for the present, I have been busy all morning refurnishing my big drawing-room, which has hitherto been kept as a ball-room. The new room is nearly ready, and is very handsome. It is to be opened as a theatre, and we are having such a pretty stage put up. Lady Harriet Fletcher has come over to spend a few days, for a change, and to help me entertain Mrs. Howland.

We had our Cabinet dinner; all men, except Lady Harriet and me, the two ladies of the house. I sat between the Prime Minister, Sir John, and the Postmaster-General, Mr. Campbell. They were both very pleasant neighbours. All were in uniform, and all full of animation and ready for the fray.

WEDNESDAY, 5TH. – In the afternoon, D. dressed in uniform, and drove in a sleigh-and-four, escorted by troops, A.D.C.s, and secretaries, to direct his faithful Lords and Commons to choose a Speaker. This did not take very long, and on his return we went and sat at the rink in delicious sunshine for a couple of hours.

THURSDAY, 6TH. – The opening of Parliament. Having to dress in the middle of the day, I was lazy, and did not appear at all till I was arrayed in my finery. His Ex. wore the Governor's uniform, like that of the Queen's Household: collar of St. Patrick, and cocked hat kept on all the time. Mrs. Howland and I, Mr. Pattisson and Mr. Curtis, went in the first carriage, Miss Blake and three children in the next. We arrived some time before the Governor-General, and I was conducted to my seat by the Gentleman-Usher of the Black Rod. I sat to the left of the throne, and down each side of Senate were rows of ladies in full dress; the Senators were on the floor of the House, and the galleries were full to the ceiling. D. drove in an open sleigh with four horses, accompanied by Mr. Howland and Colonel Fletcher. Mr. Holbeach followed with Fred. As they came up to the building twenty-one guns were fired. The Black Rod met the procession and walked backwards, bowing all the way, His Excellency getting more stern-looking every minute. When the procession arrived at the Senate-Chamber, we all stood up, and waited until the Governor-General, having taken his seat on the throne, requested us to be seated.

The Commons were sent for, and we sat in solemn silence till they came. D. then read his speech, first in English, and then all over again in French; and everything that was said was repeated in the two languages. Then Colonel Fletcher carried the speeches to the Speakers of both Houses, and so the ceremony ended, and we went away as we came. The children were much interested, but remarked upon Papa's gravity: they thought it a proper occasion to be wreathed in smiles.

SATURDAY, 8TH. – We had a pleasant dinner-party of Ministers. Mr. and Mrs. Howland seemed very happy, and she looked very smart in blue velvet.

TUESDAY, 11TH. – Mr. and Mrs. Howland left this morning in a snowstorm, and we remained in the house all day. Great arrangements and discussions go on about the coming Drawing Room: Who is to have the *entrée*? Who is to have seats? Which way are these people to come in, and which way those? Where is Her Excellency's cloak to be taken off? etc., etc. Then I – not being very well, and having meekly asked to have a tall office-stool behind me, against which I might occasionally lean, – an architect and several carpenters have been busily engaged in making a design – ground-plan and elevation – of a complicated and splendid erection, crowned by a vase of flowers, and covered with crimson, which is to appear as a part of the throne, but which is to be scooped out for me to sit on; and a request for my exact height has been forwarded to me, that all may be correct. This ceremony will be in the Senate Chamber, and both Houses of Parliament have adjourned for the occasion.

We also had a discussion as to whether we could put off our theatricals on Thursday, for Mario and Carlotta Patti, who were to have given a concert to-day, have been snowbound, and cannot get here till that day: and as 200 of the principal people here are coming to us, both the singers and the public lose a good deal.

> Giuseppe Mario, 1810-83, was an Italian operatic tenor. Appearing with him was Carlotta Patti, who, like her more famous younger sister, Adelina Patti, was a coloratura soprano.

Pepper's Ghost is also tearing its hair at the number of gaieties in Ottawa, and wrote an entreating appeal to D. to come himself on Friday, so we could not take the Ghost's day; after much consideration we keep Thursday, but try to get Mario and C. Patti to sing a song here after our play.

> Pepper's Ghost was an illusion show in which people or objects on stage mysteriously appeared, vanished, or changed. It was, quite literally, all done with mirrors.

The arrangement of our political dinners also requires some thought. We have to study which party the proposed guests belong to: which province, whether French or English – Upper or Lower Canada, their social position, etc., etc., so that the dinners may be made as pleasant as possible to the guests.

WEDNESDAY, 12TH. – Still too fine and warm, and ice bad. We are sorry, as this evening two very good skaters come to stay with us, one from Quebec and one from Montreal.

We dressed in our best for the Drawing Room, and got to the Parliament Buildings at nine. In spite of all the grand arrangements we got out at the wrong door, but everything else went off very well. The Ministers went in with us, and we stood by the throne – I with my support behind me – their wives followed, then Senators, and then the World.

THURSDAY, 13TH. – We had a great party to-night, and opened our new room. The guests assembled at nine, and after having some tea were conducted through unknown passages to their future ball-room, where they found 300 chairs arranged in rows, in front of a very pretty little stage, and a band dressed in the gorgeous uniform of the Governor-General's Guards. The entertainment began with music, and was followed by 'To Oblige Benson,' which went off admirably. People were particularly delighted with Fred's performance – he did the part of Trotter Southdown; and Mrs. Southdown was excellent, too.

Just as they finished, Mario and M. Sauret, a violin-player, arrived. They came as guests, and would hear of no terms. After a little, D. asked Mario to sing, and the audience were greatly delighted at his doing so twice. The violin-player was also a great treat. It was wonderfully kind of both gentlemen to perform for us, as they only arrived at Ottawa at five in the afternoon, and came direct from a concert. This delightful music made our party a great success. We went straight into supper afterwards, and it took some time to feed and 'speed' the parting 300.

FRIDAY, 14TH. – I kept this as a day of rest, and in the evening despatched my young party, under Lady Harriet's chaperonage, to see 'Pepper's Ghost.' She does not seem to have been a good duenna, for she said 'good-night' to the young men and maidens directly they were seated, and slept composedly through the whole lecture.

SATURDAY, 15TH. – It began to pour with rain this afternoon, and the roads were very bad for our dinner-party. We had one of thirty people – the first of a long series of similar dinners to be given every Saturday for three months. The guests were culled from all parts of Canada; we had representatives from the shores of the Atlantic, the Pacific, the St. Lawrence, Lake Huron; Upper and Lower Canadians, French, English and Scotch, 'Grits' (the Opposition) and Conservatives (the Government).

The night turned out very bad; it blew fearfully, and has blown in a large window in our new room.

WEDNESDAY, 19TH. – Two tourists came to skate, in wonderful costumes: striped red-and-yellow stockings, moccasins, bright blue blanket-coats, with embroidered shoulder-pieces, and Albanian scarfs round their waists. We asked them to dine with us before the play.

People were quite surprised and delighted with 'The First Night,' The old actor was splendidly done by M. Kimber, and the singing introduced before and during the piece was excellent.

FRIDAY, 28TH. – I took a drive in the afternoon, and at four went to the Houses of Parliament to pay my first visit there. I have a seat on the floor of the House, next to the Speaker's. The business was not very interesting, but I was rather amused, as a number of people made very short speeches, and one saw their 'tricks and their manners.'

SATURDAY, 29TH. – In the evening we had a large Parliamentary dinner. One of my near neighbours was very interesting. He is a 'workingman' member; we had met him soon after his election, when he dined in a rough coat, but now he wears evening clothes; he talked so pleasantly, and was full of information. One of our guests, a French-Canadian, made great efforts to reach the nursery when he heard the children romping upstairs, and told me he was most curious to see 'le lord.' I think he imagined Archie must be very peculiar.

> The eldest son, Archie—Archibald James Leofric Temple—was
> Viscount Clandeboye.

WEDNESDAY, APRIL 2ND. – We drove into Ottawa on wheels. D. goes in every week to have tête-a-tête interviews with different Members of Parliament. This evening there was a vote of want of confidence in the Government, but the Ministers won by thirty-three.

We had 'Benson' for the last time; very well done, and much appreciated. The children helped to warm up the audience by their shrieks of delight.

FRIDAY, 4TH. – Two men dined with us: one, the Speaker of the Legislature in Manitoba, who has lately been tarred-and-feathered by the people, and who came to relate his experiences of that operation.

> The election of the preceding summer had given John A. Macdonald's Government only a slim majority. Now in the House accusations were brought that in order to finance the election large sums of money had been accepted from capitalists negotiating for the contract to build the railway to British Columbia, promised that province when it had entered Confederation in 1871. This was the beginning of the so-called Pacific Scandal.

Dr. J. Curtis Bird, M.R.C.S., (England), had represented St. Paul's riding from 1870, the year Manitoba became a province of the Dominion of Canada. He became Speaker of its Legislative Assembly February 5, 1873, a position he occupied until a dissolution came in 1874.

The other, a Mr. Otley – a nephew of Sir Hastings Doyle's, who has been engineering near the Rocky Mountains – has walked hundreds of miles on snow-shoes, lived for months on salt pork, been eaten by mosquitoes in summer, and slept and lived, unprepared for winter, in an atmosphere 40° below zero. He came out with us in the *Prussian*.

TUESDAY, 8TH. – I went to the House, as a scrimmage was expected. First, there was great excitement over the Easter holidays – what length they should be – and then a party motion about which there was a great deal of interest. The Opposition had asked for a Committee to inquire into the conduct of members of the Government, accusing them of bribery. They lost, and then the Government itself asked for the same Committee, saying they courted inquiry. There was a good deal of irritation about the whole affair.

TUESDAY, 15TH. – The two Miss Bethunes arrived yesterday to stay a week with us, and we opened our new ball-room this evening. It is a fine room, very lofty and well-proportioned. It has not yet been painted, so we decorated it with white-and-blue twists of tarlatan and bunches of pink roses. These encircled all the windows and doors, and appeared to be twisted round the flat pillars against the wall and across the corners. The crimson throne was at one end of the room, and there was a place for the band at the other. The ante-room, hall, billiard, and tea-rooms, the passage leading up to my boudoir, and the conservatory, looked very pretty, the latter being lighted with Chinese lanterns. The large drawing-room and dining-room were both arranged for supper, and seated 140 at a time. Some 650 people were present, and, they say, all were pleased.

THURSDAY, MAY 1ST. – This week we have had lovely weather. The sun is quite hot, and I am out all day. We have put up a tent on the lawn, and every afternoon the family play football, marbles, prisoner's base, and other games, to the great delight of all.

We find Parliament is likely to sit another ten days, so we have given up all idea of moving to Quebec at present. We are rather afraid of the heat and the mosquitoes here, but it cannot be helped.

FRIDAY, 2ND. – Encouraged by the lovely weather, I put a notice in the paper that I should be 'at home' to-day, intending to receive people in the garden. But the afternoon poured with rain; so I had to sit in the drawing-room. About fifty people came, and they danced, and were apparently quite happy. Nine children took part in the amusements, the little ones liking the band, and getting quite at home with the strangers.

SATURDAY, 3RD. – The provoking weather was fine again to-day, and I am under my tent once more. Mr. and Mrs. Ryan and her daughter arrived from Montreal to stay Sunday with us. Mr. Ryan is a very pleasant Irish Senator, his wife a nice Swiss-French lady, for whom he waited forty years, she marrying someone else in the meantime.

THURSDAY, 8TH. – I saw Lady Macdonald on Tuesday, the day that Sir John made his splendid speech in the House, with which Fred was so greatly delighted.

FRIDAY, 9TH. – I advertised that I should be 'at home between three and six' this afternoon. I received in the tent, and the company sat and walked about listening to the Guards' band till after four, when they went into the ballroom and danced vigorously for the rest of the time. But I stayed in the garden and watched the dancers come out to the tea, and talked to a few of the old people, though most of them danced too.

SATURDAY, 10TH. – Mr. Coulson left us to-day. We were sorry to lose him, and, I think, he was sorry to go. He joins his regiment (60th Rifles) at Halifax.

We had our last Parliamentary dinner for this Session. The Prime Minister of Prince Edward's Island and some colleagues of his, who are here to try and arrange about joining the Confederation, dined.

WEDNESDAY, 14TH. – Fred went to dine in Ottawa, Lady Harriet was having tea with me, and D., the Colonel, and the Doctor were looking for fossils, when, to my great surprise, Lord George Campbell was announced – the Duke of Argyll's sailor son. We sent to the hotel for his things.

THURSDAY, 15TH. – Fred took our guest for a ride, and in the afternoon they went with Lady Harriet and Miss Blake to the House. We had a dinner-party, which was arranged for a young lady who is going to marry an Englishman, and who wanted to dine here before she went home. We asked two other girls, and put the smart young man between them! Oddly enough, an old shipmate of his, whom he had not seen for four years, was also at dinner.

Prince Edward's Island has come into the Confederation, so the Governor-General's dominion is enlarged; but he loses one of his titles.

SATURDAY, 17TH. – A little girl was born this day, and the Queen has telegraphed that she will be her godmother.

CHAPTER 7

On The St. Lawrence
JUNE-JULY 1873

TUESDAY, JUNE 10TH. – We left Ottawa this morning very early, going by rail to Prescott, with our whole family, the new baby included. There we got into a steamer, and sat all day on deck. We had a delightful cruise down the river, and an exciting descent of the Rapids. In one place we passed within a few inches of a wreck, and we felt quite creepy.

At Montreal we changed steamers. The children were delighted with the grandeur of the St. Lawrence boats, with their enormous saloons and state-cabins. When we were at tea we heard some music – the 'Dead March' – being played. Looking out, we saw, passing slowly in the darkness, the steamer with the body of Sir George Cartier on board. It was a striking moment – the chapel on board lighted up, the band playing, and bells tolling at sea, answered by bells tolling on shore.

> In a footnote Lady Dufferin recorded:
> *Sir George Cartier, late member for Montreal East, had died in England. He was a descendant of the famous Jacques Cartier who, in 1534, took possession of Canada in the name of Francis I, King of France.*

WEDNESDAY, 11TH. – We awoke at Quebec, and found it cold and wet. In spite of the weather and the early hour, we had a friendly welcome from the people.

MONDAY, 16TH. – The little baby's christening-day!

A large bouquet had been sent me in the morning, and beautiful flowers for the font, by Mr. Levi. The Cathedral was full of people; I had my whole six children there, and they made a very good show.

Lady 'Victoria Alexandrina Muriel May' behaved admirably, and slept soundly the whole time, in spite of a deluge of Jordan water.

Then we registered her baptism very fully: – Myself as 'Proxy for Her Majesty the Queen'; Lady H. Fletcher, 'godmother'; Sir John A. Macdonald, 'godfather'; Fred and a Minister, Mr. Campbell – as present.

Basil was, I am told, on the verge of being naughty, and won all the ladies' hearts by his wicked efforts to climb over the pew, and to knock down all the prayer-books.

We came home and rested a little, and at four I was 'at home.' The company, D., and the Fletchers went out on the platform and enjoyed themselves, listening to the band, but Fred and I were kept hard at work announcing and receiving people. We could not stir for an instant, a continuous stream coming in, and he was doubtless much tantalised as the young ladies passed him, and left him, like a sentry, tied to the door-post. I tried to drink a cup of tea, but had it nearly shaken over my dress by twenty hands, as I said 'How do you do?' and gave it up in despair. However, the A.D.C. and I did our duty, – and outside everyone was well entertained, and the affair went off well. We had a family dinner, and all, upstairs and down, drank baby's health.

TUESDAY, 17TH. – A long day of Viceregal functions. At twelve we ate a hasty lunch and started, with five children and our 'suite,' to the Ursuline Convent, where I was to give away the prizes.

There is a new Lieutenant-Governor here [Hon. René-Edouard Caron]. As he has a large family, our combined movements on State occasions require a deal of arrangement. The first fact established is, that the Governor-General and I, on public occasions, walk first; His Honour the Lieutenant-Governor and his wife follow. But the five Lieutenant-Princesses have also to be seated in proper positions, and when (as to-day) I take three of my family the A.D.C.s tear their hair! Priests met us at the convent door; the nuns did not appear. I presented at least 200 prizes, every girl in the school, I am sure having gained from one to six 'rewards of merit.' Then I crowned six of the most remarkably virtuous young ladies. Between each trayful of books we had music. The ceremony lasted two hours. One lady fainted, but the children bore it admirably, and I took them to a field to cut grass to refresh them when it was over.

We dined at six, for we had to go out early to celebrate the 200th anniversary of the discovery of the Mississippi. 'Why on earth?' you will exclaim. Well, I don't quite know why, but Laval University has to find some object for a yearly *fête*, and the discoverers were French-Canadians.

The celebration was a tremendous affair. For three hours I sat on a very hard and stately arm-chair, with my Lieutenant-Governor beside me, on my right an empty space, on the other side of which sat His Ex. and his Lieutenant-Governess.

FRIDAY, 20TH. – We christened a large new ship this morning – the *Earl of Dufferin*. The ship is on the stocks at present, and I had great difficulty in breaking the bottle, as the rope was badly hung, and when I aimed at the narrow bow it would swing away. At the third effort, however, I succeeded.

In the evening we attended a concert given in aid of the widow of a poor gunner killed by the bursting of a gun.

SATURDAY, 21ST. – We drove down to our new yacht. The Government has fitted up a vessel for us – the *Druid*. Most charming cabins are arranged for me, and everything is perfect for yachting – but I have to combine sailor clothes with garments enough for two months of Viceregal ceremonies, which would be difficult even on the *Great Eastern*. I fear Dent will go mad with the agony of crushing my things into 'bunkers.'

My cabin has a comfortable bed, a hanging-press, and a large glass, ornamented with pink ribbon and muslin. D. has an excellent cabin off it, and Dent another. The dining-room is panelled with chintz and light wood, and Fred sleeps on one of the sofas there. We have a nice after-cabin for a drawing-room, and Lady Harriet and the Colonel have small rooms off it. To-night baby sleeps on board with her two nurses, and we sail for Tadousac.

SUNDAY, 22ND. – After breakfast we went to our new house at Tadousac. It is so pretty, with red roof, green blinds, and white walls. We have a platform, upon which we sit and look out upon the St. Lawrence, and on to which all the sitting-rooms open. The children will, I think, be very happy and comfortable here until our return, for we do not remain here now.

The clergyman has not yet arrived, so there was no service. We sat on the sands and paddled a little in D.'s Rice Lake canoe – the *Lady May*. Then we returned to our ship to dine and sleep.

MONDAY, 23RD. – Such a stormy morning: Dent, my precious maid, wild about her boxes, and giving warning on the spot; myself in despair, for she is a treasure. On shore another valuable member of our household also in a tantrum about something, and when I land I must encounter her. Dent will, I trust, calm down, for I really can't bear the idea of losing her.

An address was presented to His Ex. by the Tadousacians on the occasion of his becoming a householder here.

We gave a house-warming, and had the Curé, and the Squire's agent and his daughter, and our captain to dinner. We sat on our balcony till nine o'clock and then came on board.

TUESDAY, 24TH. – We started in a boat directly after breakfast to see the salmon-fishery, and saw ten fish caught in a labyrinth.

WEDNESDAY, 25TH. – The anniversary of our arrival in Canada. We left Tadousac during the night, and had a most lovely day on board, sitting out reading; the weather perfect. We reached the mouth of the Godbout in the afternoon, and the owners, or, rather, the hirers, of that river came on board to bring us two salmon.

THURSDAY, 26TH. – We got up before six o'clock, and started for the shore. We breakfasted at the wooden huts, and fished all day. It was almost too fine for the salmon; they jumped and frisked about under our noses, and would not rise, so that after many hours' hard work there were only three fish to show. Fred caught one on his very first throw, but did no more after this hopeful beginning. The Colonel retired to bed on his return to the ship; but the swell is better!

FRIDAY, 27TH. – D. and Colonel Fletcher went off early in the morning to fish, and Lady Harriet and I met them in the afternoon. They had had very little sport, but D. had some fun with one salmon: in pursuing it he fell into the water, but held on to his fish and landed it.

We bought two little beavers from the Indians, to keep as pets on board. The crew were greatly interested in them, and we have established them in a barrel on deck, and amuse ourselves with giving them baths and feeding them. We are to start during the night.

THE MINGAN, SUNDAY, 29TH. – Found ourselves in a splendid harbour this morning, where we shall never feel the slightest movement. On one side is an island, and on the other we see a little settlement of Indian wigwams, their nicely-built chapel, and some houses belonging to the 'Honourable Company' (the Hudson's Bay). We had service in the cabin. and after lunch went ashore.

A priest visits these out-of-the-way stations once a year, and he happens to be here now; the Indians are very obedient to him. It was picturesque to see them troop to church, the women dressed in gaudy colours, with cloth caps of red and black on their heads (something the shape of sailors' red, pointed nightcaps), their babies and children with them. We followed them into the chapel, and found all the squaws squatting on one side, and the men on the other. They sang a Canticle – the women one verse, the men the next; the music was a melancholy wail, with very few notes, and the voices of the singers were thin and weak.

The Priest and the Captain dined with us. The former is a pleasant man. He is just going up to the Esquimaux, and has before him a voyage which may last three weeks. These missionary priests have hard lives.

The huts here are made of poles very lightly covered with birchbark. In each of these tents seven or eight families live. The priest in his yearly visits arranges all of a suitable age in couples, and marries them; there is a total absence of all love-making. There is also a great meeting at a place called Bersimis once a year.

The Chief had on a black frock-coat ornamented with epaulets. He called D. 'Brother.' The same man received one of our Princes when they came here, and saluted him in the same way, then showed him a medal he wore on his breast, and said, 'Ta mère; tu connais?'

MONDAY, 30TH. – We got up at six, and went in our canoes up the Mingan, about an hour's paddle. The three rods fished away, and D. caught two salmon, one a twenty-pound fish. That was all the success before eleven o'clock, though there were about ten rises. It became very hot, and we went into our tents to wait for the cool of the day.

We were just going to begin fishing again, when an Indian canoe arrived bringing us sad news. One of our footmen had gone out fishing and was drowned. We returned immediately.

We saw the place where the accident happened. He had stood at the edge of the water with his rod, and instantly slipped. He put up his hands to take off a mosquito-veil he had put on, and disappeared. The steward dived after him, but he never rose at all. A boat was got, and presently the men saw the thick end of a fishing-rod sticking up. They took hold of it, and lifted the body. He appeared to be upright in the water, the rod fast in his hand.

The Hudson's Bay Company overseer has arranged everything, and the funeral will be to-morrow.

TUESDAY, JULY 1ST. – The priest gave us a place in the churchyard here, and at two o'clock to-day the funeral took place. The flags were half-mast high, and every possible mark of mourning and respect was shown. All the crew attended, and the sailors carried the body to the grave. D. read the service.

WEDNESDAY, 2ND. – To-day we started to go up the river. The fishermen are not very fortunate. The salmon are not rising, and the greater part of those landed have been hooked by the tail or in the back. Fred caught five; one weighed 23½ lbs., and was taken in a curious way. The hook never touched it, but it was caught in a noose round the tail. Colonel Fletcher got two, but D. was very unlucky.

THURSDAY, 3RD. – The fishermen left in the afternoon and went to sleep at the Waterfall.

FRIDAY, 4TH. – Lady Harriet and I went up the river after lunch with the Captain, who is to have some fishing. The salmon will not rise; they will not be caught. We dined on the rocks, and left our gentlemen in their tents for another day, coming back with the Captain, who was, I fear, much disappointed with his want of success. We reached the ship in such a fog!

SATURDAY, 5TH. – We spent a quiet day on board, and only went ashore for half an hour to visit Mrs. Scott, the wife of the Hudson's Bay agent. She must lead a lonely life here. The gentlemen returned in the evening; they had had very bad sport. The foot of a waterfall is an impossible place to fish in.

SUNDAY, 6TH. – We had intended leaving the Mingan to-day, but it is too stormy. We had prayers on board, and then went for a walk on the island, and looked for fossils, and saw a live seal, a flock of wild duck, and three tame goats.

MONDAY, 7TH. – After breakfast we fished for trout. I caught six good ones, and was the only lucky person. We returned to our ship at three o'clock and instantly got under way.

The afternoon was lovely, and we spent it in that kind of busy idleness which distinguishes life on board ship. 3.30: Rumour that a seal is seen; rush to the side – get out rifles, opera-glasses, telescopes – fire – splash; all right! nobody hurt: seal looks up again. 3.50: Number of sea-birds to starboard. 4.15: A whale! he appears, disappears, turns up again for nearly an hour. 5 o'clock: An island! 5.10: On the island thousands of sea-gulls sitting on their eggs. 5.20: Fire at the island; tremendous excitement amongst the gulls, and instant flight of the whole colony. 5.30: Attend to the tame partridge: fetch water for her, catch flies for her. 5.50: Attend to the beavers; they refuse to come and be looked at; are they ill? Oh, the poor pets! 'Turn their box upside down' – no, they won't come out. 'Shake them,' 'put your hand in,' etc., 'Anticosti in sight'; everyone rushes to look at it. A long, low strip of land, where we are glad to see there is nothing to be seen, as many people wanted us to stay there. 6.30: Dinner. 6.50: A shower. 7.30: A beautiful sunset. 7.40: Waves getting up, passengers getting less and less frisky. 8.15: Assured that in five hours it will be calm. 8.30: Colonel Fletcher says 'good-night.' 9: Tea comes – ladies won't attempt it. 9.10: Lady Harriet disappears. 9.30: All in bed, and, I am happy to add, asleep and well.

TUESDAY, 8TH. – A new page in our Canadian history – Gaspé. This morning I came on deck, and found we were steaming up a lovely lough into a splendid harbour. A sunny landscape: hills, and white houses, and red roofs dotted about; sufficient houses to make it very gay, and not enough to make a town of it. 'Such a place for a sailing-boat,' D. thinks, and is delighted with it.

A gentleman comes on board, and we make arrangements for the morrow. We get our mail, and write our letters.

In the afternoon a deputation appears, and reads an address, to which His Ex. replies in 'suitable terms.' The deputation consists of the Mayor, the Custom House Officers, the Doctor, and other local dignitaries. They ask if we will have a drive, and promise to have carriages ready for us when we like. So at four o'clock we go ashore. On the landing-place we are met by our friends, and I find that Gaspé driving is all to be done *tête-à-tête*. The Mayor takes His Ex. in a gig, I follow with a millowner in the next. Number Three contains the Colonel and Mr. Eden (of whom more hereafter); Number Four, Lady Harriet and the Doctor; Fred closes the procession with – I don't know who; but he must have been the fifth in order of precedence at Gaspé.

It was amusing, starting off in this way, and we took a pretty drive for nearly two hours, and made ourselves as agreeable as possible to our several companions. It was rather fun, in the evening, comparing notes as to the various items of news, and the different opinions we had gleaned from our drivers. One considered Gaspé the rising place in the universe, another viewed it gloomily; etc., etc. We saw some fireworks and a bonfire in our honour on shore.

WEDNESDAY, 9TH. – A very great day. Up at six, and go ashore; tents and baggage are packed into canoes and go down the bay, while we drive to meet them. We are in our gigs again; but ours is a double one.

We are driven by the Mr. Eden of whom I spoke before. He is the 'oldest inhabitant,' a Custom House officer, and a most sanguine person. He assures us we shall catch fifty salmon, and views everything in the *couleur de* rosiest light. We do have a most lovely drive. The country is like the highlands, and we see wild hills on each side, and Gaspé Bay on the other. The road is through trees, and it would be impossible anywhere to see a more beautiful country.

In an hour and a half we meet the canoes on the Dartmouth River, and we become most picturesque! Imagine six birch-bark canoes in procession; in each two men stand upright, with long poles in their hands, while two passengers sit in the centre of the boat. We have three hours' journey in this way up a beautiful river, going up rapids and enjoying ourselves. Then we arrive at a salmon-pool, get out, and pitch our tents. We have two bell-tents, a small one for Fred, and a tent for the cook. The twelve canoe-men make one of birch-bark for themselves. We hoist our flag and take possession.

Our *chef* is capital; he works away, builds himself a fire-place, gets out his pots and pans, and soon sets before us a splendid dinner. We have soup and fish, and entrées and pudding, and are far from 'roughing it.' We have but two trials in life – one is great, the other small – 1st, the terrible flies; and 2nd, the obstinacy of the salmon, who do not rise. The gentlemen whip the pools and catch nothing, and we ladies find a few trout.

THURSDAY, 10TH. – We are all up early, and breakfast at five, get into our canoes, and proceed higher up the river. The pools we reach to-day are very lovely. Fred got a salmon – the only one. We stopped fishing at eleven; the men made a bower of branches and birch-bark, and we sat and read and ate until four, when we fished again. The last pool was so pretty – or, rather, fine. There were great cliffs on either side, and in front a waterfall with a wall of rock and trees. At eight we left and paddled down to our camp, passing through some great rapids. The worst are called the 'Lady's Steps.' Tea and bed followed.

FRIDAY, 11TH. – Again we breakfast at five, and begin our return journey. Finding an invitation from an American gentleman to go up his river, the St. John, and to stay with him, we accept. We go on board the *Druid*, wash and dress better than is possible in a tent, and in two hours begin a new adventure.

We drive for half an hour, cross a stream in a boat, walk a little way, and then meet six saddle-horses. These we mount, and ride for three hours through the forest, five miles of the way being through a burnt wood. The tall, charred trunks are all that remain of the old forest, but a beautiful fresh underwood has grown up everywhere. This ride brings us to Mr. Curtis's 'shanty' on the St. John.

I could not get on with him at first, but soon found he was very nice. It was only pre-occupation that was the matter with him – and no wonder. It seems we ought to have brought blankets with us, and the poor man is in despair, as he has a very limited supply in the backwoods. We swear we like doing without blankets, and he is happy. There was time for a little fishing, and Fred caught a salmon.

The sand-flies are dreadful here, but we try to defy them with smoky fires (called 'smudges') and curtains. After dinner we sit out of doors before a pile of blazing wood.

You remember I told you that a poor manservant of ours was drowned at the Mingan. As we knew nothing about his people, we were unable to communicate the news of his death to them, so D. ordered all letters that might arrive for him to be brought to himself. The first of these – which we have just received – was from a servant girl he was attached to at Ottawa, and dated exactly seven days after the day of the accident. In it she said, 'I have been in my new place a week, and like it very much; but I had such a dreadful dream on the day of my arrival. I dreamt you and Nowell were upset in a boat together, and that Nowell was saved, but you were drowned.' As the spot where the accident occurred is in an uninhabited region on the coast of Labrador, more than 500 miles distant from Ottawa, without either telegraphs or posts, it was impossible that she should have had the news of her lover's death when this letter was written.

SATURDAY, 12TH. – This morning we were four hours going up the river; however, we stopped five times to fish, so the time did not appear long. We have reached 'Kelly's Pool,' and are told that here salmon will surely come. D. catches one (18 lbs.) almost immediately. Mr. Curtis hooks one for me, and hands me the rod; but in so doing off it comes. Then he hooks another; I take the rod again, and enjoy myself immensely while I play the fish. I landed him, and great was my joy and pride. Colonel Fletcher and Lady Harriet each play one, but she loses hers. Then we were carried swiftly down the rapids home. Dinner – fireside – bed!

Alas! bed is not the end. There was frost to-night, and the limited supply of blankets was terrible. I woke at one, very cold, got up, and dressed in all my clothes, and lay down again; but not to sleep. I shivered till four, and at this early hour on Sunday morning might have been found sitting at a great wood fire out of doors; a tent on my right, where sleeps my friend; behind me a wooden house, where sleep my husband, brother, and the Colonel; to the left a section of a tent, jutting out of which may be seen the feet of sleeping men; one – who is awake – attends to my fire; a dog lies by, the river rolls along in the background. In this picture I may be represented reading a novel; the primeval forest extends itself on every side of me. The rest of the world got up to breakfast at seven, and we rode and drove home to our ship again. Mr. Curtis 'of Boston' was most kind to us and very pleasant.

MONDAY, 14TH. – We started in the night, and found ourselves next morning off Percé. There is the great, precipitous rock standing out by itself, with a natural arch through it, which gives the name to the place. On the mainland the red cliffs rise up above the sea, crowned with green shrubs, and the plateau on which the little town is built slopes down to the water, and ends in another great cliff. The sun shines, and everything is delightful. Colonel Fletcher and D. both made sketches. When they had finished we steamed round the rock, and got into a boat to row ashore.

A salute was fired (by the blacksmith), and all the fishing population of Percé, headed by their Mayor, Manager, and the Sheriff, met us, and of course read an address.

Percé is a most important fishing-station. It is principally owned by Jersey people who have never been to it, and their representative here is Mr. Orange. In addition to its beautiful scenery it has the merit of spotless purity (in spite of a strong smell of fish pervading the atmosphere). The houses and stores are all of the freshest white, with red window-sashes and doors; the streets are of gravel.

We were told there was a splendid view from the high cliff above the town. I only got to the bottom of the worst climb in the gig with the Mayor and Mayoress, but the gentlemen went to the top. In the afternoon we continued our journey up the Bay of Chaleur to Paspediac, off which little town we anchored at ten o'clock.

TUESDAY, 15TH. – D. went ashore at 7 a.m. and found a sleepy agent who could not rise to the magnitude of the occasion, or comprehend that it was the Governor-General who represented the 'early bird.'

Paspediac is another part of the Jersey fishing-business. Here ships are built, and in them the dried cod is sent off to its various destinations.

We were detained an hour by our engine, which had got out of order, and so did not reach Dalhousie till five o'clock. The scenery towards the end of the Bay was lovely, and the surroundings of this village reminded us of Scotland. We had not seen such high hills for a long time.

The courageous people of Dalhousie fired off some old guns which had been found at the bottom of the river, and it is a mercy no accident occurred.

The principal inhabitants met us at the wharf, but His Ex.'s hand was first shaken by a black man, who appears to be a pet jester of the neighborhood. Later, this gentleman perceived he had forgotten me, and made a dive through the crowd to shake hands with me. My gravity was rather upset by this unexpected welcome.

We walked to the Court House, and had an address presented. Then D. took a drive, and I went up to the house of a senator – Mr. Hamilton. We got on board again in time for dinner, and continued our journey in the night.

WEDNESDAY, 16TH. – We have had a rough twenty-four hours, and could not enjoy the deck until we were some way up the Miramichi river. We reached Chatham in the afternoon.

Lunch was prepared at the house of the Member, Mr. Muirhead, to which we had to pass under an arch specially erected in our honour. We returned in the evening to attend a concert given by the convent school.

THURSDAY, 17TH. – We invited Mr., Mrs., and Miss Muirhead, and two other gentlemen, to breakfast on board, and to go with us to Newcastle, a town a short way from Chatham.

There was an address, and a drive to a new bridge which is being built over the river. Then we set sail – or, rather, 'got under steam' – on our way to Prince Edward's Island, where I hope to receive letters.

CHAPTER 8

The Maritime Provinces
JULY-AUGUST 1873

FRIDAY, JULY 18TH. – This morning we found ourselves in sight of Prince Edward's Island; and very pretty it looked in the sunshine. The cliffs are low, but they show a red line above the water, crowned with green, and the whole country is much more cultivated and more park-like than anything we have as yet seen in Canada.

We anchored at ten, and got some letters from Tadousac, with good accounts of the children; and at twelve we landed at Charlotte Town.

There was a crowd, and a very pretty arch, one of the mottoes on it being 'Long courted, won at last,' in allusion to the island having just joined the Dominion.

We are staying at Government House with Mr. and Mrs. Robinson. They took us a drive through red lanes, farms, trees and ferns – country sights which are quite delightful to us, who of late have only seen forest scenery.

> William (later Sir William) Cleaver Francis Robinson, 1834-97, had been appointed Governor of Prince Edward Island in 1870. It was in no small measure the result of his wise diplomacy that that colony became a province in the Canadian Confederation. He was designated its first Lieutenant-Governor on June 10, 1873, but resigned later that year. In a footnote Lady Dufferin records: "Sir William Robinson, Governor of Trinidad, 1891."

SATURDAY, 19TH. – We walked through the town, and in the afternoon had a reception, and in the evening a dinner-party.

MONDAY, 21ST. – In the morning we started to take the first trip on the first railway made in the island. About thirty people came with us, and at a distant station we were met by carriages, in which we drove to the seashore, where we had lunch. Then we returned home by the same route, and had a little rest before we dressed for a ball at Government House.

> The Prince Edward Island Railway was not officially opened for traffic until two years later. However, Lord Dufferin was given the honour of being its first passenger on the short part completed between Charlotte-town and Little Rock. From there the party went in carriages to Stanhope, on the north shore of the island.

TUESDAY, 22ND. – We drove out with Mr. and Mrs. Robinson to do some shopping, to look at a fine view of the town, and to be photographed under the triumphal arch. Then we went off to the *Druid,* and H.M.S. *Spartan* manned yards as we passed. There was a regatta in the harbour, for which D. had given prizes, and we had invited forty people to lunch with us on board and to see the races from our ship. We had a pleasant afternoon, and as soon as the sports were over we went ashore to give away the prizes. The day was a perfect summer day.

We dined quietly at Government House, and dressed for the ball after dinner. This ball was part of the reception which the local Parliament had resolved to give the Governor-General.

It was in the Parliament Buildings, and the Senate Chamber was beautifully arranged for it. From the ceiling hung a thing like a chandelier, made of roses and moss, which spread out into single ropes of flowers, attached to the gallery all round the room, forming a light canopy of flowers above us; then there were flags and wreaths on the walls. Nothing could have been prettier. Besides a dressing-room, a little resting-place was provided for me, in which there was a large supply of refreshment!

The supper-room was decorated with green, and with a large painting of D.'s arms, surrounded by all the Canadian flags, that of New-foundland being still rolled up (it has not joined the Union). The supper was a sort of picnic, being sent by different people, and was very good.

When we left, we were accompanied by a torchlight procession to the pier; there we got into our boat, and went on board the *Druid.* All the ladies, in their ball-dresses, came out on the balcony of the house to see us off; and the arches were illuminated.

THURSDAY, 24TH. – In the morning we reached Pictou.

I must mention that the climate of Prince Edward's Island was very much more like England than that of our part of Canada, and both Lady Harriet and I felt the change. She got hay-fever and asthma, and is in bed, and I have a cold. However, I did not like to miss seeing the coal-mines of the Dominion, so I went with D. to inspect them. I saw all the above-ground part; the engines, the ventilators, etc. The principal ventilator is called the 'Lady Dufferin,' and there are two engines which go by the name of the 'Lord Dufferin' and the 'Lady Victoria.'

D. went down the mine with Fred and Colonel Fletcher. The shaft was 1,000 feet, and it took them just fifty-four seconds to get to the bottom in a lift. They stayed down there an hour and a half, while I talked to the managers at the top.

We got back to the *Druid* in time for dinner. All night there was a fearful noise going on – 'coaling,' just over our heads.

FRIDAY, 25TH. – Sailing through the Gut of Canso, with the land close to us on each side, on our way to Louisburg, where we anchor in the morning.

SATURDAY, 26TH. – There is a fog outside the harbour, so we are caught here, but have had a most pleasant day.

I looked in a book of universal knowledge, and read that Louisburg, in addition to its historical interest, is a town with broad streets and stone houses; it is, in reality, a small village, consisting of a few scattered wooden cottages. We landed at one of these, borrowed two gigs, and set off to drive twenty-five miles to the capital of Cape Breton, Sydney by name. D. drove me, and Fred the Colonel; Lady Harriet remained on board.

We drove through pretty woods, occasionally getting a glimpse of one of the several arms of the sea which cut Cape Breton in so many places, sat by the roadside to lunch, and reached Sydney in the afternoon.

It is situated on a beautiful harbour, and we found several large steamers there. The biggest was the *Hibernia,* which had just been laying the Atlantic cable, in company with the *Great Eastern.* We went on board her, and saw the machinery, and the tanks which held the cable.

We had asked to see the mayor of the town, and when a gentleman jumped out of a carriage and accosted us, we took it for granted that this was he, and accepted his offer of a pair of fresh horses and a cup of tea. We went to his very pretty house, where his English wife received us graciously. Then D. heard that a deputation was waiting for him at the hotel. There he found the real Simon Pure, and spent an extra hour with him and the other magnates of the place. We left very late, and had a dark drive back through the woods.

The weather was quite lovely, and the trip extremely pleasant. At four o'clock we bought a Sydney paper, in which we found our arrival announced. Very sharp of the Sydney Press.

> Lord Dufferin's genial host that July afternoon was the eminent engineer, Frederic Newton Gisborne, whose ingenuity had joined the Maritime Provinces by telegraph and submarine cable many years before they were united by railways and confederation. Some weeks later his nineteen-year-old daughter Ellen received a copy of Lord Dufferin's book, *Letters from High Latitudes*. It was inscribed: 'To Miss Gisborne with the compliments of the author, 1873.'

> The first successful transatlantic submarine cable was laid by the *Great Eastern* in 1866, and joined Ireland and Newfoundland. Realizing the potential of this powerful ship, capitalists were now meeting further world demands and the cable just completed had joined England to the Canadian mainland.

LOUISBURG, SUNDAY, 27TH. – We are detained here by the fog. After church we went to look at the old forts. There are scarcely any stone remains, but Colonel Fletcher's military eye easily discovered the form and plan of the fortifications in the grass.

> Louisburg was begun as a French fortress in 1720. The beautiful stone for its buildings and fortifications was brought from Caen in France, and the cost was so great that the French king inquired whether its streets were paved with gold. It was captured for the second time by the British in 1758, and demolition squads laid it in ruins. Thereafter it was used like a quarry, its stone being carried off to Halifax and St. John's, Newfoundland, and used in the construction of public buildings and bridges. It is now being restored.

MONDAY, 28TH. – We started this morning, and got on a good way before the fog came down upon us again. Fog – rain – Atlantic swell!

TUESDAY, 29TH. – Still very foggy. We had great doubts as to whether we should get into Halifax. However, with great care, we poked our nose in just the right place, and at two o'clock appeared in the harbour, to everybody's astonishment.

It was so wet we did not go ashore, and put off our landing till next morning. The Lieutenant-Governor and Mrs. Archibald came to see us, and arrangements for endless gaieties were made.

WEDNESDAY, 30TH. – At twelve o'clock we landed, on a slab of marble which commemorates the arrival of the Prince of Wales [later Edward VII] on the same day, thirteen years ago. The weather was dull and muggy, and the guard of honour made some mistake and turned up an hour later at Government House, instead of at the wharf.

I received Admiral Fanshawe, his wife and daughter and son, in the afternoon. When the day cleared up we saw we were anchored in a cheerful place close to the town. Dartmouth, which is almost a part of Halifax, is on one side of us, and woods and villas and large institutions are dotted round the Bay, while at the mouth of the harbour is a small fortified island. There is one man-of-war here, and we have just missed the Flying Squadron.

There is a question as to whether Parliament should be prorogued on August 13th or not, and the papers are advising the Governor-General, and abusing him in advance, if he does not follow each of their different counsels.

THURSDAY, 31ST. – Lady Harriet and I went a drive with Mrs. Fanshawe, and saw the North-west Arm and Bedford Basin, and enjoyed the country drive.

In the evening we held a Drawing-room at Government House, and had the pleasure of 'full-dressing' in our cabins. We got ashore in safety, and had a very successful gathering. Everyone said, 'We did not know there were so many people in Halifax.' Going back to the ship, we found ourselves in a fog, and my feathers and tulle were much the worse for it. Dent says, with indignation, 'Every day in this yacht takes pounds and pounds off the value of your clothes.'

FRIDAY, AUGUST 1ST. – This was the day of the Regatta, and, had it been fine, it would have been a pretty sight. But as there was fog and rain, little except the lunch took place.

We had a great dinner at the Lieutenant-Governor's, which was long but pleasant. One of my neighbours was the R.C. Archbishop of Halifax, a clever, amusing Irishman. The dinner had rather a funny *finale*. Mr. Archibald [Hon. Adams George Archibald; he was created a K.C.M.G. in 1886] proposed the Queen's health, and we all stood up to drink it. The band played the National Air, and at the end of the usual eight bars we all prepared to sit down. But no; the band went on – a slight smile passed down the table; eight bars more

– the band strikes up another verse; until at last, after several of these unexpected beginnings, the whole of the solemn and stately party broke out into a hearty laugh.

There was an evening party after dinner, and D. and I talked to all the strangers till 11.30 o'clock, when we returned to our ship.

SATURDAY, 2ND. – Early this morning we went to visit the fortifications, and saw three different sets of forts. We returned to the *Druid* at two, and had the Local Government to lunch. They are in opposition to the Dominion Parliament, and their papers were rather disagreeable about our visit here. But I am happy to say they have set aside all political differences for the moment, and really seem as if they could not do enough for us. The result is, that next week we have four balls, three monster picnics, three dinners, a concert, a cricket-match, and a review. Is it not fearfully kind? 'What shall I wear?' is a question I must debate seriously every day.

We dined to-night at Admiralty House with Admiral and Mrs. Fanshawe, where we met the same people as last night and a few sailors. One guest, a midshipman, was Prince Louis of Battenberg.

MONDAY, 4TH. – A day of Herculean labours! At 8.30 a.m. D. went to breakfast with Admiral Fanshawe, to see his beautiful drawings. At ten we rowed down to the Dockyard to meet him, and all went on board the *Royal Alfred*. She and the *Spartan* manned yards as we approached; we got on board and went into every hole and corner of the ship. We finished the inspection about 12.30, when we returned to the *Druid,* and prepared to receive a party at luncheon, including the Lieutenant-Governor and the Admiral.

No sooner had we finished this meal than we started for a picnic given by the Irish Benevolent Society. D. and I sailed to it in our own little boat. The rendezvous was at McNab's Island, and we were received on landing by gentlemen wearing green sashes. There was a lovely view from the door of the large picnic shed; but we had to go in and dance a quadrille. At five we had a 'cold collation' and many toasts.

We returned to the *Druid* at seven o'clock, and having re-dressed and re-dined, we left again at eight, to attend a promenade concert in the Horticultural Gardens. We did not 'promenade' at all, but sat on the centre one of three stages, a bright gaslight thrown full upon us, and an immense crowd looking on. On one side was the band of the 60th Rifles, and on the other that of the 87th. They played in turns, and we remained till the end of the performance. To-day, at any rate, we have earned a night's repose!

TUESDAY, 5TH. – Lady Harriet and I went a little shopping expedition this morning. We were given a picnic by the 87th Regiment and D. and I sailed down to the Island about five o'clock. When it was quite dark, we went out lobster-spearing. We had two boats and two great torches in each. We stood up, – with poles forked at one end in our hands, – and watched the bottom for lobsters. Presently we saw one crawling along; I made a grab at him, but missed. Then came a second; this time I was more careful, and aimed my weapon slowly at him, putting the fork right over his back, and then lifting him, kicking, into the boat. It was very exciting. We were only able to stay a very short time, but we 'grabbed' at five and brought home three.

WEDNESDAY, 6TH. – A luncheon party on board, then a visit to a great lunatic asylum, so gay and clean and quiet. D. dined with the Archbishop, and Lady Harriet and I with Mrs. Fanshawe. She had the Prince-Midshipman and some other sailors to meet us.

THURSDAY, 7TH. – In the evening D. dined at the Club, and made a speech upon the absolute impartiality of the Governor-General in party matters (there is great strife going on now), which was extremely well received. He ended by saying: 'As a reasonable being the Governor-General cannot help having convictions upon the merits of different policies. But these considerations are abstract, speculative, devoid of practical effect on his official relations. As the head of a Constitutional State, as engaged in the administration of Parliamentary Government, he has no political friends, still less need he have political enemies; the possession of either – nay, even to be suspected of possessing either – destroys his usefulness. Sometimes, of course, no matter how disconnected his personality may be from what is taking place, his name will get dragged into some controversy, and he may suddenly find himself the subject of criticism in the Press of whatever Party may for the moment be out of humour; but under these circumstances he must console himself with the reflection that these spasmodic castigations are as transitory and innocuous as the discipline applied occasionally to their idol by the unsophisticated worshippers of Mumbo Jumbo when their harvests are short or murrain visits their flocks.' D. met me afterwards at a ball at the General's, where he had to dance everything till two o'clock.

FRIDAY, 8TH. – We had a large lunch on board, and after it went to a review of the garrison and Volunteers on the common, and, as the afternoon was lovely, it was a very fine sight – red coats, brilliant staff, His Excellency and Fred riding about, cocked hats, rifles, bands, artillery, engineers, a sham fight, a large number of spectators, etc.

To-night we had a really beautiful ball, given by the Legislative Council, in the Parliament Buildings. The ballroom is very lofty, has handsome cornices, and several full-length oil portraits hanging in it. The whole of the walls were covered with white calico, striped with bands of pink; over the doors and windows were 'D.'s,' surrounded by pink-and-white flags. The curtains and all the windows were pink-and-white tarlatan, and it was all very bright and finished-looking. The supper-room was hung with real flags, and the entrance-hall was converted into a grotto of ferns. There was plenty of air in the dancing-room, and a very good band, and we really enjoyed it very much. (You know there are occasionally entertainments which are more duty than pleasure.)

SATURDAY, 9TH. – The political difficulties to which I have alluded call D. back to Ottawa, and he has had a very busy morning, writing farewell letters, and making arrangements for the long journey, which he begins to-night. If he had gone by rail it would have taken him at least seventy hours; but he luckily catches an English mail steamer on its way to Quebec, which will take him part of the way, and will leave him within twenty-four hours' journey of Ottawa.

> By May, 1873, parliamentary business was practically completed. One item only remained—to receive the report of the committee set up by the Government to investigate charges, levelled against some of its ministers, of corruption in the financing of a railway to the Pacific Coast. A Bill passed by both Houses of Parliament had granted this committee authority to question witnesses under oath. The Governor-General had given it royal assent.
>
> The Commons and Senate agreed an adjournment should take place until August 13, at which date the committee would bring in its report. Since it was thought this would be a mere formality, and exonerate the ministers, it was decided members need not return, only the Speakers be present, and a commission acting for the Governor-General could prorogue Parliament.
>
> It seemed imperative that Lord Dufferin go ahead with his plans to visit Nova Scotia. Many there were dissatisfied, and a strong anti-confederation party, advocating the province's withdrawal from the union, was building up. Dominion Day, July 1, was ignored.
>
> It was not until he reached Prince Edward Island that Lord Dufferin learned of the storm clouds that had arisen in Ottawa. The British Parliament had disallowed the Bill permitting the committee to

In Toronto: "The Lieutenant-Governor, Mr. Howland, took us to his house, which was magnificently illuminated."

In Hamilton, at the Cattle Show: "D. and I walked around the grounds and looked at the animals, while the people looked at us."

receive testimony under oath, and the Opposition was accusing Lord Dufferin of exceeding his authority. Newspapers had been publishing correspondence and information incriminating some of the ministers. If Parliament were prorogued, the committee would automatically cease to function; and it was not yet ready to present its report. The Opposition contended Parliament should be recalled and the whole matter debated by the Members. Lord Dufferin felt his presence was urgently needed in Ottawa.

There, after consultation with Sir John A. Macdonald, he decided the advice of his ministers, against whom as yet no charges had been proved, must be accepted, and prorogued Parliament. However, it was agreed a new session should be called within ten weeks, and a royal commission of three judges was set up to take over the investigation started by the now defunct committee.

In the afternoon we went to a monster picnic given to us by the citizens. We sailed down to McNab's Island in our boat, where the Mayor received us. After dinner D. made a speech, in which he 'confided me to the care of the people of Halifax during his absence.' Soon after we were conducted down to the boats and returned to the *Druid*.

At eight we went to Government House, and were met there by a torchlight procession, and a grand fire-engine demonstration, the engines preceding us, and being brilliantly illuminated. Many of the houses also were lighted up. There was an immense crowd, which we drove slowly through, back to Queen's Wharf, where a guard of honour was in waiting, and where D. said 'good-bye.' The torches all remained at the pier till we had reached the *Druid;* it was a beautiful sight.

D. and Colonel Fletcher got on board the *Nestorian* at ten, and we watched them steaming past us; both we and they sent off some rockets. And now, here am I, alone for a week, doing 'Governor-General' at Halifax.

MONDAY, 11TH. – This was a very tiring day. In the morning I had a great many things to do for D., and in the afternoon I had lunch with the Archibalds, which lasted till after four. At 6.30 had to be at the General's [General Sir W. O'Grady Haly] house for dinner.

He was too ill to appear, and we were a small party of eight. After dinner we proceeded to the theatre, where we saw 'Still Waters Run Deep' and 'Under the Rose' acted by amateurs. There were some excellent actors, and I enjoyed it. I received three bouquets, which I carried together in an enormous bunch. The best performers were Major and Mrs. Hall, Captain and Mrs. Mitchell Innes, Captain Wallace of the 60th Rifles, and Mr. Poe, who is on the *Royal Alfred*.

TUESDAY, 12TH. – Mr. and Mrs. Robinson came on board to say 'Good-bye,' and I had a lunch for fourteen people. My guests were two handsome Toronto girls and two admirers of theirs, the Lieutenant-Governor and his family (five), and Captain and Mrs. O'Grady Haly. He is the General's son and A.D.C.

It was a lovely afternoon, and after lunch we drove through the Horticultural Gardens to a cricket-match – the 60th Rifles against the Garrison.

Then we dined with Admiral and Mrs. Fanshawe, and went with them to the ball on board the *Royal Alfred*.

I did like this entertainment. The ship was close to the wharf. The deck was divided at the mast into two parts – supper-room and ballroom, – and at midnight the partition was taken down. The funnel was beautifully decorated with arms – swords, bayonets, etc. – and was surrounded by jets of gas. The supper-tables were arranged between it and the main mast, round which there was a rockery and fernery, in which water trickled and frogs disported themselves. The band sat on a scaffolding round the mast. The whole was covered in with flags, and all the companions, compasses, wheels, etc. etc. were ornamented with plants. The poop made a second ball-room, also covered, in the shape of a bell-tent, and I had a seat there, and a good view of the ball. Those who preferred Nature could gaze out in the opposite direction upon the moonlit sea. I did not occupy the chair-of-state much, but danced, and enjoyed myself.

WEDNESDAY, 13TH. – I took a long rest this morning, and was ready in the afternoon to visit some Protestant charities.

The first was an orphan-home, and the second a very interesting reformatory for boys. There are no walls, or bolts, or bars. They all learn trades, and do not leave the Home till they are able to earn their bread. We saw them hard at work, carpentering, shoemaking, tailoring, and cabinet-making. They also do gardening and farm-work; school-work is done in the evening.

This evening a ball was given to us by the 60th Rifles. It was a most successful one. The room looked like a very smart lady's boudoir, and was beautifully lighted with wax candles. I danced a great deal; we were not home till three.

THURSDAY, 14TH. – I had to leave Lady Harriet in bed with an asthmatic cold, while I delivered myself over to the Roman Catholic Archbishop. Fred and I visited his house and his Cathedral, and a convent, and went on to his country place, where he had 150 people at lunch to meet me. I got back to the ship at five (having left it at twelve), and at nine attended the Sergeants' Ball.

The political excitement is fearful, and we hear that the Opposition is going to ask for the Governor-General's recall!! So expect us home in disgrace.

SATURDAY, 16TH. – We went to Dartmouth, and visited a rope manufactory, and a skate manufactory, where I was presented with a grand box containing two lovely pairs of Acme skates, for D. and me.

We drove on seven miles by a chain of lakes, till we came to an old-fashioned inn, where we had lunch. After this we went to a gold mine, and saw the process of extracting the precious metal. This ended our sight-seeing. All day we went about in a procession of ten carriages.

I gave a dinner to the amateur actors on board the *Druid,* and afterwards went to see them do 'Caste,' which was very amusing.

MONDAY, 18TH. – We left our dear *Druid* early in the morning, and drove to the train, where the Lieutenant-Governor met us, and escorted us for about six hours on our way. We passed through 'Evangeline's' country to the Bay of Fundy, where we got into a crazy-looking steamer and sailed for St. John.

Here the Mayor, Sheriff, etc., came to meet me, and there was a great crowd on the landing. Never was I so stared at as to-day. When D. is with me I feel that I am only part of the show; but alone, I have to bear it all. At the stations people looked in at the windows, and gazed at me while I ate sandwiches (of all things in the world!); when we got to the hotel, a crowd outside eyed me, and a crowd inside stared at me, and on the stairs Yankee visitors criticised me, 'I guess.'

I went to my room for a little, and on my way to dinner I found them all still on the stairs, and they looked at me through the hinges of the door. When I came up again there was a couple walking arm-in-arm in my room, and three ladies looking into it. But I walked by them in so stately a manner that they sent me word they had only come to put some flowers there. Then the crowd outside would not go, and I had to stand at the window, and be cheered, and hear 'God save the Queen' (to which I have no right whatsoever).

TUESDAY, 19TH. – D. arrived here this morning. He left Ottawa on Friday, slept that night at Montreal, and Saturday night at some place in the White Mountains (in the State of Maine), where he found a ball going on. Sunday, he saw the scenery, and came on here at night.

This is a fine hotel, upon American principles. The cooking is excellent, and we dine alone, and are waited upon by our own servants in a 'private dining-room,' which seems to us very noisy after the ship. Our own sitting-room is comfortable. Everything is arranged so that one may require as few servants as possible. There is a large public drawing-room, and the guests also perambulate the passages a good deal.

Our maids enjoy themselves, as they dine with the company, and can have many kinds of food, while they fill their heads with the fashions. Dent gave a sigh of relief when she dressed me this morning, as she said, 'Well, I am thankful none of them have a dress like this!' 'Them' are Americans.

I was amused by seeing in the papers this telegram: 'Mackenzie has left for Halifax, to worry the Governor-General.' Mackenzie is the chief of the Opposition, and D. is the Governor-General.

WEDNESDAY, 20TH. – At eleven D. and I went to some public room, where an address was presented, and at three the Reception Committee came for us, and took us in carriages all about and around the city.

We dined almost directly we came in, and dressed for the Drawing-room, which was held in a great room in this hotel. We stayed and talked to the people when the presentations were over.

THURSDAY, 21ST. – This morning, early, we started to see the Regatta. I had a headache, and no sooner got on board the steamer, which was crowded with people, than I found that, although I might sit through four hours, I certainly could not talk and smile through them. So I went to the cabin, and lay still all the time of the races. The crowds on the shore and in the rigging of the ships made it a pretty sight. We got home in the middle of the day, and were quiet until five, when a procession of the schools came to the door of the hotel, and we stood on the steps to see them.

I believe about 4,000 children were collected, and they were to have stood around us. But the crowd was so great it was impossible for them all to get through. A small circle was formed for those who were dressed up to represent the Provinces, and they gave me a bouquet. The other children had to stand where they could. D. made a speech to the sea of heads, which few of the waves heard, but which will read well, I hope.

In the evening carriages were ready, and we drove through the town in a procession. We saw little of it till the end, when our carriage stood to let the crowd pass us. There was an immense stream of walking lights, and all the fire-engines were lighted up, and ornamented with wreaths and flowers. Some of the horses had high arches of roses over their backs. The crowd was perfectly tremendous and received us heartily. When we got into the hotel, we went to a window on the second storey to look down upon the crowd, and they saw us and cheered.

FRIDAY, 22ND. – We had a long drive of fourteen miles to Chief Justice Ritchie's house, where we were to lunch. The drive was through a beautiful country, and we had several warm greetings on our way. An arch was put up at one place, and a bouquet presented. At another private house the gate was hung with flowers, and the lady stepped out with a second bouquet for me, while a third was brought me further on.

We had lunch, or what was called a 'high tea'; but there was no tea – only champagne. Returning home we found several bonfires lighted along the route.

We reached our hotel at eight, and dressed for the ball. This was given in a new theatre, and was got up in a great hurry. The floor had to be laid down over the pit, and the decorations to be done. During the day we heard it was not nearly finished, and that it would be dull and wretched.

It was, therefore, a pleasant surprise when we reached the door and saw a brilliant room, the stage end with 'Welcome' in gas-lights over two crimson chairs, the floor lined with ball-dressed people, the boxes and dress-circle filled with spectators, draperies of red and green, flags, plants, and cages of birds (which sang, and gave a rural sentiment to the entertainment) , and a very beautiful string-band playing 'God save the Queen.' Supper was in the green-room. The ball was very successful and amusing. There were many Americans present; they dance in quite a different style from ours.

SATURDAY, 23RD. – We felt sleepy when we were called this morning, but had to be down at the steamer at ten, and could not allow ourselves any lazy indulgences. [The steamer was the *David Weston*.]

Our journey was up a splendid river, the St. John, with lovely scenery all the way. About five miles from Fredericton we were met by three steamers crammed full of children and people, who greeted us warmly, and, having once begun to cheer, felt obliged to carry it on the whole way.

Mr. Wilmot [Lemuel Allan Wilmot, 1809-78], the Lieutenant-Governor of New Brunswick, met us at the landing-place, and we had a most gracious reception at this, 'the ambitious little city,' 'the celestial city,' Fredericton.

We dined early, and went to the Exhibition Building, where the address was to be presented. There were at least 3,000 people present. The school children sang, and after the speeches we got into a carriage and drove in the torchlight procession.

The engines looked beautiful; but my pleasure was somewhat destroyed by my dread of fire. The torches were paraffin lamps, and the way in which many of them were spilt about the ground, and went on burning there, muslin gowns walking carelessly close to them, made me fear some bad accident. Rockets and Roman candles were also flying wildly about.

This Government House (where we are staying with the Wilmots, who are both most kind to us) is a very good one. The river passes the house, and a very pretty flower garden goes down to it.

SUNDAY, 24TH. – We got to the Cathedral in a close carriage. It is rather a fine one, and is quite finished, – strange to say!

MONDAY, 25TH. – The people of Fredericton had arranged a picnic for us to-day. We went first to see an interesting settlement, the property of a Mr. Gibson. [This was Nashwaak.] Eight years ago there was not a house in the place; now there are good cottages for the labourers, fine houses for Mr. Gibson and his sons, a very ornamental church, and a school.

His business is lumber. His old mother, who left our neighborhood in Ireland fifty-four years ago, was so delighted to see someone from 'home.' Her parents, having objected to her marriage, never wrote to her, and I wished they could see her now, in her son's fine house, surrounded by every comfort that money could buy her, her granddaughter playing the organ, and her son so much respected and honoured!

After this visit we got into the train, went thirty miles up the new line and half-way back again, to a place on the St. John River, where an arbour of evergreens had been erected, under which 250 people lunched.

TUESDAY, 26TH. – We left Fredericton in the morning, accompanied for an hour by the Wilmots, the Sheriff, etc., and proceeded on our way to Woodstock, a drive of sixty-five miles. At a half-way house we changed horses and had lunch. We drove all the way through lovely scenery, following the river St. John. We reached Woodstock in time for dinner, and directly afterwards went to the Court House. We finished the day by driving in a torchlight procession.

WEDNESDAY, 27TH. – We had a fine day and a delightful drive, changing horses four times in the seventy miles. We lunched at a charming little inn, and slept at Grand Falls. To our surprise, we found two arches, all the cottages illuminated, magnificent bonfires, an address, and an assembly of people in the Court House. After we had gone to bed we heard 'Rule Britannia' being sung all round the house. There was also a pretty procession of birch-bark torches. The inn was kept by a North of Ireland lady, and was perfect! The Grand Falls here are very fine.

THURSDAY, 28TH. – We started at eight punctually this morning, for we have 250 miles to go, and drove on as before, stopping to have lunch by the way, and sleeping at a little French inn. The family got up a dance when we had gone to bed, and we heard the fiddle going, and our servant instructing them in a Scotch reel, during half the night.

FRIDAY, 29TH. – We got up very early, and drove, drove, drove on through forest nearly the whole day. We saw one great fire in the wood, and were nearly choked as we passed through it. We missed seeing a beautiful lake owing to the clouds hanging over it.

We reached Rivière du Loup about five in the afternoon, and got a tug steamer to take us straight over to Tadousac [Tadoussac].

There we found the whole party of children in their dressing-gowns, just going to bed. The five elder ones are looking so fat, and rosy, and well; but my baby is a mite indeed!

SATURDAY, 30TH. – Our summer tour is now over, and I return to a prosy account of home affairs. We have done all we intended to do; and the drive of 250 miles in four days was a pleasant termination to our tour. The *Druid* was to have met us at Rivière du Loup, but was detained by storm, and only reached Tadousac this morning.

CHAPTER 9

The Fall

SEPTEMBER - DECEMBER 1873

TADOUSAC: MONDAY, SEPTEMBER 1ST. – I seized upon a fine morning to bathe with the children. It is rather late in the season for a first dip, but I could not resist trying it, though the water is at all times extremely cold here. We prepared for the bath in our own rooms, and, covered with waterproofs, ran down to the water. My costume is of the brightest orange, and is very striking. We are very quiet here, and D. very busy. He is writing the whole day long.

FRIDAY, 5TH. – We went on board the *Druid* just before dinner last night, and took Nelly with us for a little holiday. The night was rather rough, but the wind suited and we reached Quebec early this morning. We found Mr. G. Brodrick at the hotel, and D. brought him up to stay with us. He is very pleasant and gave us much English news. [A footnote records that in 1891 Hon. G. C. Brodrick was Warden of Merton College, Oxford.]

I drove him to the Montmorency Falls; the Natural Steps are very curious. The river narrows at this place, and has cut a regular staircase in the rock through which it makes its way. D. did not move from his desk all day; he was up till two, and the clerks till four, and the steamer had to wait half an hour this morning (Saturday) for the monster despatch.

FRIDAY, 12TH. – We gave an outdoor afternoon party on the platform. The amusements consisted of a band, dancing, a bear, and my children (who all arrived in the morning) to be looked at. Basil was a splendid sight, and had the air of Henry VIII, as he sat back in a small rocking-chair, with his sturdy form and rosy cheeks. The others are very flourishing, and the 'family' did us credit. I did not show my baby; instead, we exhibited the Queen's present to her godchild. It is a large medallion, with Her Majesty's head in raised gold in the centre, surrounded by rows of diamonds, pink coral, and pearls. On the back is engraved, 'Lady Victoria Alexandrina Blackwood, from her god-mother, Victoria R.'

SATURDAY, 13TH. – I had a visit from a charming lady, a Miss Florence Lees. [She later became the wife of Rev. Dacre Craven, Rector of St. George the Martyr, Holborn, London.] She has been thoroughly trained as a surgical nurse, and did nurse, and underwent great fatigues (not to say danger) in the Franco-Prussian War. She wears the Iron Cross, and another order, which only three ladies possess. After nursing twenty-two men through typhus fever before Metz, she took charge of the Crown Princess's Ambulance at Homburg. She has been sent out to visit the hospitals in Canada and the States. All anti-women-working people ought to see her!

MONDAY, 15TH. – I took the children to some athletic sports. The trees are most of them decorated with a crimson or golden branch – the first touch of autumn.

WEDNESDAY, 17TH. – A football match took place this afternoon. The Dufferin Club were dressed in blue-and-orange jerseys, caps and stock-ings; and the B Battery (the Citadel) wore red. Colonel Fletcher played on their side. The soldiers were somewhat rough, and one gentleman had his nose broken. The Dufferin Club won.

SATURDAY, 20TH. – The Stadacona Hunt met to-day. I drove out with the children to see the meet, and they were amused for a short time watching the jumping; but we felt so cold that we took advantage of a heavy shower as an excuse for returning home.

MONDAY, 22ND. – I inspected two convents this afternoon, which D. had visited without me last year. The first was the 'Bon Pasteur.' The Misses Caron and some other young ladies were there to meet us and to take charge of my A.D.C. We looked at the beautiful embroideries, admired the chapel, visited the reformatory school, besides going into every bedroom.

Having thoroughly done the 'Bon Pasteur,' we proceeded to the 'Grey Sisters,' who take charge of old people and orphan children. The Grand Vicaire was my spokeman on this occasion. He went round with me and made little exhortations – thus relieving me of the necessity of finding something to say to everybody.

TUESDAY, 23RD. – Such a wet day! We just managed to get out on the platform for half an hour, for a game of very odd football with a brick, with the children, and had to give up all hopes of dancing there in the evening.

We had a dinner party, and then a 'drum'; and as the balcony failed us, we opened our one passage, and the young ladies promenaded up and down, and drank tea, and cracked crackers, and had supper, and seemed to bear the disappointment about the dancing very well.

WEDNESDAY, 24TH. – We had a bride and bridegroom to dinner. They have been married six weeks, and are taking an immense tour, on their way to Japan and India. I am quite surprised at the small quantity of clothes she carries for so extensive a tour, and one comprising so many climates. Two serge dresses, one 'good' silk, cut square, and a black silk skirt with a white 'top'; with these, she has entered the smartest New York society, and is going round the world.

SATURDAY, 27TH. – This was a most lovely warm day, and the weekly Paper Hunt was a very gay affair. About thirty people were riding, and nearly twenty carriages following. We saw the jumping very well, and the country looked quite beautiful with its autumn-many-coloured hills, the blue river, and the gay villages with their shining spires and roofs. The riders found the sun almost too hot.

WEDNESDAY, OCTOBER 1ST. – In the afternoon I took the children out to see a collection of birds made by Mr. Lemoine. The trees in his place were lovely, the leaves being now of the most brilliant colours – some trees perfectly crimson, and others orange, with yellow ones and dark green firs all mixed.

> When Henry Atkinson sold part of his beautiful estate of Spencer Wood to the Government of Canada, he reserved forty acres, called Spencer Grange, for himself. Visitors, including the famous ornithologist, John James Audubon, came from far and near to wander through its ornamental gardens and orchid houses and to study its bird life. In 1860 this property was purchased by James (later Sir James) MacPherson Le Moine, a Quebec lawyer, who was a keen naturalist and historian.

THURSDAY, 2ND. – We were surprised this morning to find it snowing; but the day cleared up, and after our dinner the young ladies and the 'drum' generally danced out of doors on the platform. The dancing amused some, and the Boston Quintette Club, who are here now, brought their instruments and played beautifully to us. We had supper, and the people left after twelve o'clock.

SATURDAY, 4TH. – The ground covered with snow, and a dismal snow-storm still going on. This is rather early to begin winter, but we hope to see the ground once more before it disappears until May.

MONDAY, 6TH. – A very wet day; our intended visit to the Indians, and all the sports of the week, postponed. Mr. and Mrs. Rothery arrived. He is the British Commissioner who is to settle the fishery part of the Washington Treaty. His wife, George Dallas (his secretary), and a young Mr. Russell, are with him. They lunched with us.

TUESDAY, 7TH. – Fred went off before breakfast to train for the race which he is to ride. He has scant hopes of winning, as he walks a stone [14 pounds] over the proper riding weight, and his horse has just come off the grass. In fact, his only chances lie in the possible misfortunes of others.

Mr. and Mrs. Rothery dined with us, and we went to the Sergeants' Dance, where we opened the ball with the Sergeant-Major and his wife.

WEDNESDAY, 8TH. – I visited an asylum for old women, and paid a morning visit to the Ursuline nuns. The children were so astonished when a dozen cheerful ladies dressed in black appeared behind a double grating to talk to us. Basil and Hermie could not get over it, and Nelly seemed greatly amused. The key of the room into which we went was handed to us through a hole in the wall, so that nothing could be seen but the hand that held it.

THURSDAY, 9TH. – The weather was so beautiful that we could not tear ourselves away from the 'home-view,' and remained on the balcony all day.

In the evening the Lieutenant-Governor, Admiral Hillyard and twenty-four others dined with us, and we had a party. As the night was perfect, our guests danced to the light of the moon, and were much pleased with the entertainment.

FRIDAY, 10TH. – We were startled this morning by fifteen guns, – our guns saluting the General (O'Grady Haly), who arrived by the Montreal boat. We sent down the carriage, and an invitation for him to stay with us.

We have begun to prepare for our ball, and I am trying to solve the difficulties we have to encounter in moving from Quebec. All our servants, plate, etc. have to be at the ball on Tuesday night. Then all has to be packed to start Wednesday afternoon; the servants are to get to Ottawa Thursday evening, and visitors come on Saturday. Parliament meets on the Wednesday after.

We went to see the 'Stadacona Races.' I took the General, D. rode, and the jockey (Fred), was on the course before. He wore a lilac jacket and cap, weighed twenty-one pounds too much, and his horse was not 'fit.' There were twelve hurdles and seven brooks to jump. The 'favourite' threw his rider at the first fence. The remaining three had a good race, and the end was most exciting, Fred coming in a good second in spite of all his disadvantages. He rode beautifully. The weather was magnificent.

SATURDAY, 11TH. – The General inspected the B. Battery before breakfast, and we looked on. Then I assisted at the first meeting of the 'Clandeboye Football Club' – all boys under twelve. There are twenty members. They had two capital games, and afterwards elected a secretary, Archie being president.

MONDAY, 13TH. – The athletic sports were most successful, and crowds of people seemed to enjoy themselves. The esplanade was fringed with people, bands playing and flags flying.

> A keen athlete himself, Lord Dufferin encouraged all types of sport—curling, skating, rowing, yachting, swimming, etc.—giving scores of prizes and trophies for various competitions.

TUESDAY, 14TH. – The ballroom looked unpromising this morning. The decoration had yet to be done, and, worse than all, the platform, upon which we are so dependent for room, was covered with puddles. However, we set to work: sailors decorating the outside, and myself and maids the inside. Fred Ward got in three stoves which he set a-going under the tent, and with which he successfully dried the floor and roof. Still, the weather looked so bad that we got ready two of the children's bedrooms to act as safety valves should the company be unable to use the platform.

In the dancing-room I had three hooks in the middle of the ceiling, to use as keynotes to my ornamentation, and from these I brought ropes of pink, white and blue tarletane, and made the room look like a tent, with a chandelier hanging from the centre of each group of ropes. The ropes were fastened all round to the cornice, which was finished off with festoons and roses. It looked very light and pretty.

There was a heavy shower at six o'clock, and then it cleared, and everything went off well. The platform was so popular that it ended in our having almost too much room in the ballroom. The supper, too, Mr. Pattisson managed very well. The room only held sixty, and we were 330; but there was no crush, and the relays were kept quite distinct, and each sat down comfortably. The guests stayed till 2.30, having begun to dance soon after nine.

WEDNESDAY, 15TH. – We took a farewell walk on the beautiful platform before going down to the boat, where we found many of our friends waiting to say good-bye. The Lieutenant-Governor paid me a state visit at the Citadel.

MONTREAL, THURSDAY, 16TH. – We had a comfortable passage to Montreal, and were glad of a good long night on board the boat. To-day D. was kept extremely busy seeing different people. We managed between two interviews to get a little walk, and at one o'clock, he being unable to come, I went to the Geological Museum, and was shown part of the collection of fossils by Professor Dawson.

> Sir John William Dawson, 1820-99, made a thorough study of the geology and mineralogy of his native Nova Scotia, as well as of the other maritime provinces. In 1855 he became principal of McGill University, and held that post until his retirement in 1893. A voluminious writer, he published numerous books and articles on scientific and educational subjects.

FRIDAY, 17TH. – We travelled up to Ottawa, and found all the children well, and the house looking so nice. Many improvements have been made, and our principal passages have had new crimson carpets, and white paint on the doors and walls; so they look very gay and smart. After all our travels, home looks very comfortable, and we should be very happy but for political anxieties.

The Judges came to bring D. the report of the Commission.

> The Commission, which had been set up on August 14, had as chairman the Honourable Judge Charles Dewey Day. Associated with him were Judge Antoine Polette, and Judge James Robert Gowan.
>
> Their first meeting was held on August 18: and now, after almost two months of interviewing witnesses and sifting evidence, they were submitting their report to the Governor-General. This indicated that the leaders of the Government had been financially involved with one of the promoters of the railway being projected to the Pacific coast.
>
> When the famous 'short session' began its labours on October 23, a

copy of this report was laid on the desk of each Member of Parliament. Accompanying this were replicas of the despatches of Lord Dufferin to the Colonial Secretary, the Earl of Kimberley, referring to the prorogation of Parliament on the thirteenth of August, and to the setting up of the commission, together with the replies in which the imperial authorities signified their approval of the Governor-General's conduct.

SATURDAY, 18TH. – I was busy all day getting the drawing-room to look 'lived-in.' The Rotherys arrived in the evening. The weather was wet.

WEDNESDAY, 22ND. – To-night we had the Ministerial banquet, and were thirty at dinner. The only missing Ministers were Dr. Robitaille and Mr. Tilley.

> Theodore Robitaille, 1834-97, practised as a physician and surgeon for many years in his native Quebec. In 1873 he became Receiver-General in the Macdonald Cabinet. From 1879 to 1884 he was Lieutenant-Governor of Quebec.

> Samuel Leonard Tilley, 1818-96, member from New Brunswick, had been one of the 'Fathers of Confederation.' He became a Cabinet Minister in 1867, and in 1873 held the portfolio of Finance. He was later Lieutenant-Governor of New Brunswick and created a K.C.M.G. in 1879.

THURSDAY, 23RD. – We dressed for the 'opening' before lunch – low gowns, feathers and diamonds, uniforms or evening coats – and at 2.30 set off in carriages: Mr. and Mrs. Rothery, Mr. Pattisson and I in one; Lady Harriet Fletcher, my three children, etc. etc. in others, and the Governor-General in a carriage-and-four behind us. He opened a bridge on his way, which is to be called the Dufferin bridge, and then came on, and entered the House with a very brilliant staff – for he had this year a number of officers and friends in uniform accompanying him. The Senate Chamber was full; numbers of ladies on the floor, and crowds of people in the galleries. D. read the speech in French and in English.

FRIDAY, 24TH. – At last we have a lovely day. I took Mrs. Rothery, Mr. Brodrick, and Mr. Russell to see the Chaudière Falls, and we also went over a lucifer-match manufactory.

SATURDAY, 25TH. – I gave the prizes for some athletic sports. Mr. Brodrick and Mr. Rothery went to a Ministerial dinner, and brought us home much news. Lord Rosebery (who came to us to-day) dined with the Opposition, but, although they sat till twelve, they never mentioned the great fight which is coming off on Monday, and about which they were all thinking, but talked instead of Shakespeare and the musical glasses. The Archbishop of Manitoba (Riel's protector) dined with us.

MONDAY, 27TH. – The great debate began; but I did not go to the House, and D. and I had Rideau to ourselves.

TUESDAY, 28TH. – I went to the House to-day, and remained till 11 p.m. I heard Sir Francis Hincks [member for Vancouver, British Columbia], Mr. Macdonald, of Pictou (who is a very good speaker, but untrained), and a Mr. Glass [member for the city of London, Ontario]. It is supposed that Mr. Blake [Edward Blake, member for South Bruce, who subsequently became Minister of Justice in Mr. Mackenzie's Cabinet, 1875] and Sir John Macdonald are waiting for each other.

WEDNESDAY AND THURSDAY, 29TH AND 30TH. – Our thoughts and time still occupied by the debate. The first day, two speakers took up the whole time.

SATURDAY, NOVEMBER 1ST. – The weather is very wretched, and very English-wintry. It tries to snow, and succeeds in sleeting and being raw and dull.

I saw people for the first time since my return, to-day; 134 visitors came. I had Lady Harriet and Mrs. Rothery and the young men to help me, and the afternoon was pleasant, and like a party.

MONDAY, 3RD. – Mr. Brodrick left this morning. We (ladies) went to the House of Commons at three o'clock. Before the recess for dinner, there was a little scrimmage over His Ex.'s despatches, and at the end of this we adjourned for two hours.

At a quarter to nine Sir John Macdonald rose, and spoke for five hours, making a very fine speech, full of power, lively, and forcible to the end. He did not fail in the slightest degree while speaking, but when he sat down he was completely exhausted, and his voice was quite gone. Mr. Blake got up after him, but adjourned the debate in a few minutes, and will finish his speech to-morrow.

TUESDAY, 4TH. – I did not hear Mr. Blake. He spoke for five hours too.

WEDNESDAY, 5TH. – I drove to Ottawa, intending to hear the speeches and see the division, but at the Office I was told that Sir John was with the Governor-General. As the House could not sit without him, I remained in the carriage, and soon we saw Colonel Fletcher taking Mr. Mackenzie to His Excellency. Of course, we guessed that he had been 'sent for'; and the groups of two and three who stood about turned their heads curiously and nodded in a knowing way.

We took our places in the House, and Sir John got up and briefly announced that the Government had resigned. The announcement was received in perfect silence.

The Opposition, directly it was over, crossed the House to their new seats.

SATURDAY, 22ND. – This is the family half-holiday; so after dinner we went down to the ice, and exerted ourselves to learn the Dutch roll – mother and children and governesses struggling and tumbling about, but all making great progress.

MONDAY, 24TH. – There is a regular snowstorm going on. Skating was out of the question, so we went out to toboggan. The snow was soft and loose, and we were nearly choked and buried in it; but, of course, the children liked this very much.

MONDAY, DECEMBER 1ST. – D. had a party of Scotchmen for curling and lunch (St. Andrew's Day), and we drank the 'Queen of Scotland's' health. This was the opening of our new Curling Rink. It is close to the Skating Rink, and the tobogganing hill is on the other side; so we have quite a nest of amusements there.

WEDNESDAY, 3RD. – Alas for the thaw! – our Rink was just right, and now all the ice, and all the skating, disappears! It is in a terrible state – all over lumps and bubbles, with dead leaves frozen into it, which, as you know, burn holes in the ice.

SATURDAY, 6TH. – Being the twelve children's half-holiday, Saturday has now become a weekly festival. We skated all afternoon, and after tea had a great rehearsal of the children's play. Mr. Dixon exhibited a magic lantern too, which, though only partially successful, was received with shouts of delight.

MONDAY, 8TH. – Thermometer 18° below zero. The day looked dull, but we had a most delightful skate on the Ottawa – clear, smooth ice, and any amount of space. I found myself able to go more than a mile as fast as possible on the outside edge. The children enjoyed it immensely.

MONDAY, 15TH. – D. went into Ottawa, and came back in time for a short skate. In the evening we had some new Ministers to dinner. I am trying to become a Grit, but I can't quite manage it. It takes me as much time as the outside edge backwards.

I sat between Mr. Mackenzie and Mr. Cartwright; I like them both, and the latter is very talkative and pleasant. Mr. Mackenzie is very straight-forward, and very Scotch, in accent and in looks. On the other side of him sat M. Letellier St. Just, a French Canadian, and then came Mr. Vail, from Halifax, and the Haligonian Prime Minister, Mr. Almon. We also had the head of a large deaf-and-dumb institution at Belleville, who is very anxious for us and 'family' to go down there to see a pantomime done by his pupils, and thinks a journey of six hours absolutely nothing for the purpose.

Alexander Mackenzie, the new Prime Minister, had appointed Richard (later Sir Richard) John Cartwright, the Member for Lennox and Addington, his Minister of Finance. Honourable Luc Letellier de St. Just, the Minister of Agriculture, continued to hold that portfolio until his appointment as Lieutenant-Governor of Quebec, December 15, 1876.

Hon. William Berrian Vail became Minister of Militia and Defence on September 30, 1874. This position was confirmed when he won the federal seat of Digby in a by-election on October 22.

FRIDAY, 19TH. – We attended an amateur performance in aid of a charity. It was very good indeed. The first part consisted of 'waxworks' done by the beauties of Ottawa. They certainly have a talent for *tableaux,* for I never saw anything more perfectly still than they were – although they were 'on view' for nearly half-an-hour at a time. Each one was wound up in turn, and went through its performance admirably.

TUESDAY, 23RD. – I drove into Ottawa on a Christmas shopping expedition, skated in the afternoon, and dined at six, as we had to go and give prizes to Protestant schools in Ottawa. The room was very hot, but the 'exercises' went off well, and 200 people had to be sent away for want of space. Children read and sang. D. received an address, and replied to it, and we did not give the prizes, as there was not time.

WEDNESDAY, 24TH. – Gawen and Fred [Lady Dufferin's brothers, Captain Gawen Rowan Hamilton, 7th Dragon Guards, and Fred, the

A.D.C.] arrived this morning, both looking very well. They found me busily arranging the Christmas-tree. Gawen began his skating, but at present he looks very tall and shaky on the ice.

THURSDAY, 25TH. – The church was beautifully decorated for Christmas.

Lunch and a little skating filled the afternoon, and at five the children's Christmas really began. There were ten of them under eleven for tea, and very pretty the table looked, with their little fair heads all round it.

The tree came next, and was a great success; everyone seemed to get what they wished for, and the books, toys, etc. will be thoroughly appreciated during the week's holiday.

SATURDAY, 27TH. – This morning [evening] we attended a performance at St. Joseph's College. The house was beautifully illuminated outside, and we had songs and addresses, and a little French play acted by the students. It was a good night for sleighing, and the drive home was pleasant.

WEDNESDAY, 31ST. – We had our first skating party to-day, and I was able to perform the outside edge backwards and forwards quite well enough for public display. About seventy people came, but there was not enough snow for tobogganing. After the outdoor amusements we danced in the ballroom, and I think all enjoyed themselves.

CHAPTER 10

Our Second Season at Ottawa
JANUARY-JUNE 1874

THURSDAY, JANUARY 1ST, 1874. – D. had, unfortunately, a bad cold and headache, and so I was obliged to receive the gentlemen of Ottawa by myself. You remember that they pay visits to all their acquaintances on New Year's Day, and that every lady in the land remains at home to receive them. Two hundred and seventy came to see me, greeted me, passed through the drawing-room into the dining-room for tea or champagne – mostly champagne!

One very odd man appeared whom I had never seen before. He said to me, 'Ah, very sorry indeed to hear that Lord Dufferin is ill; he is such a great fellow, it really would be a pity if anything were to happen to him. . . . Do I speak to Mr. Hamilton?' Fred got him off into the dining-room, where he continued, 'I knew Mr. Conway' (our other A.D.C., whose name was Coulson) 'so well that I felt I knew the crowd, so I thought I would come to-day. Sorry His Ex. is ill; he is such a good fellow, always turning up everywhere. Awful bore this sort of thing, but one is obliged to do it.'

I have been busy the last few weeks teaching the children to act a little play, to be performed before an audience this New Year's Day, so directly the last of my visitors had gone, I rushed to make final arrangements on the stage, to visit my patient and get him up, to dress myself, and to dress the fairies.

Every member of our two families (ours and Colonel Fletcher's) between the ages of twelve years and eight months appears either in the play or in the *tableaux* which come after it, and I only wish you were here to see how well they do it, and how pretty they look!

In the piece they represent imps who, clad in the gayest attire, are invisible to mortal eye the moment they put on certain bright-coloured caps, and visible again directly they take them off. The fun of the play consists in the way in which they are supposed to appear and disappear, plaguing the life out of a gigantic mortal, who either cannot see his tormentors at all, or whose frantic attempts to catch them when he does, only lead him into the traps they have prepared for him.

My little troop entered fully into the spirit of the plot, and were so delighted with Fred's acting in the part of 'Grumps,' the troubled mortal, that they were really holding their sides with laughter, and there certainly was more nature than art in their representation of the mischievous imps.

The *tableaux* were equally successful, and though an eye was occasionally opened during the 'Sleeping Beauty in the Wood' scene, and then conscientiously shut up again with unnecessary firmness – though one infant preferred to sleep with his legs in the air, and another made an uncalled-for announcement in the middle of a *tableau vivant* – the whole performance was most charming and successful, and actors, parents and audience were all equally delighted.

SATURDAY, 3RD. – The cold has diminished, and now there are only ten degrees of frost – which is nothing. One really does not feel cold half as much here as in England. The house is warm throughout, day and night, so that one does not shiver over one's dressing, or dread venturing out into the passages, or crowd round the fires in the rooms, as one does at home. And then, when one wishes to go out, one knows – thanks to tradition and to the thermometer – exactly what ought to be put on, and one wraps oneself up like a mummy, and drapes one's face in an indispensable and most becoming 'cloud,' and thus defies the weather.

We had a delightful skating party. The ice was lovely, and while numbers of graceful performers danced over it, other young men and maidens, to say nothing of fathers and mothers, were sliding down hills in toboggans, children were digging and burrowing in the snow, and nurses and perambulators added a homely touch to the scene. You can't think how lively it looked – like an ant-hill decked in brilliant colours.

When it got too late for outdoor amusements, we came in for tea, and the young people danced for an hour.

MONDAY, 5TH. – The thermometer 53°! the most unheard-of thaw, and the snow almost entirely gone. We were, however, able to skate about two miles up the Rideau – a very rare chance here.

In the afternoon I actually drove on wheels into Ottawa, to begin a tour of inspection of the Institutions there with Miss Lees. We went first to the Gaol, which Miss Lees thought the best she had seen in Canada. We next went to the Protestant Orphan Home, a small house, with a stuffy sleeping and living room for the babies. A better house is much needed.

TUESDAY, 6TH. – We drove in a snow-storm to the Grey Nuns' Convent, and were received at the 'Mother House.' From this house we walked to the Hospital, after it to the Orphanage, and the Refuge for the Old. All these Miss Lees examined as well as she could. But she likes to turn up every sheet, and to peep into every corner, and this is the kind of inspection to which the good nuns are not accustomed. They like my perfunctory style much better.

WEDNESDAY, 7TH. – We finished the 'Grey Nuns' to-day by visiting their school and an English Orphanage. Miss Lees is going to write a book about these things, so I need not record details.

Last night we kept Twelfth Night by practising the 'Boston Dip' and Badminton.

THURSDAY, 8TH. – The weather is despairing. It will thaw, and even condescends to rain, which in a Canadian January is mean! Think of the ground being visible! and no skating! and umbrellas up! and driving on wheels!

There was, however, a sight to-day which I am glad to have seen. After the rain it froze hard for a short time, leaving ropes of beautiful clear ice hanging from the telegraph-wires, while the trees seem to be the decorations of a fairy play. Words really do fail to describe the beauty of our woods while this 'ice-storm' continues. There is a transparent sheath round every twig, the birch-tree being particularly pretty, with its small and well-known rods all cased in clearest crystal, while in the distance the trees seem to be made of silver with dazzling jewels on every branch. It reminds me of the story of the twelve princesses who used to disappear at night, and were, after much searching discovered by the owner of an invisible cloak to frequent a garden whose trees were covered with precious stones. Like the invisible soldier, I cannot resist breaking off branches and taking them home; but, unlike his, my diamonds melt.

SATURDAY, 10TH. – The skating party, postponed on account of the thaw, resolved itself into an indoor party. The young ladies came in extra smart attire, and from 3.30 to 6 they danced. After the dancing the children performed their little play and *tableaux* again with great success,

SATURDAY, 17TH. – This was a lovely day for our skating party, so warm (about 10° below freezing-point), the tobogganing hill in perfect condition, and the ice good. I skated the whole time, only stopping occasionally to watch the toboggans come down. Once Fred was left behind in the middle of the hill and rolled to the bottom; another time, three passengers remained in the snow, while the fourth sailed on to the bottom of the slide.

TUESDAY, 27TH. – Thermometer 30° below zero during the night – about zero during the day. At five o'clock the children were all ready in their fairy dresses to act their play to about fifty of their contemporaries. The guests were many of them very pretty, and all very well dressed.

WEDNESDAY, 28TH. – We have lent our ballroom for a concert in aid of our little church, and the morning was occupied in placing the 300 chairs, and in preparing the stage.

The first part of the programme consisted of vocal music by amateurs. The 'Rosa d'Erina' sang four songs. Three very pretty *tabeaux* closed the entertainment: – The Death of Cleopatra: the Expulsion of Hagar; and a group of flower-girls, Nelly being one of them. Cleopatra was very handsome, and beautifully dressed. I think they will have cleared fifty pounds.

SATURDAY, 31ST. – Saturday brings its usual skating party. The day was very cold, and we cut short the outdoor amusements, and had a very successful cotillon indoors.

Mr. Mackenzie, the Prime Minister, arrived. At the station he received a note from D. asking him to come out to us, which he did immediately, and stayed for dinner. On returning to Ottawa he found he had missed an ovation, which had been prepared for him after his very successful elections. I believe his majority will be about eighty.

MONTREAL: MONDAY, FEBRUARY 2ND. – We left for Montreal, and had a long day in the train, but with books, and short naps, we got through it very well.

TUESDAY, 3RD. – Soon after breakfast, we went up to the Rink, the two Misses Bethune and ourselves being the only privileged persons, as it is shut to the public on account of the fancy-dress ball which is to take place there to-night; we had plenty of room, splendid ice, and a most delightful skate.

At eight o'clock we went back there for the ball, and took our places on a raised dais at one end of a great building like Westminster

Hall, with an architectural roof and ornamented rafters, its shiny ice floor illuminated by a thousand lights. As soon as the band changed from 'God save the Queen' into some lively strain, we saw, from the far end, gay fancy-dressed figures gliding hand-in-hand down the ice, and passing us in couples, till at last the whole space was covered with Dolly Vardens, Nights, Knights, Queens, Savages, Red-Riding-Hoods, etc. etc. D. skated in plain clothes; I only looked on and enjoyed the scene.

WEDNESDAY, 4TH. – D. visited the High School and made a Latin oration there.

TUESDAY, 10TH. – We had a band at the Rink this morning and skated to music. We danced the lancers and Sir Roger to their proper tunes, and then some waltzed and some 'outside-edged' to the 'Blue Danube.'

I must tell you the names of some of our figures, though I fear they won't convey much to you. We execute the 'Rose,' the 'Shamrock,' and the 'Thistle'; the 'Ransom,' the 'Lily,' the 'Snail,' the 'Serpent,' a chain of 'eights,' etc. etc. I wonder if ever you will see a performance?

WEDNESDAY, 11TH. – We took the Gaol by surprise this morning, and inspected it. The women's department is most unsatisfactory; the men were much better cared for.

After dinner Fred Ward, Mr. Thompson, D. and I went to see the games at the Rink, which looked pretty, with its shining ice floor, its lights, and a quantity of flags. There were 211 entries for the races, and some of them were most exciting and amusing. The barrel-races went off with great spirit, and the boys, in all stages of creeping through bottomless barrels, rolling and struggling about, looked like strange shell-fish. Mercifully, none were hurt, for it must be a dangerous game. I gave away the prizes afterwards.

I have been elected a member of the Rink, and am the only lady who holds that proud position, being also, I believe, the first wife of a Governor-General who has ever skated here.

THURSDAY, 12TH. – D. and I left early, and were 'seen off' by a guard of honour composed of the students at McGill College – a fine looking rifle regiment. We had Mr. Brydges' car, [Charles J. Brydges was General Manager of the Grand Trunk Railway] and travelled in great comfort. We found it very cold at Ottawa. All the children in different stages of cold.

OTTAWA: TUESDAY, 17TH. – There was a very exciting game in the Curling Rink between D. and Mr. Gordon, a Presbyterian minister.

They play for the Club prize, and whoever wins to-day has to play another member, and so on, till the last man remaining gains 'the horns.' This game was very close, 'twelve all,' and the next shot must decide the winner. We all came in to watch the last strokes, and D. got 'two,' and so won, and has a new antagonist to encounter.

THURSDAY, 19TH. – We had a great expedition to-day. Our party filled two sleighs, and we started at eight o'clock in the morning, and drove three miles along, or rather on, the Gatineau river, and then eighteen miles through the 'bush,' enjoying the winter scenery.

It was a prettier drive than I had expected, being more open, less shut up in wood, and the horizon more varied than it usually is here. We saw the Gatineau rapids, rushing along black-looking through the snow; also something of the lumber-trade, for we met the little sleighs full of wood coming to market. As they were loaded, we had to make way for them, and on two occasions we met in most awkward places, when we all had to get out, and lift our sleigh sideways on to the bank, and once we had to take out the horses. Another time we were at the top of a hill, and our foe wanted us to back down it. We asked if he could not back, but he exclaimed indignantly, 'Why, there are enough of you there to lift that cutter of yours right over the mountain' – this of the great family sleigh!

We arrived at last at the house of a farmer, the owner of a cave, which cave was the end and object of our expedition. Here we lunched, and then, guided by the farmer, we proceeded on our way two miles along a lumber snow road, very narrow and bumpy. We left the carriages on a lake, and climbed up a hill to the mouth of the cave, where we took off our fur cloaks, and, each taking a lighted candle, entered the cave.

After examining a part of it, which I may call the hall and ante-room of this subterranean mansion, we proceeded on hands and knees through a very low passage to the drawing-room. We ladies had great difficulty with our petticoats, especially when in this doubled-up position we had to cross a pool of water on a narrow plank, and were greatly relieved when we were able to stretch ourselves upright again. New perils were, however, before us, and the gentlemen were astonished to find that Lady Harriet and I really did intend to descend the ladders which, in the darkness, appeared to lead down to the middle of the earth. But, as we very naturally observed to them, we had not driven twenty miles, and crawled on hands and knees to the spot, to be deterred by a small difficulty; so down we went, and saw two more large rooms in the basement of said mansion. Of course the place requires a geologist's eye to appreciate it thoroughly. It is made of – no: I won't even attempt to describe its origin.

We came out from our crawling very dirty indeed, and, returning to our carriages, drove homewards. Our sleigh was first, and we had just descended a steep hill when we heard a noise, and looking back saw the second sleigh stranded in the middle of the road, its horses galloping madly towards us. Our footman rushed in front of them, and caught hold of their bridles just as they were upon us: he was knocked down between them, but was not hurt. The gentlemen all got into the broken sleigh, and finally arrived safe home, though they were run away with at every hill on the way back. It snowed most of the day, and at the end of our drive we looked ideal Canadians.

MONDAY, 23RD. – There was a very exciting curling match to-day between D. and Hutchison for 'the horns,'

D. won by six points, and will now have to encounter another player. The boys made some calculations afterwards, in which they proved that each player had run eight miles, had thrown four-and-a-half tons forty yards, and had swept out the Parliament Buildings – pretty severe labour for one game!

TUESDAY, 24TH. – The 'Freds' – for we have no less than five of that name in our household – played a match, the winner to be the 'representative member' of the new 'Viceregal Curling Club.' Brother Fred won it.

He and Colonel Fletcher dined with the Ministers, 'in honour' of the Dominion Board of Trade, and Fred returned thanks for the ladies.

SATURDAY, 28TH. – Colonel Strange, from Quebec, and Mr. Plumb, M.P. for Niagara, dined with us, and we had an 'electric evening.' I don't suppose you could have one at home; but here by rubbing our feet on the carpet, and then touching another person, we can produce a spark, and from any hot metal, such as the fireplace, we get quite a shock.

Mr. Plumb showed us a very curious thing. We went into a dark room, and rubbed the inside of the back of a book with a fur glove, and instantly the gilt pattern on the outside was illuminated by sparks, so that the whole design was as clearly marked out as it is in the daytime. He discovered this accidentally by passing a piece of fur round his hat, when the maker's name appeared inside in letters of light. Then we tried to light the gas, and I had the satisfaction of succeeding three times myself. I held a piece of wire, or a needle, in my hand, rubbed my feet on the carpet, and touched the burner; a spark was emitted, and the gas instantly blazed up.

The children are extremely fond of charging at some unsuspecting victim with a finger or a nose, which instantly emits a perfect flash of lightning. One day I brought the baby down to the drawing-room, and Fred (who had just been rubbing his feet preparatory to trying an electric experiment) kissed her, and gave her such a shock that she cried with fright!

FRIDAY, MARCH 6TH. – The Ottawa Curling Club came and played on our rink for His Excellency's medal. They made a good score, and have hopes of winning it. Mr. Gilmour and Mr. Mackenzie spent the afternoon here and curled with D. The Premier brightened up very much during the 'roarin' game.'

SATURDAY, 7TH. – It poured, and skating was out of the question. A few ladies dropped in alone; but at last the two necessaries – men and music – arrived and we had a very nice little dance and cotillon. Hermie and Basil contribute greatly to the amusement of the company. She and Basil talk to everyone, and are always in such high spirits, that the lookers-on like having them to play with.

Nowell (D.'s valet) won the cup, and I presented it to him; it is to have his name, and 'Presented to the Viceregal Curling Club,' etc., engraved on it.

TUESDAY, 10TH. – There was tremendous excitement in the Curling Rink to-day – D. playing another opponent, Mr. Russell, for 'the horns.' They had to make twenty-one points, and five times during the course of the game they were ties, D. winning finally by one – a very honourable and unexpected victory, as Mr. Russell is 'skip' of the Ottawa Club.

TUESDAY, 24TH. – There was beautiful tobogganing to-day. The children went down in every sort of way, double and single, standing, sitting and lying. Once they tied four toboggans together, which looked like a raft covered with people – a rescue from shipwreck.

FRIDAY, 27TH. – A day of much ceremony. Diamonds, lappets, and feathers at two o'clock, when all drove to the Parliament Buildings, the Governor-General in carriage-and-four, and I in a quiet brougham, to a private entrance. I went into the Senate Chamber, which I found full of gay ladies, and soon we heard the guns which announced His Excellency's arrival. We all stood up to receive him, as he came in preceded by his Staff. He sent for the Commons, and the new Speaker made a little speech, and the President of the Senate replied to it. Then D. read the speech, first in English, then in French, and we departed as we came.

The preceding January, Parliament had been dissolved and an election called. This had resulted in a handsome majority for the Reformers and for Alexander Mackenzie's new Ministry. The day preceding the opening of the new session, on March 26, 1874, Timothy Warren Anglin (1822-96) was sworn in as Speaker of the House of Commons. A native of Ireland, he had emigrated to New Brunswick when twenty-seven years of age. The newspaper he founded there became recognized as the mouthpiece of the Roman Catholics in that province.

The famous actress, Margaret Anglin, his eldest daughter, was born in the Speaker's Chambers of the Parliament Buildings, April 3, 1876.

The Honourable David Christie had been appointed Speaker of the Senate, January 9, 1874.

On my return I doffed my finery until after dinner, when I dressed up again, and we returned to the Senate Chamber to hold a Drawing-Room; it went off very well, and was quite a brilliant affair.

SATURDAY, 28TH. – We turned out of the drawing-room to-day, to have it arranged as a second supper-room. The conservatory was hung with Chinese lanterns, and everything that was possible done to embellish the rooms for an evening-party.

There was a band, *tableaux,* and some singing in the drawing-room, supper in two rooms, and I believe people enjoyed themselves.

SUNDAY, 29TH. – We had such a nice walk on the Ottawa. The banks were lovely, clothed in icicles, and ice-grottoes, into which we got, had been formed in places. They were supported by enormous pillars of ice, and a fringe of large icicles shut us in.

TUESDAY, 31ST. – I went into the House, expecting to see Riel take his seat. [Louis Riel, one of the leaders in the North West rebellion of 1870, had just been elected to represent the riding of Provencher in Manitoba.] There was great excitement outside, but he did not appear.

We heard an amusing debate about abolishing the sale of spirits within the precincts of Parliament. We were very busy at home preparing everything for a full-dress rehearsal of a selection from the opera, 'Semiramide,' and the little play of 'One Hour,' in which I myself take part. The rehearsal was successful, the servants making up an audience.

THURSDAY, 2ND APRIL. – Mr. Charles Kingsley [the Reverend Charles Kingsley, author of *Westward Ho!*, *Hypatia*, etc.] and his daughter are staying with us, and we took them over to the Houses of Parliament, and had Sir John and Lady Macdonald one day, and Mr. and Mrs. Mackenzie another, to meet them at dinner.

SATURDAY, 4TH. – We looked on at curling to-day, and saw D. beat the 'champion,' Mr. Gilmour, twice. Dr. Grant dined with us, and he and Mr. Kingsley were very happy over geological subjects.

> Dr. James (later Sir James) Alexander Grant, 1831-1920, had been brought to Canada from Scotland when only a few weeks old. After graduating from McGill University (M.D., 1854) he practised medicine in Ottawa, and from 1867 to 1905 was physician to the Governor-General. In 1882 he became a charter member of the Royal Society of Canada.

EASTER SUNDAY, 5TH. – There was a great congregation, and we had an excellent sermon from Mr. Kingsley, appropriate to the day. He does not stammer at all in preaching, The gentlemen say that in the smoking-room he is most amusing; but he seems shy, and is therefore less brilliant, in general society.

TUESDAY, 7TH. – D. walked into Ottawa, and in the street met Mr. Laurence Oliphant, whom he asked to come to us at once, and to bring his wife. [Mr. Laurence Oliphant, novelist, war correspondent and mystic, had been secretary to Lord Elgin in Canada, 1853-1854. He was the author of *The Piccadilly Papers*, and many other books.] He is very pleasant, and she is a sweet pretty little woman, very chatty. They both belong to a curious sect, headed by a Mr. Harris. They consider themselves bound to spend all they have, not merely to give to charitable institutions, but to distribute it personally. They live in a district where they have farms, and the members all help each other all they can.

FRIDAY, 10TH. – D. curled, and nearly killed Mr. Oliphant with the exertion. I like both her and him. Their faith in what they believe, and their conscientious performance of the same, are wonderful.

FRIDAY, 17TH. – The great ball given by the citizens of Ottawa in our honour took place to-night. The dancing was in the Senate Chamber – a very handsome room – and a new floor was put down for the occasion. I suppose two thousand people were present, but there were so many passages and promenades that the dancing was not too crowded. We much appreciated our hosts' kindness and hospitality.

MONDAY, 27TH. – We were pleased to see in the morning paper that there are 900 dollars (nearly 200£.) over, after all the ball expenses have been paid, which are to be given to charities.

WEDNESDAY, 29TH. – In the evening our play came off, and was a great success. People seemed to listen with eyes and ears, and to be delighted.

After it was over I changed my dress in about three minutes, and came down to supper. Stray couples walked about the corridors, visited the conservatory, and had what is called 'a lovely time.'

When I had shaken hands with the 'six hundred,' and we were alone again, we had our supper, of which we were all very glad, for acting makes one so hungry!

SATURDAY, MAY 2ND. – D. and Fred went out hunting, and had a pleasant run.

The children tried a paper-chase. Colonel Fletcher was the fox, and the run was most exciting, the 'hounds' shrieking all the way, and having some delightfully stiff timber to climb.

A Parliamentary dinner; five expected guests failed to come, and left a great gap at the table.

THURSDAY, 14TH. – The Lieutenant-Governor of Nova Scotia and Miss Archibald arrived to spend a few days with us.

Lady Harriet is expecting her sister and uncle – a great excitement in our small world; for, though our guests are numerous, our home-circle is small. We have had very pleasant weather, and sit out a great deal, enjoying it; but as yet there are no leaves on the trees, and no plants bedded out.

FRIDAY, 22ND. – We had such a pleasant day, driving in two carriages to visit Mr. Gilmour's place on the Gatineau River, and to see his sawmills, etc. Lady Mary and Mr. Marsham, who arrived on Friday, went with us. The weather was fine, and the river very full; the rapids were magnificent, and it was interesting to see the lumber go down them.

We watched the trunks of great trees turning and twisting in the whirlpools, passing from one current to another, dashing down water-falls, disappearing in the waves, and coming up again on the brink of other rapids. We saw them reach a place where a number of men, with poles and spikes, stood by to harpoon and mark the passing monsters, sending those stamped with a 'G' in one direction, and those with a 'P' in another.

After this, a further rush down the river brought the logs to a calm pool, where they were just recovering from their exciting voyage, when they were laid hold of by an innocent-looking cogwheel, up which they marched slowly and surely into the teeth of fourteen thickset saws, which sent them in pieces on a further sail, down a small trough of water, to the stack-yard. In addition to the almost human interest of this tragic performance, we had lovely scenery to look at, a good lunch to eat, and a row home in boats; so we enjoyed ourselves much.

MONDAY, 25TH. – The Queen's birthday kept. We dressed up, and at eleven arrived in front of the Town Hall, where the firemen and engines were to be reviewed. We looked at and walked round them, and then proceeded to the review-ground.

The Governor-General's Foot Guards looked extremely well; but the weather was dreadful, and when I came to give away the colours it poured in torrents, so that the feathers in my bonnet stood on end, and I had to take off my veil and throw it away. You may imagine my mother's feelings when I turned round in the middle of the deluge and found that Archie was out in dancing-shoes!

WEDNESDAY, 27TH. – We made an expedition down the Slide to-day. D. paddled his canoe to the foot of the Chaudière Falls. Colonel Fletcher rowed there, and we took two carriage-loads, with five children – all in a great state of excitement. We found a magnificent 'crib' prepared for us – flags and green arches over it. When we were all assembled, we started at a slow and stately pace on our journey over the Slide down to the Ottawa. It takes three waterfalls to reach the level of the river, and going over these is the greatest fun. We remained on our crib for some time, and then got on to a raft for tea, which we drank out of tins, without milk or sugar; and we also ate raft-made bread, which was excellent.

FRIDAY, 29TH. – We went up the Rideau in a carriage for about eight miles, and saw the Falls, which are very pretty. Had tea there, and came back in canoes, D. rowing me. There was a beautiful sunset, and the river was lovely – the scenery much more English-like and meadowy than it usually is here. There were some rapids to run, and we ladies got out, while the Colonel and D. took their canoes down. It was quite dark when we got home.

SATURDAY, 30TH. – As the mosquitoes are, so far, harmless, had tea out of doors. We carried the things down to the rocks, and the children were extremely happy attending to the fire, and jumping about at the edge of the water. The two families were present – ten old enough for picnics.

TUESDAY, JUNE 2ND. – We drove about twelve miles into the country to the borders of 'Meech's Lake,' a pretty piece of water inhabited by swarms of mosquitoes. We drank our tea in a cloud of smoke, to keep off the tormentors, and then got into canoes (which had been brought here in a cart), and explored the Lake. 'We' means the Fletchers, Lady Mary Marsham, D. and myself.

Our expedition did not end pleasantly. It had been arranged we were to get into a boat half-way and row home. The night was very dark, and the current tremendous. Presently we came up against a beam of wood stretched across the rushing river. We knew it had an opening in it through which boats could pass, but in the dark could not find the place. The Colonel, who was rowing with D., said the ladies would have to get out, and the boat lifted over the bar. Oh, it was disagreeable! We knelt on the narrow plank, with the rapid stream swirling under it. I don't think I could have done it but for a fortunate peg in my bit of plank by which I held on, and which gave me a certain sense of security. Lady Mary was so brave; she made no fuss at all. When the boat had been dragged over the beam we got into it again. But we had several more alarms about steamers, rafts, etc., and I was thankful when we got safe home without collisions or further accident.

CHAPTER 11

Fishing on the St. Lawrence
JUNE-JULY 1874

QUEBEC: SATURDAY, JUNE 6TH. – We left Ottawa yesterday – Archie, D., and I; Nelly was up to see us off, and looked a little melancholy at being left behind. We went by train to Prescott, and had two hours to wait for the boat, which had been detained by fog. We feared this delay would disarrange our plans, and make us late for the night-boat from Montreal; but it waited for us, we made our journey successfully, and arrived this morning at delightful Quebec, where as usual we met with the most friendly welcome. People always seem so glad to see us here, and all the way up the town faces were smiling at the windows, and hats were off everywhere; it is just like coming home! In the afternoon Archie played in a football-match – 'The Clandeboye' against 'The Rovers'; I need not say who won.

D. and I had a walk in the town, and then I unpacked the English box, which has just arrived, and which astonished me with the new fashions it contained. I cannot yet decide whether to put on the bonnets forwards, backwards, or sideways.

WEDNESDAY, 10TH. – We went on board the *Druid*, and left Quebec. The day was lovely, and as we went down the St. Lawrence the colouring was beautiful everywhere. We passed numbers of sailing-vessels.

FRIDAY, 12TH. – Found ourselves in sight of Gaspé this morning. Not a ripple on the water, Mr. Eden, the vivacious harbour-master, came on board, presented me with a large Indian box which had been made for me, told us all about the salmon, etc.

D. went into the bush to see about our fishing-box. We have brought with us the pieces of a little bedroom and dressing-room, which are to be put together on the site, which D. walked eighteen miles to select. The night was very bad – rain, snow, and hail. We are glad to be in harbour.

112

Hariot, Marchioness of Dufferin and Ava, taken in Canada while her husband was Governor-General: "Society is at present my business in life."

SUNDAY, 14TH. – A fine-looking morning, but cold. We went to church, and had a good sermon – short and plain. In the afternoon we landed on the York side of the harbour, and drove along a good road.

We met a friend on the way, a farmer, originally from Cavan, who has cleared, and now lives upon, thirty acres of his own land. He and his wife have added fifteen to the population of Gaspé. He asked us up to his house, which was very comfortable: a large sitting-room, with three concertinas, books, etc., in it; a dining-room, kitchen, and nice bedroom on the ground floor, and everything very neat and clean. The view from his door – lovely.

MONDAY, 15TH. – Our two rooms were taken off in the middle of the night to their destination on the St. John River, and D., Archie and I soon went after them. We made the first part of the journey in a 'waggon,' then got on horses, and rode at a jog-walk for three hours, when we reached our fishing-box. We gave all necessary directions there, and then mounted again to cross to the York River. When we reached Mr. Reynold's camp [Thomas Reynolds was managing director of the Ottawa and Prescott Railway], which is situated on this rushing river, I got Archie some food, and then the poor little man had to start back again, and only reached home at ten at night. He was very proud of his long day, which prevented his acknowledging any fatigue. [Archie would not be eleven years of age until the 28th of the following month.]

Our host is so pleasant and kind, and we had a very agreeable dinner; Colonel McNeill [later designated as Major-General Sir John McNeill, V.C., K.C.B., Equerry to H.M. the Queen] and Mr. Monck are also here. Afterwards we sat round a fire outside, and then came in to write up the game-book.

TUESDAY, 16TH. – I fished for a short time, and caught, or rather hooked, a 'kelt' – an uneatable salmon, which has been in the river all winter. D. caught one salmon of 14 lbs., Colonel McNeill two, and Mr. Monck two; but it was considered a very bad day's sport.

This is a beautiful river: numbers of pools, a very rapid current, very clear water. The woods have a great deal of birch in them, and the look-out is much more open than on most rivers.

I have such a comfortable room, with carpet and curtains.

SATURDAY, 20TH. – Fred and Dr. Campbell arrived here very early, having left the *Druid* at 5 a.m. Colonel McNeill and Mr. Monck have most kindly gone up the river to a distant house in order to leave room for them here.

We had a beautiful day as to weather, but the river had risen so much that there was no fishing. D. and I took a walk, and Fred upset a canoe, and sent himself and two men into the water.

SUNDAY, 21ST. – We took a walk, and sat round a 'smudge' – that is, a fire of damp wood, which smokes and keeps the black-flies and mosquitoes off.

MONDAY, 22ND. – The salmon not rising. The river is too high and the current too rapid. I went down to the pool where D. was fishing in the canoe, and walked back by myself; but I am advised not to do so again, lest I should meet a bear.

TUESDAY, 23RD. – Here are the statistics of our fishing so far at York River:–

Mr. Reynolds, five fish, weighing 23, 21, 33, 28, 12 lbs.

Colonel McNeill, twelve, weighing 24, 22, 11, 18, 24, 25, 27, 25, 24, 20, 26, 14 lbs.

Mr. Monck, seven, weighing 25, 11, 26, 27, 27, 23, 15 lbs.

Lord D., three: 14, 13, 10 lbs.

Fred, two: 23, 14 lbs.

So far we have not been fortunate. Last year Mr. Reynolds caught ten fish himself the first day he went out, the average being 25 lbs. This is marvellous in the way of fishing, and I record it as an interesting fact.

THURSDAY, 25TH. – Archie arrived to-day, and Mr. Reynolds left. D. had at last a good day's fishing, and came home with six salmon: 26, 25, 14, 13, 12, 10 lbs. Dr. Campbell caught one 23 lbs, and Fred nothing.

Our mail arrived, and in the middle of his salmon-catching D. sent off despatches.

FRIDAY, 26TH. – Fred was given the best pool to-day, and D. went up to the 'Little Salmon Hole' and the 'Flat Rock' pool. Archie and I looked on at the sport.

Our lunch, which the men provided, consisted of lumberman's fare: bread fried in pork fat, and tea. We all came down in a canoe, the stream bringing us at a great pace. We found that Dr. Campbell had not even seen a fish. Fred caught two, and came home to dinner in good spirits.

SATURDAY, 27TH. – We leave to-day to go to the St. John, so we had our packing to do. Besides our clothes, there were two tents to be put up, and a sledge to be transported over the river, for carrying our goods through the bush. D. and Fred started to walk. A few minutes after they left we saw a raft coming down the stream, with a little dog upon it, and a green tree floating over his head. Then a canoe came in sight, with Colonel McNeill and Mr. Monck in it. We found that the raft contained the salmon they had caught, which they sent off with the dog as its only live passenger to astonish us. They brought home nineteen large salmon, the average being twenty-three pounds weight. Mr. Monck caught eight one day, and five one evening.

We were soon ready for our start. Archie, Dr. Campbell, and I rode – I with a jar of cream on my knee. Our road was very bad, trees lying across it, and much mud and marsh to go through.

D. met us just outside our camp, and we were all delighted with our new habitation. The men had worked very hard, and made cedar-bark paths and fir plantations around the houses. The 'village,' over which the Dominion flag floats, consists of two large tents for the men, and a wooden house divided into two rooms. The windows have green mosquito-blinds over them, and the bed, white mosquito-curtains. There is a washing-table, and lots of pegs and shelves, and a little bit of carpet, which is a great luxury in the woods. A cedar path leads to the log-house, in which there is a sitting-room, and two little 'cabins,' in which our guests sleep.

Opposite our door a bonfire burns, and when the flies are bad we have a row of smudges to smoke them away. The kitchen is in another log-house on the other side, and from it we soon had an excellent dinner.

Nowell (D.'s valet) has made all these arrangements, and, in spite of many bites from the untiring flies, he works away with great good-humour and skill.

MONDAY, 29TH. – The first fishing on our own river. The fishers drew lots for the pools, and Archie and I went to see D.'s success. He only brought two home when we returned to dine at two o'clock. The others had not seen a fish. So D. and Dr. Campbell resolved to go down towards the mouth of the river, the fish being only now on their way up. There is a little house there, in which they intend to sleep to-night. Archie went to fish in a lake close by, and brought home fourteen trout. Some of these we ate for tea.

WEDNESDAY, JULY 1ST. – Dominion Day! We had several flags flying and a great bonfire in the camp. D. and Dr. Campbell returned; they seem to have enjoyed their trip.

THURSDAY, 2ND. – D. was up at a nameless pool, and caught five salmon before two o'clock. He was coming home when he caught the last, so he determined to bring it down to the house. I was hungrily watching for the fishermen's return to dinner, when I saw the canoe arriving with D. hanging on to a salmon. This was very exciting, and we saw the creature brought ashore without a gaff.

D. wanted me to fish in the afternoon. So about five o'clock we went again to the nameless pool. I stood up in the canoe, a man at each end keeping it steady with poles, and began to throw my fly. The fish did not come, so we changed the bait, and tried 'Jock Scot' and 'King Coffee.' This royal personage was large and gaudy, and had, alas! a very big hook. 'A rise!' 'He's on!' Then I stand firm, and my friend jumps several times up in the air; but I hold him well in hand, and suddenly he spits out my fly, and is gone!

Again we go up and down the pool with 'King Coffee,' and then we try the 'Silver Doctor,' and at seven o'clock another fish is on! This one simply tugs; he keeps a steady pull on all the time, and I do the same by him, and take care to give him no rest, but wind him up every time he attempts to lie quiet; once he jumps, and they say he is a large one.

This game goes on for some time, and then my friend thinks he will take me down the rapids. I am still standing in the canoe, but keeping firm by pressing my knees against the bar across it. We went down half a mile hand-in-hand like this, and I began to feel that it was a question which of us would be exhausted first. A salmon-rod with a fish at the end of it is no joke! I began 'to wish he were dead,' and to say to myself that I never would go through such an anxiety again, for the fish is never safe till he is in the boat. At last we gaffed him, and brought him safely to his death, weighed him, and found him twenty-six pounds – the largest caught here this year; so I am very proud of my success. The nameless pool is now the 'Countess Pool.'

SATURDAY, 4TH. – We packed up, and went down in canoes towards the *Druid*, fishing on the way. The salmon would not rise, and we had only three to show at the end of a long day. We left our boats in the evening, and drove to Gaspé, where we got on board the *Druid*, after saying farewell to our fishermen, etc. We meant to start at once, but there was a fog outside, and we did not get off till four in the morning.

TUESDAY, 7TH. – A fog, – and the *Druid* at a standstill all yesterday, we not knowing where we were till three o'clock, when the mist rolled away suddenly. We anchored at night about fifteen miles from Tadousac, and came in there early this morning. The children were out looking for us, and Archie went ashore to fetch Nelly and Terence for breakfast, and to show off his steering.

We landed after breakfast, and found Hermie and Basil with outstretched arms at the top of the stairs, waiting to give us a warm welcome. Then we saw the baby: such a fat fairy, so pretty, with golden hair curling all over, and large, dark grey eyes. Such a merry, happy little thing; she stands at a chair, and crawls about everywhere.

FRIDAY, 10TH. – After breakfast we got on board the *Druid* – the Fletchers, Lady Mary Marsham, ourselves and Nelly – and started up the Saguenay. At two o'clock we stopped to fish for trout, but were not very successful.

Then we proceeded on our journey, and saw a most lovely sunset, which turned the Saguenay hills into gorgeous masses of purple and blue with golden backgrounds. This arm of the sea is considered one of the great Canadian sights; it is a reft in the rocks, and the water is very deep right up to the sides. There are two enormous cliffs or capes, called 'Trinity' and 'Eternity;' but it was very dark when we passed them, and we hope to see them better on our return.

SATURDAY, 11TH. – We are anchored in Haha Bay, and D. and Colonel Fletcher started early for a day's salmon-fishing in a small river near. We ladies followed later, and found the fishers had had splendid sport. We were able to watch them, and had some exciting and terrible moments to go through! D. hooked a salmon in a pool, and the creature seemed very strong and large, and after tugging more than half an hour he insisted upon going down the rapids. D. had on great wading-stockings and boots, and ran or stumbled through the water over rough, round stones. At the foot of one rapid he nearly got the fish in, but the gaffmen were inexperienced, and made a dash at it, which frightened the salmon, and sent him off down a second rapid; then there was another long pause, another attempt on the part of the gaffmen, the hook came out of his mouth, and he was gone! However, we brought home seven salmon, and were all very happy, and very hungry for dinner at nine o'clock.

Branches were being planted all along the road, in honour of the Roman Catholic Archbishop's visit. He comes here once in five years. D. was able to present each of the priests with whom he was to stay with a salmon, which was very acceptable. The Comet, and a splendid

Aurora, appeared for us to look at after dinner. In the night we start again.

SUNDAY, 12TH. – We reached Chicoutimi this morning. We sent a note ashore inviting ourselves to breakfast with the Prices, and when we were dressed found Mr. Price waiting with his carriages to take us to his house. The Prices are a happy family of four girls and six sons, all unmarried, and all living together. We found their house charming. As you enter the gate you see through the trees the beautiful blue water, with large ships upon it; and the tide, when high, comes right up to the edge of the parapet. It is a delightful summer residence. They always have a large party in the house, and have lovely rides and drives, and boating excursions for their guests.

They gave us a good breakfast, which we ate ravenously, enjoying all the country fare, and the wild strawberries and cream! Afterwards we walked to a waterfall, and then returned to our steamer, and waited on board, while D. received an address. When we left we fired two guns as we passed the Prices' house, saluted with our flag, and exchanged pocket-handkerchief waves! The weather is fine and we are enjoying our sail immensely.

> The father of this large family, William Price, had died in 1867. When only twenty-one years of age, in 1810, he had been sent to Canada to purchase lumber. Later he returned and established his own lumber mills, which in time extended from Quebec City to the Saguenay River.
>
> His home, Wolfesfield, near Spencer Wood, was built close to the Ravine St. Denis, up which General Wolfe had his troops climb during that memorable night, September 12-13, 1759.
>
> Two of his sons who entered their father's business, Price Brothers and Company, were called to the Canadian Senate.

In the afternoon we passed under the cliffs 'Trinity' and 'Eternity,' and went quite close to them. Trinity rises straight out of the water, 1,500 feet high, a straight wall of rock. D. fired at the cliff, and we threw stones, without being able to hit it; it looks so much nearer than it is in reality.

We reached Tadousac at nine, and Archie was on the sands waiting for us, Terence awake in bed, and the others asleep and invisible.

MONDAY, 13TH. – In the evening we went on board the *Druid*, hoping to sail; but there was a fog, which continued all night, and which kept us at anchor.

TUESDAY, 14TH. – We could not see our house when we first got up, but the mist cleared away suddenly, and we immediately prepared to start. Then there was great waving of handkerchiefs from the balcony to the steamer, and from the steamer to the family on shore. About two o'clock we reached Murray Bay, and went ashore to see this rival seaside place. We took a long drive in two carriages, D. and I leading the way, and the Fletchers and Lady Mary following. We had beautiful weather, and thought the place quite lovely. The ground seems to have been cut into terraces and mounds by the action of the water, and there are the St. Lawrence, the Murray River, the mountains, and some very picturesque houses to make up the landscape. After driving for nearly three hours, we dined on board, and saw a beautiful aurora. At twelve we started again, and found ourselves on the morning of Wednesday, 15th, at St. Anne. We drove off early, in two gigs, to see some celebrated falls. The drive was nine miles, and we passed wood-carts almost by hundreds drawn by oxen and horses.

At the end of the drive we followed a woman who was to guide us to the Fall. She brought us up to a pretty little one, which we decided was scarcely worth all the trouble we had taken to see it. But, happily, I had been told a great deal about the St. Anne Fall, and felt sure this could not be the right one. We questioned the lady, and as she admitted there were some 'little' falls above, we determined to go on. The walk was tremendous – up such a hill, in the bush, and with pouring rain coming down upon us. However, we struggled on, and were rewarded by finding ourselves suddenly in front of the Falls. The water was rushing from a great height down a narrow gorge, forming six great steps or waterfalls, each one with a still pool at its base. They were six separate falls, and yet but one flow of water. By the time we got back to our carriages we were very tired indeed, very wet, and ready for our lunch, which we were to have in a cottage.

The yacht's cook's mother-in-law lived on the road, and he begged to be allowed to give us our lunch there. Nowell tells us that when he and the cook arrived they found the poor people busy with their summer cleaning; the man had two cans in his hand, and when the cook suddenly announced to him that the Governor-General was coming to lunch with him, he dropped both his cans, fell back into his chair, and shrieked 'Jamais!'

When we arrived, we found a flag at the gate, and one on the house, and the man and his wife – he not sixty, she seventy-two, and just married to him, *en seconde noce* – waiting to receive us.

The first room of the cottage was a big kitchen, with a good cooking-stove; and the room behind was also very large and clean. In three corners were beds, surrounded by chintz curtains hung from the ceiling. There was a large stove, some chests for clothes, and a cupboard with glass door containing china. A table in the middle of the room was spread for lunch.

The old lady talked to me, and seemed amused at our having so many people to wait upon us. The cook gave us an excellent meal, ending with wild strawberries, cream, and maple sugar! We soon after said a warm farewell to our hosts, and drove back to the wharf. We ought to have seen a church at St. Anne celebrated for miracles performed there, and in which about 100 lame people have left their crutches. But we had not time to visit it.

> From Murray Bay the *Druid* steamed up river sixty-five miles to the village of Ste. Anne de Beaupré, which lies twenty-one miles east of Quebec city. Settlers established themselves there about 1657, and the chapel built in honour of Ste. Anne became a shrine. It is now famous throughout North America as a pilgrimage centre.

About eight in the evening we reached Quebec, and just as we landed the most awful shower I have ever seen came on, accompanied by thunder and lightning. The streets were literally flowing with water, and every spout was spurting forth little waterfalls.

CHAPTER 12

Ontario and the Lakes
JULY-SEPTEMBER 1874

WEDNESDAY, JULY 22ND. – Our mail arrived at Quebec yesterday evening, and as soon as we had read our letters we embarked on board the *Druid*, and began our Western tour. We arrived at Trois Rivières, and the Mayor came on board at eight o'clock this morning and took us ashore, where we found awaiting us a magnificent array of firemen, some in helmets and plumes, and some in full Zouave Costume.

We drove to the Town Hall, a new and very large room for a town numbering only 9,000 inhabitants, and there we had an address in French, to which D. replied in the same language. We went on to the Roman Catholic Cathedral, to a House of Providence, to the Ursuline Convent, and to the English Church, at the same time seeing the town. All this we accomplished by 9.30 o'clock, when we returned to our steamer, and a cannon announced that the Governor-General had gone.

He soon after emerged from his cabin as an unofficial tourist, and we started in three carriages to see the Waterfall of the place. It was twenty-four miles off, and we had to be back at 7.30, so we had no time to lose. When we got to it, we found a very pretty fall, though not, I think, quite worth the journey. Close to it there is a curiosity in the shape of an enormous hotel, buried in the bush, like the palace of the *belle au bois dormant,* and into which no mortal guest has ever stepped – the produce of some incomprensible speculation. We rowed six miles of the way back in a big, slow thing called a 'scow,' got into our carriages and returned to Trois Rivières. There we were met by a number of young ladies and a pile of bouquets.

THURSDAY, 23RD. – We travelled by train as far as Kingston, and thence by steamer.

FRIDAY, 24TH. – After a calm night on Lake Ontario, we landed at Toronto this morning. We had heard of guards of honour, etc. to meet us, but found only the hotel-keeper of the Queen's, who said our luggage was in our rooms (it had arrived by train the night before). He ushered us into carriages and drove us to his hotel, where we found very comfortable rooms arranged for us.

Colonel Cumberland, the provincial A.D.C., having made all arrangements for us, we did not even know where we were to go. But it now turns out he had engaged rooms for us at the Rossin House. However, a friend of the Queen's telegraphed to the proprietor of that hotel, and he came to meet us, carried off our luggage, showed us into the Rossin House carriages, and drove [us] to his rival establishment. Our steamer was in an hour earlier than it was expected, and Colonel Cumberland was walking up and down his verandah waiting for the proper time, and so missed us.

D. received an address from the Town Council, and walked about to see the improvements in the town, and at five we had tea at the Lieutenant-Governor's.

> The Honourable William Pearce Howland, who had entertained them
> at Government House on their previous visit, had completed his
> term of office November 5, 1873. Their host now was his successor,
> John Willoughby Crawford, who held the position until his death the
> following May.

SATURDAY, 25TH. – Archie joined us. Directly after breakfast we drove to the railway-station, accompanied by a guard of honour. There we found a very smart pilot-engine, ornamented with flowers and branches and flags; a second one, equally gay. Then a sort of open carriage, with a canvas awning, with red pillars, and green boughs twisted about, and bouquets in the lamp-stands. Next this we had a very comfortable railway-carriage, with chairs and sofas, but when we passed stations we went into the open one, and smiled sweetly.

The first place we stopped at was called Newmarket; here we got out, and mounting a stand, received two addresses. Then we got into carriages, and drove through the town, passing under four or five triumphal arches, to lay the foundation stone of a church.

All the country had come into the town, and almost every house had decorations and people in the windows. D. laid the stone, upon which 'Straight Forward' was engraved, was given a silver trowel, and drove back to the train.

The corner-stone laid was that of the Christian Church, a denomination strong in the United States, but with only a few congregations in Canada.

At the request of the Prime Minister, the Honourable Alexander Mackenzie, their railway, steamboat and other travel arrangements had been made by their aide-de-camp, Colonel Cumberland. He was then general manager of the Northern Railway of Canada, over whose line their trip from Toronto commenced. As the first railway in Canada West, it had begun operations from Toronto to Allandale in 1853, and later to Collingwood, thus linking Lakes Ontario and Huron. By 1874 the line had been extended through Barrie and Orillia to Washago.

Allandale station was famous for its excellent dining-room; and rhyme claimed

> The Barrie scene would please the Queen
> Going by rail from Allandale.

The luxurious hotel on Couchiching Point frequently served as a rendezvous for the executives of the Northern Railway.

The next ceremony was lunch at Allandale, in a very fine station on the borders of Lake Simcoe. It is a junction for Barrie, of which it has a lovely view. We went on there in the train, and passed under a fine arch close to the station, to receive addresses from the corporation, and one from the clergy of all denominations in the place. There was a great crowd, and all the people we have seen to-day seem well-to-do; so well-dressed and flourishing-looking.

Here we left our smart train, and got into a 'special' steamer, in which we had the most delightful voyage across Lake Simcoe; the air delicious, and the scenery beautiful; green, clear water, and wooded islands, and a very distant shore. The day warm, but this travelling perfection.

About five we came to a curious place, called the Narrows, where the steamer passes under two bridges, and through a grass cutting. Having only a foot to spare on each side, it is necessary to go very fast so as to be able to steer. Just before we got here four steamers decorated with flags and filled with people came out to meet us, and D. and I stood on the bows and bowed, and the people waved their handkerchiefs and cheered. Then we went in procession through the

Narrows. Soon we came in sight of the hotel at which we are now staying. It is built on a promontory [Couchiching Point], and is a sort of garden in the bush. The grounds are laid out with grass, flowers, fountains, and with summer-houses hanging over the water.

Having got through the Narrows, we are now in Lake Couchiching, and this is the Couchiching Hotel. We passed it, however, for the moment, and went on to Orillia. Some Indians in canoes came out to meet us; their flags were larger than their boats, and one man kept making furious gesticulations of welcome with a drawn sabre.

Orillia gave us a great welcome; there were four or five arches – immense erections – one of them rather different from the ordinary pattern. It was castellated, and ornamented with wheat, and with animals of the country, stuffed – a deer on the top, birds, foxes, etc. in various recesses. Then there were all sorts of mottoes and good wishes, and the name 'Killyleagh' appeared, having been inspired by an old shopman from Belfast.

This place is on the edge of the settled country, and on the outskirts of the grant now set apart for emigrants. We drove through the town, then returned to the steamer, and made our way to the hotel. We dined privately, and afterwards were ceremoniously presented to all the people in the house; we then 'repaired' to the larger dining-room, where there was dancing. We also had fireworks, and a band playing till eleven o'clock, when at last we went gladly to bed.

SUNDAY, 26TH. – We went by steamer to church at Orillia. Towards the end of the Litany the poor old clergyman fainted; another clergyman finished the prayers, and we left.

D. went to see the Rector, and found that he was dreadfully disappointed that the sermon he had prepared had not been read; so we are going to ask for a copy of it. It seems he had been ill all night, and the doctor fears apoplexy.

MONDAY, 27TH. – There was a regatta this morning, and an Indian canoe-race. I gave the winners of this last their prizes, and afterwards we started in our small steamer up Lake Couchiching.

The first place we stopped at was an Indian reserve called Rama. They had put up a platform and flags, and fired off guns. The chief [Joseph Benson] and his 'young men' met us on the wharf, and when we got on the dais they all stood round. The Wesleyan missionary [Reverend Thomas Woolsey] read an address, to which D. replied that he was glad to hear his children were content, and that it was the intention and endeavour of the Government to keep faith in every particular with the Indian subjects, in whom their great Mother, the Queen, took a special interest, etc. Then he presented the chief with a History of the Holy Land, illustrated, and we looked at the babies, who were being carried about on a novel sort of cradle. It is a flat board, on which the child lies; at the top there is a hood, which can be thrown back in the house, while out of doors it is raised, and has generally a shawl thrown over it. It is a most convenient cradle, as it can be set up against a wall, or hung up on a nail, or in a tree, the child being quite safely tied into it. It also goes flat against the mother's back as she walks along.

We looked at the plain little church, went into one of the houses, and distributed pipes and beads, and then said good-bye. They sang 'God save the Queen' in Indian. These are the Ojibbeway Indians. The missionary, his wife, and two nice children came with us to the next place – Washago.

This is only a temporary railway-station, but there was lunch in a car, an address, a guard of honour, and a foundation stone of a church to be laid.

> Barlow Cumberland, Colonel Cumberland's son, tended to many of the arrangements for the viceregal tour. In his book, *A Century of Sail and Steam on the Niagara River*, pages 53-55, he amusingly recounts the insistence of the Presbyterian minister at Washago that Lord Dufferin lay the corner-stone for his church. Agreement was reached that they would delay their schedule for fifteen minutes. But after his token stone, three inches square, perched on a rocky knoll, had been 'truly laid,' the minister's prayer became so lengthy that 'the Governor and Lady Dufferin and their Suite quietly slipped away and going to the carriages, which were waiting near by, drove away.'

After this we got into carriages to drive fourteen miles, and stopped twice – at Severn and at Gravenhurst – to receive addresses. At each place where this occurs D. makes a speech, instead of reading a formal reply.

When we left our carriages we got on to a steamer covered with flags, and steamed along a lovely place called Muskoka Bay, into Muskoka Lake, and then through a curious, narrow river, in which we twisted and turned round islands, and had only just room to move. Sometimes we appeared to be going straight ashore, and then turned suddenly to one side and were saved. This river brought us to Bracebridge. [This was the north branch of the Muskoka River.]

Bracebridge is an entirely new town, on the border of the New Muskoka Grant. It has grown wonderfully, considering that eight years ago the white man had not set his foot there. A band and a crowd met us on the wharf, and we drove under seven or eight arches before we came to the dais. The houses here are remarkably neat and finished-looking; the population is almost entirely English.

When we returned to the steamer I had an interview with a very charming emigrant. I was much interested in her, and in her husband's history and their present life. He was valet, and she was lady's-maid, with Sir William and Lady Anna Stirling-Maxwell; they married, and made up their minds to come here.

> Sir William Stirling-Maxwell, 1818-78, a Scottish historical writer, a trustee of the British Museum and the National Gallery, was an ardent collector of works of art. He was Member of Parliament for Perthshire for twenty years. On the Keir estates he inherited, he was interested in the breeding of shorthorns and Clydesdale horses. In 1877 he married as his second wife the Honourable Mrs. Norton, a poetess and writer, sister of Lord Dufferin's mother.

Of course, neither he nor she knew anything in the world about farming. But they took the grant of 200 acres of uncleared land (in fact, of forest), and set-to to make a home. They have been here five years, and have two fine boys, and she was so merry, and so happy and courageous. They do everything for themselves, and are getting on well. Their land is good, and, if only the railway comes to it, Bracebridge will become an important town.

TUESDAY, 28TH. – We slept on board, [the *Nipissing*], and started at SIX this morning, sailing through Lakes Rousseau and Joseph. As we passed the lock between the two, D. stepped ashore to speak to the few men there. His visit was quite unexpected, but one of the men made him a very good speech, though he trembled so over it that he could scarcely stand.

I can't describe the delightful travelling on these lovely lakes. We stopped at Rousseau, where we visited the church and a poor Icelandic family, and landed at the Summit House, where we got into carriages. The drive was seventeen miles long, and was right through the free grants, where any man coming out and wishing to take up a farm, receives 200 acres of forest free. As we drove along we saw settlers in all stages of their existence.

First we went into a neat cottage, where we found a County Down man; he seemed delicate. All his sons had set up for themselves, and I think the work was too much for him alone.

Then we saw a Parisian jeweller – the merriest man! He was turned into a hard-working farmer, and sees everything in *couleur de rose*. He had two nice boys. Again, we saw a Canadian and an Enniskillen man living opposite each other, and both happy and content. They all say the land is good, though there is much rock in parts of it.

The finest family we saw was that of an old soldier from Meath. He and his wife had nine children, all beautifully dressed in white frocks with sashes, and in the house one wall was covered with books. The man was loud in his praises of the country. The whole is more thickly settled than we expected; it is through a fine forest, and no part of it is far from a lake.

Finally we arrived at Parry Sound, where we had addresses and arches, and a 'sail' in a steam-tug; then we went on board the *Chicora*, our new home for a fortnight.

She is a very large steamer, and was formerly a celebrated blockade-runner known as the *Letter B*. Now she has storeys of cabins built on her deck. We have her all to ourselves. This was Archie's birthday, so he dined with us.

During the American Civil War, ships of the North blockaded certain Southern Atlantic ports in an attempt to prevent arms and ammunition being shipped in and to stop the export of cotton. When the mills of Lancashire began to suffer for lack of raw material, blockade-runners were built by Lairds on the Mersey. One of these, the *Let Her B*, a powerful, schooner-rigged steamship, ran from Charleston to a secret port in the Bahamas, where she exchanged her cargo of cotton for arms. Her speed, and the rapidity with which she could be loaded and unloaded, made her a highly profitable investment. Although once her masts and boats were shot away, usually all the blockaders saw was the name painted on her stern, *Let Her B*.

When the war ended, she was brought to Canada, and, under a new name, *Chicora*, became the finest ship in service on the Upper Lakes. When rebellion broke out in the North-west, in 1870, Colonel Cumberland used her for the rapid movement of troops from Collingwood to the site of the present Port Arthur.

A year after she took the Dufferins on their cruise, she was brought to Lake Ontario, and for many years this trim, graceful ship, about which still clung an aura of romance, was a familiar sight on the

Toronto-to-Niagara run. And as late as 1916 the blockade-running bell, inscribed *Let Her B,* still hung by her octagonal wheel-house, with its columned sides and graceful, curving cornice.

WEDNESDAY, 29TH. – We left Parry Sound early in the morning, and about twelve o'clock found ourselves off Collingwood.

Nine steamers came out to meet us, with flags and passengers. They turned and followed us to the town. There we had addresses, and arches, and a drive. Two little girls dressed as 'Britannia' and 'Canada' stood at the corners of the principal arch.

When we left, the steamers followed us out for some way, and there was a great farewell, with cheering and shrieking of engines, as we parted company.

Our next destination was Owen Sound. The feature of the visit was a drive. I found myself behind four horses and postilions, an outrider in uniform in front of us, and about forty vehicles following us. We drove through the town and under arches out to a waterfall. The country is beautiful; the finest trees we have seen in Canada, and everything park-like.

We returned on board for dinner, and during that meal went on to Presqu'ile, where there was a magnificent bonfire and a string of lamps. While taking in wood we walked to the bonfire, and were given a letter and a jar of honey.

THURSDAY, 30TH. – We went into Killarney (the Indian name of this place signifies 'here is a channel'), and sailed up very narrow passages to reach it. The Indians were collected on the wharf, and one of them made a speech to His Ex., stopping at the end of each sentence to have it translated into English. D.'s reply went through the same process. We spoke to the women and distributed knives, pipes, tobacco and beads.

At one o'clock we came to another Indian settlement – Manitoulin. The Indians here seemed very poor, and the one who made the speech spoke much to this effect: – 'We are glad to see you; our wives and our children are glad to see you, our father. We have come far to see you, and have brought our wives and children to see you; and we are hungry, for we have had nothing to eat.' D. ordered them a barrel of flour and a hundred-weight of pork. When he replies to the Indians, they give a grunt at the end of each of his sentences, which has a most peculiar effect.

They sometimes give me presents of their work, which I immediately pay for. At this last place there are Episcopalian and Wesleyan missionaries; and at Killarney we saw a Roman Catholic priest, who came to our steamer, greet his flock in a very affectionate manner.

The evening was a little rough, but we stopped at Bruce's Mines for the night.

FRIDAY, 31ST. – At six in the morning we went ashore to see the copper-mines, which are not flourishing, though the ground appears to be covered with the mineral and we picked up a great many specimens.

On our way to Sault Ste. Marie we passed through a curious place called the Devil's Gap. There are a number of islands so close together that it is impossible to see the way till you come straight opposite the channel. One we passed through seemed only large enough to hold our great steamer.

We stopped a few minutes at Garden River, where a fine-looking Indian chief danced for us. Then we reached Sault Ste. Marie, where we went some way in a boat to lay the stone of an Indian school, [The Shingwauk Home] and had lunch in the carpenter's shop, which the ladies had ornamented and made very smart.

Archie was very ill all day, and frightened us in the afternoon. Luckily, we found a good doctor here, who has kindly promised to come on with us in the steamer.

SUNDAY, AUGUST 2ND. – We arrived at the mouth of the Nipigon River this morning, and went a little way up it in boats to see a Hudson's Bay settlement. The gentlemen visited a store there, and came home dressed in white blanket-coats and red caps, looking very picturesque.

In the afternoon we found ourselves off Michipicoten Island, which is supposed to be rich in agates. But all those on the surface have been already picked up, and we only saw a few small specimens. The old gentleman who keeps the Lighthouse gave me a good one.

MONDAY, 3RD. – Our next stopping-place was Nipigon. We passed some high rocks and curious-shaped hills and anchored at a little Hudson's Bay settlement at the mouth of the river. Our first business in the morning was to rush to the store and make purchases for our fishing and camping-out expedition – knives, blankets, tin plates, mugs looking-glasses, flies, etc. There were a good many Indians sitting about, and D. did the portrait of one girl, who giggled tremendously over it.

The next thing was to pack our canoes. We had five. Ours was painted white, with Union Jacks on the bows; and into it got D. and

I, the Fletchers, Archie, four men, and all our blankets, luggage and tents. The second held the Freds, Dr. King (who is looking after Archie), Captain Wilson (our guide), Mr. Dixon (Archie's tutor), and four men, with a good deal of their luggage. There were three more canoes with baggage.

Our journey was a good specimen of the canoe and 'portage' journeys one reads about. Whenever we came to rapids we landed, and walked to the head of them, the canoes and all the things being carried by the boatmen. We had one portage soon after we left the *Chicora;* when in our canoes again we came to a peninsula with a rapid rushing past it which we thought might be our camping-place. This was not our destination, so we had to cross the rapid and portage again. This camping-ground was on the banks of a small arm of the Nipigon, and we thought it damp, so we pitched our tents on the top of the hill. The night was cold and a heavy dew fell.

D. and I have an 'American officers' tent,' which is most comfortable; Archie was allowed to have a little corner of it. Colonel Fletcher has a funny little tent, which comes out of his carpet-bag, and holds him and Lady Harriet. All the other gentlemen sleep in one large marquee; and the men have three more tents.

TUESDAY, 4TH. – We got up early as we had a portage to make at once; and after a cup of coffee we set out. All the gentlemen had to carry things, and stumbled along with loads of blankets on their backs.

When we got to the end of this rather long portage, we had breakfast, and started off again; the day was very hot. We saw some beautiful rapids and had three more portages. At the end we found a party of Americans – three doctors. Straight across the river was another camp of Americans, with a lady in it.

At the site of our permanent camp three branches of a rapid met, and swept down the river together. Here I stood out upon a rock and fished. On one side of me was D. lashing the water; then Fred Ward, barefooted, in the middle of the stream; then Archie, with (tell it not in Gath!) a spoon at the end of his rod (poaching, in fact) ; then Fred and the Doctor also fishing. None of us made great bags, as the fish (of which there are quantities) were perfectly gorged with shad-flies, and had no room for our delicate bait. The cook, who carries about iron bars and sets up a fire-place wherever we go, provided us with an excellent dinner, and we sat around a bonfire till bedtime.

As this was our permanent camp, we made ourselves very comfortable. The whole floor of the tent was spread with fir-boughs, which are laid down most carefully and scientifically by the men, and make a most delightful carpet and spring mattress.

WEDNESDAY, 5TH. – Alas! it rains. Lady Harriet and I spent the greater part of the day in my tent. D., Colonel Fletcher, Fred Ward, the Doctor, and Captain Wilson went off to see Lake Nipigon, which is about sixty miles long.

THURSDAY, 6TH. – To-day we de-camped, began with a portage, and arrived at the beginning of another long one just before lunch. You have never seen such appetites as we all had! We were ravenous, and cleared every plate.

We ran some exciting rapids, and camped at 'Alexander Camp.' I wish you could see Archie catch a trout. The instant he gets it ashore he hugs it in his arms, and seems to think that the danger of losing it only begins on land. His coat suffered greatly in these struggles.

FRIDAY, 7TH. – Off we are again, tents and baggage, and pots and pans, packed for their last trip in the canoe.

We had a pleasant voyage down to the *Chicora*, and found her beautifully ornamented for our reception, a triumphal arch at the top of the companion, and green wreaths over all the doors and hanging from the chandeliers. We lunched, devoted an hour to a tremendous wash after four nights of camping-out, and, arrayed in a little extra finery as a reaction, went to call upon Mrs. Crauford, a lady who had sent us a jar of most delicious fresh butter.

D. has been doing several portraits of Indians. The translations of their names are curious. We made the acquaintance of 'Naughty little Woman,' of 'She who cries with Joy,' and of 'The Cloud that is past.' We have just sailed, and the ever-rough surface of Lake Superior lies before us.

SATURDAY, 8TH. – There was a fog on the Lake, but we got off early in the morning, and arrived at Silver Islet in four or five hours. The island is a mere rock, originally seventy by eighty feet. But it has been artificially increased fifty-seven times that size by breakwaters and docks built all round it. A Canadian company first began to work the mines, but, getting into difficulties, sold them to an American company, who are now making a great deal of money. There is great expense in keeping out the water, as the 'Islet' only just rises above the surface of the Lake. We went over from the mainland in a tug, and saw all that could be seen without actually going down the mine. The silver is in fern-like patterns in a sort of white quartz. The 'Captain' of the undertaking is a 'Frew' from Co. Down, and talks of going home this year to put up a monument to his mother in Bangor Churchyard. You see, we are constantly meeting successful people from that renowned County!

We proceeded on our journey, and passing Thunder Cape – high basaltic rocks, in places very precipitous, a fine piece of scenery – got into Thunder Bay. We landed at Prince Arthur's Landing – quite a new town, four years old. Every house was decorated with green, and a quantity of flags about. D. went out for a drive; but as I always shirk strange horses when I can, I returned to the steamer. We asked some gentlemen to dinner, and sat on deck and looked at the fireworks on shore.

SUNDAY, 9TH. – We went to church in the morning, and afterwards to Fort William, a Hudson's Bay settlement, where we lunched with Mr. Macintyre, his wife, and their daughter. It came on to thunder and rain heavily, and we were glad to get back to the *Chicora* in a tug.

MONDAY, 10TH. – We had to start at five o'clock in the morning, having seventy miles to drive. Some of us were in sort of *char à banc*, drawn by four horses, which we changed four times *en route*, and the rest of the party were in smaller carriages. We got safely to Shebandowan, where we found about 120 Indians, who had come down from the woods to be paid their annual stipend.

They were more savage than those we have seen before. Two medicine-men sat on the ground and drummed, or 'tom-tom'd,' and sang in a dreary, monotonous tone. One of them was painted green and yellow; their profiles were handsome, but their full faces hideous. The interpreter was bad, so D. was not able to say very much to them; but he presented them with tobacco, pipes, knives, pork and flour, which they probably preferred to conversation.

We did not get back to the sleeping-place till after nine. We dined at once and went early to bed. We slept in a cottage, and the Fletchers in a tent.

TUESDAY, 11TH. – We were again called at five, and found a wet morning – such a wet morning! We breakfasted and drove in our shaky wagon for five miles to the borders of the Kaministikwia River, where we got into canoes to paddle sixty miles. Had the day been fine we should have enjoyed it immensely; but the weather was perfectly awful, a thunder-shower lasting till one o'clock wetted us to the skin.

During this downpour we had to get out of the canoes eight times to make portages, and you may imagine how miserable we were walking through narrow paths in dripping woods, our clothes heavy with rain. The worst bit of walk led to a magnificent waterfall; it is 120 feet high, and very grand.

These were the Kakabeka Falls on the Kaministikwia River, fourteen miles west of Fort William. The name was derived from an Indian word signifying 'high falls.'

When it became clear to the officials of the North West Company that their wilderness headquarters at Grand Portage was in United States territory, they removed, in 1802, about thirty miles to the north-east, and rebuilt an old French fort at the mouth of the Kaministikwia River. This new post was, in 1805, named Fort William, in honour of William McGillivray, a partner in the North West Company, who had become its chief director in 1804. This fort passed into the hands of the Hudson's Bay Company sixteen years later.

The route the trappers took up the Kaministikwia River, by Lake Shebandowan, and by many streams and portages, until they reached waters flowing westwards, became known as 'the Dawson Route' when, in 1868, Simon James Dawson charted the best of the long-used routes for travel by larger boats.

Prince Arthur's Landing (now Port Arthur), located three miles from Fort William, was named in honour of Prince Arthur, afterwards Duke of Connaught. Here his regiment, commanded by Colonel Wolseley, landed in 1870, and proceeded by boat and portage over 'the Dawson Route' to Fort Garry, now in the heart of Winnipeg, and then on to the scene of the Red River rebellion.

At one we lunched and the rain ceased; we lit a fire and dried our cloaks. A dish of hot potatoes brightened us up, and we got on pretty well till 7.30 p.m., when we reached a place where a steamer [the *Jennie Oliver*] was to meet us. But we found the steamer had given us up and left ten minutes before! We were in despair at the idea of a further ten miles' paddle; but the canoe-men bore it with great good-humour, and immediately started to race, by way of enlivening the time, and it was pretty to see our five canoes shooting through the water. Our patience was rewarded, for some wise friend sent the steamer back. When we met her we were comforted by a cup of the best hot coffee I ever tasted.

We had promised to visit an Indian mission on our way. But the children had all gone to bed when we arrived. So we just peeped at their little dark heads as they lay asleep. We reached the *Chicora* about nine, and took off our damp things at once. But none of us caught cold, or were really hurt by the wetting.

THURSDAY, 13TH. – We reached Sault Ste. Marie early this morning, having made a quick passage from Thunder Bay. Captain Wilson, before giving up his post as guide, took us down the rapids here, which are very long and exciting. Then we bade farewell to him and to the Doctor. They have been a great addition to our party and we were sorry to say good-bye. Dr. King is an Englishman, but has joined the United States Army.

We had a pretty sail down Lake Huron, and arrived at Mackinaw late in the evening, anchoring in a little harbour which only just held us.

FRIDAY, 14TH. – A delightful voyage down Lake Michigan.

SATURDAY, 15TH. – This morning we came in sight of Chicago. A tug came off with our Consul (Mr. Warwick) in full uniform, who told us the arrangements made for our reception.

We lunched early, and immediately after the Committee of Reception came on board. The President of the Committee is from Co. Down (Mr. Dickson), and his wife was a Miss Reid, and was at Killyleagh the day of our marriage. He is very happy here. Another member is from Killinchy (more Co. Down).

When D. had spoken to all the committee, we adjourned to the immense drawing-room of a gigantic hotel. There we were introduced to the Mayor [Colvin], who made a speech, to which His Ex. replied; then to the President of the Board of Trade [Mr. George M. Howe], to the Presidents of the St. George, St. Andrews, and the Caledonian Societies, who all made speeches, which were all replied to; also to the Governor [Beveridge] of the State. I think there must have been more, but I cannot remember them. Then we got into the first of sixty barouches to drive through the town. We saw the extent of the fire of 1871, and the wonderful way in which the city has risen from its ashes; also the effects of a second fire last July; streets, churches, etc. in ruins.

What I think is really beautiful here is a drive by the shores of Lake Michigan. The water is a lovely delicate blue-green colour, there is no land in sight, the beach is charming, and the lake is covered with ships. This drive forms part of a pretty park, in which there are small lakes, zoological gardens, etc., and lots of people about, in carriages and boats, sitting, walking and picnicing – the most Hyde Park-like thing I have seen on this continent.

We visited the Waterworks, and passed twice under the river through massive tunnels. The Consul sent me some beautiful flowers and fruit. I can hardly believe I am here, and shall certainly not realise it until I see the celebrated pig-killing machines, of which one has always heard.

Mr. Dickson, and his wife, the Consul and his sister, General Sheridan, and the President of the Board of Trade, dined with us on board, and at ten we drove to the hotel where we are to stay – the 'Palmer House.'

It is a palace: marble staircases, broad passages handsomely carpeted, and furnished with crimson-satin sofas and chairs; chimney-pieces from Italy, in lofty rooms beautifully furnished; pier glasses – every luxury in fact. Each bedroom opens into a sitting-room, and off mine there is a bath-room with hot and cold water laid on. The bedroom has velvet-pile carpets with Aubusson patterns, plain crimson curtains, and chairs – such as I wish I had in my drawing-room at Clandeboye.

When we arrived we were presented to the manager, were seated in a comfortable room, and were 'elevated' to our flat. The manager walked along and talked amicably to us. Pointing out the sitting-room he said, 'This is the young gentlemen's room'; then, laying hold of D.'s arm with both hands, added, 'I don't know whether you are to be counted among them, my Lord.'

SUNDAY, 16TH. – Such a breakfast! No wonder Americans despise our efforts in the way of hotels. Being out of the Dominion, we arranged to have our meals in the public rooms, so we went to breakfast in an enormous hall, and sat at a small table. There were quantities of black waiters to attend upon the people, and a lengthy bill-of-fare to select from. Everything was very good of its kind – tea, coffee, milk, eggs, and cookery, all of the very best, and it was amusing to see how it was all managed.

I went to a church which was in mourning for a bishop, and we had a curious sermon in his praise. His industry, his good manners, his beautiful French, the graceful way in which he could pay a compliment, etc., were all set before us with much gesticulation; but, in spite of all that, we received the impression of his having been a really good man. Everybody uses fans in church, and the singing was 'done' by two men and two women.

The manager of the Hotel has placed the most magnificent flowers in my room, 'with his compliments.' I have, you see, lost one of my prejudices already – that against the American hotel system. And I think their ladies dress well; they have quite the French knack of putting on things.

At five o'clock we went into the Park for a little. All the German population were out, sitting on the grass, rowing in boats, eating their dinners, and spending the day there. A band played during the afternoon. The drive by the Lake was crowded with carriages.

MONDAY, 17TH. – After breakfast we got the manager to take us over the Hotel. There are 200 women- and 125 men-servants, and 18 cooks. Outside the kitchen is a carving-room, in which all the joints are on hot plates, with their own sauces in tins before them. Regulations for the servants were written up on the wall. The first was, 'No servant is ever to tell a guest there is none of anything until he has first been to say so to the manager.'

A washing-up room came next; then the enormous kitchen, in which were two large 'kettle-drum' cauldrons for soup, six broiling places, an oven for beef, one for mutton, another for veal, etc. etc., and places in the same way for each different vegetable. We were there between meals, and saw the chops, cutlets and chickens being packed in tins ready for cooking; when ready they are slipped into an ice-cupboard in the kitchen till required.

The store-rooms are regular shops. We also visited the bake-room, where excellent bread is made; the pastry-room, laundry, larders; and finally the bedrooms. Even the top ones are smartly furnished, and there are eleven miles of good carpet down in the hotel.

One drawing-room is in the Egyptian style; green and crimson satin furniture, the chimney-piece and the corners of the chairs and sofas carved into black and gold Sphinxes. One bedroom is done in pink satin and black velvet; but every part of the house is most gorgeous. The bar-room is very large, and has ten or twelve billiard tables. They gave us delicious lemonade there, and I was just enjoying it when a message came to say the 'Board of Trade' (to which I had not intended to go) did expect me. So I had to go and get my bonnet at once.

The Mayor, Governor, and other officials conducted us thither, and we met in a small room at the Exchange, which was what D. expected. But what was our surprise at being taken into the enormous Exchange Room, and to find it crowded with people. D. and I were put upon a platform before them, and the President, knocking with a hammer for silence, said: 'His Excellency the Governor-General of Canada will now address you.' D., who was taken quite unawares, made them a very good speech. He had to speak at the top of his voice, for it was very noisy outside, and there was some telegraphing machine passing through the room, which kept up a constant racket. But he was heard, and what he said was well received. The governor of Illinois said a few words; then the President asked anyone who wished to be presented to pass by the 'north' side of the platform, and we shook hands with all who came up.

We next adjourned to the Grand Pacific Hotel, where the Board of Trade gave us a luncheon. This is another palace, and I never saw an entertainment better done, or with more taste. A band was stationed in the passage, which played 'God save the Queen,' and other music. The lunch was cold, with the exception of hot turtle soup and coffee. The table was T-shape, and we sat at the top, having no one opposite us. A row of black waiters stood at the end of the room. They wore white aprons, black tail-coats, and white gloves, and looked so funny 'at attention,' their white paws crossed over their chests; when a signal was given, they all marched in to serve.

Again we got into our carriages, and drove to the Stockyards. The machine, into which a pig walks alive at one end, and comes out a ham at the other, had just stopped working, but it was fully explained to us. There were yards full of cows waiting to be sold.

I enjoyed the drive there, and was surprised to find miles of boulevards – broad carriage-drive, the edges beautifully finished off, trees planted on either side, parts of it park-like, and parts filled with flowers. There are beautiful villas and streets, in which each house has its own bit of lawn and garden. I had thought of Chicago only as a money-making place; I am delighted with it.

> Chicago had followed a plan, drawn in 1853, for the Toronto waterfront by the versatile Frederick William Cumberland. Its development was gradual, and not completed until rubble from the great fire of 1871 provided the necessary fill to round out the magnificent conception.

I had an hour's rest after my return, and then dressed to receive. The manager sent Lady Harriet and me bouquets for the occasion, and when we went into his drawing-room the flowers were a beautiful sight. One table was covered with bouquets, which were afterwards presented to each lady as she came in; the chimney-pieces, etc., all over flowers.

A number of people came, amongst them another Killyleagh man, Murdoch by name. He only left ten years ago, and has 'seen nothing equal to it' (Killyleagh) since. He took to printing, about which he knew nothing, and seems to be flourishing.

TUESDAY, 18TH. – D. and the other gentlemen drove off early to see the 'Prairie,' and Lady Harriet and I went an expedition over the shops. The first we 'did' was Field & Lighter. Gloves are 10s. a pair; a muslin dress, much trimmed with imitation lace, £30; and the making of a plain dress, £6, which is not cheap.

Then we went to a china-shop (all came from England), and to a toy-shop, where I made a few purchases for my family. We were shown a confectioner's, or 'candy-shop,' and we saw the picture painted in England, and sent by the 'Graphic' as a memorial of the Chicago fire.

Another sight was very curious. People here often keep their own money, instead of putting it into banks, and we visited the safes. There are small rooms, the walls of which are lined with pigeon-holes, each having a strong door and lock of its own. Persons hire these boxes, have their own keys, and sometimes go twenty or thirty times a day to use their money. Ladies also hire these safes for jewellery. The outside door weighs five tons.

D. enjoyed his visit to the Prairie, or 'Perairer,' as they call it here. He shot one 'chicken' – a prairie fowl; the others nothing, but they saw the country, which was what they wanted.

On their return we dined, and prepared for our departure. The hotel-keeper again presented us with bouquets and enormous baskets of splendid fruit. Mr. Murdoch came to say good-bye to his Killyleagh friends.

We travelled all night in a Pullman car, and slept very comfortably.

The journey to Windsor was over the Michigan Central Railway.

WEDNESDAY, 19TH. – We arrived at Detroit this morning. D., Fred Ward, and Colonel Fetcher went to Windsor and Chatham. [Here their party was met by Alexander Mackenzie, the Prime Minister.] At both places D. had warm receptions, and Colonel Fletcher tells me he made excellent speeches. At five o'clock Lady Harriet, Fred and I crossed the river in a steamer to meet D. at Windsor.

We all returned together, and were magnificently 'received' at Detroit. The steamer stopped at the foot of a fine, very wide street going straight up the town [Woodward Avenue]. It was crowded with people, flags flying from most of the houses; there were companies of United States troops, fire-engines, police, a military band, and people sitting in the windows. We drove in procession through a great part of the town, D. going first with the Mayor, Mr. Moffatt. At one place the procession reached completely round the square, the head and tail of it meeting and passing each other.

We returned to the Town Hall, which was illuminated, heard a speech of welcome from the 'Orator' of the town, and D. made a very good reply. Two other speeches followed, all expressing the warmest friendship to England and Canada. After dinner some singers came and serenaded us [at the Russell House].

THURSDAY, 20TH. – This morning at 8.30 we left Detroit, and getting on board a most comfortable little steamer [the *Steinhoff*], went up the St. Clair River to Sarnia. Mr. Mackenzie, the Prime Minister, who comes from Sarnia, was with us. We had a pleasant journey through lovely scenery, and in beautiful weather.

Mr. Mackenzie was evidently very anxious that Sarnia should distinguish itself, and looked much pleased when four steamers, crammed with people, and covered with flags and green boughs, came out to meet us. The river here joins Lake Huron, and is at this point very narrow, Port Huron, an American town, being straight opposite.

At the wharf we found a pink-and-white pavilion erected, and close by it a very large stand upon which hundreds of people were sitting. On the other side were two tents carpeted, and arranged for a reception. D. as usual replied to two addresses, and then no less than ten were read to him by chiefs of different Indian tribes, to which he replied in one speech.

Sarnia (the ancient name for Guernsey) is a small place, but there was an immense crowd in it, people from the country, and a trainful from London. We got into carriages to drive through the town. As we passed under the second arch, a large cheese was lowered into the carriage, as a present.

After the drive we came a couple of miles in the steamer to the railway-station [at Point Edward, the terminus of the Grand Trunk Railway], over which some very comfortable rooms were arranged for us.

FRIDAY, 21ST. – We ventured on to Lake Huron this morning, and were punished for our temerity. The sofas and chairs danced about the cabin, the band rushed to the side, the reporters sat drooping upon the stairs, I lay on the floor, and we were all glad when at four o'clock we landed at Goderich.

We drove to the house of our host, Mr. Cameron [Malcolm Colin Cameron, M.P. for South Huron], and about five o'clock, somewhat giddy, and not at all hungry, we sat down to a great luncheon. When it was over, at the Town-Hall, built in the centre of the Square, we held a sort of reception. Then we went to see some salt-works. In searching for oil, they found salt of the best quality. Salt water is pumped into shallow iron tanks, which are heated so that the water evaporates, and leaves the whitest, most sparkling salt.

Back again to our house, dress instantly for dinner, and for the ball which comes after. Dinner is my greatest trial on these occasions, for I really can't be hungry so often in the day.

SATURDAY, 22ND. – We had to breakfast at eight, and leaving our kind hosts, Mr. and Mrs. Cameron, go on our way. We stopped for 'five minutes' at Mitchell; next at Stratford, which town had been promised 'two hours.'

In Berlin [renamed Kitchener in 1916], a German settlement, we were met by the usual number of carriages, and some horsemen, who preceded us into the town. A German glee club sang 'Die Wacht am Rhein.'

Guelph was our last station, and resting-place for Sunday. D. went for a drive, and I came up to Mr. Leman's house, where we stay. In the evening we drove to the Town-Hall to see the illuminations, and to hold a full-dress sort of Drawing Room, which went off very well. On our return we had supper, and this time we were really hungry. I have a most charming bedroom here, everything so pretty. The hostess is very lively and pleasant.

SUNDAY, 23RD. – We went to a large, new, and rather pretty church [St. George's Episcopal]. You can't think how we bless the Sunday!

MONDAY, 24TH. – D. had to be out at nine to drive over a model farm. I remained quiet until eleven o'clock, when I joined him at the [Great Western] railway-station. We had only a short distance to go, but stopped three times on the way.

At Preston we heard an address read with great emphasis, and D. was presented with a native suit of clothes. Galt came next, and our object here was to visit Miss Macpherson's Home. She brings waifs and strays out to Canada, and gets them adopted by farmers or placed as servants. We drove off with Miss Macpherson to her Home. The children were all at the door, and looked well and healthy.

Lady Dufferin recorded on June 19th, 1872, that Miss Macpherson
and 107 of her 'street Arabs' were fellow-passengers on the *Prussian*.

We visited Harrisburg, but Brantford is our real stopping-place.
There we were met by guards of honour, both foot and horse, a band,
and a great crowd. Half an hour was given us for lunch at the hotel
[the Kerby House]. Our rooms are most comfortable. The people who
generally live in them furnished them for themselves, and have turned
out for us.

Lunch over, D. turned the first sod of a railway [the Brantford,
Norfolk and Port Burwell]. I laid a stone of a young ladies' college
now building [Presbyterian Young Ladies' College]. His Ex. replied
to the address presented to me in a speech about young ladies, which
I recommend to all those whom it may concern. D. from his speeches
is daily becoming more known to the people, and they receive him
better and better as we go on, and that is very pleasant.

The Blind Asylum came next and we got home an hour before
dressing-time. The Mayor, Clergyman, President of the Senate, Captain of the Guard, etc., dined with us – a party of eighteen.

TUESDAY, 25TH. – You lazy people who amuse yourselves all day, can
scarcely imagine how difficult it is to me to find minutes to write in.
I seize two or three moments before our early breakfast, enough in
which to scribble down dry facts, but I have to leave out many little
things which I might tell you if I were not so hurried, and which I
long to have a record of myself.

We were in our carriages by nine o'clock, and, followed by forty-six
other vehicles, started to visit the Indian Reserve – 52,000 acres – on
which the Six Nations live. Outside the Reserve is the oldest Protestant church in Canada, called the Mohawk Church. In it is a service
of plate presented to the Mohawk Indians by Queen Anne. The tomb
of the great Indian warrior, 'Captain Brant,' is in the churchyard. We
had thirteen miles to drive, and at the entrance found an arch – 'The
Six Nations' Welcome' on one side, and on the other, 'The Six
Nations are gratified; come again.' We were met by Indian people,
most of them in European clothes, but a few with feathers.

The interpreter is a clever, fine-looking man. He was beautifully
dressed in well-made, tight-fitting tunic and breeches of deerskin, with
silver ornaments. The sleeves were short, finished off with fringe, and
over the rest of the arm there was a long gauntlet of wampum; a
slouchy black felt hat finished off his costume. He looked magnificent
on horseback.

Close to the 'Council House' were a number of old warriors 'got-up' in paint, feathers, etc., in our honour. Several curiosities were laid out for our inspection, and when all was ready we passed into an enormous arbour erected for the occasion. We sat on a dais, and listened to an Indian speech, which was translated to His Ex., who replied in English, stopping at the end of every sentence for the interpreter to put it into Indian. The words of the language are very long, and the Indian speech took twice as long to deliver as the English one.

When this was over, the old chiefs shook hands with us, and there was a great rush of women, many of whom presented me with things. One pinned a little silver brooch into my dress. She was a handsome-looking person, and wore a large straw hat and a great cloak, underneath which one saw cloth gaiters, worked in beads. The next ceremony was a war-dance; seven men took part in it. Then the Indians gave us a great luncheon and some excellent tea.

After leaving, we drove on to the farm of Mr. George Brown, editor of the 'Globe,' [the *Globe* newspaper of Toronto], senator, great 'champion' of the Grit party and amateur farmer. His place – Bow Park – is so called because the river forms a bend there. He goes in for Shorthorns, and has 300 of them. What surprised me was to see a second crop on nearly all his fields. This is his method: to cut the green food, and carry it to the cows, and so to get second crops from off the whole farm. When we had looked at each beautiful but expensive animal, we adjourned to a tent, and had dinner.

Mr. Brown proposed His Ex.'s health very nicely. He was one of D.'s opponents during the Pacific Scandal, and he said: 'There may have been a time when some of us may have differed with and found fault with the Governor-General's policy. But now that we have the means of understanding and knowing him better,' etc., etc. Everyone laughed, and enjoyed the allusion.

The drive to Brantford brought us there at eight o'clock, and I had at once to dress for a reception at the Town-Hall, which went off very well. But you see that, as D. says, we 'work our passage.'

WEDNESDAY, 26TH. – Off at 9 a.m. as usual. We drove to Paris, where we were received by the Mayor and the people, and drove a mile and a half, at a foot's pace, to the railway-station.

> This station was on the Great Western Railway. The numerous
> railways, which formed a network throughout Southern Ontario,
> gradually became absorbed in the two main lines, the Grand Trunk
> and Great Western Railways.

The town is prettily situated, and takes its name from the gypsum in its neighborhood, of which it makes plaster of Paris. The station was beautifully decorated: at one end was the platform, raised, carpeted, covered in with flags and hung with green garlands and bird-cages, and all the telegraph-posts down the railway-side twined with green and joined with garlands.

Addresses, of course, were read, and then we shook hands with numbers of people; amongst others, with a woman who came from Clande-boye a year ago, and who seemed almost mad with excitement at seeing us.

Woodstock was our next destination. We drove out to the place of Mr. Alexander, senator, where a great public picnic was given in our honour. [This was at 'Rokewood,' the home of Honourable George Alexander.] D. had to reply to an address from the county [Oxford], and to return thanks for his own and for my health, which were proposed separately at lunch; mine by a farmer, who did it rather well, referring to [King] William's speech on revisiting Holland, when he said that the welcome would have been greater if 'Mary had been with me.' We met here a Southern gentleman, Mr. Fearn, whom we had known eleven years ago in England; and the three pretty Misses Alexander.

Then on to Ingersoll, a great cheese-making place. There was an arch made of cheeses, the motto on it being, 'Cheese, the making of Canada.' We drove out in procession to a cheese-factory, and saw the whole process of converting new milk into cheese in five hours. The Sunday milk has to be used for butter, as for the cheese-making it must be quite fresh.

> Lord Dufferin's reply to an address was timely and humorous. He said:
> "I am well aware that the cheese factories in Ingersoll possess a
> world-wide reputation, and that sometimes even our neighbours, when
> they want to sell their cheese to the best advantage, find it in their
> interest to let their customers understand that they are of the Ingersoll
> quality."
>
> One large cheese, on being cut into, was found to contain numerous
> bottles of champagne.

We always feel glad when we approach our sleeping-town, and at 6.30 to-day we got to London. We had been here two years before, but the people gave us as warm a reception as if this had been our first visit.

It was almost dark when the address-ceremony was over, but the streets were crowded, and we were conducted by all the people to Major Walker's house. Over the gate was a beautiful, illuminated arch. I had a room furnished with the prettiest specimens of Canadian maple furniture I have ever seen. Mrs. Walker is a German [Laura, daughter of Jacob Hespeler], and very nice. She gave us a quiet dinner, for which we were so thankful to her.

D. had to go out to a 'concert,' and found he was expected to speak – for the ninth time to-day!

THURSDAY, 27TH. – We were routed out directly after breakfast to go and open, and name, the 'Victoria Park.' Then we proceeded to the Town-Hall, where we held a reception and ate a lunch. It was given by the town, and there were about 1,000 people in the room. D.'s health was drunk, and he made a very good speech in reply. We got off to the train by 1.30.

In an hour we arrived at St. Thomas. We had a drive, and saw a wonderful wooden railway-bridge [on the Canada Southern Railway], and were taken to the railway-station, where we were introduced to heaps of people. Then, just as we were getting into our carriage, the Mayor, horror-stricken, exclaimed: 'But the lunch! you must come and lunch.' D. consented to run in for a moment, and got through three speeches. On the return to the carriages Colonel Fletcher says the Mayor was in despair – 300 or 400 dollars' worth of lunch, and nobody to eat it. He had been there fifty-six years, and never received a Governor-General before, and said: 'I know you will never come back.' It was quite touching, and I really longed to eat some of the lunch.

Simcoe is a pretty rural town, which had made great preparations for us – no less than nine arches, and every house streaming with flags, and yards and yards of red and blue and white stuffs. We went to stay with Mr. and Mrs. [Duncan] Campbell, at their charming little country-house.

> This was 'Lynwood.' Archie, a son of the Campbells, had been married to Col. Cumberland's daughter, Helen, the previous year.

We had to turn out after dinner to see fireworks and illuminations, and to be introduced to people. In the night there was a real fire, caused, I fear, by these honours to us. The Freds both worked hard till two in the night, carrying buckets, and helping to put out the flames.

FRIDAY, 28TH. – We drove to Waterford, first visiting the schools at Simcoe. There, and at Dean's Corner and Welland, we stopped for addresses, and at four we got to St. Catherine's. It is near Niagara, and celebrated for mineral waters.

The arches here were of new patterns. One represented a ship with the yards manned, and a large boat, filled with people, hung from the centre of it. One was made of carriage-wheels, one of chairs; and across the street, in one place, a man was slung, apparently sitting in an umbrella. One flag had: 'Hamilton – Killyleagh Castle, County Down – For Ever,' written on it. The prettiest arches to look at were some with mottoes in very large-headed tin nails on red cloth. The Royal Arms were also done in this way, and were quite lovely.

We drove slowly through the crowd to the hotel. Being very tired, I escaped a dinner given by the town; nor did I go to the fireworks, which were really beautiful. D.'s arms were done, and great bouquets of coloured 'candles' finished off the display. When he came back, I held a reception with him.

I have only given you the slightest account of our doings and of the kindness we meet with everywhere. Even the short-hand reporters have been unable to keep up with the descriptions they ought to write, so you must forgive me.

SATURDAY, 29TH. – D. went to the Welland Canal Works, and Lady Harriet, Fred Ward, and I met him in the train a short way from St. Catharine's, where we went to see a great bridge which Colonel Gzowski has 'thrown' across Niagara River.

I told you two years ago that we saw it being built. This time we crossed over it, and on our return stopped in the middle, and waited to see the way it opens to let ships pass. We stood on an immense piece of it resting on three piers; the two ends were detached by machinery, and we swung on the centre pier straight up and down the river. It was beautiful to see how easily it worked, and curious to look at our train left standing at the edge of a precipice. Then we swung back, and the rails and all joined together again.

Opposite the Falls we got into carriages, and drove down to see them again. The second visit lifts Niagara in my estimation above all disappointment; and, after great experience in waterfalls, I can say that none approach it. We saw it in beautiful sunshine, with a perfect rainbow joining the Falls. When we had quickly admired them, we proceeded in our train to the town of Niagara [Niagara-on-the-Lake], which is fourteen miles away. Here we stopped at the door of Mr.

Plumb, who is to be our host for a couple of nights, and having had a cup of tea, went on to the Court-House.

SUNDAY, 30TH. – We drove to church, and went into the Rectory afterwards to see Mrs. McMurray, who is a celebrity in her way. There is an account of her in a book called 'Winter Studies and Summer Rambles in Canada,' by Mrs. Jameson. She is an Indian half-breed; her father was an Irish gentleman of good family, but she spoke nothing but Indian till she was fifteen. Dr. McMurray, a missionary, married her. She is now a very tall old lady, with a good deal of the Indian peeping out; but as she is proud of her nationality, that is as well.

> Charlotte Johnston, whose mother was an Indian princess, had married in 1833 William McMurray. The year previous he had been appointed a missionary to the Indians at Sault Ste. Marie. Later, Dr. McMurray became rector of St. Mark's church at Niagara-on-the-Lake.
>
> Mrs. McMurray's sister was married to Henry Rowe Schoolcraft, who from 1836-41 was superintendent of Indian affairs for the State of Michigan. He became famous as a writer on Indian life and customs.
>
> Anna Brownell Jameson, wife of Robert Sympson Jameson, Vice-Chancellor of Upper Canada, wrote with great respect and affection of these sisters and their mother. She visited in their homes in 1837 while on her memorable trip to the head of Lake Huron, a trip delightfully described in the book mentioned by Lady Dufferin.

We made a round on our way home, to drive through an oak park on the borders of Niagara River. The quiet of Mr. Plumb's place is delightful. It is a red brick villa, with a Mansard roof, and a large new dining-room just added on. He has three sons and three daughters at home. [Josiah Burr Plumb had married a daughter of the Honourable Samuel Street of Niagara Falls.] He himself is an M.P., American by birth, Canadian by adoption.

We see peaches and grapes ripening in the open air, and the weather and climate in summer are delightful in this part of the country.

MONDAY, 31ST. – We left Niagara in a steamer, and crossed Lake Ontario in most lovely weather.

The chief excitement of this trip was caused by my maid. She was rushing to the waiting-room to fetch a parcel, when the steamer went off without her, and she ran about the wharf gesticulating in the most excited manner. We put back for her, and got her on board on the verge of hysterics. I kept safely away until she had had time to calm down.

We went to the Queen's Hotel at Toronto, and in the evening I took a walk in the streets with D. As we were walking along, a man looked over his shoulder, and said: 'It is quite pleasant to see you going quietly like that,' and then entered into conversation with us respecting our tour, and especially about our reception by the Americans.

D. and Fred went to a theatre after dinner, where D. was recognized, and received with cheers. The actors, who were in the midst of a tragic part, could not imagine what the noise was about.

> The Dufferins, unfortunately, were not able to be present at the gala performance given at Mrs. Daniel Morrison's new theatre. The Grand Opera House, on Adelaide Street just west of Yonge Street, a magnificently appointed building, was officially opened three weeks later, on September 21, 1874.
>
> An advertisement in the *Globe* stated:
>
> *Under the patronage of His Excellency and the Countess of Dufferin, Mrs. Morrison has the honour to present Sheridan's Great Comedy,* The School for Scandal, *as lately revised and played in the London theatres, where it has reached the unparalleled run of over six hundred nights.*
>
> This play, first produced almost one hundred years before, in 1777, was written by Lord Dufferin's great-grandfather, Richard Brinsley Sheridan. Mrs. Morrison herself took the part of Lady Teazle.
>
> It was further stated that 'the elegant prismatic Sunlight Chandelier will be lighted by electricity every evening at a quarter to eight o'clock.' The Grand Opera House continued as one of Toronto's leading theatres until the mid nineteen-twenties.

TORONTO: TUESDAY, SEPTEMBER 1ST. – D. looked at a regatta, and lunched with a rifle-club. I did nothing until the evening, when we dined with Mr. Howland. Although the dinner was rather long, it was very pleasant.

WEDNESDAY, 2ND. – D. went again to the Regatta, and to give away the medals won. In the evening he dined at the [Toronto] Club, and made (people say) an exceedingly good speech. The hearers were quite enthusiastic, and besides continual cheers during the speech, they stood up and cheered for fully five minutes after he had finished.

In speaking of our tour, D. said, 'Never has the head of any Government passed through a land so replete with contentment in the present, so pregnant of promise in the future. From the northern forest border lands, whose primeval recesses are being pierced and indented by the rough-and-ready cultivation of the free-grant settler, to the trim enclosure and wheat-laden townships that smile along the Lakes; from the orchards of Niagara to the hunting-grounds of Nipigon; in the wigwam of the Indian, in the homestead of the farmer, in the workshop of the artisan, in the office of his employer – everywhere have I learnt that the people are satisfied: satisfied with their own individual prospects and with the prospects of their country; satisfied with their Government, and with the Institutions under which they prosper; satisfied to be the subjects of the Queen; satisfied to be members of the British Empire.'

THURSDAY, 3RD. – Hitherto we have been hot. To-day we were very cold, and had our first experience of this sort of tour in wet weather.

Whitby was the first place we stopped at. Soldiers held a tarpaulin over our heads, while an umbrella-covered crowd stood around us. Then we drove to the High School. The poor children had taken great pains with their decorations; there were V.R.s and D.s in every pane, garlands on the walls, and children in white standing out in the rain.

Next we went to a college [Ontario Ladies College] about to be opened. An arch at the entrance was prettily done. Children in pink, white and blue stood all round the top of it, forming a lovely decoration – if only the sun had shone upon them! This college is called 'Trafalgar Castle,' and the house was built as a private residence [by Sheriff Reynolds], but had to be sold. There was another address, and presentations in the drawing-room.

Bowmanville came next, but the rain poured so heavily that we hurried through three addresses as quickly as possible. At Port Hope the rain ceased. But I conceived a dislike to the horses provided for us, and as we went jogging uncomfortably along I disliked them more. D. made me get out and return to the station. I missed seeing the town and also a fatal accident.

In the Fletchers' carriage, which was second, there were also some spirited horses. Of course there was a great noise, a crowd, bands, escort of cavalry, shouting, etc.; in fact, all the things which, combined

with fatigue, have made me terribly nervous during our various processions through towns. The carriages stopped, and just as they were
going on, a poor woman rushed forward to look, and got between the
first and second carriages. The horses could not be pulled in, and she
was knocked down and killed. I fear she has many children.

At five o'clock we reached Cobourg, had an address – or two – and a
drawing-room afterwards. The rest of the evening, wonderful to say,
was unemployed. We are in a most comfortable hotel [the Arlington
Hotel].

FRIDAY, 4TH. – We left the house at 8 a.m., and went by train for
half an hour to Rice Lake, where we got into a steamer. Rice Lake is
so named because of the wild rice which grows there. We had one
address as we passed through the locks at Hastings. The reeve there
was a most amusing old man, and told us he had been waiting fifty
years for a nobleman to come and see him.

The final object of our expedition was an iron-mine [the Marmora
Iron Mines], and we had to go a short way in a train to reach it. I did
not expect to care the least about it, but it was really an interesting
sight.

We found ourselves at the top of an enormous hole or cavern (these
words are too small for it), 140 feet deep, and large in proportion,
perfectly open, and light as day. The men looked like imps as they
worked below, and it was a sort of thing one sees represented, in
miniature, in a fairy play. The sides were walls of iron; but, alas! the
coal is in the States.

When we returned to the steamer [the *Isaac Butts*] we found a
barge tied to its side, covered in with green – a floating arbour – in
which lunch was laid. And very glad we were of it, as we breakfasted
at 7.30, and it was now past two. The managers of the mines, steamers, etc., are Americans, and we were their guests. Colonel Chamblis
and General Fitzhugh, with their wives (two sisters), were our hosts.
They live in the hotel, and are charming Southerners.

There was great anxiety about the time of our return, as a banquet
and ball were to follow. I had said I would not dine, and was glad I
had refused when I found we did not reach Cobourg till 7.30, after
eleven hours' outing. We were met by a torchlight procession. As my
carriage was drawn by men, and not by wild horses, I enjoyed it. The
firemen presented me with an enormous bouquet as I got out of the
carriage. All the other ladies had to rush home to dress, and Lady
Harriet and I enjoyed a quiet tea.

We went down to look at the dinner-table, which was beautifully arranged. It was shaped to represent the deck of a yacht, and two pillars which supported the ceiling of the room acted as masts, the rigging being properly arranged from them. There was a tiller and a bowsprit – in fact, the idea was completely carried out, and in front of D. stood a cake, on which was inscribed the word 'Foam.' [This was the name of the yacht in which Lord Dufferin went to Iceland.]

D.'s health was drunk, and the company were delighted with his reply, which brought all the guests to their feet. The dance was in the same room, and was very pretty and successful. I was at it for a short time.

SATURDAY, 5TH. – At our posts at 9 a.m. A tender farewell to Cobourg, and a warm 'How do you do?' to Belleville.

The station was three-quarters of a mile from the town, and we had a slow march all through to where the addresses were read. Then out to a great institution for the deaf and dumb. The building is on a fine site, and is airy and cheerful. The pupils were collected in a large room, and on the wall, in green letters, was written, 'Accept our silent welcome.' Dr. Palmer, the head of the institution, brought forward some untaught children just arrived, and showed us how he began to teach them so as to give them their first ideas. It was interesting to see their expressions of dawning comprehension.

A deaf-and-dumb teacher next came forward to show us the sign-language, and in pantomime told us a story. It was a wonderful piece of acting. He afterwards (in the same way) told the story of Christ stilling the storm. I don't think the reading of the passage could be more impressive than the way in which he conveyed the narrative to us by signs. I thought, when he began, that, coming after the comic story, it might seem irreverent. But it had a most solemn and reverential effect. D.'s speech was interpreted into signs as he spoke it, so we saw the method well. No word is spelt; every sentence is in signs. They all 'did' 'God save the Queen' in this way before we left.

This interesting entertainment made us unpunctual for the first time during our tour, and we had to cut Napanee very short so as to get to Kingston at the right time about six. We had to drive some way, and go in a steamer to Mr. Cartwright's, where we stay.

> Their host was the Honourable Richard (later Sir Richard) John Cartwright, Minister of Finance. To his home they went on the steamer *Maude;* the same vessel took them through the Thousand Islands the Monday following.

I felt very unready to go back to Kingston after dinner. But it had to be done, and through rain and lightning we returned there, to hold a reception. There were a great many people in a brilliant room, and after we left the 'young things' danced. I have forgotten to mention that Brother Fred left for England on the morning of the 3rd.

SUNDAY, 6TH. – Kingston is prettily situated, almost at the beginning of the Thousand Islands. Sitting under the trees here and resting is delightful.

MONDAY, 7TH. – We have had a lovely journey through the Thousand Islands, a comfortable steamer all to ourselves, with one full of people following us. When we came in sight of Brockville, a hundred small row-boats came to meet us. Each one had a lady in it, and a flag; it was a pretty sight.

When landed we got into a carriage, and the horses immediately stood upon their hind legs. As continual experiences of this sort have spoilt my nerves, I got out and took a lower place behind two lambs. These, however, had the misfortune to run their noses up against a flag, and shied fearfully. I was really delighted to think that this was my last drive.

Here D. made a speech, in which he gave some account of our reception at different places, and said, 'During the six weeks my tour has occupied, I believe I have received something like one hundred and twenty addresses, every one of which breathed a spirit of contentment, loyalty, and kindness. In fact, from first to last, no harsh, desponding, or discordant note has marred the jubilant congratulations of the nation.

'But the demonstrations with which we have been honoured have not been confined to mere vocal greetings. It would be impossible to describe either the beauty or the variety of the triumphal emblems which have glittered on either hand along our way. In addition to the graceful and picturesque decorations of evergreens, flags, tapestry, and prismatic canopies of colour from window to window, with which the towns were gay, we have passed under a number of the most ingenious and suggestive arches. There was an arch of cheeses, an arch of salt, an arch of wheels, an arch of hardware, stoves, and pots and pans, an arch of sofas, chairs and household furniture, an arch of ladders, laden with firemen in their picturesque costumes, an arch of carriages, an arch of boats; a Free-trade arch, a Protectionists' arch, an arch of children, and last of all – no, not an arch, but rather a celestial rainbow – of lovely young ladies! Indeed, the heavens themselves dropped fatness, for not unfrequently a magic cheese or other comestibles would descend into our carriage. As for Lady Dufferin, she has been nearly smothered beneath the nosegays which rained down upon her, for our path has been strewn with flowers.'

We had a reception in the Victoria Hall, and then returned to the train. We stopped at Smith's Falls, where there was a charming little reception, though we did not go farther than the station. We stopped in the same way at Carleton Place, and D. made his last speech. Two Ministers, M. Letellier and M. Fournier, met us at Smith's Falls, and at Ottawa all the Ministers came to the station. They are all pleased with the success of the tour, and delighted with the Toronto speech.

A fine guard of honour met us at Ottawa. The Governor-General's guards looked splendid, and even *our* Colonel was satisfied.

We gave a sigh of relief when we got home. The house looked so nice: a cheerful little fire (merely for the look of the thing) in the drawing-room; Fred's office grown, and with a fine glass side to it; my bedroom re-papered and new-carpeted, and looking so large after all the various rooms and cabins I have slept in; the quiet so charming, and the idea of not having to catch a train in the morning, of not having to reply to an address, of not having to visit three or four towns before we go to bed again, and of having 'got through' with flying colours – delightful.

We asked our faithful reporters and Colonel Cumberland to dinner, and we congratulated each other all the time. So ended our tour of 1874, which has been very delightful, though I am so glad of a rest now.

CHAPTER 13

Winter and Spring
SEPTEMBER 1874 - MAY 1875

OTTAWA: TUESDAY, SEPTEMBER 15TH. – We opened the Dominion Rifle Match. I fired the first shot, and am said to have made a bull's-eye – which some people won't believe, in spite of my having received an engraved silver tablet in commemoration of the event!

SATURDAY, OCTOBER 3RD. – D. went out hunting. They had a very good drag for about twenty minutes, and then a bagged fox was let loose. But he sat quietly looking at the hunt, and refused to stir. The man near him gave him a kick, upon which he ran at him, and after him with open mouth. At last he bolted into a wood, and so was altogether a failure.

SATURDAY, 10TH. – We have received invitations from New York: one to D., from some of the principal men there, inviting him to dinner on Monday, 19th; and one from Mrs. Wilson, asking if she might issue invitations to meet me on the same afternoon.

MONDAY, 12TH. – We set off on our journey to New York, leaving about ten in the morning and travelling all day and all night till we got to our destination the next morning.

TUESDAY, 13TH. – When we arrived the town looked gay and bright – so many creepers and trees, and bits of gardens and lawns. But the day was dull and cold. We had visits, made some engagements, and took a good walk down Broadway. Mr. Duncan sent us a box for 'Madame Angot,' to which we went, and enjoyed it much.

We are at the Brevoort House, which is comfortable, but very dear. Our rooms and one fire are $18.50 a day, and the servants' board and lodging will be ($5) 1£. a day each.

Dinner is made disagreeable to me by the menu having a price attached to each thing. I do not like, when eating my soup, to know that my share of it is 75 cents, and that my potato costs 30 cents. Seeing the prices enables one to be economical, if one wishes, but it makes that virtue even more disagreeable than it usually is.

WEDNESDAY, 14TH. – Mr. Sam Ward called, and I believe some engagements are made with him. I went to do a little shopping, wanting, among other things, a dark parasol. I was asked 6£. for a very ordinary black one, with a little silver at the handle.

In the afternoon I set out on a round of visits, and found the distances immense. I had to go to 74th Street, which is miles away, and D. started to walk there, and pitied himself very much. In the evening, having had an opera-box given us, we took the Fletchers to see 'Ruy Blas.' The performers were not of the Patti order. The box we had was very open, and had none of the privacy of an English one.

THURSDAY, 15TH. – This evening we went to a theatre owned by Mr. Stuart, and were much amused by a thoroughly American piece from Mark Twain's novel of 'The Gilded Age.' The house was very full, and the people seemed especially pleased at the jokes which alluded to the corruption of their own Legislature. The heroine shoots her false lover with a revolver, and the last act caricatured a Yankee court of justice, with its appeal to the feelings of the jury, and its verdict of 'Not Guilty,' though the murder was completely proved. The principal actor was excellent – Raymond by name – and the woman was good in the tragic parts, but looked much too wicked in her innocent days at the beginning of the play.

Mr. Stuart told me he made 20,000£. a year by his theatre. He is getting up Sunday concerts, to 'relieve the loneliness of the Sabbath evening.'

Ladies go to theatres in bonnets, and were not very smart at the opera.

FRIDAY, 16TH. – I saw Sir Edward Thornton, who called, and at the appointed time D. and I started for General Wilson's house in 74th Street. I was in a morning gown and bonnet, but found my hostess in a low dress. Everyone else, however, was like myself, and only those took off their bonnets who (I suppose) looked best without them. I had to do duty, standing at the door all the time, and shaking hands with everyone, for two hours. Mr. Sam Ward sent me a most lovely bouquet of pink and yellow rosebuds for this reception.

Sir Edward Thornton, 1817-1906, who had held various diplomatic posts abroad, was from 1867 to 1881 British envoy at Washington. He had served as arbitrator in several boundary and fishing disputes.

Samuel Ward, 1814-84, a prominent politician, was interested in legislation affecting financial matters. He was known as a genial host and a brilliant conversationalist. His sister, Julia Ward Howe, was an ardent worker in organizations advocating the emancipation of the slaves. She was the author of the "Battle Hymn of the Republic."

Samuel Langhorne Clemens, 1835-1910, wrote under the pseudonym Mark Twain, a term, meaning two fathoms deep, used by leadsmen taking soundings on the Mississippi. He was just then becoming well known and recognized as a humorist. *The Gilded Age* had appeared only two years before.

SATURDAY, 17TH. – We drove through Central Park to Jerome Park, where the races took place. We were in the Jockey Club stand, opposite the Grand Stand, and the horses passed twice between the two, so that we saw both the beginning and the end of the race very well.

Sir Edward Thornton dined with D. and me, and we took him to a theatre in which we had been given a box. We had not been there three minutes before we found it was such a piece which we could possibly not stay to see. Imagine the history of the temptation and fall of man in burlesque upon the stage!

SUNDAY, 18TH. – We went to an unsatisfactory church to-day: little service and much sermon. I walked home, and met all the world doing the same. As a crowd, the Americans are better dressed than we are, but I do not think that they excel our best-dressed people, such as appear at Ascot or Goodwood; and they are not, to my mind, so pretty.

We dined with Mr. A. T. Stewart, a Belfast man, who came out here at sixteen, and must be very rich. His palace is entirely of white marble. In our honour the dinner was at six instead of at three. A silver dish-cover lay before Mr. Stewart; at each course it was removed, the dish of food put in its place, to be looked at for a minute, then taken away to be helped, and the cover replaced.

When it was over we saw the picture-gallery and the house. I liked Mrs. Stewart – she seemed simple and natural. We sat in each room in turn; a little in the drawing-room, a short time in the library, a few minutes in the billiard-room, a little while in her bedroom, etc. The latter is very beautiful, and I suppose it is slept in, but it does not look as if it were.

> Alexander Turney Stewart, 1803-76, was born in Lisburn, Ireland. With a small inheritance he purchased Irish laces and opened, in 1823, a dry-goods shop on Broadway in New York City. A shrewd trader, he prospered and eventually owned the largest retail store in the world. This was later purchased by John Wanamaker.
>
> His house, which so impressed Lady Dufferin, was reputed to be the finest mansion in America.

There was a lady there who was just like a conventional Yankee on the stage. She announced, first, that she had told her husband she would never put on black for him, as she meant to marry again as quick as ever she could. She next proceeded to tell me her domestic troubles, and how she had to get a policeman to turn her cook out of her house. When she had got so far, a more fashionable person came up, and would talk 'opera' to me, so I heard no more.

MONDAY, 19TH. – I walked in the streets, and paid a number of visits, and in the evening went to the opera with Mrs. Stevens. It was 'Ruy Blas' again, as Albani, who had just arrived, was too unwell to sing. C. Yznaga was the young lady of the party, and there was a stream of young men passing through all the time. No one seemed to dream of listening!

D. was dining with thirty gentlemen at Delmonico's; the dinner went off well, and there were no speeches.

> Madame Albani was the stage name of Emma Lajeunesse, a Canadian operatic and oratorio singer, who was born in Chambly, Quebec, where she received her early musical education from her father. Following study in France and Italy, she had made her London debut in 1872. Now, two years later, she was to appear on the New York stage.

> Lorenzo Delmonico, 1813-81, was of Swiss origin. In 1834, about two years after he came to the United States, he, with his uncles John and Peter, established in New York City a restaurant, Delmonico's. It became famous for the fine quality of its food and service. In 1876 it was located at Broadway and 26th Street.

TUESDAY, 20TH. – D. had a breakfast given to him by Mr. Sam Ward, which he liked immensely, and in the evening a dinner, which he also enjoyed.

THURSDAY, 22ND. – We started off before nine in the morning to a railway-station, where we were met by Mr. Dudley Field, and went by train to Tarrytown [twenty-five miles north of New York City].

There a coach-and-four, driven by Mr. Dudley Field, junr., awaited us. We were glad to see the country; there were pretty villas all along, and a capital road. The view ought to have been lovely, but a fog hung over the Hudson, and hid its opposite bank. We returned by road to Irvingstown, where we saw Washington Irving's 'Sleepy Hollow,' passed in front of Cyrus Field's house to see the view, and then stopped at Dudley Field's, junr., for lunch, or rather breakfast, for we had only a cup of tea before starting. Then we drove back to the station and returned to New York.

> David Dudley Field, then sixty-nine years of age, was a lawyer who had been counsel in many important cases involving constitutional issues. He succeeded in obtaining adoption of a Code of Civil Procedure.
>
> His brother, Cyrus West Field, fourteen years his junior, who had amassed a fortune in the paper business, helped to promote the first submarine telegraph cable between America and Europe. Although a few messages were transmitted in 1858, that cable ceased to operate, and it was 1866 before complete success was achieved.
>
> Stephen Dudley Field, Junior, then twenty-eight, had just started on his career as an inventor.

FRIDAY, 23RD. – Another country day. This time we took the ferry, and went over to Orange Valley, where Mrs. Yznaga lives. She gave us Spanish and Cuban dishes; the first, 'gumbo,' a curious gelatinous soup, with oysters, chicken, sassafras leaves, and red pepper in it. Then a dish with rice and tomatoes in the middle, grilled chicken and fried bananas round; then various sorts of light pastry, and chocolate to drink. We returned about four o'clock. Our party consisted of Miss Stevens, Madame van Hoffman, and Bret Harte.

> Francis Brett (usually known as Bret) Harte, born in Albany, New York State, in 1836, had gone to California at the age of eighteen. Here, after brief attempts at mining, he turned to writing, and as editor of the *Overland Monthly* became a prominent literary figure. He returned to New York in 1871.

We dined with Mr. and Mrs. Morton, and met Mr. and Mrs. Duncan, Mr. and Mrs. Randolph Robinson, General Taylor, and Consuela Yznaga. We dined at 6.30, as we were all going on to the opera. They gave us a very pretty dinner, and we only missed the first act of 'Lucia,' and enjoyed the rest very much. Albani, who sang for the second time here, was very well received, and we are proud of her as a Canadian.

SATURDAY, 24TH. – We went with Mr. Duncan to see Mr. Belmont's picture-gallery, and on to the house of a gentleman who is rich, and collects pictures. D. then went with Mr. Bierstadt to see his pictures, and afterwards made a round of galleries.

In the evening we saw 'The Romance of a Poor Young Man' acted by Mr. Montague, whom the young ladies here call 'a lovely man.'

> August Belmont, born in Europe, came to the United States at the age of twenty-one and established a banking business. This became very prosperous and brought him great wealth. He was noted as an art connoisseur and sportsman, and twice served his country as its minister abroad—to Austria and to the Netherlands.

> Albert Bierstadt, 1830-1902, was brought to the United States from his native Germany when one year old. He became a painter of landscapes and historical subjects.

SUNDAY, 25TH. – D. had to leave for Washington before nine o'clock, so we dined quietly with some very nice people. It amused me to observe in what way their dinner differed from one we should give. Their house is handsome and comfortable, and they are very rich. But their table was large for the number of people, and had absolutely nothing on it – not a bonbon, a flower, a bit of china, a candle, a bit of food – so it looked very bare. We had oysters, soup, fish, an *entrée*, cold beef – as a compliment to the Sunday – and a hot pudding. The cloth was then taken off, and we sat at a mahogany dessert-table once again.

MONDAY, 26TH. – D. went to Washington, where he arrived at six in the morning, and was just settling down to a quiet sleep in his train-bed, when he heard Sir E. Thornton had come to meet him, so he had to jump up at once. Sir Edward gave him a cup of tea, and took him a walk, then breakfast, and then a drive to all the sights. He saw the

President, who was very civil and called upon him, and Mr. Fish, and then started for Baltimore, where he slept.

> Ulysses Simpson Grant, 1822-85, during the American Civil War co-ordinated the movements of all the armies of the North to defeat the Confederate forces of the South. He received the surrender of their armies from General Robert E. Lee at the Appomattox Court House on April 9, 1865. In 1868 he was elected the eighteenth President of the United States; he was re-elected in 1872.

> Hamilton Fish, 1808-93, an American statesman, was born in New York City and practised law there. As United States Secretary of State from 1869 to 1877 he negotiated settlement of the *Alabama* Claims with Great Britain and of the north-west boundary dispute.

WEDNESDAY, 28TH. – In the morning Mr. Cyrus Field came for us, and we went to see the Normal School. At nine precisely music struck up, and 1,200 girls marched in. A chapter in the Bible was read, and a hymn sung. The President got up and said: 'Young ladies, I present to you the Earl of Dufferin, Governor-General of Canada, and his Lady'; and D. said a few appropriate words.

Our next visit was to a common school, and the children's department was very interesting. There were 1,150 collected in one room, and they marched with an air of solemnity that was amusing. At a signal from the mistress the 1,150 heads went up in the air, at another, there was clapping of hands; at another, singing. There are 2,500 children at school in that one building.

FRIDAY, 30TH. – D. dined with Mr. Stoughton last night, and I went about eight o'clock to fetch him. The landlord of our hotel went with me, and sat by me in the carriage. Then I realized how wanting I had been in not shaking hands with him when I first arrived.

We travelled all night, and though the beds themselves were comfortable, the night was not. The engine kept up a perpetual shriek, and the train went more like an animal than a machine – in jerks and with varieties of speed.

When we reached our destination – the Revere House, Boston – I rested, but D. put off his nap, and took a walk. We drove in an open carriage through the town. There are some handsome buildings, pretty public gardens, and a common, on which a great many good houses look out. We visited Bunker's Hill and Harvard College. The Memorial Hall, built to the memory of the former students who were killed in the War [the Civil War], where the young men dine, is very handsome.

We visited Mr. Longfellow, and found him in a nice old-fashioned house, where Washington was living when he took command of the American army. The poet's study is a plainly-furnished room, with a large orange-tree standing in one window. He is a most charming and loveable old man. He gave me one of his poems as a souvenir of my visit, and he invited D. to dine at the Club dinner to-morrow, so we remain for that. Just as we were going out of the house his daughter Alice appeared, and he introduced her to us.

> Henry Wadsworth Longfellow, the beloved poet of Boston, was then sixty-seven years old. He lived in Craigie House, on the Cambridge side of the Charles River. This picturesque home had been given to them as a wedding present by his wife's father, the Honourable Nathan Appleton.
>
> With her sisters, Alice is mentioned in "The Children's Hour":
>
>> Between the dark and the daylight,
>>   When the night is beginning to lower,
>> Comes a pause in the day's occupations,
>>   That is known as the Children's Hour.
>>
>> .   .   .   .
>>
>> From my study I see in the lamplight,
>>   Descending the broad hall stair,
>> Grave Alice, and laughing Allegra,
>>   And Edith with golden hair.

We have our meals in American fashion here, in a public room. There are numbers of small tables for ten people; sometimes we are alone, sometimes there are other people at our table. At every meal the first ceremony always is to place a glass of iced water before us.

In the evening we went to the Boston Theatre – a fine one, with spacious entrance-hall. The theatre itself, very large and beautifully decorated, finer than any we saw in New York. The piece was 'Belle Lamar,' a story of the War, interesting and well put upon the stage. Here they have a farce both before and after, while in New York there was only one piece given in each theatre.

SATURDAY, 31ST. – We drove this morning to Dorchester Heights, to see some more of the city, and at 2.30 D. went to his Club dinner. He has been very lucky to be here for it. It takes place only once a month, and he met at it Longfellow, Lowell, Emerson, Dana, Dana junr., Holmes (the Autocrat of the Breakfast Table), etc. They have all promised him books as a remembrance of the occasion.

> Ralph Waldo Emerson, 1803-82, lecturer, essayist and poet, settled in Concord, Massachusetts, twenty-three miles north-west of Boston, in 1835. Here, near him, gathered a group of writers. Companionship with them and with other authors in and near Boston led him in 1855 to become one of the founders of the Saturday Club.
>
> It was to this Club that Longfellow had invited Lord Dufferin. Here he met, among others, James Russell Lowell, 1819-91, a poet and essayist who had succeeded to Longfellow's chair as Smith Professor of French and Spanish at Harvard University. He became a leader among the mid-nineteenth-century authors, and was first editor of the *Atlantic Monthly*. This position he held for four years, from 1857 to 1861.
>
> Richard Henry Dana, a poet and journalist, was then eighty-seven years old. His son, Richard Henry Dana Junior, then fifty-nine, was a lawyer, a specialist in admiralty law. When but twenty-five years old, he had published *Two Years Before the Mast*. This book, which became an American classic of sea adventure, embodied his experiences during a trip from Boston around Cape Horn to California, 1834-36.
>
> Oliver Wendell Holmes, 1809-94, had graduated in medicine and been a practising physician in Boston before becoming, in 1847, Professor of Anatomy and Physiology at the Harvard Medical School. This position he held until his retirement in 1882. His light, witty articles, first published in the early issues of the *Atlantic Monthly*, appeared in 1858 in book form as *The Autocrat of the Breakfast-Table*. His numerous lectures, addresses, essays and poems constitute a large collection.

I took a walk in the town, and in the evening D. and I went to the Museum Theatre. It is not so fine as the Boston, but it is uncommon in one way. You pass through a museum to it – statues, pictures, stuffed animals, etc. The play was 'Arkwright's Wife,' by Tom Taylor – very good indeed. The heroine was pretty and graceful.

> Tom Taylor, 1817-80, an English dramatist and author, wrote and adapted about one hundred pieces for the stage. From 1874 to 1880 he was editor of *Punch*.

SUNDAY, NOVEMBER 1ST. – We tried two churches before we could get a seat, and the third we attempted to enter turned out to be a Universalist church. It is one of the Old-English chapels, and the service was our Liturgy very slightly altered, and a sermon upon All Saints' Day. This service is intended to suit everybody, whatever their opinions may be. In many places in Canada where they cannot support a number of different sects, they have these Universalist churches.

We had to dine at four – American system! However, it will enable us to go to bed early, and prepare for thirteen hours' railway tomorrow to Montreal.

MONDAY, 2ND. – The day passed much more pleasantly than I expected, and we really enjoyed the journey. We had a comfortable compartment to ourselves, passed through beautiful scenery (seeing the Green Mountains and several rivers), and had two most excellent meals. Generally they only wait [at the meal-stations] ten minutes for dinner, but, thanks to our 'high office,' they gave us half an hour.

OTTAWA: SATURDAY, 7TH. – I have had nothing particular to relate since our return here. But to-day I took Mr. Hepworth Dixon, who is staying with us, his son, and Lady Harriet, to the steeplechases.

Four horses started in each race; the first was for the Governor-General's Challenge Cup, and the only fall was that of a man of fifty-seven – rather old to do 'jockey.' His horse swerved at a pole, and the rider lay still for several seconds on the ground and frightened us; but he got up and walked about all the rest of the day. We saw the same horse ridden by a jockey proper in the last race. He swerved at the same place every time he came round to it, and so lost the race. There was constant variety in this race, for the order of the running changed every few seconds.

WEDNESDAY, 18TH. – Colonel Fletcher got his recall from England to-day, and I fear they will all have to leave in February. Lady Harriet will be a terrible loss to me; she has been my constant companion, and was always ready to do everything and to enjoy everything with me; the most sympathetic person I have ever met. We had many things in common, and I cannot bear to think of her departure yet.

SATURDAY, 21ST. – The new General (Commanding the Canadian Militia), Selby Smyth, and his A.D.C., Mr. Miles Stapleton, came to stay till Monday. The A.D.C. looks very 'jolly,' and will be an acquisition to Fred, I think. But the really exciting question is: 'Does he look as if he would dance the Boston?' which all the young ladies have been practising.

Colonel Barnard and a very big and pleasant Chief Justice – Begbie, from British Columbia – came to dinner. The latter has been out there sixteen years, and has, I believe, succeeded in making the law respected by Indians and other 'wild men.' He gave us an amusing description of the difficulties which occur from the Indian plan of families and property descending in the female line.

SATURDAY, 28TH. – A heavy snowstorm during the night and nearly all day. The children, with the help of Colonel Fletcher, Mr. Dixon, and a ladder, have erected in front of my window an enormous and hideous snow-man, who will remain an eyesore to me the whole winter, unless some kind friend assassinates him. I was threatened with a wife for him, but I am in hopes that a judicious suggestion I have made as to the appropriateness of making the pair stand as spectators over the Skating Rink may induce the builders to model the statues there. The creature has a carrot nose, and lips of the same material, coal for eyes, and an old hat on his head; he is eight feet high, and stands right in my way, hiding my view of the Parliament Buildings. In the evening he was illuminated with red and green fire.

TUESDAY, DECEMBER 15TH. – There was some very good tobogganing to-day. The new slide is most exciting, for, the natural hill not being considered sufficiently steep, a great addition has been made to it. A long flight of stairs now leads to the top of a high wooden slide, and, as this is almost perpendicular, the toboggan starts at a rapid rate down it – and its occupant has both the length and the excitement of his slide greatly increased. To-day the wooden part of the slide is a sheet of ice, so the toboggans rush down it at a tremendous pace.

FRIDAY, 18TH. – Gwen and Katie arrived about five o'clock, looking extremely well. [These were Lady Dufferin's two younger sisters, Helen Gwendoline Hamilton and Mary Catherine Hamilton.]

CHRISTMAS DAY, FRIDAY, 25TH. – An ideal Christmas Day – the weather lovely, twenty degrees of frost, and a bright sun. The children had received presents from their governess and nurses in the morning, and were in great excitement. After breakfast they came down, and we introduced Nelly and Hermie to a dolls' house, which delighted them. Hallie had dressed a number of inhabitants for it, and it is a charming toy.

In the afternoon, everyone, except me, went out and had a pleasant afternoon skating and tobogganing. I found plenty of work at the Christmas-tree, which was ready directly after tea. The only *contre-temps* of the day happened just as the children were jumping with excitement to go in to see it. The gas went out, and we had to wait more than half an hour for it to recover. In the meantime we got up a dwarf, who amused them much. The tree was next lighted up, and was greeted with cheers. The fifteen children – the eldest eleven years old – were all perfectly delighted, and were much too pleased with the treasures they had received to feel inclined to play games afterwards. They simply sat on the floor absorbed in their new possessions, with sighs of perfect happiness. The youngest of the party was one of the happiest; she ran about the floor pulling a sheep after her, and looked such a pretty little dear. The big people also went away laden. We were fourteen at dinner, with governesses, secretaries, etc., and in the evening we played games.

FRIDAY, JANUARY 1ST, 1875. – We were more or less busy in the morning making the arrangements for the children's play, and from 2.30 to 4.30 His Ex. and I were 'at home' to receive visitors. We had 211 gentlemen, who said 'How do you do?' had a glass of wine or a cup of tea, and passed away. We refreshed ourselves with a cup of tea when the reception was over, and then I dressed for the evening, and helped to paint the actors.

The play took place upon a small stage erected in the anteroom to the ball-room. Mr. Dixon wrote the piece and painted the scenes. 'Pussy-cat, Mew-mew' was the name of the play, and it went off very well. Fred was excellent in the part he undertook, and was well made-up, with red stockings, red knickerbockers, a brown blouse, and red wig. Fred Ward was the master-magician, in a dressing-gown covered with mysterious signs. Nelly looked very pretty in white tarlatan and gold, a crown on her head, and a wand in her hand. Archie was a prince in green and silver; Terence, the 'Man in the Moon,' in red. Hermie, a pink fairy; and all the others in the same style of costume in different colours. Terence's first appearance was through the full moon, and he did his part very well. All have much improved in acting since last year.

The *tableaux* were very pretty. I had to be behind the scenes, and so only managed to see one myself, which I will describe to you.

The foreground of the stage was painted in dark colours to represent a cavern, and the back opened, displaying a brilliant grotto in gold and silver and red. Hermie stood on a raised rock of gold at the top; beneath her sat three little ones, with baby in the centre, who was enchanted with her position. Terence lay at their feet in his red moon-costume, and grouped beneath were Archie, Nelly, Maud, Edward, etc. They were lighted up with various coloured fires. Baby amused us so by giving three cheers in the middle of the performance. The other *tableaux* were scenes in a tournament: the Encounter, the Result, and the Coronation of the Victor.

FRIDAY, 22ND. – D. played the final game of the curling-match with Colonel Fletcher, and won a cup presented by me.

We had a large children's party, and repeated the play. Directly it was over we had tea for sixty-five children, who seemed very hungry and very happy, and after that dancing and a few games till eight, when the little people left.

MONDAY, 25TH. – D. started for Montreal. I copy the following out of his letters: –

'We had not left Ottawa ten minutes before the train came to a stand, and all our sweepers had to jump out. By their exertions we got on another few hundred yards, when a second stop occurred.

'This kind of business went on for nearly an hour, at the end of which time the Parliament Buildings were still in sight. After a little, however, matters improved.

'On arriving at Montreal we found our rooms looking very cheerful, and a nice little supper ready, for which those marvellous ladies [my sisters] were again quite ready.

'TUESDAY, 26TH. – We started at eleven o'clock for the Rink; found the Bethunes, Miss Campbell, Mr. Maxwell, and a couple of nice Englishmen. With these playfellows we passed a couple of hours very pleasantly, and executed a brilliant lancers.

'At 2.30 the two Freds and I and Nowell went to have a game of curling, preparatory to a match to-morrow with four of the oldest members of the Montreal Club, whose united ages, I believe, amount to something like 350 years. We did not play well, and got a bad beating, though we ended by winning the last two ends, the latter of which was an end of four. The girls went out walking with Colonel Fletcher. Maxwell and the other two young men I have mentioned dined with us, and at ten we went to the ball. It was a nice large, square room, with beautiful music, excellent parqueterie, and very jolly. Gwen looked very well, and I liked her dress. As you may suppose she got lots of partners.'

MONDAY, FEBRUARY 1ST. – The great event of the day was the opening of the new theatre here – the first one at Ottawa. The house is really very nice, and the state box a comfortable and convenient one.

TUESDAY, 9TH. – A great curling-match was played between our Club and the Renfrew Club, for a medal presented by the Caledonian Club. Four of ours had to go to Renfrew, and four of their men came here; so the winner could not be announced till the two games were over. The two Freds and Messrs. Baker and Dixon went early to Renfrew, and D., Nowell, Colonel Fletcher and Robertson were the team who remained here. The game began at ten, and they had to play for three hours. The V.R.C.C. were at one time five behindhand, but they finally won by one; and an hour later we heard by telegraph that at Renfrew they were ties, so we won the medal by one shot. This is the first public match our club has played. The boys got home to dinner, and we talked curling and played whist all evening.

FRIDAY, 12TH. – We had a large dinner-party to-day – married Ministers and their wives. A great division was expected in the House; so they went off there after dinner, and they amnestied Riel during the night. [But he was never allowed to take his seat in the House.]

WEDNESDAY, MARCH 31ST. – My baby boy [Lord Frederick Blackwood, born 26th February, 1875] is now five weeks old, so I was able to be present at the second representation of the 'Maire of St. Brieux,' of which the first performance had been extremely successful. It is an operetta, written by Mr. Dixon, whom you know well by name, and composed by Mr. Mills, the organist in Ottawa. The music is very pretty and the whole play excellent. It is very interesting to bring out a new thing on one's own stage, and even the author and composer must have been satisfied with the actors and singers who played in it. The prima donna, Mrs. Anglin, both sang and looked charmingly, and the Maire himself, Mr. Kimber, was quite perfect.

I asked the actors to keep on their costumes during the evening, and they made the party look very gay and pretty, the girls' coloured petticoats and high, white caps, and the men's bright-coloured clothes, being very effective.

SUNDAY, 25TH. – Baby was christened by the name of Frederick Temple.

TUESDAY, MAY 11TH. – We leave for three months' holiday in England, and had quite a sad parting with the seven little ones. General Selby Smyth met us, with his A.D.C. at the gate, and at the station there was a crowd of people to wish us adieu and *bon voyage*. The day was lovely. At Montreal we were met by General O'Grady Haly, (the General Officer Commanding H.M. Forces in British North America), who is to be Administrator during D.'s absence.

WEDNESDAY, 12TH. – A torrent of rain falling all day. We left Montreal early, and spent ten hours in the train, reaching Quebec about six in the evening.

FRIDAY, 14TH. – A very stormy night, slates blowing about, and we go on board to-morrow!

SATURDAY, 15TH. – Such a dreadful morning: snow, rain, and cold wind of the bitterest description. D. sent to beg the Mayor not to bring the steamers out to accompany ours, as it was impossible for any ladies to go in them. The Lieutenant-Governor came for us, and drove us down to the *Polynesian*. One steamer did go with us for a little way with a band on board. They played 'He is a Jolly Good Fellow' and 'God save the Queen,' and cheered us when we parted. This was about 1 p.m.

At three we stopped suddenly, and on sending out to inquire we found we were ashore! We got off soon, but at four we were stuck again; this time we were told we could not get off till high-water, at two o'clock in the night. We have a very comfortable sitting-room on deck, with a warm-water stove in it, and next to it the smoking-room, in which we have our meals privately. Our sleeping-berths are comfortable.

SUNDAY, 16TH. – Awoke to find ourselves stuck. No hopes of getting off till 4 p.m., at high-water. One of the boats went out to do something, and could not get back. Another was sent after her, and now both, with a large proportion of our crew, are gone. I suppose when we do get off we shall go after them.

TUESDAY, 18TH. – In the afternoon we sighted a field of ice, which looked pretty in the rosy evening. Some small pieces floated round the vessel, and during the night we got into quite a thick part of it, and had to stop.

WEDNESDAY, 19TH. – Loose and large pieces of ice all round us – some, dirty brown-looking lumps, others white, and all rough and ragged. A fog over all, a wet deck, a ship stopped on its voyage – such are the pleasures we find on this May day. About five we began to move slowly through the ice. It was a fascinating employment, that of watching the great 'Juggernaut' we were in cutting and pushing its way through this field of ice. Sometimes we went through great pieces, just as a knife cuts through a wedding-cake, sometimes the piece resisted us to a certain degree, and we had to push it slowly aside before we could get on.

THURSDAY, 20TH. – I awoke about five in the morn, hearing the vessel crunch up against the ice; at ten we were free, but in a fog; the steam-horn blew all day.

As soon as we got far enough south we turned the corner of the ice, and went on our way rejoicing, in spite of a great deal of fog, and fog-whistling.

CHAPTER 14

An Uneventful Season
OCTOBER 1875-JULY 1876

Shortly after arriving in London, Lord Dufferin was the guest of honour at a large banquet given by the Canada Club. Replying to the toast, 'The health of the Governor-General of Canada and prosperity to the Dominion,' he said:

If to love a country with one's whole heart, to feel that in each of its inhabitants one possesses a personal friend, to believe in its future implicitly, to take a pride in everything that belongs to it—its scenery, climate, its physical and moral characteristics, its very sports and pastimes—be any test of loyalty to its interests, then I feel my devotion to Canada can never be called in question. [Cheers.] . . .

If at the end of the next three years, I shall be able to complete my term under the same happy circumstances which have hitherto characterized its duration, if I can carry with me home to England the consciousness that the people of Canada regard me as having been a faithful, loving, and devoted servant to the Dominion; if, at the same time, I am fortunate enough to have merited the approval of my Sovereign and countrymen at home, I shall consider few public servants will have ever reaped so honourable and so dearly prized a reward. [Loud cheers.]

Then the Dufferins returned to Ireland, to their own home, Clandeboye, a few miles east of Belfast. Cheering tenants welcomed the travellers; the horses were unhitched, and stalwart men pulled their carriage, while flags fluttered from the turrets of the house.

In this ancestral home, with its many art treasures brought from Italy and the Mediterranean, the Dufferins rested from official duties. From its windows vistas opened to quiet pools, while, from its own

169

special hill, Helen's Tower, built by Lord Dufferin, in her lifetime, as a tribute to his mother, looked out over the pounding surf of the Irish Sea. In it oak panels were inscribed with some of her poems.

Twelve miles to the south was Killyleagh, Lady Dufferin's girlhood home. This beautiful Norman castle, built in 1177, and reputed to be one of the finest still-inhabited castles in Ireland, had come into the possession of the Hamiltons about 1600. Its walls had resounded to trumpet calls, and its wide courtyard witnessed archery contests and mediaeval tournaments.

In its drawing-room, thirteen years before, Hariot Hamilton had become Lord Dufferin's bride. Resplendent in wedding finery, they had driven north to Clandeboye, so tenants might share in their happiness. There, school children had strewed their path with flowers. To Killyleagh they now went to visit Lady Dufferin's mother; her father, Archibald Rowan Hamilton, had died in 1860, two years before her marriage.

October saw them returning to duties in Canada. There, seven children eagerly awaited their arrival.

FRIDAY, OCTOBER 22ND. – I sent you a post-card from Londonderry telling you we were off on our return to Canada after our holiday at home. We got on board on a very disagreeable evening, but we thought the wind was lessening, and that we should probably have a calm passage. We talked of seeing land on Thursday and reaching Quebec at the latest by Tuesday.

Thursday, however, found us very near Ireland, in a regular storm, which lasted two days and two nights, during which time we scarcely made any progress. In twenty-four hours we made only forty knots, and the captain said he had never been so delayed in his life. We were obliged to remain below, rolling perpetually. Later we saw some beautiful icebergs; and now that I have seen field-ice, icebergs, fog, and a storm, I do not wish for any new experience of life at sea.

We got to Quebec this morning, and found the weather beautiful, but very cold. One steamer, which left the Monday before us, arrived yesterday with her bulwarks washed away, and having lost three boats. Our *Prussian* received no damage; she is such a good sea-boat.

The General [General O'Grady Haly], Lieutenant-Governor [Honourable René Edouard Caron], etc. came to meet us, and our landing at this lovely place was very pretty. It was so gay and sunny, and the Canadian air does feel so exhilarating. The children sent letters of welcome to meet us at Father Point, begging us not to stop on the way anywhere. We go on by the boat this afternoon, and reach Ottawa at four to-morrow.

TUESDAY, 26TH. – Colonel and Mrs. Littleton [of the Grenadier Guards, later Lord Hatherton], who have come out with us in place of Colonel and Lady Harriet Fletcher, reached Ottawa yesterday, and are at the hotel. They came to lunch, and to see their house.

THURSDAY, 28TH. – Lawn-tennis, and a drive. The Littleton children came to tea, and quite won the hearts of mine. They expected to see 'the King of Canada' in a crown and train, and still think that at some future time he will appear in full dress.

WEDNESDAY, NOVEMBER 3RD. – The new tennis-court has been begun. It is to serve the purpose of a supper-room as well.

SATURDAY, 13TH. – We are proposing later in the season to give a fancy ball, and are already deep in millinery-talk.

THURSDAY, 18TH. – We skated for the first time this year, on the Rideau, where we had swept a place.

We had a great dinner to-night for the Judges of the Supreme Court (sixty-two guests), and had a large T-shaped table spread in the ball-room for it.

In proposing the health of the Chief Justice, the Honourable William (later Sir William) Buell Richards, and his colleagues, the other members of the newly constituted Supreme Court of Canada, Lord Dufferin said:

As during the Saturnalia, the Roman slaves were allowed to buffet their masters with impunity, so a Governor-General may be permitted for once, on a festive occasion like the present, to give his Prime Minister advice, instead of receiving it. The advice I would tender Mr. Mackenzie and through him to the Parliament and people of Canada is this: that, inasmuch as pure, efficient and authoritative Courts of Justice are the most precious possession a people can enjoy, the very founts and sources of a healthy, national existence, there is no duty more incumbent on a great and generous community than to take care that all and everyone of those who administer justice in the land are accorded a social, moral, and I will venture to add, a material recognition proportionate to their arduous labours, weighty responsibilities and august position.

MONDAY, DECEMBER 6TH. – Lovely day, and the skating-ice simply perfect. We have had a man from Montreal to teach us to flood it properly, and the result of his instructions is excellent.

THURSDAY, 9TH. – There was great excitement at receiving a box directed to me from 'the Queen.' It contained a pretty doll, dressed in the smartest blue velvet gown, for Victoria. She was delighted, and carried it about all the evening.

SATURDAY, 11TH. – We asked Miss Kingsford, Miss Patrick and some of the other good skaters to come to-day, that we might practise our figures. This was a real, true skating-party, with no temptations to toboggan or dance, and it was very pleasant. We worked away at roses, double roses, thistles, lilies, snails, etc., and then we came in, had some tea, and talked about – the fancy ball.

MONDAY, 20TH. – On Saturday we had the same people as last week, but as the thermometer was about 20° below zero, skating was a doubtful pleasure. Sunday was still colder, and to-day the weather is no milder.

TUESDAY, 21ST. – During the afternoon a sudden and comfortable change in the weather. They say there was a jump of 76° in the twelve hours. Certainly it became very warm, and a complete thaw set in after a very 'cold snap' indeed.

FRIDAY, 24TH. – The snow is quite off the tobogganing-slide, and the Skating Rink is spoilt for the present; but it has begun to freeze again.

I was very busy all day with Mrs. Hall, arranging the Christmas-tree. At five o'clock Gwen and Russell [Russell Stephenson, to whom her sister Gwen was married in October, 1875] and Fred Ward arrived. They met at Prescott. Gwen looks extremely well. During the severe frost in Montreal her hot-water pipes burst, and she was nearly frozen.

SATURDAY, 25TH. – A wet Christmas Day in Canada! We went to church under umbrellas! However, it cleared up afterwards, but was at no time a nice day. At five o'clock the Littleton children came, and after tea the tree in the ball-room was lighted up, and the shrieking 'brats' were admitted to it. The tree was really very pretty. It was placed just in front of the Throne. Its natural eccentricities of shape were concealed by ropes of many-coloured crackers and glass balls, and it was covered with small presents, and surrounded on the floor

by larger ones, the whole being bounded by a paling of gaily-orna-
mented curling-brooms. On the floor were also to be seen four toboggans, presented by His Ex. to different people – one very lovely one
for me. When the first excitement had a little subsided we began to
take the things off the tree, and I am happy to say the children appeared well pleased with their presents.

WEDNESDAY, 29TH. – There was a great deal of curling to-day: in the
morning a match between D., F. Ward and Russell Stephenson, Mackenzie, Fred and Colonel Littleton. We also drew for the match for
my cup.

I anticipate great amusement in seeing Mrs. Littleton and Gwen
watching their husbands play: they are both very excited over a game,
and offer much advice, and groan and triumph alternately – the ladies,
I mean.

SATURDAY, NEW YEAR'S DAY, 1876. –We received our visitors between
twelve and two to-day – 225 gentlemen. The day was very mild – most
sad and un-Canadian; but at any rate the weather was decidedly interesting to talk about.

My children had invited all the workpeople and their children to
come to tea and to see their play, 'Little Nobody,' written by Mr.
Dixon. He has taken great pains with the scenery, which is quite
beyond that of a mere amateur stage. There is a street and a castle,
with a background of sea and sky, followed by a magnificent transformation scene, in which a silver-dressed fairy stands behind a star
of many colours, the rays of which gradually part and open, leaving
her supported on each side by minor fairies of the female sex, while
two male fairies sit in cars underneath. This is the last scene of the
play, and while this gorgeous sight is in the background the active
performers in the piece are grouped in the front. We had an appreciative audience, filling the room.

TUESDAY, 11TH. – A very important curling-match took place in our
rink, between the four 'Fredericks' of the Vice-regal Club and the
four 'Jameses' of the Ottawa Club. Alas! the Jameses won by one.
There was tobogganing after lunch. A lovely day – about zero.

WEDNESDAY, 12TH. – The married men of the Curling Club had a
match against the single ones. The best bachelor was absent, and
'little Campbell' (who is very short-sighted, and never plays) took his
place. He was a great element of amusement. In the first place, he
made by accident two most beautiful shots; then he fell in front of

a stone while sweeping. The bachelors were beaten by 18 to 2. There was much tobogganing in the afternoon, and a frightful upset, Fred and Colonel Littleton coming in with their noses scraped by the icy snow.

THURSDAY, 13TH. – The bachelors determined to try and regain their laurels to-day, and marched in procession to the Rink. They were dressed in white blanket-coats, wore kid gloves, and orange-flowers in their button-holes. Their fate was, however, as sad as yesterday.

MONDAY, 17TH. – We had a large children's party in the evening. When the fifty-five children and their mammas had arrived and seated themselves, 'Little Nobody' began, and went most successfully till near the end. In the middle of the last beautiful fairy transformation scene there was a fire, which might have been very bad. The man attending to the lime-light held a candle under an indiarubber pipe containing gas. The pipe melted, and the gas burnt furiously. There were people rushing about, water flowing, and a great scrimmage going on, during which the imperturbable queen of the fairies continued her speech. Darkness ensued; then we lifted the curtain and threw a rose-light over the scene. But of course the grand effect was spoilt, and the author and the carpenter burnt their hands a little.

WEDNESDAY, 19TH. – We begin to feel that the fancy ball is near. I have been writing out programmes. There are to be singing-quadrilles, valses, and lancers. The dancers have to learn and to rehearse their parts, and we expect this will be a very pretty feature.

TUESDAY, 25TH. – Spent a great deal of time over a most troublesome business – that of getting 150 parts copied for the singing-quadrille; that is, thirty copies of each figure. You may imagine the confusion and the difficulty of arranging all these separate bits of paper. Fred Ward does the hardest part; but I help – and dream of it.

In his book, published in 1878, *Canada under the Administration of the Earl of Dufferin,* George Stewart Junior thus describes the opening weeks of 1876:

The social season at Ottawa, which began on the first of January, 1876, with the performance of a fairy extravaganza at Government House, and continued till late in the spring, was an unusually gay and brilliant one. A Grand Fancy Dress Ball was given at Rideau Hall in February, and for weeks before and for many months after it had been held, it was the favourite topic of conversation throughout Canada. Fifteen hundred invitations were issued and nearly all of them were accepted. The dresses and costumes were of the most elaborate and costly character, and the affair passed off with great éclat. One very pleasant feature in this magnificent entertainment was the performance of a singing quadrille, happily executed.

Actually there were a number of these singing quadrilles, where the music was supplied by the dancers themselves, supported by a piano. The music, ingeniously harmonized to the dance steps, was based on nursery rhymes—"Hickory, Dickery Dock," "The Man in the Moon," "Sing a Song of Sixpence," "Jack and Jill," "Ride a Cock-horse," and many others.

SATURDAY, 29TH. – The thaw was so decided this morning that we gave up all idea of outdoor amusements. At two we rehearsed 'School,' which is to be our next play. As soon as the people had collected afterwards we danced, and I made the elderly people join. Waltzes and a cotillon wound up the day.

SUNDAY, 30TH. – The Comte Louis de Turenne arrived, and we took him a snow-shoe walk.

MONDAY, 31ST. – We all – D. and I, the Littletons, the Freds and Comte de Turenne – started in a private car for Montreal.

Although Lady Dufferin heads this chapter 'An Uneventful Season,' it was a busy one socially. Because of the many events scheduled to take place in Ottawa, their stay in Montreal was less than a week.

WEDNESDAY, FEBRUARY 2ND. – A stormy, snowy day, extremely cold, and no admittance to the Rink. In the evening there was a fancy dress ball on the ice. The Count, the Littletons, and those who had not seen this before, were delighted with the sight. I danced a set of lancers and some other things with D.

THURSDAY, 3RD. – Some good skating in the morning, then a grand lunch at Mr. Ryan's, which our three Fredericks had to leave early, as they were going to join the fourth Frederick in playing against four Jameses. We meant to go and see the game, but when we arrived we met our party coming out, victorious and radiant.

SATURDAY, 5TH. – We left Montreal by the morning train taking with us the Comte de Turenne and Gawen. [Her brother, Colonel Gawen R. Hamilton.]

TUESDAY, 8TH. – The Marquis and Marquise de Bassano arrived this afternoon, just as we were finishing a labourious rehearsal of part of 'School.'

WEDNESDAY, 9TH. – A cold, windy day; however we went out and skated. The Comte de Turenne is working hard at the outside edge. The Cabinet dinner took place to-night, and the new Ministers came for the first time in their uniforms. The dinner was in the ball-room, and we had a band to play during the evening.

THURSDAY, 10TH. – In the morning we had some skating and curling; the day was beautiful and mild. After lunch we went to the opening of Parliament.

On our return the energetic gentlemen had a great afternoon's tobogganing. Madame de Bassano and I rested, as we had to dine at seven, and be present at the Drawing-Room afterwards. I never saw so many people at one before, and I must have made an enormous number of curtseys. The boys went to a dance after the Drawing-Room.

FRIDAY, 11TH. – A complete thaw, with pouring rain. The Bassanos left, and in the afternoon we rehearsed the first two acts of 'School' – very successfully. Mr. Kimber and Miss Fellowes remained for dinner, and in the evening the other twenty-eight singers arrived, and we rehearsed the singing-quadrilles, lancers, and waltz. The lancers went beautifully, and the waltz is very pretty.

SATURDAY, 12TH. – This was such a lovely day, so bright and so mild that it was doubtful whether there would be any skating. Guests kept telegraphing from Ottawa, 'Can I bring my toboggan?'

> Since the telephone had not then come into use, the telegraph served as an instrument of rapid communication for those fortunate enough to have that convenience at their disposal. Rideau Hall was in New Edinburgh, a village now within the boundaries of the City of Ottawa.

Fortunately, we were able both to skate and to toboggan, and as it was very pleasant for the lookers-on, we remained out till past five, and had a most successful party. This is the last we can have before our ball, which now draws near.

Our new supper-room, with its red-and-white tent, let down inside the tennis-court, and the shields bearing the arms of the various provinces hung round its walls, will be very pretty. The ball-room is wreathed in roses.

WEDNESDAY, 23RD. – The American painter, Mr. Bierstadt, and his wife are staying in the house with us, and he has begun to paint me a picture as a remembrance of his visit. It will be a nice thing to have. We went out and saw the great curling-match of the year, for His Ex.'s medal. Montreal won it. The sixteen players had lunch with us.

We dressed for the fancy ball at nine – all our household in costumes of the same period – and walked in procession up the room. The dresses of our guests were beautiful, and there was great variety in them. The singing-dances and the new supper-room were much admired, and when people went away at 4 a.m. they seemed extremely pleased.

Under the title 'The Governor-General's Fancy Ball,' the *Canadian Illustrated News* of March 18, 1876, in an article several columns long, reported:

There never was so splendid a ball on this side of the Atlantic as that given by their Excellencies on the 23rd ult. It has not often been excelled, even where silks and satins are more indigenous to the soil than in this young Canada of ours.

As for preparation. There has been one long, golden, glorious harvest reaped by the tradesmen during the past three months, and many a hungry, slender purse has found itself filled by deft fingers working in silks, satins and velvets, to say nothing of leather and collodion.

The issuing of some 1500 invitations gathered celebrities from all parts of the known and unknown world. The noble proportions of the splendid room, with its exquisitely delicate tints of colouring on ceiling and walls, were brought out to the fullest extent by hundreds of wax candles, grouped round the sides, in addition to ordinary light afforded by gas chandeliers and brackets. Festoons of roses hung in graceful curves round the pilasters from the floor to the ceiling, while at the far end of the room stood, on a dais of three crimson steps, the throne surmounted by an imperial crown.

The Vice-regal party walked in procession through the room to the dais. Their Excellencies, their Staff and household represented the

Court of King James V of Scotland, Viscount Clandeboye and Lady Helen Blackwood personating the characters of Lord Darnley and Princess Mary—better known as Mary, Queen of Scots—when children.

The artistic disposition of the Vice-Royal party, with the richness and beauty of their dresses, accurate in every detail, made a picture of the living likeness of the age represented. His Excellency's costume, though very rich, was perhaps the plainest in the room; but the good taste that marked its selection made his plain black and gold-clad figure more distinctively the figure there. He had on a black velvet cap with white feather, fastened by a diamond aigrette; he wore the stars and collars of his orders.

The countess, in whom the charm of youth is blended with that of maternity, looked the prettiest woman in the room, while her magnificent dress showed to advantage the graceful figure, which has so often won compliments and admiration for its charming owner. Her Excellency had a petticoat of crimson satin, white satin train, with two rows of gold embroidery, crimson velvet robe, bordered with ermine, crimson velvet hat, white feather banded with shamrocks in diamonds, ruff edged with gold.

Their Excellencies' three eldest children, whose childish grace and handsome dresses added to the interest of the scene, sat at the foot of the throne, while the rest of the group was composed of visitors to the Hall and members of the Staff.

One of the funniest things was the supreme indifference on the part of the two royal pages, sons of His Excellency and Colonel Littleton, Terence Blackwood and A. Littleton. During the performance of the opening quadrille, they comfortably ensconced themselves in the two State Chairs, and with drawn swords were most delightfully engaged in a dire though luxurious combat. The clash of steel was covered by the music.

The Toronto *Globe* of February 24 devoted nine columns to an account of the ball, naming hundreds of guests with their costumes. As well it described the supper-room, "dazzling with massive gold and silver plate," while down the long tables gleamed the gold spurs and roses presented annually to the Lord and Lady of Clandeboye — the tribute by which the Hamiltons of Killyleagh had held the barbican of their castle from their kinsmen, the Earls of Dufferin, whose property line had run through it.

SATURDAY, 26TH. – It snowed hard – in fact, I have never seen the snow round us so deep. The Littletons have to be dug out every day, and the road to their house is on a level with the palings.

MONDAY, 28TH. – The French members of the Commons gave a beautiful ball in the new Library at Ottawa, to which we went. The room, an enormous round building, was very well lighted. I believe 1,500 people were in it, and there was no crush at all. Numbers of people wore their fancy dresses.

> The design for this circular library first appeared in 1859, in a ground plan prepared by Frederick William Cumberland, who later became one of Lord Dufferin's aides. Only a small part of its south wall touched the Parliament Buildings proper. However, it was not erected for over fifteen years. Its peculiar isolation, even though directly connected, allowed it to be preserved during the fire which destroyed the main Parliament Buildings in 1916.

WEDNESDAY, MARCH 1ST. – The Comte de Turenne arrived for the play. The actors dined early, in D.'s room. Then I went to dress for Mrs. Honeyton, in the 'Happy Pair.' Then the 'School' arrived, and began to dress in one room, and the men had another, and the guests came crowding in, and got off their things in the school-room, and there was painting and curling and excitement going on everywhere.

Fred and I began the performance with 'A Happy Pair,' and had a very warm audience, which was pleasant. 'School' is a difficult piece for amateurs; but I must say it was an unequivocal success. Every part was well done. It was quite new here, so the audience liked it immensely.

I was really surprised when I came into the supper-room to see how handsome it looked. It certainly is a much-needed addition to the house, enabling us to give supper to a large party at once. Afterwards I went into the drawing-room, and said good-night to all the beaming crowd.

TUESDAY, APRIL 11TH. – Such a lovely day. We play tennis, walk, lunch, practise some music, drive into Ottawa, and go to a birthday-party of the Littletons, where there was to be a magic lantern. I took six children, and Victoria enjoyed her first party immensely, and applauded every slide. When a somewhat undraped statue was exhibited, she exclaimed that 'Hallie would pip (whip) her.'

MONDAY, 17TH. – Gwen, Miss Abbot and I drove into Ottawa in the morning, and after lunch walked to the river Rideau to see the ice coming down. We stood watching great blocks go over the Falls; but after a little found that a new bridge immediately over them, upon which we had been a few minutes before, had been partly carried away. We sat down where we could have a good view of the river, and saw such a *smashing*, and heard such a *crashing* of timber. There was great excitement – men and horses hard at work cutting and dragging away what could be saved from the wreck.

THURSDAY, MAY 11TH. – The waters of the Ottawa are six feet higher than they have been for years, and there is more ice to come down; there are floods everywhere.

TUESDAY, 16TH. – The weather deserves to be recorded, fine, bright and sunny, unlike anything we have had before this month. A few mosquitoes were able to appear, but they are not strong enough either to buzz or bite.

THURSDAY, JUNE 1ST – 103° in the shade. I was 'at home,' and received my visitors in the garden from four to six, when it was cooler and very pleasant.

WEDNESDAY, 7TH. – D. and I, Nelly, the Smyths, and Littletons, left by steamer at seven o'clock in the morning, and landed at Buckingham at eight. There we saw a waterfall, *en passent*. The river Le Lièvre, a large tributary of the Ottawa, rushes through a narrow passage, and the water tumbles over rocks and stones. Nelly was delighted, and kept up a fire of joyful exclamations, which helped us to like getting up so early.

After driving through the village of Buckingham, gaily decorated with flags and arches, we got out at a wharf, and found a small steam-launch ready to take us up the river. We had twenty-five miles to go, and were to be four hours doing it. There were some swift rapids in the river. We were told the steamer was too heavily laden, and that some of us must get out. We had a good deal of trouble landing the gentlemen, D. only remaining with us.

The small engine puffed away, but we made no progress, and we got very frightened. The bell-rope which the pilot used for giving his orders had burnt through, a lace curtain having caught fire early in the day. When he called out his orders the stoker did not always seem to hear.

D. tried to reassure us, but when we looked out and found we remained exactly in the same place – off a great rock – we ladies were in an agony of terror. Then the boat began to turn round, and the gentlemen on shore were frightened too. They feared that while we had this powerful stream broadside on, we should be toppled over. Nelly and I were both in tears. It makes me laugh now to think of Nelly's face, the tears pouring down, as she exclaimed: 'Oh! it will be so horrid to be drowned.' However, we did get to shore, and there landed, so that the steamer was light enough to get up the rapids, while we walked, and got into her above them.

It was three o'clock before we landed, still trembling, and had lunch on the shore. After that we had to walk a mile and a half to see the Fall, the object of our expedition. The walk was rough, and we had some climbing and steep places. About six we returned to our boat. When we asked for something to drink we found that everything had disappeared from our basket. Lucky for us that drinks had been preferred to silver spoons!

We found a large bonfire burning at Buckingham, and a crowd of people. There we got into the carriages, and prospered till we came to a steep hill with a precipice on one side, in the middle of which our horses jibbed, and when they got us well to the edge of the 'precipice,' Nelly and I escaped through the window (a large one). The horses were led down the hill, and D. reproached us for leaving him alone in his peril. We got back about eleven, very tired!

MONDAY, 12TH. – Packing day! Very hot, and everyone melting and busy. Boxes and bags yawning all over the house. A holiday for the children.

THURSDAY, 15TH. – We started early in the morning by train to Prescott, there got into the steamer, and had a pleasant voyage to Montreal, where we changed from one steamer to another, and came on to Quebec.

QUEBEC: FRIDAY, 16TH. – Arrived early, and landed at eight; the Lieutenant-Governor and a guard of honour came to meet us, and we found the children waiting breakfast. It was very hot, and we did not go out till evening. D. and I then walked over the scene of the late Fire – desolation over a large space.

SATURDAY, 17TH. – We went to see the temporary accommodation arranged for the sufferers; charities have taken in some, and drill-sheds and barracks hold others. In the evening we went to see the 'Busy Bees' perform. They are the officers and soldiers of the B Battery, and represented on this occasion the Christy Minstrels, singing songs, etc.

In 1844 Edwin P. Christy, a banjoist and actor, advertised: 'Christy's Far-Famed and Original Band of Ethiopian Minstrels, whose unique and chaste performances have been patronized by the élite and fashion of all the principal cities of the Union.'

His was no idle boast. This troupe, with blackened faces, singing Negro melodies, while Christy as interlocutor interspersed jokes, became famous. In their earlier days, Christy, or some member of his company, composed most of their songs. But later, the ones that were to live and be so appealing were from the pen of Stephen Foster. Christy secured from Foster the right to sing these prior to publication. This gave Foster an immediate and appreciative audience. In the eighteen-fifties the minstrels toured England, receiving great acclaim.

MONDAY, 19TH. – Three strangers dined with us: a Frenchman, an Austrian, and an Englishman. D. enjoyed it, as he heard something of European politics. I was 'at home,' and saw many old friends in the afternoon.

TUESDAY, 20TH. – At ten o'clock there was a parade on the Esplanade; then D. presented some medals and prizes won by the Battery.

WEDNESDAY, 21ST. – The citizens of Quebec gave a great dinner to the Governor-General to-night. The room was most beautifully arranged, and the stage, at the far end of it, looked like a garden, with real flower-beds in the foreground, and a painted shrubbery behind them.

There was one long, straight table, at which the principal guests were sitting, with the Governor-General in the middle; and four more long ones ran down the room towards the gallery. About 200 gentlemen were present.

D. and his speech were immensely well received, and he spoke very well. He began by saying, 'I cannot help remembering under what various conditions, in how many vital emergencies, at what supreme epochs in its history, during the last 300 years, my illustrious predecessors must have had occasion to harangue the citizens of Quebec. In a thousand vicissitudes of fortune, in perpetual alternations of triumph and despondency – when hordes of savages were lurking round your palisades; when famine had prostrated your strength, and the unaccustomed rigours of an Arctic winter had benumbed your faculties; when novel forms of pestilence devasted your homes, crowning your clergy and your sisterhoods with the aureole of martyrdom; when foreign leaguers assaulted your independence, and hostile cannon threatened your battlements – Viceroy after Viceroy has appealed to your patience, your fortitude, your charity, your patriotism, and never once, whether in good fortune or ill fortune, as your history tells us, has the appeal been made in vain.' At the end he proposed the toast of 'Prosperity to Quebec.'

FRIDAY, 23RD. – We visited the Sillery Convent, and then walked into a place belonging to Colonel Rhodes. He has underground gardens, which supply flowers, mushrooms, winter salads, etc. The Colonel, who entertained us most hospitably, has made quite a name for himself as a practical gardener here. The view from his house is lovely.

On our return home we had a long visit from the Bassanos, who were delighted with our platform. After dinner the soldiers had some very good theatricals.

SATURDAY, 24TH. – D. went down to the steamer to say a few words to the Canadian rifle-team, now starting for Wimbledon. I was 'at home,' and the lovely morning turned into a bad afternoon – thunder, showers and wind. Though I had many visitors they were all uncomfortable. Some feared for their gowns, some disliked thunder, and some thought it would frighten their horses; and I sincerely sympathised with them all.

MONDAY, 26TH. – We saw the procession of Jean Baptiste pass through the town on the way to the church. This is the great festival at Quebec. We returned home in time to see Gwen and Russell off to Montreal, and Gwen was obliged to continue waving her handkerchief to the children for several miles down the river.

In the evening we attended a concert given by the Jean Baptiste society. An address was presented to D., a great bouquet and gilt china jar to me, and fireworks were sent after us as we departed.

TUESDAY, 27TH. – A busy day, preparing again for departure. I made time to call upon Lady Belleau, and took four children to see the Ursulines. It is a great treat to them to visit the nuns in their cage, and to receive maple sugar through the bars.

WEDNESDAY, 28TH. – We got off in the *Druid;* a lovely day, and everything on board very comfortable. We enjoyed sailing calmly on the beautiful river. Mr. Gregory, the official who furnishes the yacht, presented me with a key and a list of goodies, which he bought for my special benefit, and had locked up for me.

FRIDAY, 30TH. – Arrived at Gaspé at eight o'clock, most fortunate in having had so good a passage. Bad news of our river: they say it is much too high for fishing. We went up to it, however – an hour's drive and three hours on horseback – Archie being the only one who really enjoyed this. Our servants had made our huts look very nice, and after lunch we went out to try the river; but the news was too true – the water was much too 'heavy.' We returned home to dinner – and mosquitoes. Let me say at once that these torments are ever present, and are quite intolerable.

SATURDAY, JULY, 1ST. – Having no hope of salmon here, D. and Fred went off to the York River, where they had been invited to fish, and which is an earlier river than ours. I sat all day in mosquito-armour reading, Archie took charge of smudges, and occupied himself in various small devices for killing time, and at eight o'clock D. and Fred returned. D. had caught five salmon and a grilse, the average weight of the salmon being 24 lbs., the largest one 28 lbs. Fred had one salmon of 26 lbs. and a large trout of 5 lbs. His salmon had been foul-hooked, and took him two hours to kill.

MONDAY, 3RD. – As it has rained again, we resolved to return to our comfortable and mosquito-less *Druid*. D. and Fred went up to the York. This time D. got one, and Fred five, the largest 32 lbs.

TUESDAY, 4TH. – Three hours' driving and walking brought us to our pool, called Miller's Landing. I soon had the pleasure of a rise. I stood up in the canoe to throw the fly, and sat down to manage my rod when the fish was on, for it would be no joke to upset the boat in these swift rivers. I landed my victim with success, and he weighed 21 lbs. I tried once more, and caught another, 24 lbs. D. and I then had lunch, and I returned home at four, while he fished on, and brought two more salmon home in the evening.

We had a jolly little dinner when we met again, and enjoy being comfortably on board after our experiences of the 'Bush.' The owner of this river, with his party, caught fifty-seven salmon, averaging 23 lbs., the first week he was up here.

WEDNESDAY, 5TH. – We went ashore 'to shop,' and D. visited two schools. After lunch we fished for 'Tommy cods.' We sat in the boat and fished over the side. The excitement was in the variety of the game – sea toads, flat fish, Tommy cods, smelts, blue-fish. We brought home a bucketful.

SUNDAY, 9TH. – We went to church in the morning, and in the afternoon took a most lovely walk. The weather was beautiful.

MONDAY, 10TH. – This morning Fred and Archie started for the Bush, and D. and I went to fish the lower pools, intending to sleep here, and to follow them to-morrow.

D. went on foot taking with him a little boy to act as guide. On the way, this boy told him his father had been drowned two months ago, about twenty miles up the river, having slipped into a rapid as he was pushing some felled wood into the stream, and that his body had never been found. To-day, when fishing from a canoe, as he was looking over the side, he saw lying in about fifteen feet of water, the body of the poor man. It was in the same condition as on the day of his death, having been preserved in the ice-cold water.

WEDNESDAY, 12TH. – D. did not go out this morning, and sent in his stead our captain, a nice old man, who has never caught a salmon in his life. He returned at two o'clock highly delighted with a twenty-pounder he had landed, and which we have sent off to his wife.

SATURDAY, 15TH. – I went up the river with D. and Fred to catch trout. D. was anxious to make up his forty salmon [at that date he had landed thirty-eight], but he was only able to capture a grilse. When we returned to the ship, we dined, said good-bye to all the men, and started for Tadousac.

MONDAY, 17TH. – We were in sight of Tadousac about one o'clock, and immediately shrieked from our steam-whistle to report ourselves to the children. They came down to the beach to meet us.

TUESDAY, 18TH. – We keep Archie's birthday to-day, so a haycart, a buck-board, and a horse were ordered, and D. and I, five children, and Mademoiselle packed into the cart. Archie rode, and Fred, Mr. Dixon, and the provisions came in the buck-board.

We drove to a place where there is a small waterfall and a mill, lunched there, stayed till it was time for a cup of tea, and then mounted our carts and drove 'round the Concession.' The buck-board broke down, and we had to borrow a cart. As the road home was very rough, the fun of the expedition consisted chiefly in the fearful bumps we got! All our plates and cups were smashed, and I felt much bruised and shaken; but the children enjoyed it immensely.

THURSDAY, 20TH. – We left Tadousac to-day, and had to say good-bye to Archie, who now goes to school in England – so the first break in our home circle is made. Parting with him took off rather from the distress of parting with the others; though even from them we shall be away some time. We left in a great shower and thunderstorm, and had to anchor some hours in a fog.

OTTAWA: MONDAY, 24TH. – Delighted to get to Rideau in the evening. Found the weather cool enough for fires.

25TH-29TH. – The week has been spent in arranging for our departure for the Grand Tour. A great difference of opinion exists as to what we shall want *en route*. Some say take provisions, others say don't. We decided, however, in the first place, to have a box made to hold plates, cups and saucers, knives and forks, tea, salt, etc. Then we take cases of preserved meats, a basket of eggs, some butter, Devonshire cream, and jam, and we have a refrigerator in our baggage-car. So we shan't starve, as we can add our own delicacies to the tough antelope-steaks we are to get on the way. [These were preparations for the forthcoming trip to British Columbia.]

Mr. Reynolds has taken the greatest pains about our comfort in the railway carriages. Fred Ward arrived Saturday night, so we are now ready for our departure.

CHAPTER 15

Across the Continent and Along the Pacific Coast

AUGUST-SEPTEMBER 1876

Over the caption, *British Columbia in a Pet*, the front page of the *Canadian Illustrated News* of September 9, 1876, carried a timely cartoon. A benign, bearded Uncle Aleck (Alexander Mackenzie, the Prime Minister) is bending solicitously over a peevish, pouting young woman, and saying: "Don't frown so, my dear, you'll get your railway by-and-bye." To which Miss British Columbia replies: "I want it now. You promised I should have it, and if I don't, I'll complain to Ma [Queen Victoria]." It was unrest and dissatisfaction in the Pacific province that lay behind Lord Dufferin's trip.

When, in 1871, with a flourish of trumpets, British Columbia entered Confederation, the Dominion of Canada committed itself to build a railway across the continent—the project to be commenced within two years and completed within ten. Both sides should have known such an undertaking was impossible, since six hundred miles of unsurveyed mountains barred its path.

Despite diligent surveys, the route it was to take had still not been determined. Appeals to the Colonial Secretary, Lord Carnarvon, had extended the time to sixteen years, with the understanding a railway would be commenced on Vancouver Island, from Nanaimo (where coal had been discovered) to Victoria. This would eventually be pushed northward, crossing islands and narrow straits, until linked to the suggested terminus of the transcontinental line at Bute Inlet.

These so-called Carnarvon Terms had only increased the dissension. Parliament passed a bill agreeing to the terms; the Senate threw it out. An alternative suggestion, that the province be given $750,000 and allowed to build the Vancouver Island Railway itself, was rejected.

British Columbia was talking of secession, or even annexation to the United States.

Isolation, distance and false reports had bred misunderstanding and mistrust. Prime Minister Mackenzie was baffled by this unsolved problem, bequeathed to him by a former Ministry. Lord Dufferin was asked to make the long trip across the continent, to listen to complaints, ascertain opinions, while reassuring a discontented people that Canada would keep faith with them.

SUNDAY, JULY 30TH. – I must begin my account of this Grand Tour one day before its actual commencement, because upon this Sunday, when even our rugs were rolled up in their straps, and only finishing touches remained to be put to our piles of luggage, a blow fell upon us. Dr. Grant called to inform me that Mrs. Littleton was ill, and that in bed she must remain for at least ten days.

I went over to see her, and found her dreadfully disappointed, but a little comforted by the hope of following us when she recovers. To me, and indeed to us all, as a party, she is a great loss – she is always so cheery, and so ready to enjoy everything.

MONDAY, 31ST. – We breakfasted comfortably, and went to the station at 10.30. There we were received by the Governor-General's Guards, and by a great many friends who came to wish us 'good-bye.' We have a whole Pullman to ourselves, and 'two drawing-rooms'; these last are small, square cabins, where four berths can be made up. My lucky maid inherits Mrs. Littleton's, and as it can be opened into mine I also have some additional space. The three gentlemen – Colonel L. and the two Freds [Captain F. R. Hamilton, A.D.C., and Captain Fred Ward, A.D.C.] – sleep in the Pullman, and we all live in it by day, when the top berths shut up and disappear, and the under beds turn into seats for four.

At Prescott we lunched in the station, and then returned to our 'house-upon-wheels,' and really began to live the life that is to be ours for seven days. Here I was introduced to the American reporter, who comes with us to give an account of our tour in one of the New York papers. During the day he became so enthusiastic over the delightful prospect before us, that he made known to me, through Fred, his desire to invite a charming young lady of his acquaintance to share the enjoyment of the trip, assuring him that, if only I would lend her the shelter of my name, no more active chaperonage would be required of me; and that her mother – too delicate to undertake such a journey herself – would be perfectly satisfied with this arrangement for her daughter. He proposed, with my approval, to telegraph at once and arrange for the girl to join our special train at some station on the way. Hard-hearted, prim Englishwoman that I am, I felt obliged to discourage the scheme!

Our next amusement was our five o'clock tea. Mr. Reynolds had made us a most ingenious 'portable kitchen,' and we all sat and watched our kettle boil, and were extremely particular about scalding our teapot, etc. We had an excellent cup of tea, in spite of the watching and the number of cooks; so we set two proverbs at defiance with impunity.

I have a comfortable chair (between the railway-couches), and I sat in it, did a little work, read and talked till eight, when we reached Cobourg, where we had supper or dinner, whichever you like to call it. The evening is the least pleasant part of the day; the light in the cars is not sufficient to read by, and we do not always feel inclined for games.

TUESDAY, AUGUST 1ST. – We slept pretty well, though often awoke for a moment by the unusual sounds and shakings. We crossed in our train to the American side by means of a ferry opposite Sarnia. [The Grand Trunk Railway tunnel under the St. Clair River was not opened until September 1891.]

When we were dressed, and our carriage turned into its day condition, we got ready our breakfast; the public had theirs at Sarnia. A most excellent meal we had: fresh-boiled eggs, which Fred Ward superintended; tea, Mr. Reynold's home-made bread, our own butter and Devonshire cream, potted meat, a cold chicken, raspberries, and jam! We enjoyed it all very much, which accounts for my telling you so much about it.

We were so warm and so dusty by the end of the day, that the sight of Lake Michigan, and the pleasant fresh air from it, as we passed close to it into Chicago were very delightful. Crowds of people were bathing, and we longed to join them.

When we arrived at the Palmer House Hotel, we were shown into the most gorgeous suite of rooms: a drawing-room with marble statues, satin curtains, embroidered chairs, gold and carving and pictures; a dining-room furnished with pretty light wood, oh, so smart! a bedroom too splendid to sleep in, and with a magnificent satin cover over the bed; a bath-room off it, and a large room, with two 'unique' beds in it, for a dressing-room. We settled into these magnificences as well as we could, but I think we rather agreed with my maid, who said that at the end of a long day in a train one did not feel inclined to be 'bothered with so much splendour.'

WEDNESDAY, 2ND. – The Count de Turenne breakfasted with us, and drove with us to the station. Mr. Palmer took a tender farewell of 'Mr. and Mrs.' Dufferin, as he called us, and Mr. Forrest and his daughters (old acquaintances) also saw us off, and I was introduced to Mr. St. John, the 'Globe' reporter.

> Frederick Edward Molyneux St. John was born in Newcastle, England. In 1870, when thirty-two years of age, as special correspondent for the Toronto *Globe*, he accompanied Lord Wolseley on his expedition to the Red River.
>
> The account of the trip with the Dufferins, which he was now reporting, was published in 1877 in two volumes under the title, *The Sea of Mountains*. Shortly before his death in Ottawa in 1904, he was appointed Gentleman Usher of the Black Rod.
>
> Two other special correspondents also accompanied the Dufferin party—Mr. E. Horton of the Toronto *Mail*, and Mr. J. B. Stillson of the New York *World*.

The Chicago morning paper speaks of me as 'Her Royal Nibess,' and says that I do not wish my 'hubbie to go to see the "Nausty" man,' Brigham Young. [Twenty-nine years earlier, in 1847, the Mormons, under the leadership of Brigham Young, had settled in Utah and founded Salt Lake Ctiy.] It also reports that we went to bed early to 'save gas,' and that 'if our money holds out' we shall go to the Centennial [at Philadelphia].

We had rather a pleasant day; it was less dusty, some of the country rich and well cultivated, vineyards to be seen, and nice little homesteads; we saw some prairie land, and in the evening stood outside our car to cross the Mississippi [at Burlington]. There is a beautifully light bridge over it, 2,260 feet long. It is a sensation to see this river, of which one has heard so much; and a great river can't help being striking, but there is nothing grand in the scenery at this point.

We lunched and dined at stations, Burlington being the principal one at which we stopped. After dinner we played whist, and all agreed we had got over the day very well.

THURSDAY, 3RD. – We had a very bad night – stopping so constantly it was almost impossible to sleep – and I was not, therefore, in good condition for trying the 'hotel car,' which was put on. There seemed to be an excellent meal provided; but the room was hot, and smelt of food, and I longed for our own little quiet breakfast.

At ten we reached Omaha, and crossed the Missouri – such an extremely muddy river, it excites no desire to bathe in it. Carriages awaited us here, and we drove up to our hotel, and chose our rooms. They really are very good for this last point of civilization, before the prairie begins.

D. and I took a drive to see the town, and we sat on the steps of the High School while he made a sketch of the view: low hills in the background, the Missouri twisting about through muddy-looking plains, and the small town in the foreground.

We took another walk later in the day, and saw our first Chinaman – a neat young man, all in black, with his coat cut after the fashion of his country. The streets of Omaha are very new, with bridges of loose planks between the footpath and the street. The houses are low and square-looking; but there is a fine post-office. The Mayor called upon D., and one resident Canadian presented an address.

FRIDAY, 4TH. – We left Omaha in the morning, and had a most delightful day. The weather was perfect: warm enough to sit with every window open, and yet fresh and pleasant; no dust, and a most exhilarating atmosphere. We are rising all day, going slowly over the Rocky Mountains; the train moves at an easy sort of jog-trot, and we thoroughly enjoy everything.

We passed through the Platte Valley, the river Platte running at some distance from us all day. The scenery, if not beautiful, is interesting: a great sea of land, very flat, but with a good soil, and giving one an extraordinary idea of the capabilities of the country and of the room in it.

We lunched at Fremont, and dined at Grand Island. There is a difference of opinion as to the food at these stations. My idea is that it is excellent; the reporters and my maid think it is disgusting. This difference of opinion can be explained. If you require a meat dinner, you will find it bad; but I want neither meat nor wine, and can live upon the things which we get good everywhere: tumblers full of iced milk, good bread, butter, eggs, fish, and iced cream! – the latter, at the most unpromising stations, rivals Gunter. We generally have a table reserved for us, and at Fremont a very smart negro, with a beautiful peacock-feather fan, brushed the flies away while we lunched.

SATURDAY, 5TH. – We slept much better last night, and I did not even

awake when we were stopped by – the grasshoppers! They get on the
rails, and, being squashed there, oil them, so that the engine can
scarcely pull the carriages along, as the wheels don't bite.

When we did awake, we found ourselves on the Rocky Plains, a
delicious wind blowing, and not bringing the dust to us. When we
look back from the train it does not appear desolate: great plains of
dull-coloured grass, broken by rocky mounds, which present a white
appearance to the eye; in fact a part of the Rocky Mountains. We
have risen 3,600 feet since we left Omaha, and I suppose the delicious
air makes everything appear *coleur de rose*.

We have seen flocks of cattle, and four antelopes. The curious
thing is, that you see cattle apparently quite near, but on consideration
you realize they must be very far away, as you cannot make out the
details; a man on horseback that you fancy quite close, looks like a
stone moving. There are no trees or houses, or any object by which
to judge distances, and the atmosphere is wonderfully clear.

This is very like being at sea: the wind whistles round the car, and
the land round us is flat, with white-crested waves of rocky sandhills,
while the air is most exhilarating. But I must not, under its intoxi-
cating influence, fill up my journal with rhapsodies.

We lunched at Cheyenne, and were met there by the Governor of
the territory [Wyoming, organized in 1868], Mr. Thayer. There is a
large hotel at Cheyenne, and it is 'quite a place.' After leaving it the
scenery became lovely.

First, we had the interest of the plains, with its little prairie dogs
to watch, the gophers – a sort of ground-squirrel – and an occasional
antelope; then the plain broke up into undulating hills and heaps
of rock, a few scattered trees, and the magnificent range of Rocky
Mountains, with patches of snow relieving their blueness, in the distance. Some of the 'heaps of rock' look like ruined castles, for the
stones are piled one upon another. I think the views enchanting, and
I breathe the air with pleasure. At Sherman we reached our highest
point (8,263 feet), and soon after we went over a sort of skeleton
bridge, without a parapet, across a ravine.

The wind, of which there is a good deal, blew off the lid of our
precious kettle, but luckily we stopped a moment after, and it was
rescued.

SUNDAY, 6TH. – The scenery early in the day was ugly; sandy, desolate
plains – 'the Artemisian Desert,' it is called, or 'the Alkali Plains.'

Breakfast and lunch, at Evanston, were served by 'John Chinaman.'

They wore clean white blouses, loose blue trousers, and stumpy embroidered shoes, their long pigtails twisted round their heads and fastened up. Their height, their dress, their hair, and their singularly mild expression, make them very feminine looking.

> The pigtail, or plaited queue of hair worn at the back, was introduced into China by the Manchu conquerors about 1644 A.D. This fashion persisted until early in the twentieth century.

At Evanston there were some very Indian Indians, dressed in brilliant rags, waiting for gifts of food, and a number of boys with arrows. The Colonel set up a coin on a stick for them to shoot at, and one split the stick. He also knocked the cork off a bottle without touching the bottle.

The guide-book told us that after leaving Evanston we were to watch with 'full breath and anxious heart' for the magnificent scenery through the Echo Canyon. By evening we came down hill through the valley, starting from a great upland of the Uintah Range of the Rocky Mountains. On one side were green sloping banks, while on the other were gigantic hills of rough, red stone, twisted and tilted and tumbled into every sort of strange form – castles and pulpits, monuments, – all kinds of devices seemed to stand before us.

For several hours we had a little stream close to us, and as the day became very hot, the river seemed most refreshing, and added a foreground of fresh green to the magnificent views in the distance. We passed the Thousand Mile Tree, – 1,000 miles from Omaha, – and close to it 'the Devil's Slide,' a curious geological formation: two natural walls of rock down the side of a hill, with just sufficient room between them for 'Him' to slide through.

A short time before we came to Ogden we came through the Rocky Mountains, passing quite close to patches of snow, and looking back upon a much more rocky appearance than the mountains have from the other side. Do you understand that from Omaha the country gradually slants upwards towards these mountains, and that the railroad mounts to a height of 8,242 feet, after which it suddenly descends? Do you realize that now the rivers flow the other way, and that we have crossed the Great Range?

An American general came to have tea, or rather iced water, in our car, and stayed till we reached Ogden. We part from our car and our two conductors here; the lines of railroad change, and we have to get into another car.

The trip to the West Coast was over a number of different railways. They began their journey on the Ottawa and Prescott Railway; from Prescott to Sarnia, and on to Detroit, the Grand Trunk Railway; the remainder of the way to Chicago, the Michigan Central Railway; from Chicago to Omaha, the Burlington and Quincy Railway; from Omaha to Ogden, the Union Pacific; from Ogden to Oaklands, the Central Pacific (now known as the Southern Pacific).

We had arranged to sleep at Ogden, and on arriving there, at six, we visited our rooms. They were frightfully hot, for the weather is very warm. The village is in a valley, and there are stony hills straight opposite the house. This is on the way to Salt Lake City, and this place is almost full of Mormons. So, of course, when Fred and I took a little walk, we fancied every two women we saw together were colleague-wives, and every house to us seemed to have several entrances for the various ladies of the family.

MONDAY, 7TH. – We had every door and window of our rooms open, and so spent a tolerably cool night. All the morning we sat on the platform of the station. The thermometer was 99° in the shade. In the afternoon, D. and I went for a drive up the Ogden Canyon, the same thing, in miniature, as the Echo Canyon, through which the railway goes. Our driver gave us much information as we went along, showed us the house of a bishop who owns eight wives and forty children, one of the wives busy clothes-washing at the back door. Our reporters went to Salt Lake and interviewed Brigham Young.

Under their 'prophet,' Brigham Young, 1801-77, the Mormons left Nauvoo in Illinois and established a settlement in Salt Lake City, 1847. Young proclaimed the doctrine of polygamy, but ultimately this was abolished by the Government.

Ogden has no time of its own, but keeps 'East' time for one train, and 'West' time for the other. A perpetual sum of mental arithmetic goes on, and we were constantly forgetting by which time we ought to go, and trying to remember whether the 'left-hand clock,' or the 'right-hand clock' was ours.

About three years later Sir Sandford Fleming suggested 'time zones'— a concept which was adopted by international agreement, and became known as 'standard time.'

We left in the evening, and found our new carriage very comfort-able though it has only one 'drawing-room.' We sat at the end of it – the last of the whole train – and passed by moonlight along the banks of the Salt Lake.

TUESDAY, 8TH. – We are going through the Alkali Plains, and the dust is dreadful: a large, rough dust, covering everything in a second, and very painful to the eyes. As I write this my paper is like a ploughed field, and, the wind being very high, one can only see a few yards for the clouds that surround the carriage. The only thing that grows on these plains is sage, and a 'sage-bush' here is the worst name one can apply to any vegetable growth.

WEDNESDAY, 9TH. – We got up at six this morning in California, the sandy desert changing into a mountainous district covered with pine and oak, parts of it laid bare like a great quarry by the mining for gold. As one looks back upon the country through which one has just passed, it seems perfectly impossible that the railway should really have made its way through such steep and perpendicular rocks, which seem more fitted for the Alpine traveller with his helpful stick than for an immense long train like ours.

The point of interest is 'rounding Cape Horn.' There is a 'path' just wide enough for the railway round a precipitous rock, and one looks straight down upon the valley far beneath. I find the skeleton bridges very trying to the nerves; one can see through them, and they make no attempt at having sides, and are so weak-looking, and so high from the ground.

The country now begins to look rich and park-like, and at the stations the most enormous peaches are offered to us at twopence apiece. We lunched, very badly, at Colfax, where there was a grizzly bear at the station, and then returned to our carriages for a hot, dusty afternoon. However, we felt that our long journey – of nine days – was near its end, and packed up the things in our 'house-on-wheels' ready for our arrival at San Francisco.

Mrs. Littleton telegraphs that she can't come at all. I am so sorry.

Having washed off the dust, and made ourselves as smart as possi-ble, we prepare to 'land' at a small station called Oaklands. Captain Chatfield, the captain of H.M.S. *Amethyst;* Mr. Booker, the English Consul; and Mr. Walkem, a British Columbian, came 'on board,' and escorted us to our hotel.

We got into a large ferry-steamer, which took us over to San Fran-cisco. Our hotel is the 'Palace,' and is enormous. It is built round

a court, which is loaded with American flags; there must be at least
five hundred hung about. We took a walk while our luggage was being brought up; but oh! it was so cold. I had on my light 'train'
garments, and the wind blew through and through me. I saw many
ladies in furs, and have now ordered out mine. The climate of San
Francisco is treacherous, for it is a promontory, and its climate is
different from the rest of California.

Captain Chatfield, who has kindly made every arrangement for our
comfort on board the *Amethyst,* dined with us, and we went to the
play, and saw the 'Geneva Cross.' We enjoyed the play, though I, at
any rate, began to feel the effects of having risen at six and travelled
day and night for many days.

THURSDAY, 10TH. – Breakfasted in the enormous dining-room, and
were glad of a fire in our sitting-room. Received visits from Mr. Bradford, the artist; Captain Chatfield; and a lovely basket of flowers, with
'Welcome to California,' from an old North of Ireland friend. [Wil-
liam Bradford made a specialty of painting Arctic whaling scenes.]

At one o'clock D. and I, the Colonel and Fred Ward, drove off to
see the sights. We went to Woodward's Gardens to see the sea-lions
fed, but were too late for this; so we resolved to go at once to the
Cliff House. This is an hotel overhanging the Pacific, and is a great
resort of the people here. To get to it you drive through the Park,
a place which has been reclaimed from a sand-heap, specimens of the
original desert being plentiful on all sides; every morsel of earth has
been carried to the spot.

The balcony of the Cliff House, overlooking the Pacific Ocean, is
charming. Close there are some great rocky islands, upon which sea-
lions are basking in the sun, and pelicans stand combing out their
feathers. I counted seventy-one sea-lions to be seen at once; some
were dry, and of a real lion colour, others which were still wet looked
quite black. They made a noise very like that of hounds in a kennel,
and it was most amusing to watch them climbing about the rocks,
jumping in and out of the sea, and enjoying themselves generally.
The pelicans, too, were flying about, and taking headers into the
water.

We lunched at this hotel upon its celebrated fare: oysters, 'Porter-
hall steak,' and omelette, and then drove home. The streets are pure
sand, and there are windmills for pumping water everywhere; you see
ten or twelve of them in two or three streets.

One curious thing here is a car in which to go up and down hill without horses. There is an engine on the top of the hill, which winds and unwinds a wire rope, and this is attached to the carriages. As the rope is invisible, this unexpected movement of the carriages has an odd effect. [San Francisco's famous cable car, still in use.]

General McDowell, the hero of Bull's Run, dined with us, and we took him to a special performance of 'Brass' in our honour. We had a good box, and enjoyed that very ridiculous play.

D. and I took a walk, and our return found a staunch old man from Killyleagh. He is connected with both our families, having been called Hans after D.'s grandfather, and having been taken on board my grandfather's ship when he was thirteen. It is extraordinary how he remembers everybody of that day – the very old times. He put me through such an examination as to my great-aunts, uncles, and cousins, that I felt some self-satisfaction at having passed it. He thought me like my family, but said the ancestors did not come out so clearly in Fred.

This man has been mining for forty-five years, and now declares he is going back to the 'old place' to buy a little property and die there. I dare say 'going home' is a dream of his, and that he expects to start by every steamer; but the gold-fever is difficult to shake off, and, even if he does go, I fear matter-of-fact Killyleagh will be dull after years of Californian gambling.

This interview ended, we had to begin to prepare for departure. The gentlemen had to get into their uniforms, and there was great agitation over a missing bit of uniform, and a frantic rush to the tailor to make up the deficiency. We breathed again, and were all gloved, booted and spurred, the luggage and servants gone, when I peeped into His Ex.'s room and discovered an enormous bath-sponge unpacked! Happy thought! Push the sponge into the arm of His Excellency's fur coat. D. came in and I told him on no account must he put on his fur coat. But the despotic ruler of the Canadian Dominion declared that not for all the sponges of the sea would he consent to be cold with a fur coat at hand. We had to submit to a vulgar newspaper parcel. It was lent the shelter of the fur coat till we got to the boat, was received with respect by a gentleman in uniform, laid with care by His Excellency's side, extricated by one of his Aides-de-camp, and conveyed to the proper quarter by one of the seamen.

We sent two men-servants on by the mail-steamer, so the party on board the *Amethyst* consists of D. and I, Colonel Littleton, the Freds, Miss Alexander (my maid) , and 'John.'

The captain has taken a large slice off his cabin, and divided it into two. If I were not afraid of using a wrong mathematical term, I should say the slice is an equilateral triangle, that a small angle at the top is my maid's room, and that D. and I, two iron beds, and a large chest of drawers, inhabit the base of the said triangle. Captain Chatfield has been so kind in making everything nice – pictures on the walls, muslin-covered dressing-table, etc. We remain at anchor till the morning, and are, consequently, very bold and brave and perky, and dine below, and play whist and enjoy ourselves.

SATURDAY, 12TH. – 'A change comes o'er the spirit of my dream': it appears to me that the Pacific is a nasty ocean. I get on deck, and lie and sit and doze all day; the men look pale, and are not in good spirits. [Lady Dufferin here quotes from 'The Dream' by Lord Byron.]

SUNDAY, 13TH. – The Pacific is even nastier than I imagined, very much nastier than the Atlantic, and the Captain's cabin the least nice place one could possibly be in. The screw thumps and vibrates directly under it, and the pitching is longer, and in it one has to perfection that delightful sensation of being held in mid-air which is so very trying to the inner man.

MONDAY, 14TH. – Got on deck, and lay in a cot swung under a tent of flags; everyone better, but not well – not by any means. I should have felt very low about myself, had I not heard the Captain say that we 'shipped green seas' nearly the whole way over; so I feel I had a right to be ill.

TUESDAY, 15TH. – Things look better. I dress, and sit down and eat, and soon begin to walk, and to look about with pleasure. We coast all the way, and there are strange, dangerous, isolated rocks sticking up out of the sea. About three we arrive at Cape Flattery, and directly after passing it come to a narrow channel (ten miles) between Vancouver [Island] and the mainland. We have the sun, smooth water, and before us a splendid snow-capped range of mountains.

We reached Esquimault at nine, dropped anchor, and the screw ceased, so that we shall have a quiet night before encountering British Columbia. The mail steamer has not arrived, and they say we are twenty-four hours sooner than we were expected.

WEDNESDAY, 16TH. – After a peaceful night I came on deck, and found myself in a beautiful harbour, very small, but very deep; two men-of-war besides our own, gaily dressed with flags; flags and banners on land, beautiful mountains in the distance, charming weather.

The early morning was spent in waiting about, messages coming and going; some anxiety felt about the mail steamer, which is two days late. However, at twelve she arrived with our servants, who are announced as the 'Hon. F. Nowell and the Hon. G. Dame, Aides-de-Camp to His Excellency.' If they had arrived first, as they should have done, I believe they would have been received by the whole city.

We were to land at one, and at that hour the Staff went off in one boat, while we followed in another, and remained a short way from the ship while the salute was fired.

Then we stepped ashore, and were received by Sir James Douglas and a number of residents, and got into the carriage which was to drive us to Victoria.

> Sir James Douglas, at that time seventy-four years of age, in 1843 had founded, on the site of the present city of Victoria, the first Hudson's Bay Company post on Vancouver Island. He retired as chief factor of that company in 1858; but seven years before he had been appointed governor of Vancouver Island. In 1858 he became as well governor of the new colony of British Columbia and administered that mainland colony with firmness and vigour during and after the days of the gold rush.

We grew into an enormous procession before we reached that city (it is three miles distant), numbers of carriages and riders joining us. At one point along the route there rode out from the wood a party of magnificently-dressed archers, such as you have *not* seen off the stage: green-feathered hats, green velvet coats, breeches, big boots, bows, arrows – really very handsome-looking people. They formed an escort the rest of the way. Further on we picked up a band of horsemen with red ribbons across their breasts – a company in green – bands – some militia – an army of small boys, each carrying a bright-coloured flag – my 'bodyguard.' The men who wore the coloured sashes saluted in a curious fashion, by putting the hand to the mouth. We went over two bridges, both ornamented with green and various flags and devices, whence we saw a number of the Indian canoes, which here are shaped like gondolas, full of people, and covered with flags. The Indians were singing, and we were sorry we could not stop to look at them longer and to see them nearer.

Then we passed through the Chinese quarter of the town, and saw a number of the men and a few of the funny little women. The Chinese put up their own arches, and they were very prettily designed.

They hung up lanterns in some, and on one there was quite a house-ful of little images.

When we entered Victoria there was an address. D. replied from the carriage. At present the feeling here is British, but anti-Canadian, on account of the railroad, which can't be made yet; so it is not all plain sailing. We were told that on one arch there was written, 'Our Railroad or Separation.' The Governor-General was obliged to refuse to go under it, though he said he would do so if the 'S' were turned into an 'R'; and one man who found we were making a turn to avoid the street with the obnoxious arch jumped about as if he were mad, and when he met us above the arch he jumped again, and shrieked, 'Three groans for Mackenzie.'

I think every one of the 5,000 inhabitants of Victoria must have been out in the streets, and we drove at a foot's pace to the Government House, which has been lent to us during our visit here. The drive lasted 2½ hours.

> The Honourable Albert Norton Richards, a younger brother of Sir William Buell Richards, Chief Justice of the Supreme Court of Canada, had only a short time before received his appointment as Lieutenant-Governor of British Columbia. He had not as yet moved into Cary Castle, then Government House, and had offered it for Lord and Lady Dufferin's use. The former occupant had been the Honourable Joseph William Trutch, the first Lieutenant-Governor appointed after British Columbia entered into Confederation with Canada in 1871.

When we got to the door, we stood while the procession passed, and D. had an opportunity of stopping a carriage full of Chinamen, and thanking them for their reception of him. At last everybody was gone, and we looked about. The house is nice and comfortable; there is a good ball-room, small drawing-room, large billiard-room, and excellent bedrooms. We have a Chinese cook, who is, I grieve to say, highly British, having cooked for six Governors, but he is very good in his homely style; Ah Sâm is his name. Then I have a comfortable sort of housekeeper, a housemaid with a Chinaman under her, our own four servants, a coachman, and a gardener. But I have had to write so much to-day that I will finish my description to-morrow. We were very tired and glad to go to bed early.

In the evening the Chinese quarter of the town was illuminated, and all their houses were opened; people went in just as they liked, and were given tea and sweetmeats.

Lord Dufferin "danced all night at a ball, never flagging till four in the morning, and being pronounced 'a brick' by the young ladies of Montreal."

THURSDAY, 17TH. – This Government House is built on a rock, but a nice garden has been made; the drawback to it is the want of water. Every drop, both for house and garden, has to be brought in barrels; so there is not much to spare, and the grass is all burnt up. From the windows there is a view of a magnificent range of mountains, a little wanting in variety of outline, but extremely high. Mount Baker stands by itself, and is a splendid sight. Between us and them there is the sea.

D. interviewed people from ten till five. They are very angry with Canada, and he has hard work. About five I got him to come and take a little drive. We called on the Lieutenant-Governor – Mr. Richards – drove through the city, and as our drive was unofficial, went under the obnoxious arch, and round the 'park,' Beacon Hill; from the coast-road there is a very fine view of the mountains. Captain Chatfield came to stay with us. There is a bright sun, but a cold wind. It seems to me a trying climate, and the many changes of temperature and food, and the long journey, have rather knocked me up.

Chief Justice Sir Matthew Begbie dined with us. He is a very big man, very amusing, and *the* whist-player of British Columbia; however, on this occasion D. and I beat him thoroughly. His mind was, I suppose, distracted, for I found afterwards that he had planned to serenade us, and had arranged for some young ladies to come up at 9.30 to sing with him at our windows; so he was all the time listening for the sound of wheels, while he was attending to the trumps with his eyes. At last D., who had just gone away to do some business, heard voices in the garden, and with well-feigned astonishment rushed in to tell me. We brought the singers in, and gave them tea.

FRIDAY, 18TH. – We had a dinner for the Lieutenant-Governor and his wife. The other guests were Mr. and Mrs. Bunster (he is the Dominion M.P.), Mr. and Mrs. Roscoe, Senator and Mrs. Macdonald, and the local Prime Minister, with his wife, Mrs. Elliott. [The Honourable Andrew Charles Elliott was born in Ireland, but had come to British Columbia in 1859.]

SATURDAY, 19TH. – D. kept busy till within ten minutes of dinner-time. He is working very hard. At five o'clock I gave him up, and took the Commodore and the boys a drive. We went to the Gorge. The roads here are good, and the drives pretty.

In the evening we had a Drawing-room at the Parliament Buildings. The officers of the fleet helped to make a brilliant Court, and it was very largely attended, and was most successful. Six Chinamen came, and their names greatly tried the gravity of the A.D.C., who had to read them aloud.

MONDAY, 21ST. – I walked for an hour with D., and the whole of the rest of the day he was shut up with various people. One deputation stayed from two till six. I was 'at home,' and the Commodore helped me to receive my visitors, for Fred was deep in invitations, and the others were with D. In the evening we had a dinner – Mr. and Mrs. Trutch, Mr. and Mrs. Crease, Mrs. Grey, Mrs. O'Reilly, the Ministers Smith and Vernon, and the Mayor (Mr. J. S. Drummond).

> Having the use of Government House enabled the Dufferins to extend that warm hospitality which had become known as a feature of Rideau Hall. It was said that Lady Dufferin had a way of setting at ease even the humblest with whom she came in contact, and the art of inspiring in them a feeling of confidence and liking. Women especially were attracted to her and she won admiration by her unaffected ways. She dressed plainly, but prettily.
>
> That some of their guests were hostile to the Dominion Government was well known. A few months before, Robert Smith, now dining with the Dufferins, had moved a resolution to the effect 'that if the Pacific Railway be not commenced before January, 1876, British Columbia be allowed to sever her political connection with Canada and become an independent Province under the protection of Her Majesty's Government.' He had also suggested that the province should claim from Canada $30 million as compensation for non-fulfilment of treaty obligations.
>
> Another guest, Hon. Forbes George Vernon, the same age as Lady Dufferin, thirty-three, had been born in her native Ireland, at Clontarf Castle. He had become Chief Commissioner of Lands and Works in his adopted province.

TUESDAY, 22ND. – As usual, the morning was spent by D. in seeing deputations and visitors of all kinds.

We had an afternoon-party, and I received the guests in the garden. We had a band there, but in a short time adjourned to the house, and danced. D. was released about four o'clock, and was able to lead off the ball. Six Chinamen came, and looked on with great interest. The party broke up at 5.30, and we had a dinner, beginning at 6.30, and had afterwards to attend a concert held in the theatre.

WEDNESDAY, 23RD. – I have just received such a funny visit. Our cook,

Ah Sâm, has been lately married, and said he would like me to see his wife; so she came this morning. The door opened, and in walked a Chinese lady, dressed in black satin, wearing bracelets and rings, and with her hair wonderfully done. And supported by her came a little creature with a baby face, who evidently could not walk alone on account of her tiny feet, her hair very much dressed, and ornamented with what appeared to be a cap of many-coloured cut papers. She wore a blue tunic with embroidery on it, black satin petticoat, bracelets and earrings, and had rings on her bits of hands. This was the bride.

We got her into a chair, for she seemed at first incapable of even shaking hands without help. She appeared to be on the verge of tears, and half covered her face with a red silk pocket-handkerchief. Ah Sâm kissed my hand, and brought in a tray full of presents: two packets of fireworks (which will be awkward to travel with), some gimcracks they use in their churches, a Chinese *crêpe* handkerchief, and some shell frames. We looked at these, thanked him, and then he went away.

We began to talk to the bride, who by this time had somewhat recovered. She was really a very pretty little thing, with a bright complexion, pretty eyes and teeth. She answered us very nicely in English, and quite understood D.'s jokes as to the respective merits of her hairdressing and mine.

Poor baby that she is, she has only been married a week, and has not known Ah Sâm, who is an elderly and very ugly gentleman, much longer. When leaving she kissed my hand, and then made a set curtsey at the door, just like a child who had learnt its lesson.

At twelve o'clock we went in carriages to see a regatta, which was to be held at the Gorge. Its shores are rocky mounds and wooded banks, and there were knots of people in every direction. A number of boats were dotted about, and arranged in three groups were twenty large canoes, filled with Indians, and covered from stem to stern with flags. It is impossible to conceive anything more brilliant than the scene was, with a bright sun shining over all. As soon as the Indians saw the Governor-General approaching, they set up an extraordinary howl, and jumped about, stamping and clapping.

We got into a man-of-war's boat, and rowed about amongst them, being greeted by each set with fresh contortions and acclamations. There were about seventeen people in each canoe. Most of them had their faces painted, – bright red being the favourite colour. Some had a streak across the face, others patches on their cheeks, some were almost covered with it. Some had down sticking all over their heads, and looked as if they had slept inside a feather-bed.

There were some excellent races, four or five of the large canoes in a race, the men paddling with all their might – eighty strokes a minute – leaving quite a sea behind them.

There was a most exciting squaw race; one crew consisted of rather nice-looking young ones, but these did not win. Many wear handsome silver bracelets, and a certain young lady, Amanda by name, has promised to try and procure me a pair.

The Commodore came home to dine with us, and we had a party. We were obliged to dismiss our guests early, as we embarked after they left. We drove to Esquimault, and when we got into the boat the three men-of-war suddenly illuminated. At the end of each yard a blue-light burst into flame, and every port was lighted up. There were also some rockets.

THURSDAY, 24TH. – I was awoke about seven by the thump, thump of our screw, and found we were again on our travels. We passed through most lovely scenery; part of the time we were in a narrow channel, and could almost touch the rock on one side. About four we reached Nanaimo, and anchored in its harbour. We went out to fish for salmon, being unsuccessful.

FRIDAY, 25TH. – Directly after breakfast we landed at Nanaimo; the inhabitants gave us a kind reception. A large square place was decorated with flags and evergreens, and at one end the school-children were placed. There was an address, then a song, written for the occasion. We went to the coal-mine, looked down it, and came on board our ship again.

We left at one o'clock, and proceeded on our journey north, reaching Tribune Harbour in three hours. The gentlemen rather expected to get some shooting, and appeared in sporting clothes. D., the Captain, and I went in one boat, and landed where there was an Indian house. The inhabitants promised to show us grouse and deer, but directly they had put us in the track they went off at a gallop with their own guns. We tramped on through the narrow path, climbing over fallen trees, our only pleasure being the beautiful view over the bay in which the *Amethyst* was anchored. When sunset was approaching, we turned back.

SATURDAY, 26TH. – We started in the middle of the night, and when we came on deck in the morning we found ourselves in Bute Inlet. The scenery here for forty miles is perfectly lovely. The channel between the outer belt of islands and the mainland is narrow, and the water very deep. On every side rise pine-covered hills, exhibiting the greatest variety of form and outline, and some of them capped with snow.

Unfortunately the weather was bad, and got worse every mile we went, so that sometimes we only saw the tops of the mountains for a few moments before the mist descended upon them and they were lost to view.

Bute Inlet is expected to be the terminus of the Canadian Pacific Railway, so the Governor-General came out of his way to see the harbour.

In his book, *The Sea of Mountains*, Mr. St. John, the special correspondent for the Toronto *Globe*, said:

The course lies up a long, narrow strait for about a hundred miles. On either side the mountains rise straight from the water's edge and tower high up into the clouds.

In Victoria they have taken with bad grace Mr. Blake's perfectly justifiable remark about a 'sea of mountains.' [This was said by Honourable Edward Blake during a speech in the House of Commons.] But he might with truth have spoken of Bute Inlet as a sea of mountains in a gale of wind. It is marvellously beautiful in its wild grandeur, so lofty, rugged, and defiant are the mountains that wall in the calm, narrow strip of pale green sea, but it almost takes one's breath away when regarded as a railway route.

And Lord Dufferin was later to say:

I only wish that Waddington Harbour at the head of Bute Inlet was a better port. In fact it is no harbour at all and scarcely an anchorage.

The water is the most beautiful green. We saw several glaciers and cascades coming down the mountain. Directly we anchored we set out to fish. I never saw so many fish jump so close to one before; however, they would not look at our tempting spoons, and we caught nothing.

On shore we saw a most picturesque figure – an Indian wrapped in a scarlet blanket, and with a conical hat on his head, perching upon a large stone, his arms clasped round his knees. He looked like an enormous robin redbreast. D. went to speak to him. He was in the act of making a 'dug-out' – a canoe carved out of a tree – which lay on the shore in its unfinished state. D. looked into his hut – a miserable place open at two sides; a woman and three children, and a quantity of dried fish were in it. We gave the man what tobacco we had in the boat.

SUNDAY, 27TH. – Another misty and rainy day. We had service on board, with good singing. We at this time were still in the Sound, but for about three hours in the afternoon we were in the open sea, and there were doubts whether we should not have to keep out to sea for the night, to avoid a nasty bit of navigation in the dark. But the good ship *Amethyst* went very fast, and we had the pleasure of anchoring at eight in Safety Harbour, and having a quiet dinner. We found our tender waiting us here.

MONDAY, 28TH. – We started as usual about daylight, passed through narrow channels and beautiful scenery. At ten we had some gun-practice, and saw shot, shell, and case fired at the rocks on shore. The sailors equipped themselves for war, with swords and pistols, and the doctors prepared for broken legs and various wounds.

We arrived at our anchorage about four o'clock, and, as usual, this sporting community prepared to fish and shoot. The bear-hunters shot a goose, the large boat-load caught six trout, and the Commodore and D. took a tremendous walk through the bush. It rained, and I remained in the boat.

TUESDAY, 29TH. – The weather has been desperately bad, pouring rain and much fog. Our tender piloted us into Metlacatlah; here we are safe at anchor.

Metlacatlah is one of the most successful of Indian missions. It is entirely the work of a Mr. Duncan, who has lived amongst them, and is regarded by them as their father and friend. We fired a cannon directly we arrived, and Mr. Duncan came off to see us. He is very pleasant – bright and enthusiastic, good and clever – quite a model missionary. He has not only taught them their religion and the three R's, but has shown them how to build, taught them how to trade, to make soap, to sing, and is their chief magistrate.

He came to Metlacatlah from Fort Simpson with fifty Indians, setting up a new village on this spot; now there are eight hundred living here. When he first came the Indian exercised horrible heathen rites and ceremonies, dressed in blankets, wore painted masks, and knew no law. Now Metlacatlah is quieter than a white village; the

Indians themselves are police, and they form a council, which settles all their local matters.

Mr. Duncan amused us by telling us how he once bought a schooner to take furs to Victoria; he started as its captain, and his crew were Indians. Neither captain nor men knew anything about the sea, and the voyage is a difficult one, and somewhat long, for they were out a month.

WEDNESDAY, 30TH. – It was delightful, after yesterday's rain, to find a lovely morning, and to see the beautiful scenery to perfection. But I must tell you about our visit to the village.

We started in boats directly after breakfast, our Staff dressed in red, to please the Indians. As we approached the shore they fired off two cannons, and we found a respectable guard-of-honour ready to present arms; a boarded place had been prepared on the grass for us to stand on.

They had received no notice of our intention to visit them before our arrival last night, so the greater part of the inhabitants were absent on their summer fishing-tours, and we saw only about a hundred. These were remarkably well dressed; the men in cloth clothes, the women in neatly-made prints, with bright-coloured handkerchiefs on their heads and shawls over their shoulders. They were quite Dutch in their cleanliness.

Mr. Duncan presented me with a silver bracelet, made by the Indians, and two silver napkin-rings. He gave D. a lynx robe, and a beautiful black wolfskin, with its head and teeth perfect. The animal was shot outside his door in the winter.

His assistants, Mr. and Mrs. Collinson, gave us some spoons carved out of horn, Indian rattles, and a carved box with a set of teeth, and green eyes staring out of a face on its side; so I had quite a cargo of gifts. Mrs. Collinson teaches the girls and trains them for servants, or rather for wives. We saw the 'Council Room,' and in it a peculiar fireplace, which they have in all the cottages, and which D. would like to put into some large hall somewhere. It is a good-sized square, in the very centre of the room, with the chimney directly over it. Everyone in the room is thus able to get an equal share of the fire, and it looks most cheerful with people sitting all round it. In this room Mr. Duncan and his Indian colleagues carry on the business of the place.

The Prison stands opposite; it is a funny little tower, painted black below and white above. It is divided into two rooms, the 'black' prison being more disgraceful than the 'white.' On the top of this building there is a stand for the band! The Church comes next, and is quite new, having been built entirely by Mr. Duncan and the Indians. It is 120 feet long by 60, and is 50 feet high. It is made of cedar and cypress, and is, I suppose, the only building of the kind to be seen anywhere by people so lately savage. It holds 1,200 people, and is very handsome inside. Of course it is made of wood, and is perfectly simple; but the proportions and the simplicity together give quite a grand effect.

The School is another good building. The pupils all learn to read English, which they prefer for reading to their native tongue – their own words are so very long. They translate what they read into Tschimchyau.

After making the tour of the village we returned to the platform. The people collected and sang 'God save the Queen,' some English songs, and then a song about Metlacatlah, composed by Mr. Duncan, and set out to the air of 'Home, Sweet Home'; also some English and Tschimchyau hymns. An Indian read an address in English, and the chiefs signed it in our presence. D. replied, Mr. Duncan taking down his speech, and translating it afterwards. He speaks their language perfectly, while many Englishmen only learn a jargon called Chinook, which is a sort of 'pigeon English,' intended for trading purposes, and quite unfit to explain the mysteries of a new religion.

Close to the wharf there is a large, empty room, which is used for stray Indians who arrive here, and who may have sickness among them. Mr. Duncan has put up a saw-mill, and I think I told you the Indians make soap; the traders used to ask them a dollar for a piece the width of a finger! This manufactory is not working at present, and the Indians came off in canoes to the ship, and asked for soap, instead of money, for furs. Great exchanges were made by the men on the ship – furs for old clothes.

We were obliged to leave this most interesting place at one o'clock, as we were to visit Fort Simpson, the most northern station of British America on the Pacific coast. We went there in our tender, the *Douglas*. Fort Simpson borders on Alaska; the view is beautiful.

Unfortunately, the Governor of the Fort and the missionary [Reverend Thomas Crosby of the Methodist Church] were both away, and few of the Indians were at home. Mrs. Crosby, the missionary's wife, took us through the village, where we saw for the first time some extraordinary monuments put up to Indian chiefs. The subjects are, I suppose, symbolical, but to us they appear grotesque. [The Dufferins were seeing totem poles for the first time.]

The most curious one we saw was an enormous bare pole, on the top of which was carved and painted in gigantic size a grinning head. The body was that of a bird with its wings spread out, and on each wing and on its breast a naked baby or imp; underneath was nailed a longcloth apron ornamented with buttons. Another pole had a dog at the top and a queer face carved below. These poles are said to cost the Indians about 300£. apiece – that is to say, they will give away blankets to that amount for the privilege of putting one up.

We had a very short stay here, and were soon in the *Douglas* again, on our way back to Metlacatlah. Mr. Duncan and Mrs. Collinson dined with us. An Indian chief came with them in order to present D. with the hat his father used to wear in the feasts and dances. It is 3 feet high, made of strips of thuja-bark plaited together; and jointed so as to sway about with every movement of the dancer. The man valued it very much, and Mr. Duncan told us that, although he has known him for years, he never saw the hat before.

THURSDAY, 31ST. – There was a thick fog, which only lifted at 9.30; after which the day was beautiful, and we had a splendid passage over to Queen Charlotte's Islands. I suppose this is the wildest place I shall ever be at. It is solely inhabited by Indians, and as yet there is no missionary amongst them. But Mr. Collinson is coming here.

We anchored opposite a village, which, in the distance, looked like a forest of bare poles. Every house seems to have one; they are highly valued, as symbols of rank. Some are carved the whole way up with grotesque figures and faces, some are painted. In many houses the door is a part of the pattern of the pillar, and is an oval hole, through which you see the picturesque Indian figures appearing. When a man dies, his friends destroy his house, leaving the framework and the pillar, and make a little hut for the dead body to lie in, with a blanket nailed before it. We saw one with two canoes outside, ready to take the owners across the 'silent lake.' On one house were two figures with tall hats and frock-coats – missionaries, evidently.

FRIDAY, SEPTEMBER 1ST. – The Freds and I went to a little trading settlement, and had great fun bargaining, buying silver bracelets and carved bowls. It was amusing on board to see the buying and selling going on, furs, bracelets, old clothes, soap, tobacco, and biscuits being exchanged, while hideous faces, painted black or red, looked up from the canoes. We are off again; you may see by my writing that the screw is at work.

SATURDAY, 2ND. – We were able to enjoy the evening, but the night was somewhat rough. A fog this morning, and many doubts as to whether we should have to go out to sea – an unpleasant prospect. We had just turned back, when we met our little friend, the *Douglas*, and she undertook to show us the way. We were off Vancouver Island, and wanted to pass between it and the mainland. The fog came on very thick, and we lost sight of the *Douglas*, and stopped again. Then the mist suddenly lifted, and we were able to go on full speed.

The fog this morning detained us so long that we found it impossible to get to the harbour, in which we had intended to stop the night. It was suddenly determined to anchor in Alert Bay. We had an hour to spare before dinner, so we landed to see the Indian village there.

We found a great number of people sitting in front of their houses. But they did not appear much interested in us, though they had fired off two cannon on our arrival, and had whitewashed their homes on the chance of our coming. The trader who lives there explained it all. They had been having one of their most savage orgies, and had been singing, dancing and feasting for six days. This very morning their 'medicine-man' had been out on the rampage, and in his tantrums had bitten six people; this they consider a great honour. The moment the man-of-war came in sight, they quieted down, hid their drunken people, and allowed their medicine-man to escape into the woods.

Drink is at the bottom of much of the misery. In Canada there is a fine of $500 for selling spirit to Indians, but here they get it from American traders.

SUNDAY, 3RD. – We had a lovely day, and after morning service went through the last danger on this route – the Seymour Narrows. There are several whirlpools formed by a rapid tide in this narrow channel, and an American man-of-war was lost in them not long ago. We anchored in Tribune Harbour, and took a nice walk over the cliffs, returning in time for dinner.

MONDAY, 4TH. – This is the last of our voyage in the *Amethyst*. When we arrived at Burrard's Inlet we saw the *Rocket*, and the sight of her told us our mail was in. Not having heard for a long time, we were all delighted. In the evening, by another steamer, two more mails arrived. When I went to bed I had quite a headache from reading letters. I had forty myself – so many from the children.

CHAPTER 16

British Columbia, California and the Salt Lake City
SEPTEMBER - OCTOBER 1876

The many interviews Lord Dufferin had in Victoria made him aware of the bitter hostility that existed between the people of the mainland of British Columbia and those on Vancouver Island. Originally these two had been separate colonies, with the island capital at Victoria, while that of the mainland was the Royal City of New Westminster. Both colonies became overburdened with debts, and in 1866, as a measure of economy, the British Government joined them, keeping the mainland name, British Columbia, while adopting the island capital of Victoria.

Debts still piled up, and longing eyes were cast eastward to the newly formed Dominion of Canada, which, upon Confederation, had assumed some of the debts of the Atlantic provinces. The governor, Frederick Seymour, was opposed. But after his death in 1869, union with Canada was approved, and Confederation followed in 1871. With it came the promise of the transcontinental railway.

But the mainlanders were definitely against the scheme now being proposed, which would take the railway through wild, unpopulated country to Bute Inlet, and from there on to Victoria. Of what use to them was a railway from Nanaimo to Victoria? Let the people there transport their coal by sea! Also, they pointed out, that northern route would demand finding passes through *three* mountain ranges, where little exploration had been done.

They were demanding that the railroad come from the east along the Thompson River and down the Fraser to a terminus somewhere on Burrard Inlet. In this way only *two* mountain ranges needed to be crossed. Also, there, towns had sprung up during the 'gold rush,' and the famous Cariboo Trail, built between 1862 and 1865, had opened up the country for 480 miles north from Yale, the head of navigation of the Fraser. This stupendous engineering feat had been carried out under the direction of Clarence Moberly, who had received his training under Frederick William Cumberland in Ontario. But, as the mainland held thirteen of the twenty-five seats in the British Columbia Legislature, so far they had thwarted the hopes of the people on Vancouver Island.

Now Lord Dufferin was to hear, and see, their side of the problem.

TUESDAY, SEPTEMBER 5TH. – The repose of a sea-life is over; posts and telegrams, addresses, replies, arches, bands and salutes are alive again.

Almost before we had finished our breakfast we were hurried into boats, and put on board the *Douglas*, and in her we steamed along for an hour, reading up the news in the papers. Later we got into boats and canoes, and landed in the bush, where we went to see a great tree cut down. Our host, Mr. Raymur, had chosen a tree near the water, and he made many apologies for its small size. But as it was 250 feet high, and about 6 feet in diameter, we thought it enormous. It had been partially cut through, and we stood by to see its overthrow. Two men were working at it. They stood each upon a spring-board, on either side of the tree. These boards were narrow planks stuck into holes about 12 feet up the trunk. They say the lower part of the trunk is too hard to repay the labour of hacking through it. The spring-board gives the workman great power with his axe.

In about ten minutes the monster began slowly to bend to one side, and then a crashing and a great thud upon the ground announced its downfall. According to its rings it was 400 years old, and planted in the reign of King Edward IV.

We set off again in our boats to the *Amethyst*, where we had a lunch still more hurried than the breakfast. The *Douglas* towed us in the ship's boats, and as we went very fast, and the water was full of pieces of timber, we had quite an exciting voyage, trying to avoid a blow from one of these.

We landed at a wharf, and got into carriages, which took us eight miles over a corduroy road through the primeval forest. Our destination was New Westminster.

At that time the city of Vancouver did not exist. A picture, taken four years later, on the site where the business centre of that city now stands, shows seven yoke of oxen hauling out a recently felled giant tree.

When we arrived within the precincts of the city we were met by the Mayor, a guard of honour, and a band, and passed under arches decorated with flags. There were some very pretty devices, and two rather amusing ones. D.'s motto was happily combined with the great political question of the day – 'which route the Pacific Railway is to take' – 'Per Vias Rectas, The Fraser Valley.' Another had 'Speed the Railway' written upon a board, above which a little train moved along as we passed.

We had a short way to drive, and turned up a grass hill, at the top of which a series of platforms were arranged, covered in with flags, and decorated with evergreens. The view over the Fraser River, the town, and the distant mountains was quite beautiful. The whole town was out, and there was besides a great assembly of Indians. After various varieties of white men had presented addresses, been replied to, and shaken hands with, we looked down the hill, and saw a mass of flags marching up. The bearers of these gay banners were all Indian chiefs, or great men, followed by a set of Indian Volunteers, who had got themselves into a very smart blue uniform, and were commanded by the owner of an old red coat and a pair of epaulets. The chiefs formed into a circle, D. went down and shook hands with them, then returned to the platform and listened to the speeches of four, every sentence translated by an interpreter into English.

When it was his turn to reply, D. spoke one sentence, which was taken up by five interpreters, who each, in turn, put it into some new Indian tongue. The process was long, but interesting. These poor people have been waiting here for the Governor-General for nearly three weeks, and have taken great pains to get themselves up for the occasion.

There was lunch in a tent, and after we walked down to the river, and saw three good canoe-races. One set of boats had twenty-one Indians in each. At six o'clock we made a move to go to the steamer upon which we sleep. On our way we passed under a Chinese arch, and got out of the carriage to speak to some of the people. After parting with the officials, seeing a great sturgeon in a fishmonger's, we went in to look at it. He showed us more than a hundred salmon he had in store, and asked if we should like to see some caught that night; which invitation we accepted.

D. had a long talk with various gentlemen on business before dinner. After it we stood on the roof of our drawing-room on the steamer to see a beautiful torch-light display by the Indians in canoes. We steamed up a little way, and then back, the canoes following, their torches looking very brilliant in the darkness and reflected in the water. Some men on foot, also with torches, ran along the banks, and the town was illuminated. Before the lights disappeared there was cheering, and 'God save the Queen.'

After this we retired into private life, and prepared to go out fishing. Conducted by our friend the fishmonger, Mr. Herring, we got into a boat, Mrs. Herring coming with us to do the honours. We followed Mr. Herring, who, in a second boat, put down a great net, which we saw him take in. We caught six fine salmon and a sturgeon, and it really was great fun. When we landed we walked under the Chinese arch again, and were amazed by their lanterns, which had little animals going round and round inside, jumping and moving their legs – so cleverly managed. Sir Matthew Begbie joined us here, and goes with us for some way. All glad to get to bed.

WEDNESDAY, 6TH. – Our steamer started at night up the Fraser River. She is a stern-wheeler, and has capital accommodation.

The scenery of the Fraser is lovely. It is impossible to convey an idea of the *luxe* of beautiful views there is in this country. Until we reached Yale the only event of the day was to be called out to see some magnificent one. We stopped a few minutes at Hope, a charming little place, and got to our destination – Yale – in the afternoon. A coach-and-six (in which we travel for a week) took us up to Mr. Oppenheim's house, where we are to sleep. On the way we stopped to receive a Chinese address, written on pink paper, and an Indian one. The decorations were wonderful for such a small place; the most original being a live horse, with a cloth over it, on which was written, 'Good, but not iron,' in allusion to the celebrated railway.

The Oppenheims had a banquet for us, cooked by a Frenchman from Victoria – very good, but so plentiful that Nowell managed to suppress some dishes behind the scenes. Mrs. Oppenheim, though French, is like a motherly English woman, and I liked her very much.

THURSDAY, 7TH. – After breakfast we started on our journey. Unfortunately, it rained on and off all day, but the wet was not sufficient to damp our enjoyment. Just before leaving, an Indian woman brought me a pin made of a gold nugget.

We set off in a large carriage, which held six inside and three on the box. The servants had gone before us, and D. and I, the Commodore, the Chief Justice [Sir Matthew Baillie Begbie], the Colonel and the Freds, went in this coach, drawn by four horses. We had forty-four miles to drive, and the road is a wonderful piece of engineering: a wall of rock on one side, and a great precipice upon the other, almost the whole way, with every now and then a sharp turn round some fearful bluff, where, looking forward, the road seemed to end, and there was nothing but the river to be seen, a hundred feet below. We were following the Fraser all day. The river itself is muddy, but very rapid, with mountains almost precipitous on either side.

It was very curious to see the little Indian fishing establishments on the way. Wherever there was a rock rising above the water, there you were sure to see a scaffolding, upon which were hung rows and rows of dried fish, and near it a sort of spring-board jutting out into the water, upon which a man stood over the stream, and dipped a net, shaped like a snow-shoe, into it. We saw one man bring up a large trout, and cheered him from the carriage.

Another curious thing we saw was a sort of house in which the Indians winter. A large hole is cut in the ground, and covered over with a round roof; in the top of this there is a hole, through which a notched pole is stuck, and by this the people go down – and through it the smoke comes up.

We lunched at a place called Boston Bar, and D. took several portraits of Indians there. They were a different type from those we have seen before: instead of very fat faces, they have thin ones, and large, but not coarse, mouths. As we approached our camp we saw a most beautiful mountain view; down the sides of the precipitous hills there were streaks of light green, the rest being very dark fir; light clouds of mist floating about, and the river, far below, flowing rapidly along. We got out at one place to look at Hell's Gate, where the Fraser rushes through a very narrow pass. We passed several teams of sixteen oxen, and some with twelve mules, drawing two waggons fastened together.

When we arrived at our sleeping-place, which had been arranged by Captain Layton [George Richard Layton, the Lieutenant-Governor's private secretary], a village came in sight! Our tents are on the side of a hill, 800 feet above the river, and when we walked up the little path made to them, we found a large dining-room tent, carpeted, the walls hung with chintz, and ornamented with green; and out of this my bedroom, fitted with every luxury! Outside the dining-room a row of ten tents – one for each gentleman, to sleep in – and a public dressing-room.

A great camp-fire is burning, the Chinese cook is at work at another fire, and a lovely view lies before us. I was tired after the long journey, and was glad of the good dinner we had. After it we sat round the fire; the Indians joined the circle, and passed a stone pipe from one to another.

I have retired from the fire to write this, but it is impossible to do justice to the day so hurriedly. I have not mentioned a waterfall, perfectly straight, down an enormous high cliff. The road really is rather awful, and I got great credit for my courage in driving over it.

FRIDAY, 8TH. – We breakfasted in our spacious camp at seven o'clock – to the tune, alas! of a pattering rain – and in half an hour set off on our drive. The rain kept on all day more or less. The road was, I thought, rather worse than before, being equally precipitous and narrow, and much softer and more slippery-looking. Before we reached Lytton we met a great assembly of Indians, who had built an arch close to a little church they have there. There were about 500, of whom 200 men and women were on horseback; numbers of foals were following, and the neighing and excitement among the horses was as great as that among the men.

An Indian had met us about three miles from the town, and said, 'Tayee?' (chief). 'Yes,' was the reply from our carriage, and off he started on his way to tell them we were coming. Such a motley and picturesque assembly; every sort of colour and dress; curious caps, made of handkerchiefs tied on in every possible way; fur caps, made apparently of a whole animal, though some were merely a strip of fur tied round the head; and every face a study. The women rode astride, but had a blanket so neatly laid over the knees, and tucked into the stirrup at each foot, and sat so well, and were so much at home on their saddles, that they looked charming. Sometimes there were two on a horse, and many a mother and child sat together on one. The men's saddles were often a good deal ornamented.

The missionary read an address, and 'God save the Queen' was sung in Indian. We visited the Church, and shook hands a good deal, and then rode on, the troop after us, to Lytton, where D. ordered beef and flour for the Indians. Here the whites had an address and an arch, and we stopped for a few moments. After we left it the Indians followed for some way, and we handed out tobacco to the women who came nearest, young and old being glad of it.

You can't think what a pretty sight it was! We were two large coaches-and-four, and a great procession of these curious riders, talking and laughing, following after us. Their horses are small, but good, have plenty of work, and are never ill. We have now left the Fraser River, and are on the Thompson.

Although a great many people were involved in making arrangements for the pleasure and comfort of the Dufferins and their party on the 250-mile trek into the interior of British Columbia, few names are recorded in this journal. But, despite their varying political viewpoints, the members of the Dominion Parliament and Senate, as well as those of the provincial house, were most assiduous in their efforts.

Among these was Edgar Dewdney, a surveyor, who seventeen years before had come from his native Devonshire. Successively he had been a member of the provincial and then of the federal house. In later years he was to become Minister of the Interior at Ottawa, and in 1892 Lieutenant-Governor of British Columbia.

Another was Clement Francis Cornwall, a forty-year-old lawyer, who had been summoned to the Senate when British Columbia entered Confederation. This scion of British aristocracy claimed descent from a son of King John, who had been created Earl of Cornwall. His home was at Ashcroft.

The large coach in which the Dufferins rode along the Cariboo Trail into the interior of British Columbia is one of the prized possessions of the New Westminster Historic Centre, which occupies the old home of Captain Irving. In 1964 a special addition was completed and in this the coach is displayed.

We arrived at Mr. and Mrs. Cornwall's house after a twelve hours' drive, and in a pouring rain, rather tired. I am sorry to say Mr. Cornwall is not at home, having most unfortunately had a bad accident on his way here to prepare for us. His horse shied on the road over which we have just come, and he went over a precipice, happily in one of the least dangerous places to be found on the way. He broke his leg, while his companion rolled down twenty-five feet, and escaped with a few scratches. Mr. Cornwall had to be taken back to Victoria to have the leg set. Mrs. Cornwall has a very young baby, and her brother and sister-in-law are helping her to do the honours. They have made D. and me very comfortable in their house, and were most kind. The rest of the party are lodged elsewhere.

SATURDAY, 9TH. – We left the Cornwalls' before 10 a.m., and again embarked in our coaches. At last the sun shone upon us. The country here has low hills and rolling plains which to a stranger look barren, but which really support cattle all the year round, and certainly produce the best beef and mutton I ever ate. One carries away from this district the idea of a great sandhill of a yellowish tinge, cut into terraces, valleys, mounds, and apparently carved all over by ancient watercourses. Could it be irrigated, the land would be valuable; but as it is there is scarcely any cultivation, and the only crop is bunch-grass. Though it produces such good beef, I can't tell you how many acres it requires to feed one cow, and the animal has quite a walk to take between one tuft of grass and another.

We had not left our starting-point long when, with shouts and drums and neighing of horses, we were surrounded by a cavalcade of Indians. The next half-hour was one of the greatest excitement. I never saw anything so delightful as the sight of these men, women, children, waving their flags, horses and foals galloping up and down the low hills, around us, while our two coaches drove steadily along the road.

Some of the figures were interesting to watch. There was one man with a square drum, which he beat as he galloped along, his legs keeping time, and his body dancing on the saddle. The chief was a remarkably handsome old man, with a majestic air and a fine seat on horseback. He wore a red uniform. Several women had babies before them, and bigger children tied on behind. You may imagine how the baby's head wagged as its mother galloped along!

After much cantering and skirmishing we arrived at an inn and a shop, where we got out of the coach to speak to the people, and to buy them flour, sugar and tobacco.

These Indians are very bright and intelligent-looking. We shook hands with a great many, and particularly admired the 'British General' – the handsome chief. I looked to see if the babies' heads were all right. I found one poor old lady who had been galloping along in this furious fashion with her hand and arm swelled with rheumatism. I got her a warm shawl at the store. The whole assembly followed us a mile or two, waved their flags and disappeared.

After passing through arid plains, we suddenly came upon a glassy sheet of water, into which, and out of which, the river Thompson flowed. We got on board a steamer, and as usual found every comfort and luxury surrounding us: pictures in our cabins, books of poetry on the tables, rocking-chairs, and good beds. We steamed along for three hours, when we arrived at Kamloops.

From Ashcroft the Cariboo Trail continued northward through Cache Creek, Williams Lake, and Quesnel, and on to the gold-fields at Barkerville. However, the Dufferin party turned eastward to Savona's

Ferry, following the Thompson River to where it emerged from
Kamloops Lake.

They had crossed the Cascade Mountains and emerged into the
'bunch-grass' country. Although the road they travelled was a dangerous,
hazardous one, a stage-coach had been running once a week for
seventeen years over the greater part of it — and without an accident.
When the longed-for railway was finally built, this was the route
chosen.

On one bank of the river we saw a quantity of white men and
Indians on horseback, and on the other about five hundred wild
horses were being driven down to the water. D. landed and drove up
in a coach-and-four to a platform, where he found me, I having
walked. I was presented with a bouquet by a young lady who had
been a school-girl at Clandeboye when I was married; our meeting
was quite exciting.

There were addresses, D. went a short drive, then returned to the
steamer. A deputation kept him for some time, and Ah Sâm (our
cook) got so impatient, and so fearful that his dinner would be
spoiled, that in spite of everyone, he sounded a gong (upon a tin
pan), as a hint to the people to go.

SUNDAY, 10TH. — We had prayers before breakfast in the cabin, and
soon after steamed across to the opposite shore to visit the Indians.
There was rather an interesting 'Pow-wow.' They have had a land
grievance in this province, which is serious to them, and they set it
before the Governor-General in a grave and dignified manner. They
seemed pleased to have the opportunity of seeing him, and, although
he made them no promises, they felt they had secured a friend at
court.

I must tell you a story of Ah Sâm. Captain Layton had slept on
shore last night, but as we start very early to-morrow he wished to
have a cabin in the steamer. So he said to Ah Sâm: 'You take your
mattress, and put in on the floor somewhere, as I am going to sleep
here to-night.' 'Oh,' says Ah Sâm, 'me workee hard, Captain Layton
no work; me want good bed; if Captain Layton get in first, he have it;
if me get in first, me have it.' So at nine o'clock the whole saloon was
disturbed by the snores of Ah Sâm, who retired very early indeed to
make sure of keeping the bed. He is a great character, and always
takes his boots off in the coach, lest he should be made to walk up the
hills.

MONDAY, 11TH. – I was awoke by the stern-wheel, which is immediately behind my cabin, and which shakes one more then any screw. We were starting, and about seven stopped at a place where most of the party landed to shoot. The steamer went on, and the Commodore and I breakfasted at nine, and went out fishing at Savernagh's [Savona's] Ferry, in the Thompson River. The trout were only beginning to rise when the steamer whistled for us, and we had to go back. The sportsmen had had a beautiful walk, and brought home five and a half brace of the 'sharp-tailed grouse,' and we all enjoyed our morning.

We embarked at noon in our coach, and parted with the Chief Justice at Câche Creek, on his way to Cariboo. I then got on the box (or 'fore-top,' as we call it, having just coming from the *Amethyst*) to see Mr. Tingley drive; this was an easy part of the road, so I thought it a good place to take a front seat.

We got to Mr. Cornwall's at six, and all dined there, D. and I remaining to sleep.

TUESDAY, 12TH. – We got away early; a beautiful bright morning. On the road we met many Indians, and shook hands a good deal. The old ladies are so animated; they shake both hands before you, talking all the time, and continue the motion when you give them tobacco, saying, or rather making a noise like, 'tu-choo.'

At Lytton we caught up the second coach; some of the passengers had felt the heat so much it made them sick, but we did not mind it at all. D., the Colonel and the Commodore stopped and bathed in the Thompson. We are returning the same way we came, and are enjoying the beautiful scenery in the fine weather.

Having plenty of time to spare, and passing one of those fishing-stations I told you of, we scrambled down the bank to see the man at work. His implement was like a long landing-net, and he stood on the most rickety little spring-board platform over the rushing stream, and put his net into the water, drawing it down stream as far as he could reach. When he felt a fish in it, he let go a string, which allowed the net to run down the frame, and to shut up the fish in a regular bag. Our gentlemen tried to do it, but they nearly tumbled into the river and could not manage it at all.

I again got on the box, and drove over the worst piece of the road – such awful turns, and such a precipice at the edge of the narrow road! It certainly requires good driving, and the coachman has to work hard all the time. We reached our camp at six, and in an hour were at dinner and a splendid camp-fire.

WEDNESDAY, 13TH. – I got up at six to look out at a curious effect of fog. We are about 800 feet above the river. The morning was bright and lovely, all the mountains clear, and an extensive view lay before me. But when I looked down at the Fraser, instead of its muddy stream, I beheld a beautiful river of soft cloud! This layer of fog must have been 200 to 300 feet thick, as we could tell by the trees on the banks, and it was the prettiest thing I ever saw in the way of mist.

We had a successful journey back to Yale, and D. and I sat on the box for the last hour of the way. The driver and all the Yaleites were delighted that we had enjoyed the trip, and were not frightened. And the coachman's testimony to my courage during the perilous drive to Kamloops was 'that I hadn't a scare in me.' We drove down to the steamer *Royal City*, and had the Oppenheims to dine with us.

THURSDAY, 14TH. – The stern-wheel awoke us about 6 a.m. It gives the most odious motion to the steamer. About eleven we got to New Westminster, which D. thinks should be the terminus of the new Pacific Railway. The Mayor came on board, and presented me with photographs of all the arches. The Commodore left us here, and we went on a little farther to join the *Douglas*, upon which steamer I have been scribbling this.

We had a very smooth passage of about twenty miles to Victoria, where we found it raining heavily. This only made our drawing-room, with its fire and lights, look more than ever comfortable after all our travelling. Then the delight of finding a mail waiting, and a nice quiet hour for reading our letters!

FRIDAY, 15TH. – Fred Ward, who is 'housekeeper,' has ordered up the prisoners from the Penitentiary to 'pluck chickens' for the ball; it is the custom here, and this morning, when we walked into the ball-room, we found six prisoners, with chains to their legs and an armed man standing over them, polishing the floor.

D. was, as usual, shut up with some argumentative Victorian till 4.30 p.m., when I got him out for a little drive, and we walked home.

SATURDAY, 16TH. – After lunch we went to a rifle-match. His Ex. gave away his medals, and we saw some 'company' there. The Commodore joined us, and we walked home. In the evening we attended an amateur concert.

MONDAY, 18TH. – Prisoners all busy, preparing for the ball. Fred brought the head gardener into the drawing-room to give him some directions about flowers, and was about to take him into the dining-room, when he said: 'I can't leave that man here; he's a convict.'

We visited the High School, received an address, and replied. D. presented some medals for competition, which were unexpected, and gave great pleasure. We then called upon the ex-Governor, Mr. Trutch, to see his mother, an old lady of seventy-seven, who is dying to come to the ball, but cannot get her doctor's permission to do so.

I rested in the afternoon, and at seven we had a merry little dinner in a small room. There was a rumour that the great Ah Sâm was drunk, and that the supper would be very bad; but the dinner was all right, so we felt some hope. The guests were invited at 8.30, and soon after nine D. and I came down to open the ball. The room is a very nice one, and we had had all the windows taken out, and a sort of corridor tent of canvas, lined with flags, put up the whole way round the outside, which added greatly to the available space.

I must say I enjoyed the ball very much, and I think everyone else did. We all danced from 9.30 till three without intermission, and as fathers, mothers, daughters and sons are all equally dancing-mad here, and as we had a great number of naval officers, and were in ourselves an element of novelty to the Victorians, and they were new to us, there was a great deal of spirit in the ball. When everyone else had gone, we had some more supper and a talk; the former was very good, and Ah Sâm had been maligned.

TUESDAY, 19TH. – We breakfasted at eleven, and had to start immediately after for the Esquimault Dockyard. The Commodore went on first, and received us there with the officials belonging to it. D. was to drive in the first pile of a new dry dock. When this ceremony, which was performed by the aid of steam, was accomplished, we went over the stores, and then to lunch. The croquet-ground was covered in with sails and flags, and the tables were laid on it. Our health was drunk, and D.'s reply was very successful, containing a little chaff about the way in which he had been shut up every, and all day with the male portion of the population of Victoria – which amused them immensely.

When all was over we went to see the *Rocket* – a gunboat – and then drove home, the Commodore returning to the *Amethyst*.

WEDNESDAY, 20TH. – Such a day of labour! D. very busy from 7 a.m. preparing for a very important speech; at eleven the deputation came, and he spoke till 2.30; then lunch, and off to the Cathedral to attend the christening of a baby – 'Frederick Temple Cornwall.' Then on to a public picnic on Beacon Hill. There were numbers of people there, and we stayed an hour, and said good-bye to all we knew. Fred and I then came on board the *Amethyst,* and D. went back to Government House to see that the speech was ready for the Press. Some mistake had been made in reporting it, and he found it in such hopeless confusion that he did not get away till quite late, missing the dinner on board, and half the performance which was given for us. The officers had got up some songs and glees, and afterwards we had some Christy Minstrels, which were very amusing.

Lord Dufferin delivered his masterly speech, lasting two and a half hours, and reputed to be his most brilliant while in Canada, to a small audience of thirty or forty persons, principally members of various committees he had met. He assured them he had come solely as their Governor-General, to become acquainted, and to learn of the physical features, capabilities and resources of the province. He had not come on a diplomatic mission, or charged with any announcement either from the Imperial or the Dominion Government. In forthright language he reviewed both sides of the railway question and compared the suggested terminal locations, Bute Inlet and the Fraser Valley, both of which he had visited. He said, in part:

There is, I admit, one mission that is strictly within my functions to fulfil — namely, the mission of testifying by my presence amongst you, that the Government and the entire people of Canada, without distinction of party, are most sincerely desirous of cultivating with you those friendly and affectionate relations upon the existence of which must depend the future harmony and solidity of our common Dominion.

You consider yourselves injured, and you certainly have been disappointed. Canada has been accused not only of failing to accomplish her undertakings, but of a wilful breach of faith in having neglected to do so. . . . Railway enterprise in the United States was being developed to an astounding extent. One transcontinental railway had been successfully executed and others were being projected. It had come to be considered that a railway could be flung across the Rocky Mountains as readily as across a hayfield. . . . Unfortunately one element in the calculation was left entirely out of account, and that was the comparative ignorance which prevailed in regard to the mountain ranges and passes. In the United States, for years troops of emigrants had passed westward to Salt Lake City and to the Golden Gate; every track and trail through the mountains was way-worn and well-known. The location of the line in that neighborhood was pre-determined by the experience of persons already well acquainted with the locality. . . .

Canada undoubtedly pledged herself to that which was a physical impossibility. The mistake she made was in being too sanguine in her calculations. But remember a portion of the blame for concluding a bargain, impossible of accomplishment, cannot be confined to one only of the parties to it. The mountains which have proved our stumbling block were your own mountains, and within your own territory. It is impossible to forget you yourselves are by no means without responsibility.

It is asserted that the new Government is an enemy to the Pacific Railway. I believe this to be a complete misapprehension. I believe the Pacific Railway has no better friend in Canada than Mr. Mackenzie. His position was undoubtedly a very embarrassing one. His Government inherited responsibilities which he knew, and which the country had come to know, could not be discharged. . . .

During the whole of the period I was in constant personal communication with Mr. Fleming [Sandford Fleming, chief engineer of the surveys]. Over and over again he has explained to me how unexpected were the difficulties he had to encounter, how repeatedly, after following a particular route, his engineers found themselves stopped by an impassable wall of mountains and how trail after trail had to be examined and abandoned. . . .

Mr. Mackenzie has offered you a very considerable grant of money. To fulfil a special item in the Carnarvon Terms, *he has adopted the only course left to him, in proposing to discharge his obligations by a money payment. Every single item of the* Carnarvon Terms *is at this moment in the course of fulfilment. . . .*

Most earnestly do I desire the accomplishment of all your aspirations; and if ever I have the good fortune to come to British Columbia again, I hope it may be by — rail.

THURSDAY, 21ST. – The morning was lovely, and D. having finished his business was able to enjoy himself. The Commodore took me for a row, and we went on board the *Douglas,* where there was a party to see us off. We started at twelve, accompanied by the little steamer, and had much waving of handkerchiefs before parting with her.

I regret to say I was not able to appear at dinner, and that, one by one, those who sat down disappeared from the table. We had a very rough night, and half the officers and sailors were ill. The mail steamer *Dakota* started an hour after us, bent upon beating us.

SATURDAY, 23RD. – Beautiful weather, and all decidedly better.

SAN FRANCISCO: SUNDAY, 24TH. – Anchored at 7 a.m., and have won the race against the *Dakota*. We stayed on board for church, and then said a temporary 'good-bye' to the ship and her officers, and came ashore to the hotel.

MONDAY, 25TH. – At twelve o'clock we went on board the *Amethyst* again, the ward-room officers having asked us to lunch with them. They received us most hospitably; we are sorry to part.

After our farewells, General McDowell met us, and we went by train with him southwards for an hour. At the station we had a carriage-and-four and drove to Mr. Sharon's. [This was Belmont, the home of Senator William Sharon.] He was a miner, has twice been a millionaire, twice lost all, this being his third enjoyment of a great fortune. He owns a gigantic hotel, another almost as big in San Francisco, a large house in town, this country place, a big house in Washington, not to mention various little mines and railways. He is considered the merchant-prince of 'Frisco.

The guests are General Sherman [one of the heroes of the Civil War], a very pleasing man, and Mr. Cameron [at that time Minister of War in the United States] and his daughter. General McDowell does most of the honours and he marshalled us in to dinner, I going with our host, Mr. Sharon. I told him I liked his hotel, and tried to look as if 14,000,000,000 dollars – a sum he named – conveyed a definite idea to my mind. There was no plate, no luxury whatever here. No table could have looked less wealthy, and the dinner itself was simple.

The ball guests were coming by train, which was an hour and a half after I was ready. I danced the opening quadrille; the bandmaster stood close to me, and called out the orders, 'Ladies' chain, set to partners, cross,' etc., in a loud voice. The waltzes were slow.

Mr. Sharon took us to the train, in which we returned with the rest of the company to San Francisco.

TUESDAY, 26TH. – Fred Ward and I went to church for the purpose of standing as godfather and godmother to Francis Ward's baby, born the day we reached 'Frisco. I held her the whole service, and as she was awake I had to nurse her, and to do the 'goose-step,' all the time.

Mr. Miller, navigating-lieutenant of the *Amethyst*, came to lunch and brought some charts, in order that we might choose some anonymous places to which we might give names. Future maps will show the 'Dufferin Range' and the 'Countess of Dufferin Range' of mountains 'Dufferin Island,' 'Chatfield Island,' 'Hamilton Cape,' 'Littleton Cape,' 'Ward Cape,' and Mr. Miller is to be immortalised too.

We asked our reporters to dine with us, and they, ourselves and the Commodore had a delightful evening. D. and I agree that we would have come the whole journey for the sake of seeing the Chinese Theatre.

We went with the necessary appendage of a policeman. The pit was full of Chinamen, as was the gallery, with the exception of a small place, where about fifty women sat. The actors played in front of the musicians. A Chinese play is not an affair of hours, or of days, but of months. You can have about six hours a night of it as long as it lasts. We went for half an hour, and stayed two, and then left most reluctantly.

The music is of the bagpipe order. D. was charmed with the minor key and the barbaric tunes. When we arrived the stage was occupied by a company of aristocratic Chinamen, and it was evident an important council was being held. The councillors were magnificently dressed in gold and embroidered satin and various-shaped head-dresses. The acting *we* might consider stagey, but it seems to suit the dress and the people. They did it with such an air!

Having torn ourselves away from the theatre, our guide took us to see the 'Joss House,' or Chinese church. We mounted a winding stair till we reached the top storey, where we found the place of worship. Two candles and three night-lights were burning in front of idols. It is not at all imposing, being small and crowded.

This ended our last day in San Francisco, and to-morrow the return journey begins.

WEDNESDAY, 27TH. – We had to cross in a ferry to the railway-station, where we found our Pullman ready. The grizzly bear at Colfax looked miserable with the heat. He received grapes thankfully. Enormous bunches here are to be had for five cents.

THURSDAY, 28TH. – On the Alkali Plains; the acrid dust disagreeable to the eyes.

FRIDAY, 29TH. – We breakfasted at Ogden, then started for Salt Lake City. Salt Lake was in sight almost the whole way, and was of a deep, bright blue. On the other side of the carriage the hills were red and orange and brilliant yellow, autumn having already put the sumach plant into her gorgeous livery.

The city is a wonderful creation. The streets are broad, so that the tramway which runs down the middle does not interfere with one's carriage-wheels. At the side runs a little open stream of rapid-flowing, clear water – a most refreshing sight in a naturally dusty place. Green trees grow along the banks of this artificial ditch, and the watering of the arid plain is the greatest work the Prophet has performed.

The first thing to be seen was the Tabernacle, in front of which a temple of granite is being built. The service will be held there when the congregation is small. The Tabernacle is a huge edifice with a great flat dome. There is no support to the arch inside, of which fact the Mormons are proud. It holds 12,000 people, and we found it decorated with garlands and hanging bunches of flowers. There is an enormous organ, which we heard played, and from Brigham Young's pulpit you can see every seat in the vast circular room. The acoustic properties are perfect.

SATURDAY, 30TH. – We had to leave early in the morning, and were, as our hotel-keeper playfully remarked, 'sent off with fireworks,' the illumination being the burning of a rival inn. The whole roof was on fire, and the goods were being thrown out of the window.

We breakfasted at Ogden, and then, in our comfortable 'house-upon-wheels,' began to ascend the Rocky Mountains.

SUNDAY, OCTOBER 1ST. – It was difficult to believe that this was Sunday, for when we arrived in Cheyenne all was bustle at the railway-station, and in the town the shops were open. The only 'Sabbath' look was given to the place by the laziness of the men, who sat about and drank beer. The 'West' seems to me to be very careless in religious matters, and the only church we could discover in this town was a Roman Catholic one. We and our two cars were left here.

> As on the trip westward, the party travelled over a number of different railway lines. There was no road that had a continuous right-of-way from the Pacific coast to the Canadian border.

MONDAY, 2ND. – We slept 'on board,' and started at five in the morning. About nine we reached Denver, a town surrounded by mountains. It has its own political excitements, and a torch-light procession of Democrats marched past our hotel this evening, while a Republican one formed close by and set off in the opposite direction. It is wonderful how these rival processions are managed without collision. [1876 was election year in the United States.]

We heard of a young man who came down from the mines a week before with 1,900 lbs. weight of gold, worth about 16s. an ounce. He

had an escort of twenty men, to each of whom he paid $200 (40£.).
We were shown a nugget weighing about 145 ounces.

TUESDAY, 3RD. – We were glad to leave Denver this morning. D. had a
talk with a hunter, who is known as Oregon Bill. He gave us his
photograph, in which he is depicted with an Indian scalp hanging
from his belt.

We travelled through the ugliest country it is possible to conceive:
a flat plain, without the smallest variation the whole day. Our only
excitement was seeing a calf dragged along by a lasso, and numerous
prairie-fires at night, illuminating the landscape in every direction.

WEDNESDAY, 4TH. – The country still ugly, though when we got to Missouri a few trees and some castor-oil plants were to be seen. I think
we found this almost the longest day of our tour.

THURSDAY, 5TH. – Arrived at St. Louis early, and found that it is
the day of the year to be here – the best day of the Great Fair. The
town and hotels are crammed, and some residents good-naturedly
turned out to give us their rooms. We found two mails awaiting us,
and after reading them went off to see the show.

There is a fine, uncovered amphitheatre, where we saw trotting-
horses and four-in-hands; a band played, and the seats all round the
course were filled. There must have been 30,000 people there, and
crowds outside and all through the grounds. It is a great holiday here.

D. took me a walk through the town, which is one of the nicest I
have seen in the States – solid-looking, and with very handsome residences. The hotel is comfortable.

FRIDAY, 6TH. – We left St. Louis early, and stood outside our train to
examine the great bridge over which we had to pass. It crosses the
Mississippi and the Missouri, the two having joined into one muddy
river. The bridge is built on three piers, and is, I believe, a wonderful piece of engineering work. The carriage-way is over the bridge,
the railway through it. The whole looks light and airy, and suggestive
of a 'smash'; but it is, of course, really very strong.

We read our newspapers, and I went for the third time through
all my letters! Letters are never more appreciated or spelt through
than when one is travelling.

SATURDAY, 7TH. – Soon after breakfast we crossed the St. Clair in our
train, on a large boat built for the purpose, and being now in Canada,
the 'Grand Tour' ends.

D. and I spend Sunday at Toronto; on Monday morning I go to Montreal and he to Philadelphia. Friday, I hope to see my children, and am planning holidays and 'great larks.'

Lord Dufferin's visit to the Centennial Exhibition in Philadelphia was a private one. In a speech given in Ottawa after his return, he had high commendation for Canada's exhibits there and for 'the many prizes we have taken away, especially in the agricultural competitions.'

CHAPTER 17

Our Fifth Winter and Summer in Canada

OCTOBER 1876 - JULY 1877

FRIDAY, 13TH OCTOBER. – The 'Grand Tour' being over, I quite forgot I had still to keep up a Journal, and, suddenly remembering it, I find myself at the end of a week with no notes, and the necessity of remembering how I have spent the time. We arrived in Toronto last Saturday night, and were very hospitably received by the Macdonalds at Government House. I liked them all very much.

On Sunday D. and I went to church in the Cathedral, and in the afternoon a few people came to see us – Lady Macdonald, old Mr. Chapman, etc. The Howlands, Mowats, Colonel Cumberland, and Mr. Crooks, dined.

The Honourable Donald Alexander Macdonald, Postmaster-General of Canada from 1873 to 1875, had, in May 1875, been appointed Lieutenant-Governor of Ontario. Mrs. Macdonald had died in 1869 and his daughter was hostess at Government House.

With the others of the same name — Sir John and Lady Macdonald — Lady Dufferin was better acquainted. Sir John had been Prime Minister during their first months in Canada. However, in 1876 they were living in Toronto on St. George Street.

Edward Chapman, professor of mineralogy and geology at University College in Toronto, is here designated as *old*. He was fifty-five, only five years older than Lord Dufferin.

The guests at dinner included the Howlands, who had been their host and hostess on their visit to Government House four years before. Oliver (later Sir Oliver) Mowat had become Prime Minister of Ontario in 1872. Mrs. Cumberland was not present. She was in England with their daughters, and Colonel Cumberland expected to sail in a few days to join them. Hon. Adam Crooks, a forty-nine-year-old lawyer, who was Provincial Treasurer, was there alone; his wife had died eight years before.

On Monday morning I had to be up at 5.30, to catch my train to Montreal, and D., whom I left behind, started at eleven *en route* for Philadelphia. In spite of our recent long tour, Alexander [her maid] and I both thought this the longest journey we ever made. We got to Montreal at 9.30, Mr. Mackenzie [the Prime Minister] having been with me as far as Prescott. Russell [Russell Stephenson, her sister Gwen's husband] met me at the train, and I found Gwen in her own house, looking very well, and all her surroundings so pretty and comfortable. Gwen and I spend quiet mornings together. One afternoon we went a lovely drive up the mountain. We visited her chief friends, having tea with Miss de Rocheblave (a French-Canadian lady who has many friends in England) and Mrs. Stephen, one of my sister's best and kindest friends.

Mrs. Stephen was the London-born wife of George Stephen, who, in 1850, had emigrated from Scotland and entered a cloth manufacturing business in Montreal. In 1876 he was president of the Bank of Montreal. Joining with his relative Donald Smith (later Lord Strathcona) and other colleagues, their company completed the St. Paul and Pacific Railway and the Canadian Pacific Railway. He served for eight years as president of the latter line. In 1891, he became Baron Mount Stephen.

We breakfasted early this morning, and I left by the train for Ottawa.

FRIDAY, 20TH. – Two days of Indian summer; such lovely weather. We drove in the afternoons, and remained in the garden till five. The Council and Ministers are making arrangements to give D. a grand reception on his return; we expect him on Monday or Tuesday.

TUESDAY, 24TH. – Sunday was wet and gloomy again; so was Monday, on which day D. returned. Four aldermen went to meet him at a station thirty miles off, and when he arrived at Ottawa there was a platform, a guard of honour, an address, and a carriage-and-four to bring him to Government House. The children were very happy

listening to the guns and watching the four greys, and we all stood
at the door to receive the Governor-General.

He was so surprised at the sight of his baby, who is much grown
and improved, and admired Victoria, whom later in the evening
Nelly dressed up in the most artistic manner as the 'Queen of Sheba.'
WEDNESDAY, NOVEMBER 1ST. – The Count de Turenne arrived this
morning to pay us a visit. He returns to France next month.

At three o'clock we went into town – a large party: seven children,
accompanied by three parents, a nurse and the Count – to see Tom
Thumb.

> Charles Edward Stratton, a midget born in Bridgeport, Connecticut,
> joined the P. T. Barnum circus organization in 1842, when but four
> years old. Barnum gave him the name 'General Tom Thumb,' dressed
> him in a uniform, and exhibited him in the United States, in England,
> and on the continent of Europe (1844-47). Until his teens he was only
> 2' 1" tall, and weighed about fifteen pounds. At maturity he was
> 3' 4" high and weighed about seventy pounds.
>
> In 1863 he married Lavinia Warren, a dwarf also in Barnum's
> troupe. He lived until 1883.

We filled two boxes, and the delight of the children made it very
amusing. Basil jumped up and down, pounded the cushions, shouted
'hurrah,' and roared with laughter; and they all clapped and cheered
in company with the rest of the spectators, who were mostly children.
The dwarfs did some little plays, one having a man in the part of a
'mischievous monkey' in it, who once made a dash at our box, and
was received with shrieks.

The Littletons dined with us, and the Count told us funny stories
about his tour. The weather is very bad – almost pitch-dark, and wet.

SUNDAY, 5TH. – We were surprised when we got to church to have the
sermon first. It was explained in the evening that this was a hint to
people who came late. It was rather unfortunate that on this day it
happened the Governor-General was two or three minutes late, and
of course could not imagine what had happened when he found us in
the middle of the sermon.

TUESDAY, 19TH DECEMBER. – The children did their Christmas shopping.
I think it is the event of the year they like the best. They each go
with a few shillings, and with a list of about sixteen people, for whom
they expect to buy handsome presents.

"The opening of Parliament [1873] . . . D. drove in an open sleigh with four horses."

Lady Dufferin from a drawing by her husband: "D. drew a good deal and finished some very nice sketches."

CHRISTMAS DAY, 1876. – The children's voices are heard very early, rejoicing over presents they have received from their nurses.

The whole family, except the absent Archie, dined at our lunch, Baby and Victoria for the first time. The Littletons came to tea, and there was a round table with ten very happy faces at it. Then came the tree, which looked very brilliant, and gave universal satisfaction. Everyone seems to have got just what they wanted, and the clamour of musical instruments resounding through the house ever since sounds cheerful, if not pretty. When the pleasures of the tree were exhausted we had snapdragon, and then a 'Yorkshire wassail-bowl,' in which we all drank Archie's health with cheers.

SUNDAY, 31ST. – Gwen's baby was christened to-day.

MONDAY, JANUARY 1ST, 1877. – A hard day. At ten the children re-hearsed their play; at twelve His Ex., the A.D.C.s, and I, having dressed ourselves smart, sat for two hours receiving all the men in Ottawa. Exhausted by two, we lunched, and I then packed off my family to bed, promising faithfully to call them at four.

At three a servants' children's party commenced, and mine joined them for tea; after which they acted a little play with great success.

FRIDAY, 5TH. – I had my annual children's party to-day. Seventy-eight of them came at five, and mothers besides. After the play, which was acted again, there was tea: two long tables down the dining-room, and one outside for the grown-ups. The magic lantern came next, and then we cleared away the chairs, and the children danced about, and amused themselves.

SATURDAY, 6TH. – We had a skating-party, and final representation of the children's play, 'Fifine, the Fisher Maid,' which went off extreme-ly well. They like the appreciativeness of a grown-up audience.

Victoria was very funny; she would run on to the stage and exhibit her shoes, bracelets, etc. to the spectators; at last I had to draw her back, as she was taking the interest off from the real performers. When the curtain was drawn up again at the end, she came forward and made a nice little curtsey, and said 'Good-night, everybody.'

There was a scene in the play in which all go down to the bottom of the sea. I managed this by having green tarlatan, upon which fishes were pasted, drawn up slowly in front of the children to a cer-tain height above their heads, showing the depth of the water.

TORONTO: WEDNESDAY, 10TH. – We left Ottawa for Toronto yesterday, on the most lovely Canadian morning, to stay with the Macdonalds.

After lunch we set off for the Town Hall, and had an address from the Mayor and a reply from His Ex. This was the one about which one of the aldermen said, when discussing the question of our reception, and the expense of it, that 'a nice little speech from the Governor-General would cost nothing.'

People were presented to us after it, and then we went to tea at the Macphersons'. There was a very pleasant dinner of thirty people here in the evening.

> Hon. David (later Sir David) Lewis Macpherson came to Canada from his native Scotland in 1835, when seventeen years old. He became a successful railway contractor, working in association with Sir Casimir Gzowski.
>
> Called to the Senate in 1867 at the time of Confederation, he became its Speaker in 1880. For several years he served as a member of Sir John A. Macdonald's Cabinet. Chestnut Park, his large estate, with its spacious house, lay to the north of the city and east of Yonge Street.

THURSDAY, 11TH. – D. and I went to the Mechanics' Institute to receive an address.

> The beautiful building of the Mechanics' Institute, designed by Frederick William Cumberland, a life member of the organization, was located at the north-east corner of Adelaide and Church Streets. For its more than one thousand members, it provided free library service from its over eight thousand volumes, and educational lectures during the winter season. Its reading-room was declared to be the best in the Dominion. As well, evening classes offered training for apprentices recommended by railway officials. The Mechanics' Institute was merged with the Toronto Public Library in 1883.

A ball given in the evening was nicely managed, and handsomely done. We received the guests with Mr. and Miss Macdonald, and then walked through the room to the dais prepared for us. I sat there most of the evening talking to different people, and His Ex. danced everything till early next morning.

FRIDAY, 12TH. – After breakfast D. and I visited the rooms of the Art Union Society of Toronto, and in the afternoon we went to the Curling and Skating Rink [their new building was being opened on Adelaide Street], where an address was read, to which he replied in very happy terms. They presented him with curling stones and brooms, and me with a beautiful pair of skates.

I skated a little and D. curled. He had a dinner at the National Club, and made a very amusing speech. Alluding to his duties as a constitutional governor, he likened himself to 'the humble functionary we see superintending the working of some complicated mass of chain-driven machinery. This personage merely walks about with a little tin vessel of oil in his hand, and he pours in a drop here and a drop there, as occasion or the creaking of a joint may require; while his utmost vigilance is directed to no higher aim than the preservation of the wheels and cogs from the intrusion of dust, *grits,* or other foreign bodies.' The 'Grits' being the party now in power, this joke on their name was much appreciated.

The weather is very cold; there is so much wind we feel it more than at Ottawa.

SUNDAY, 14TH. – Before church we visited the Sunday-school, and then had a long service in the Cathedral. After it we drove out to see Mr. and Mrs. Gzowski in their pretty house.

> Their 'pretty house,' named 'The Hall,' stood in large grounds, a short distance north of the lakefront on Bathurst Street. Later it served as a part of the Toronto Western Hospital. Part of the land became the Alexandra Rose Garden.

After lunch Fred and I drove out with Mr. W. Howland to the General Hospital [then located on Gerrard Street East, between Sackville and Sumach Streets]. It is a fine one, and we went all over it, and on to tea with Mrs. Howland.

MONDAY, 15TH. – We four ladies – Miss Macdonald, her sisters and myself – dined alone, the gentlemen being at the [Toronto] Club dinner given to His Ex., where he made another important speech.

TUESDAY, 16TH. – Such a lovely day at last. In the afternoon there was a pleasant little skating party at Government House, and in the evening we went to see 'Arrah na Pogue' at the Theatre. When the play was over we drove back, changed our dresses, and went off to the railway-car, where we meant to sleep.

THURSDAY, FEBRUARY 8TH. – In the afternoon I attended the opening of Parliament. The Senate Chamber was crowded, and all the dresses, etc. looked very handsome. The Speech was a rather long one.

In the evening we had a large Drawing-room in the Senate Chamber. There must have been 800 presentations, and the room got quite crammed.

THURSDAY, 15TH. – We had an evening rehearsal of some plays we are getting up, and all the actors came to dine first. Of course there were several things to be improved: the gas did not go out when it should, etc.; but by working hard we got it all right.

FRIDAY, 16TH. – We had the dress-rehearsal. Both pieces were immensely successful. D. was delighted; the dresses capital, and in 'Our Wife' very pretty.

The 'Loan of a Lover' came first, Mr. Kimber and his sister doing the principal parts, and doing them admirably. Colonel Littleton and I, Mr. Brodie and Mr. McLean, did the smaller parts. The songs were all well sung, and we put in a few additional ones. The two Freds looked magnificent in 'Our Wife.' Fred Ward acted extremely well; his part is most amusing, and suited him exactly. Mr. Kimber was at his very best; indeed, we had a very strong cast for the whole play.

SATURDAY, 17TH. – A rehearsal of 'The Scrap of Paper' after lunch, and then a skating party. There was no snow on the top of the slide, and consequently no tobogganing; and it was too cold for much skating, so we began to dance early.

WEDNESDAY, 21ST. – The day of our theatricals. The weather is beautiful, almost too warm. Great misfortunes happened to-day. Miss Lea [later Mrs. Anna Lea Merritt], who is staying with us to do a picture of me, took hartshorn by mistake, and nearly choked herself. Then D. got a bad headache; and at seven we had no gas at all! I was in despair. The order was given to collect all the candles and lamps in the house, and our cook, who was preparing a supper for 400, was left in sudden darkness. His wife was furious, and of course a couple of lamps had to be returned to him. You may imagine my feelings; all the passages and dressing-rooms in a miserable light; for by eight o'clock only a glimmer of gas had appeared. The stage was lighted up with candles, which dripped over us, and had to be replaced between each scene. It was so depressing.

People declared they were delighted; and certainly they did not mind the want of gas half as much as I did. At the end I felt much more tired than usual, owing to the worry.

WEDNESDAY, MARCH 7TH. – On Friday, the 2nd, there was a great curling-match between our club and Belleville for a medal. It was very exciting, the V.C.R. [Vice-regal Curling Rink] being behind-hand at first; but we finally won by two points. We have to play once more before we can keep the medal.

SATURDAY, 10TH. – Such a magnificent day. The trees sparkle like diamonds, and every twig and branch is encased in ice. Against a bright blue sky they are too lovely. A large Parliamentary dinner in the evening.

WEDNESDAY, 14TH. – D. went into town, and after he got out of the sleigh slipped upon the icy pavement, and fell very heavily on a step. Some men picked him up, and put him on his feet; but he could not stand, and fell again. They then carried him into a shop, where he lay on the floor for quite twenty minutes before he could recover his breath. Two doctors came, and bandaged him up tight. They said no bones were broken; but he was severely bruised and shaken, and in the evening suffered great pain if he moved.

Of course he had to go to bed, and missed the 'Scrap of Paper.' It went off very well, and people were delighted with it, and so interested in the story. There were no hitches at all; the only drawback was D.'s absence.

FRIDAY, 16TH. – D. very poorly all day, and quite unable to move. Colonel and Mrs. Hewitt came for the large military dinner we gave. [Colonel Hewitt, R.E., at this time was Commandant of the Military College at Kingston, Ontario.] There were fifty-four at dinner, and the room looked very well. D. so disappointed to miss it.

WEDNESDAY, 21ST. – About 11 p.m. Mr. Brodie drove up to say that he, General Smyth, his son, etc., had been burnt out, and had lost every-thing – two theatrical suits for Saturday into the bargain!

SATURDAY, 24TH. – We had the last performance of the 'Scrap of Paper.' D. was able to be at it, and in the house we had the Stephen-sons and Hewitts. There was a very large audience, and the piece was a great success. Between the acts we had some very good singing and playing.

MONDAY, APRIL 30TH. – D. and I were the recipients of a great honour to-day, The cabmen of Ottawa, having benefited by the gaieties at Government House this winter, got up a testimonial and an address for us, which they presented themselves.

They came at two o'clock – fourteen very respectable-looking men. They read an illuminated address, and then presented D. with a handsome stick with a gold top and inscription, and me with a silver card-case on which is inscribed: 'Presented to Her Excellency the Countess of Dufferin by the Hackmen of the City of Ottawa, as a token of esteem. April, 1877.'

When the presentation was over, D. showed them the house – our sitting-rooms, etc. – and gave them dinner in the ball-room. Directly the wine was poured out they all stood up and drank the Queen's health.

SATURDAY, MAY 12TH. – We left home, D. on his way to the Centennial Exhibition at Philadelphia, and I to pay a visit (with Fred) to Gwen at Montreal. We had Mr. Reynolds's car, and parted from D. at Prescott. We had four hours to wait, but passed the time very pleasantly, walking and sitting by the riverside.

SATURDAY, 19TH. – After a delightful week with Gwen, Fred and I returned to Ottawa to-day, and the baby came down to see us off, as merry and amiable as usual.

MONDAY, 21ST. – In the evening Fred, the Littletons, and I walked to the Reynoldses', and sat on the steps of their house watching the procession on the water in honour of the new Pope [Leo XIII]. There were a quantity of canoes with torches, which were very pretty, and the Roman Catholic houses in town were illuminated. The night was fine, and we enjoyed the walk and the fine view from Earnscliffe, the Reynoldses' house.

Earnscliffe, the large limestone house overlooking the Ottawa River, located not far from the mouth of the Rideau, was built about 1855 by John McKinnon, the first president of the Ottawa and Prescott Railway. He died in 1866 and two years later the property was bought by Thomas Reynolds, managing director of the same railway. Throughout this narrative Lady Dufferin has mentioned the latter gentleman a number of times, commenting on his thoughtfulness for their comfort when they left Ottawa over his railroad.

Twenty years later, in 1888, Earnscliffe became the residence of Sir John A. Macdonald. After his death in 1891, Lady Macdonald continued to live there for some years. Eventually, after having been leased to various persons, it was purchased in 1930 by the British Government. Since then it has been the residence of the United

Kingdom High Commissioner. From time to time additions have been made to the original structure.

TUESDAY, 22ND. – D. arrived from New York at 1.30, and we spent the afternoon out of doors.

SATURDAY, JUNE 2ND. – Mr. Ford came to stay till Monday.

> Francis (later Sir Francis) Clare Ford, 1828-99, was a British diplomat who had served in various embassies abroad. At that time he was agent for his Government on a commission which had been in Halifax studying United States fishing rights.

THURSDAY, 7TH. – Before lunch an assembly of ecclesiastics arrived: 'His Excellency the Apostolic Delegate to Canada,' the Bishops of Ottawa, Newfoundland and Prince Edward Island, with all their acolytes.

The first-named is Bishop Conroy, of Ardagh, and is sent here by the Pope to arrange various matters in this country. He is a very pleasant man, and after 'doing' a quantity of institutions, he came with all the others to dine here, and he and his chaplain remained the night.

We dined in the ball-room, and were about fifty-five people – Ministers, Priests, Supreme Court Judges, etc. The Delegate has been *fêted* and worked so much in Canada, that he seems to be longing for privacy and rest.

FRIDAY, 8TH. – The Bishop was off at 7.30 to have Mass in town; he returns to lunch, goes back to hold a *levée,* and then dines here.

TUESDAY, 19TH. – All the last week we have had the most delightful weather, and not a mosquito to destroy our pleasure.

We left Ottawa to-day and had to be up early, and to breakfast soon after seven. The children were all dressed in time to see us off. Our travelling-party consists of Nellie, Fred, ourselves; Mr. Johnston, who comes as far as Montreal; and Colonel Stuart, whom we take with us in the *Druid* for a few days. We reached Prescott at ten, and then got on board the river-boat and spent a very pleasant day.

The *Druid* as nice and comfortable as usual. Nellie sleeps in the cabin next to us, and originally intended for my maid. Fred and Colonel Stuart have the two cabins in the fore part of the vessel.

WEDNESDAY, 20TH. – We got to Quebec directly after lunch, and as soon as D. had dismissed the guard of honour, we went to the Citadel, and returned to dine on board the *Druid*. Dinner being over, we again started on our journey.

GASPE: SATURDAY, 23RD. – D. and Fred went off for a little fishing, and brought back two salmon and three trout. D. was the lucky one. The men say we are a week late (always the case with salmon-fishing!); so we shall have to go up and live in the bush, instead of in our comfortable ship.

MONDAY, 25TH. – Mr. Reynolds, Mr. Middleton, and the Molsons came to see me in the afternoon, and after dinner D. and I went over to their yacht. They expect to sail in the morning, and are leaving the fishing in disgust. Mr. Reynolds has only caught five fish, and Mr. Middleton nine.

The only lucky person has been Colonel McNeill; he got thirty-three salmon in the York, and last night there came a letter from him to say that he had just reached the Matapedia, and in one evening's fishing caught four salmon, averaging 29½ lbs. in weight.

TUESDAY, 26TH. – D. and Fred have gone up to the house, so we shall not see them till to-morrow. Colonel Stuart is fishing down here, and will dine on board.

WEDNESDAY, 27TH. – All the morning preparations for our departure were being made, and at two o'clock we got off. We drove in a buggy for two hours, and then got on to horses. We only got at a foot's pace, but Nellie enjoyed it.

We arrived at five o'clock at the camp and found the river very low, but the water beautifully clear. We had a good account of the fishing. Tuesday afternoon D. caught six salmon and Fred four, and yesterday D. caught four and Fred six; besides, they have several trout. Nellie and I welcomed them home about eight o'clock, and saw the fish displayed on the rocks. Then we dined, and sat at the camp-fire till bedtime. Nellie amused herself making 'smudges,' and filling saucers with moss and violets. The flies are not so bad as usual this year.

SATURDAY, 30TH. – D.'s morning's fishing produced three salmon, and Fred came home with two, and thirteen beautiful trout. After lunch we again went out in the canoe. At one moment I was to be seen standing on a small rock in the middle of the river, Nelly upon another, and D. on a chair, which we had brought with us and planted in the stream. We were all lashing the water, but were most unfortunate, and only brought home one trout.

TUESDAY, 3RD JULY. – I went out with D. and while fishing for trout had an adventure with one. I hooked him at the same time that D. had on a salmon. I was standing on a small rock in the middle of the river, and had neither landing-net nor salmon-killer with me. The salmon, however, wished to go down the rapid, so D., his men, and his canoe, had to pass under my rod, and between me and my trout. When I had tired the fish out, the difficulty was to capture him; but I managed to get him on to my rock, and to unhook him. And I had another on before D. came back.

He had arranged to go far up the river and sleep, so he started off at eleven o'clock, and after lunch Nelly and I went out with Fred. As the salmon would not rise, we both fished for trout, and had great fun. To our surprise, on returning home we found D.; no fish had arrived so far up the river, so he did not stay, and we arranged to go 'out' to-morrow.

WEDNESDAY, 4TH. – All busy packing. D. stayed at home, and I went out for an hour, and caught ten trout – one 3½ lbs., and the others smaller. I fish with a beautiful little bamboo rod which with the reel only weighs six ounces.

It was a lovely day; I was quite sorry to leave our camp, as I enjoyed it very much this year, and we were less troubled with flies than usual. We had the Captain to dine with us, and started immediately after dinner.

THURSDAY, 5TH. – A beautiful day, and a lovely sunset and double rainbow. 'A rainbow at night is a sailor's delight,' so we hope it will be fine to-morrow, when we ought to reach Tadousac.

FRIDAY, 6TH. – Arrived about eight in the morning; a most beautiful day, the children all well, and enjoying the seaside very much. We sat out on the balcony, and walked on the rocks.

SUNDAY, 15TH. – We have spent a very pleasant ten days. The weather has been lovely, and we have sat out the most of the day. We were able to bathe occasionally, although the water is always cold here – quite icy.

D. drew a good deal, and had finished some very nice sketches, which yesterday met with a sad mishap. We went on a fishing expedition up the Saguenay, in the *Druid*. We breakfasted on board, and then had a pleasant voyage of two hours to the fishing-grounds. When we got back, D. found he had left all his sketching things and finished drawings below high-water mark at the fishing-place. He sent a man in a canoe to look for them, who found them, soaked and spoilt.

We are now returning to Ottawa to prepare for a tour in Manitoba, to which we are all looking forward with great pleasure.

Manitoba, which had become part of the Dominion of Canada in 1870, was the only province the Dufferins had not visited. No railway linked it to either Ontario or Quebec. Their trip was to be a long, roundabout one, through the United States.

CHAPTER 18

The North West
AUGUST 1877

MONDAY, JULY 30TH. – We left Ottawa this morning in good spirits and in smartish clothes, which we put on for the guard of honour and the friends who come to see us start. Once really off, we arrayed ourselves in cooler and more suitable travelling garments.

TUESDAY, 31ST. – The train behaved in an extraordinary manner during the night. It rushed along at a furious pace for a couple of miles, pulled up with a frightful bump, stopped to shriek, went on again after three or four jerks, and in this way kept us thoroughly awake. But a good breakfast in our own car and an hour spent outside it in the fresh morning air quite revived me.

We had such a dusty day: five minutes sufficed to cover tables, sofas, our faces, hands and hair with the dirtiest powder. We were so glad when we arrived at Lake Michigan, and felt the cool breeze from over its surface, and saw hundreds of people bathing in the refreshing water. At Chicago we got into carriages, and drove rapidly to the luxurious Palmer House, where we dined, and enjoyed the quiet and cleanliness. We returned to our Pullman much the better for our outing.

WEDNESDAY, AUGUST 1ST. – We had a pleasant day in the train, passing through a good deal of 'bush' and half-settled country. As we got near St. Paul we crossed a pretty lake, and then came in sight of the Mississippi, on which the town is built.

At the station a dozen gentlemen came on board, and took us to the hotel in carriages; we enjoyed a night 'on shore.'

THURSDAY, 2ND. – We breakfasted at 8.30, and almost directly after held a little reception. A number of gentlemen were presented to us;

one made a speech, to which D. replied. They told me afterwards they were 'more than delighted' with his 'remarks.'

This affair was scarcely over when I was hurried off to make a tour of the country. In the first carriage D. and I, General Johnston, and Mr. Rice went. They were both pleasant men, citizens of this town; the latter had been for many years in Congress, a person to whom everyone appealed for information. The second carriage contained General Terry and the Littletons. General Terry is the officer who was in command when General Custer attacked the Indians, and lost his life. [June 25, 1876, at the battle of Little Big Horn, in Montana.] Four more carriages followed, with Nellie, the A.D.C.s, and more gentlemen.

We drove to Minneapolis, through flat country, sometimes bush, sometimes prairie, and sometimes beautiful cornfields. Minneapolis is younger than St. Paul, the latter being about thirty years of age. It is, I think, more flourishing-looking, and the residences, surrounded with lawns and flower-gardens, look charming and comfortable.

We went to see the St. Anthony Falls, a series of rapids and an artificial 'slide.' The water was wearing away the rock, and the hand of man has intervened to keep it in check, and to prevent the lumber interests being injured by Nature. Then we went over a flour-mill, the flour here being a great *spécialité*. This mill turns out a thousand barrels a day, some of a peculiar, very white quality, which makes the most delicious bread; it contains the most nutritious parts of the wheat, and is made by a newly-invented process.

Into our carriages again, and off to see the Minnehaha Falls. 'From the waterfall, he called her "Minnehaha" – "Laughing Water." ' The season has been very dry, and there was little water coming over the Fall. But I am glad to have seen it, as Longfellow's poem [*The Song of Hiawatha*] is one of my earliest recollections. When we returned, General Terry came with us, and we went to the Fort.

It is beautifully situated on a high cliff at the junction of the Mississippi and the Minnesota. We were saluted by soldiers; then the officer in command took us to the top of a tower, looking over the rivers. We enjoyed the cool, refreshing air, and the lovely view.

When we left we crossed the Mississippi in a sort of ferry-boat, which was made to go backwards and forwards by the current of the river itself; the flat boat was pulled in a slanting direction, so that the stream acted upon it, just as the wind does upon a sail, and moved it across.

We reached St. Paul about eight o'clock, and said good-bye to our kind entertainers. Nellie [aged twelve] came home in tremendous spirits. In her carriage there was a doctor, who had laid himself out to amuse her, and whom she thinks very 'witty.' At the Fort she was interested to hear there was an officer with a wooden leg. So when one came up to speak to her, having decided that he was all right, she asked him to show her the gentleman with the wooden leg. He replied he was the one; in her confusion she could only think of asking him if it hurt still.

After supper we were serenaded by a band; everyone has been so kind, and we have enjoyed our day.

FRIDAY, 3RD. – We left the hotel early, and once more got into our train. We journeyed all day, through swamps, lakes and prairie-lands. In the evening we went through some burning woods. They must have been on fire in about a hundred places, but the flames had not yet joined into one devastating sheet.

SATURDAY, 4TH. – I was awoke by the most disagreeable bumping and jolting, and soon discovered we were off the line. It took us two hours and many shakings before we got on again. We were now travelling through the flattest of flat prairies, very ugly and very green. About ten o'clock by the new time – for our watches are called upon to change their opinions as to the hour at every place we get to – we found ourselves at Fisher's Landing, and the steamer ready to take us down the Red River.

We have to leave our house-upon-wheels and embark upon the boat, which friendly hands have decorated with flags, wreaths of leaves, and flowers. The steamer [*Minnesota*] is a stern-wheeler, such as we had on the Fraser River. She draws very little water, and certainly has an extraordinary passage to perform. The river, which to all intents and purposes is the Red River (the first few miles it is called the Red Lake River), is very muddy, very narrow, and extremely sinuous. It twists and turns itself about. Think of a braiding-pattern, or of a zig-zag path up a steep hill. Or imagine sailing through hundreds of small ponds all joined together, the second concealed by the curve of the first, and you may form some idea of it.

I can only tell you that we go from one bank to the other, crushing and crashing against the trees, which grow down to the water-side. The branches sweep over the deck, and fly in our faces, and leave pieces behind them. I had just written this when I gave a shriek as I saw my ink-bottle on the point of being swept overboard by an intrusive tree; D.'s hat was knocked off his head by it.

The consequence of this curious navigation is that we never really go on for more than three minutes at a time. We run against one bank, our steam is shut off, and in some mysterious manner we swing round till our bow is into the other. Then we rebound, and go on a few yards, till the sharp curve brings us up against the side. Our stern wheel is often ashore, and our captain and pilot must require the patience of saints.

I told you when the last branch came on board. Well, I have been writing as fast as possible since, and now we are ashore on the other side. So you may easily believe we travel seventeen miles for two that we make. Were it not a lovely day, and had we not a delicious air, I don't know how bad our language might not become.

We were told at St. Paul that we should be eaten with mosquitoes; that no oil, no veils, no gloves, no leggings would keep out the devouring monsters. Fancy our delight, then, to find there are none, and that we are able to sit gloveless on deck and write.

We breakfasted early, and were hungry for a one-o'clock lunch, which was more elegant than substantial. Sardines were the *pièce de résistance*, and ice-cream the most attractive dish to be procured. I hope dinner will be more suited to our appetites.

This 'Red Lake River' is forty miles to travel, though the distance is only twelve from point to point. When we reached the Red River itself, we found the stream wide enough to go straight down, but quite as muddy and uninteresting. Trees come down to the water's edge and behind them stretches the prairie.

Alas! alas! towards evening the mosquitoes appeared. At dinner (a very good one) we were eaten while eating, and were glad to leave the lighted saloon, and sit on the bow of the steamer in the air. The night was dark, the river looked gloomy and mysterious, and we sat there and watched the black reflections in the water. Our steamer whistled, and in the distance we heard it answered. Slowly we turned a point, and saw another boat [the *Manitoba* from Winnipeg] approaching. It looked beautiful in the dark, with two great bull's-eyes, green and red lamps and other lights on deck, creeping towards us. We stopped, and backed into the shore, that it might pass. It came close and fired off a cannon, and we saw on the deck a large transparency with the words 'Welcome, Lord Dufferin' on it, and two girls dressed in white with flags in their hands. Then a voice sang 'Canada, sweet Canada,' and more voices joined in the chorus. They sang 'God save the Queen' and 'Rule, Britannia,' and cheered for the Governor-General as they began to move slowly away. He had only just time to call out a few words of thanks before they disappeared into the darkness.

It was very striking, and we scarcely recovered from our surprise and bewilderment before the thing was gone.

SUNDAY, 5TH. – At Pembina the American troops were drawn up to receive us. We went ashore and up to the Fort, where we spent about an hour. A little way further, we passed the line, and found ourselves in Canadian territory again. The first town was Emerson, and we landed there. The storm in the morning had knocked down their pretty arches. We found a guard of honour (militia), and a strange one of Indians – some in red coats, some in blankets, some with painted faces, feathers in their hair, beads, medals, etc. Others were more quietly got up; but they formed a picturesque group. D. received two addresses, one from the Indians.

D. spoke to the Mennonites (Russians): they are getting on very well, and want to have more of their people out here. They are good settlers, and in addition to the virtues of sobriety and industry they add the advantage of bringing money into the country.

We were stationary all night, as we did not want to reach Winnipeg till a reasonable hour in the morning. At five o'clock the gentlemen got up, and went out duck-shooting.

We heard Nellie describe her papa to a girl, who asked her to point out the Governor-General, as 'the gentleman in the chimney-pot.' She was very anxious to get Colonel Littleton to tell her the Freemason secrets, and, failing, said, with a sigh of relief, 'Well, I dare say when women get their rights we shall know them.'

My only difficulty is in keeping her at all smart on these occasions, for no sooner is she dressed than she visits the coal-hole, or climbs into some unthought-of place, and returns to me, each of her exploits marked by stains and smudges.

MONDAY, 6TH. – We came in sight of Fort Garry about ten o'clock. The Red River appears to divide the town in two, but we left it, and turned into the Assiniboine, round the corner of which we found a wharf. Some people came on board to see the Governor-General. He arranged for me to start half an hour before him, and go the City Hall, where we ladies sat till the noise of bands and shouting announced his arrival.

The town of Winnipeg is rapidly increasing, and to-day, with its decorations of transplanted trees and flags, it looked gay. Addresses were read and answered, and then I got with D. into the carriage, and drove to 'Silver Heights,' where we are to live.

It is quite five miles from town, along a prairie road, which is a little rough when the weather is dry, but which is simply impassable when there has been rain. The mud here is, from all accounts, fearful. The Lieutenant-Governor, Mr. Morris, told us it once took him nine hours to go eight miles, and two days to do twenty-two miles.

> The Honourable Alexander Morris had been appointed Lieutenant-Governor of Manitoba and of the Northwest Territories in 1872, when forty-six years of age. Previously he had served for three years as Minister of Inland Revenue in the Government of Sir John A. Macdonald.

'Our house' is a cottage, and lent to us by Mr. Donald Smith [later Lord Strathcona, chief commissioner in Canada for the Hudson's Bay Company], who met us at the door, introduced us to his daughter, and showed us our accommodation. The A.D.C.s are in a smaller cottage close by, and the men-servants sleep in tents. A fine reception-room, and two ante-rooms, carpeted, papered, and furnished, have been added to the house for us, which we regret, as the place is really too far away to entertain in; nor have we the china, or the knives and forks, wherewith to give a ball or dinner!

We are near the end of the road, and on the other side of it is the Assiniboine River. We sat on its banks, had tea on the balcony of the house, and spent a quiet evening. There is a long programme for this week.

TUESDAY, 7TH. – We went into town to call upon Mrs. Morris, the Lieutenant-Governor's wife. The Government House is surrounded by a wooden palisade, and has a brick gateway, which forms a nice old-fashioned court in front of the house.

In the evening we went to a 'Parlour Entertainment' – songs, speeches and change of costume – very well done, and amusing. Driving back we realized more fully than we had done before the disadvantage of living so far from the town. The road is a sort of track on the prairie, and we soon found we were off it. We asked the other carriage to go first, and the driver replied he had no lights; our man said his lights dazzled him, so finally the other carriage did go first. It took us over an hour to get back, and if the four other nights on which we have to go into Winnipeg are dark or wet, I don't know what we shall do.

WEDNESDAY, 8TH. – An Indian was sent by a chief, who lives twenty-six miles away, to ask when the Governor-General would visit him. The messenger was a fine-looking man. His hair was long, and he wore a fillet round his head with eagles' feathers fastened into it. He had a red cloth tunic embroidered with beads, with quantities of ermine tails hanging from the seams, each tail sewn into the centre of a circle of beads. Round his neck he wore a large necklace of bears' claws, moccasins on his feet, and European trousers, which were generally hidden by a large blue blanket, which he pulled round him in graceful folds.

Mrs. Littleton asked him about his religion. He said he had none – that the Indians were here from the Creation, that there was one Great Spirit, but that he found 'religion' cost money, and so it was better not to have any.

We drove into Winnipeg to see some games. The most desperate shower came on, and we bundled into our carriage as quickly as we could, but not before we were much damaged; feathers out of curl, dresses dirtied. The people were wonderfully good-tempered, and it was amusing to see some holding a bit of sail over them, soldiers with wheelbarrows on their backs for shelter, and others sitting under the shade of a big drum.

THURSDAY, 9TH. – We started off to visit the Archbishop on the other side of the river at St. Boniface. He and his clergy received us at the Palace, where two addresses were read. Then we saw the church, and went on to a convent.

It is of this church that John Greenleaf Whittier speaks in his poem, "The Red River Voyageur":

Is it the clang of wild-geese?
  Is it the Indian's yell,
That lends to the voice of the north-wind
  The tones of a far-off bell?

The voyageur smiles as he listens
  To the sound that grows apace;
Well he knows the vesper ringing
  Of the bells of St. Boniface.

The bells of the Roman Mission,
  That call from their turrets twain;
To the boatman on the river,
  To the hunter on the plain!

The Grey Sisters have about thirty children under their care; in these thirty there are representatives of eleven different nationalities. Each child had a little flag with 'Welcome' written in her own tongue upon it. There were Canadian French, English, Irish, half-breeds, and different Indian tribes.

We were asked at nine o'clock for the ball at Government House, and went punctually; but 'in honour of us' the other people were late, and we stood about a long time before the dancing began. All the ladies were well dressed, and the dancing as at Ottawa or London. Six years ago, at a ball here, ladies would have come in moccasins, and danced nothing but the Red River Jig. This state of society would have had some charm for us. The Jig was danced for us; it is exactly the same as an Irish Jig.

The supper was good, and the table prettily decorated with flowers. The fruit had to be imported, as none grows here yet. The Roman Catholic and English bishops both came to the ball for a few minutes.

FRIDAY, 10TH. – We held a reception at the City Hall at three o'clock. It did not last very long, but as we had to attend a concert in the evening we decided to dine at the hotel, and not to drive out to Silver Heights. The hotel-keeper insisted upon giving us our dinner free.

Mrs. Littleton and I went over the Fort [Fort Garry], and through the Hudson's Bay Stores. The room full of buffalo robes smelt horribly; but I bore it, being determined to see all I could.

The concert was 'classical,' and its great merit was the shortness of it. Nellie spent the afternoon at the Government House, where there are three children; but she dined with the grown-up people, and enjoyed herself very much.

SATURDAY, 11TH. – There were races to-day at Buffalo Park. What we most enjoyed seeing was a man lassoing a wild cow. He rode beautifully, and sent the lasso round her horns. After holding her thus, and riding about a little, he laid her gently over on her side, unable to get up. Three buffaloes were on the field in a state of semi-wildness. We were surprised to see how fast they could run, and how well they could jump, for their big heads do not give them a very active appearance.

MONDAY, 13TH. – We drove over to St. Boniface to see a rifle-match. I fired a shot, which was off the target, but which was marked a bull's-eye, and then the match began.

In the evening we had a visit from eight or ten Indians, who came to dance and sing before us. Their faces were elaborately painted, and they came up the road uttering the most extraordinary cries. They hung their drum upon some stakes they brought for the purpose. Then half of them sat down, and the others danced round, while the sitters beat the drum, and the whole company shouted. D. promised to go to their camp in the morning.

TUESDAY, 14TH. – His Ex. had to lay the foundation-stone of a ladies' college. The Bishop of Rupert's Land is building a girls' school. He is already the head of a very successful college [Bishop's College] for boys, and after the usual ceremonies attendant upon laying a stone we drove to see it. The Bishop gave us lunch, and then we returned to the hotel at Winnipeg, where we dress for the ball given by the citizens. We dined with the Governor, and were escorted to the ball by a torch-light procession. The city hall was beautifully decorated.

WEDNESDAY, 15TH. – We have had a pleasant day on the prairie. We managed to shake off our sleepiness after the ball, and to be ready for an early start. D. and I got into a small phaeton, Mrs. Littleton, Nellie, and Alexander into an ambulance waggon, and our three gentlemen mounted their horses, and off we went, with a twenty-eight-stone-weight gentleman in a buggy to guide us. We went through Winnipeg, and on to the illimitable prairie.

It is covered with long grasses and wild flowers, and is as flat as the sea, parts of it so swampy that our horses seemed to have difficulty in pulling us through it. It has a peculiar smell, and there is a delightful air upon it, and one begins to feel the freedom-of-the-savage raising one's spirits. We drove in this way for three hours (the servants following), our only adventure being the fall of Captain Smith's horse, and his narrow escape of being run over by the ambulance.

Have I told you we are bound for the Penitentiary at Rockwood [now called Stony Mountain Penitentiary]? The building is erected on 'the big, stony mountain,' which is really only a rise of eighty feet above the level of the prairie. It is limestone rock, and descends quite suddenly on the other side – like a precipice – back to the great plain-level.

When we got within half a mile of the place, we were met by some gentlemen, who said they wished us to arrive in a vehicle peculiar to the country – namely a Red River cart. These are made entirely of wood, and this one was ornamented with boughs, and was drawn by eighty oxen! D. and I, Mrs. Littleton and Nellie got in, and our eighty beasts, each conducted by a man with ribbons round his hat, began to move off. It was such fun, and looked so pretty and picturesque. Sometimes an ox would become a little troublesome, but he was soon brought to order, and I felt like a barbarian princess as I drove along in this carriage of primitive magnificence.

We passed through a beautiful triumphal arch, made of grain, with a spinning-wheel, plough, and other agricultural implements on the top of it. D. here got out, and answered the address, then we returned to our triumphal car, and drove on, attended by a crowd, to the doors of the prison. A handsome arch had been put up about a hundred yards from it, and fifty yards nearer to the house was another. These two were connected with chains of green rope, hung from poles with flags on them, and a new road ran between the two, which is the first part of a road to Winnipeg. I was asked to open it, and was presented with a spade. I emptied some earth out of a smart little barrow, and then we all went in to lunch.

Our hostess is a half-breed lady, pretty, and very nice, and her husband, Mr. Bedson, is the warder of this prison. They gave us an excellent lunch, and the usual toasts. In his speech D. told them that he much preferred going to gaol in a cart to leaving it in one.

After this we walked on the prairie, to breathe the delicious air, and looked at the prisoners' garden; but when I proposed to look at the prison I was told all the people were asleep. We were dreadfully sleepy ourselves, and were actually in the enjoyment of 'forty winks' in our very comfortable bed-rooms when dinner was announced, about nine o'clock. The guardians of the penitentiary had arranged some fireworks, and we sat upon the prairie watching them until bed-time.

THURSDAY, 16TH. – At eleven o'clock last night there was the most beautiful cloudless, starlit sky, but I was awoke by a terrific thunderstorm, peals of thunder, and flashes of vivid lightning. We breakfasted at eight, and went over the building. It is quite new; at present very expensive, as there are fourteen officials to fourteen prisoners.

We said good-bye to Mr. and Mrs. Bedson, and drove off over the prairie again. About two we reached St. Andrews, one of the oldest settlements in the province. D. replied to an address, and Nellie and I were presented with bouquets in pretty Indian 'roggins.'

A very good lunch, on the teetotal principle, was given us, and our healths were drunk in water. Two mottoes in the luncheon-room were: '*Kit Atumiskatinan*,' which means 'we welcome you,' in the Cree language; the other was –

Native, or English, Canadian we,
Teuton, or Celt, or whatever we be,
We are all of us loyal in our welcome to thee.

In 1840, Rev. James Evans, a missionary of the Methodist Church, was appointed general superintendent of the Northwest Indian Missions, and stationed at Norway House. Here he invented the system of syllabic characters still in use among the Cree Indians. The books of hymns and texts which he printed were the first examples of printing in the Northwest.

A story is told that when Lord Dufferin heard of James Evans' work, he said: 'Why, what a blessing to humanity is the man who invented that alphabet. I profess to be a kind of literary man myself, and try to keep up my reading of what is going on. But I never heard of this before. The fact is, the nation has given many a man a title, and a pension, and then a resting place in Westminster Abbey, who never did half so much for his fellow creatures.'

I gave the prizes at a ladies' school, and after this we got into our carriage, and drove five miles more along the banks of the Red River to the 'Little-Stone Fort' where we slept. This is one of the Hudson's Bay stores, and is quite a fortified place. We all enjoy the air so much, and have had another very pleasant day. I have written this out on the balcony while our rooms are being prepared. We have our own cook and provisions, so we are not such an invasive army as we appear. D. is drawing, Nellie climbing up everywhere to look into everything, the others walking about seeing the sights. It is a very restful evening after our journey. [They were at Lower Fort Garry.]

FRIDAY, 17TH. – We got into our waggons and started on our way, rejoicing in the beautiful weather. When we had gone about five miles, we came to signs of festivity: flags flying, and sounds of music, Indian warriors dancing in time to the band, and uttering their own extraordinary shouts. This band are pagans (from economical motives), and are not good friends with the Christian Indians we are on our way to see.

We went slowly, followed by the crowd, through the town of Selkirk, to the place where another large arch, surmounted by railway implements, was erected; for this is the spot where the Great

Pacific Railway is to cross the Red River. We got on a platform, had an address, and went through the regular business of presentations, etc.

> Because of records of dangerous flooding by the Red River, Sandford
> Fleming, the chief engineer of the new railway being built by the
> Government, felt that Selkirk was the safest place to cross the river.
> Later, after the Canadian Pacific Railway Company had come into
> possession of the road, they found it safe to cross much farther south,
> closer to Winnipeg.

We drove on towards the Indian Reserve, and at its entrance were saluted by a large deputation. One was a splendid man, with a large necklace of feathers, bare legs, and squares of beaded cloth gracefully covering the rest of his body.

We stopped for lunch soon after, and spent a couple of hours pleasantly sitting about on the grass, before we walked on to the grand 'Pow-wow' place. The chief is called by the unromantic name of 'Henry Prince,' and is a gentleman in a fine red coat, with two enormous medals on his breast. We went into the school, heard a hymn sung and saw a canoe-race. We walked all round the camp, to visit the women and children. The little babies have their legs packed in dry moss, and are then tied on a sort of back-board. D. had two guns and two watches to present to chiefs, and on his own behalf he gave four bullocks for a feast. We left them all in good spirits, while we had a pleasant drive back, getting to 'Stone Fort' at six o'clock.

SATURDAY, 18TH. – We had a long drive home from 'Stone Fort' and got to Silver Heights in the afternoon.

SUNDAY, 19TH. – The Bishop of Rupert's Land preached at Winnipeg, and came back to lunch with us.

MONDAY, 20TH. – Another expedition! The first thing we heard this morning was the sound of rain, and the day looked most unpromising. However, we started about ten, the four gentlemen riding, Mrs. Littleton and her maid, Nellie and I in the ambulance drawn by four horses. We got on very well for the first three hours, when we came to some fearful swamps. Our horses plunged through water and mud, the wheels of our carriage sinking, first on one side and then on the other. Two or three times the horses in the carts sat down in despair, and once they sunk so deep in the mire that the whole caravan had to stop and help to pull them out. The rain came on in torrents, and there was thunder growling overhead. Altogether it was not a nice day for camping out.

We expected to reach our destination at two, and to lunch there; but owing to our adventures in the bogs we did not get there till five, and were all wet and famished. The Lieutenant-Governor had arrived before, and he gave us shelter and tea, which revived us. Then the rain cleared off, we made up a nice fire, and things began to look better. Our cook had been in the most unfortunate cart, and had been over his knees in water most of the day; but the moment he arrived he lit his fire, and made us a dinner of good soup, mutton chops and potatoes.

It was next discovered that three tents had been left behind – three out of six; however, we managed very well without them. D., Nellie, and I had one tent. Mrs. Littleton and her maid another (our maids take the expeditions in turns – mine came last time), and the three gentlemen the third. We had stretcher-beds, with buffalo-robes and blankets on them, and dry hay on the floor; so we were really very comfortable. Our camping ground is near water, half river, half swamp, and as we can get wood, water, and milk, we shall return here for another night on our way back. I rather dread going through those bogs again!

TUESDAY, 21ST. – We were awoke rather early by the noises of camp-life; wood being chopped up, conversations going on in every tent, etc., and I had some difficulty in keeping Nellie in bed till the orthodox hour of seven, but, as I am much afraid of her being over-tired on this expedition, I have to insist upon this.

The weather was much better – the sun shone, but the wind was very cold. It was nearly ten before everything was packed, and we were on our way to the Mennonite settlement. Four of those men met us on horseback, some way from their farms, and rode before us through their Reserve. You know the Mennonites have left Russia for conscientious reasons, in the same way they left their native land, Germany, and settled in Russia, because they will not fight, and these two countries require their subjects should serve in the army.

The Mennonites are most desirable emigrants; they retain their best German characteristics, are hard-working, honest, sober, simple, hardy people. They bring money into the country, and can settle in a woodless place, which no other people will do. Necessity (in Russia) has taught them to make a peculiar fuel – cakes of manure, mixed with straw – which is kept a whole year to dry thoroughly, and which looks exactly like turf. With this they go through the long Canadian winter without wood or coal. They speak nothing but German, and are Lutheran, to which form of religion they add the Quakers' non-fighting doctrine.

They dress in the plainest and least decorative fashion; the women, from their birth to their graves, tie up their heads in coloured hand-kerchiefs fastened under their chins, and wear dark-coloured stiff gowns, the baby's being made after the same fashion as its mother's. The men shave, and wear black stocks round their throats. Partly in consequence of this unbecoming costume, all the people, men and women, are plain. One hundred and twenty families arrived in Canada three years ago and settled on this bare prairie one autumn day. For a week they had not a roof to cover them, and slept under their carts; then they dug up the sods, and with them made rude huts, in which they lived through one of our long and severe winters. This is, therefore, their third year here. Now I will tell you how we find them situated.

We drove about five miles through their Reserve, which is eighteen miles square, and in so doing passed through five or six villages of farmhouses. They are not in streets, each house being surrounded by land. The houses are cottages, very plainly built, roofed with thick hay thatch, the walls wooden, but covered with plaster. Next to, and opening into the living-house is a large building in which the cattle spend the winter.

Everything looks neat; home-made wooden furniture, flowers in the windows, nice gardens, etc. Each family is given 160 acres of land, and the way in which they work their farms enables them to do so very advantageously.

Supposing there are twenty families in a village, they put all the land together, and mark out the different spots which are best suited to particular crops. Thus, all the pasture is in one part, all the potatoes in another, and so on. Each man, however, works his own share of each crop, and has his profit to himself. Their church is most simple – plain deal forms without backs, and no ornament any-where.

After driving through these prosperous-looking villages, and pass-ing through great corn-fields, we saw before us on the open prairie an arbour erected, and in front of it at least 700 people. The men stood on one side, with specimens of their farm produce before them, corn grown from Russian seed, from Canadian seed, flax, etc. The women

on the other side showed their garden produce. The babies and children were out too. In the arbour were three girls, with lace handkerchiefs on their heads, and trays with glasses in their hands, ready to
offer us some Russian tea, which was most refreshing after our cold
drive.

The arbour was prettily hung with garlands of flowers and bunches
of corn mixed with poppies, and there were tables all round it, and
little Christmas-trees on which hung bouquets with some German
lines of welcome wrapped round each, the whole most charmingly
done. Mr. Hespeler, the Mennonite agent who arranged the whole of
this immigration, was with us, and acted as interpreter. The Mennonites' most learned man [Mr. Jakob Peters] read, and Mr. Hespeler translated, a very nice address, and D. replied in a speech
which delighted them greatly. They never cheered, but when anything pleased them they lifted their caps. In allusion to their peculiar
tenets he said:

> You have come to a land where you will find the people with
> whom you are to associate engaged indeed in a great struggle,
> and contending with foes whom it requires their best energies to
> encounter. But those foes are not your fellow-men, nor will you
> be called upon in the struggle to stain your hands with human
> blood – a task so abhorrent to your religious feelings. The war to
> which we invite you as recruits and comrades is a war waged
> against the brute forces of nature; but these forces will welcome
> our domination, and reward our attack by placing their treasures
> at our disposal. It is a war of ambition – for we intend to annex
> territory – but neither blazing villages nor devastated fields will
> mark our ruthless track. Our battalions will march across the
> illimitable plains which stretch before us as sunshine steals
> athwart the ocean; the rolling prairie will blossom in our wake,
> and corn and peace and plenty will spring where we have trod.
> . . . In one word, beneath the flag whose folds now wave above
> you, you will find protection, peace, civil and religious liberty,
> constitutional freedom and equal laws.

We walked around, muttered a few lame German sentences, and
were as speechlessly polite as we could be. This being over, after a
song from the school-children, Mr. Hespeler asked us over to his
camp-fire, where we had Rhine wine and German cake, and where he
gave hot coffee to the women from a distance. Nellie made love to all

the babies, and having nursed one for some time, its mother presented her with a cucumber. It was very pleasant sitting by the fire and seeing the people enjoying their coffee on the grass. After an hour and a half spent here we walked to our camp, a quarter of a mile off. Some women showed us their houses, and then we dined, and sat round our own fire. Presently we saw fireworks rising from the other camp, so we got up an enormous torch, which was seen and responded to by a distant cheer, and one line of 'He is a jolly good fellow.'

The only other thing I have to say about the Mennonites is that the great proportion of those here are young, and that everybody has at least six children. Think what a gain they are to this country: in three years to have eighteen square miles of country settled by such people.

WEDNESDAY, 22ND. – We all slept very comfortably, and longer than we did the first night. We were packed up about ten, and set off to drive through some more villages. Mr. Hespeler showed us the domestic arrangements. The only fault is that the stables open into the living-rooms. The inhabitants will gradually leave off this nasty plan, but it is their devotion to their cattle which makes them wish to have them so near. The village herd and the village schoolmaster are the only two paid labourers in the Mennonite vineyard; the clergyman receives no pay. School is not kept during the three summer months.

We reached our new camping-ground early in the day, and the gentlemen went out shooting. They got a mixed, but not a good bag – prairie chicken, snipe, plover, duck and a bittern, the latter quite delicious to eat. In the evening we sat over our camp-fire, and Mr. McKay told us some interesting stories of his life. I must introduce him to you, for he is (to use a Yankee expression) the 'boss' of our party. He arranges everything for us, provides the horses, carriages, tents, beds, etc.

The Hon. James McKay, M.P. (in the local Parliament), has been a mighty hunter in his day, but as he now weighs 320 lbs., he leads a quieter though still a very active life. He has a pleasant face, and is very cheery, and a thorough 'good fellow,' but so enormous! It is curious to see him filling up his buggy, and driving on before us, steering us through the bogs, and making signs to our driver to avoid dangers on the way. His boy of eleven rides on a pony with him, and promises to be as large. I never saw such a fat boy.

Mr. McKay is a half-breed. His parents had some French blood in them, and he speaks the three languages, but I believe he talks Indian at home. He has lost one thumb, and besides this gun-shot wound he has had several other narrow escapes of his life. One day he and an English gentleman killed seven grizzly bears; there was a bag! Mr. McKay shot four, and the Englishman three. But what seems to me the most wonderful feat is that he once killed a mother and two young cubs with a lasso. He had no gun with him, and the great bear came towards him on her hind paws; he quickly threw the lasso over her head, and, turning his horse quickly away, pulled her over on her back, and strangled her; then he killed the cubs too.

He said he had thought nothing of it, as he had killed a black bear with a lasso when he was fourteen years old. 'Jemmie' (his fat boy) is always practising picking things off the ground when he is on horseback, with a view to future excellence with the lasso. Mr. McKay knows a great deal about the Indians, and it was interesting to hear him talk of them.

THURSDAY, 23RD. – We had about twenty-five miles to drive home, and as we got a good deal shaken we were very tired at night and ready to go early to bed after reaching Silver Heights. The younger gentlemen, however, having gone to Mr. McKay's to see about some shooting, found dancing going on, and amused themselves by trying to learn the Red River Jig.

CHAPTER 19

Manitoba
AUGUST-OCTOBER 1877

SATURDAY, AUGUST 25TH. – Mrs. Morris and her daughters lunched with us, and we had a visit from an American Professor, who has come here to study the manners and customs of the 'hopper' [the grasshopper].

MONDAY, 27TH. – The gentlemen went out shooting for the whole day, and came back well pleased, though they were unable to find half the birds they shot.

We ladies lunched with the Morrises, and met Mr. Macpherson and Mr. Campbell, who have come all the way here by water (three weeks in canoes) ; we are going over part of the same route, so they were able to give us some hints. Mr. Macpherson did not like it, and three weeks of pork and canoe-made bread made him ill. They fortunately had lime-juice with them.

TUESDAY, 28TH. – We drove through pleasant country, a wooded prairie, making our way towards the Winnipeg River, and did twenty-nine miles in the day. Our camping-ground is on the banks of a winding stream. A cart, containing the men's food and bedding, broke down on the way, and did not arrive till very late. My maid is ill; she has been so for a few days, but said nothing. To-night she has a fearful headache.

WEDNESDAY, 29TH. – Alexander is still very ill, and naturally thinks everything horrid, camp beds too hard, tin cups nasty. I hope she will like this life better when she is well.

We expected to go through a number of swamps, but the weather has been so dry that happily there were none to speak of. We had not gone more than two miles when a whole cavalcade of horsemen met

260

us. They rode beautifully, and galloped by us for over two miles, firing a *feu-de-joie* every few minutes. When we got near St. Andrews we found the people had made an impromptu avenue of trees fully a mile long, and at the end of it an arch decorated with arms and welcomes.

About five we reached our camping-ground, having driven thirty miles, and having had one little interval of prairie-shooting on the way. When the horses were unharnessed we all set to work: the gentlemen pitched the tents, we picked up sticks, and made two fires. Then I made four beds, and plucked a duck for dinner! This meal was highly appreciated by us all, and we sat round the fire and listened to some of Mr. McKay's stories. At seven in the morning a bear was seen quite close to our camp!

The prairie-fowl shooting is very odd. The birds remain in the grass quite close to the sportsman, and stare at him till he makes them get up, and then sometimes they flop down again before anyone can shoot. Yesterday, the mother of a brood which had been ruthlessly shot down sat calling for her young, and looking about quite close to us.

THURSDAY, 30TH. – Travelling on the Dawson route. A hot day, and the road dusty and extremely rough. We were very tired by two o'clock, when we stopped at a sort of half-way house to rest and have lunch. The hostess was a Norwegian, with five children – four most charming, pretty little girls, the fifth, a baby, seven days old! She had got up to decorate her room for us, and to make flags. She seemed such a nice person, and wept bitterly when we left. Of course she was very weak, and lives in a lonely place, and was glad to see someone to speak to. Her prospects are not good, as her husband is delicate, and does not seem to get on. They are going to move to the Pembina Mountains, where they have taken up a farm of 160 acres. Neither he nor she knows anything of farming, and when they reach the place they will have to build a house. We named the Norwegian baby Frederica.

The other children had made a train in the yard, with a piece of stone for an engine, snow-shoes and boxes for carriages, etc. When D. saw it he asked for tickets, which one child instantly produced, and which everybody, entering into the spirit of the game, bought. They immediately took the money to their mother, and we were able to please them with some little necklaces we had for the Indians. Johann Nord is the father's name.

We did not get to our camping-ground till six, and then we had some new experiences, for there was no water and no food for the horses. We had to dig for the former, and Mr. McKay tried to take the horses somewhere for better grass, but they would not leave the carts, where they hoped to find corn.

We are in Keewatin now. It is governed by a council, and has not a Lieutenant-Governor of its own, though Mr. Morris is what is called the 'Administrator.'

FRIDAY, 31ST. – Before lunch we did about seventeen miles, and as the road was rough we were glad of the rest in the middle of the day. When we started again, we were told we had only nine miles to go, and thought we should have an easy afternoon. It proved a hard one. We had five miles of swamp, and a road made with rough-hewn trunks of trees. When first made this sort of perpetual bridge is not disagreeable, but when time has worn furrows in it the jogging of the ambulance waggon upon it is not to be described!

When we had been knocked about as much as we could bear we got out and walked a couple of miles. But almost the whole journey was over a corduroy road, and as we had to go at a foot's pace, it was very fatiguing.

A 'corduroy' road is a Brobdingnagian imitation of the material worn by rough little boys, and when an occasional 'cord' has broken away altogether, when another has got loose, and turns round as the horse puts his foot on it, or when it stands up on end as the wheel touches it, the corduroy road is not pleasant to drive many miles over! In consequence of our slow progress, it was quite dark when we reached our camping-ground, and the cook did not arrive till half-past seven.

SATURDAY, SEPTEMBER 1ST. – Ten or twelve miles of rough road brought us to the North-West Angle, where we found a beautifully decorated steamer on the Lake of the Woods.

There were a few Indians about; one who is always called 'Colonel Wolseley,' because he was guide to Sir Garnet [Wolseley], on the Red River Expedition.

We had to part with Mr. McKay here, and put ourselves into the hands of twenty-six canoe-men. They all came on board at the North-West Angle, which is a morsel of the United States mixed up with our land.

We had such a pleasant afternoon in the steamer. The Lake of the Woods, about which we had heard nothing, proved to be quite lovely:

islands innumerable, rocky and wooded, a great variety of shapes and sizes, sometimes far away, and sometimes so close to the steamer as quite to darken it. We lunched and dined on board, and did not land till it was dark, and the setting-up of our camp was most difficult.

I found we were close to the house of one of our Ottawa brides, who has come out here with her husband. She was a Miss Ashworth, and he a Mr. Fellowes. We went up to see her, and found her very happy and cheerful. She has one neighbour nine miles away, and a second eighteen miles off.

SUNDAY, 2ND. – We had such a pleasant day once we had got into our canoes and were well started. The weather was lovely, and the River Winnipeg beautiful. We have two large and two small canoes. The first big one carries D. and Nellie and me, and eight men, and a good deal of luggage; the second, Colonel and Mrs. Littleton, and eight men. The first small one had the two A.D.C.s, Nowell, and six men; and the other small one held three servants and six men – that is to say, there ought to be six men in the two small ones, but two left us, so our servants take it in turns at the paddles.

We were most comfortable, and lay back reading and looking at the scenery, and occasionally doing a little sleeping. Sometimes the men sang the Canadian boat-songs which sound so delightful on the water, and sometimes they cheered themselves up by racing the other canoes. Our tents, luggage, and provisions are distributed over all the boats. In the middle of the day we landed to lunch, and at five we stopped on a piece of ground where Sir Garnet Wolseley and his troops once camped. Nellie and I had a nice bathe, and returned to find our camp full of activity. Our twenty-four men, and four gentlemen and three servants hard at work chopping wood, putting up tents, mending canoes, cooking dinners, and making beds. The latter is a most important office. The bed-maker gets a quantity of dry grass and small branches of fir, which are laid one over the other so as to form a spring mattress. A buffalo-robe goes over that, and then blankets *ad libitum*.

We had a dinner of hot soup, curry, stewed beef, duck and prairie chicken, and a blueberry pudding, our cook having got up early to pick the blueberries. The soup and beef were carried here in tins, the game has been shot on the way. Monsieur Beselin, our cook, has done so well. When we were driving he used to arrive sometimes long after us, when it was quite dark, and in five minutes' time he would be hard at work, and our dinner well under way. Mr. McKay, who is a great traveller, said he never saw a man who could produce a dinner so expeditiously, and get his things packed up again so quickly. In addition to this, he is always in good humour, and in the daytime now he paddles away with a beaming countenance.

Strange to say on the banks of a splendid river, we have no good drinking-water. We have brought no wine so as to lessen our luggage, and have no milk (except preserved milk). Tea is our principal beverage, but without milk it is not very nice. We also have chocolate (which makes us thirsty).

MONDAY, 3RD. – The gentlemen bathed, and we got off on our travels by 8.30. We had another delightful day. We made two portages, and at the end of the second we lunched. After we went over such an exciting rapid: it was a great dip, the upper part of the water being quite smooth, and we seemed to slide over it, and then plunge into a stormy sea, the canoe gallantly rising to the waves. At this one there were great cries of 'Back Water!' and energetic signs made to the canoes behind us to avoid a certain rock on the way. Later we had another exciting descent, where the stream carried us at a fearful pace sharp round a rock.

The scenery is beautiful: the Winnipeg seldom looks like a river, but nearly always like a lovely lake full of islands. They are rocky and wooded, and sometimes steep precipices of rock. The foliage is varied (not all pine), and the delightful weather helps to make it all charming.

We camped at five, and the usual busy scenes were enacted. I watched the way the men kneaded their bread, and then I made a loaf. They use a little baking-powder, and pour the water actually into the sack of flour, and do all the kneading in the top of it. Then they spread the dough out in a frying-pan, and put it before a good fire. A very nice sort of cake is the result. Pemmican soup is another of their dishes, and really it is not at all bad, and it is very (excuse the word) 'filling,' which is a great advantage.

It is wonderful how quickly these men put up our tents, especially as they have to cut down trees to make room for them. I don't think they were half an hour getting them up to-night, lighting all the fires, and unpacking all the things. Each crew has its own cook and mess.

We stopped at a small Mission, to get some milk. It is called the 'White Dog Mission,' and a half-breed clergyman lives there. His wife has been ill a year, has never seen a doctor, and is now on her back in a birch-bark tent, where she thinks she has more air than in a house. We were sorry we had no doctor with us to help the poor thing, and such cases make one realise the hardship of living in these lonely parts.

TUESDAY, 4TH. – At one most lovely waterfall the river is about half a mile wide, and the fall stretched the whole way across. It is really an enormous rapid. We portaged across, and got into our canoes again at the foot of it. There was one rapid which D. went down but would not allow me to try, as there was some danger that one might be swept into a whirlpool and upset. But all the canoes got safely through.

We have just camped at a portage for the night. We are 'bounded on the north' by a waterfall, flowing from us; on the south by a great rapid and a wood; wood on the east, and an island filling all the space between the Rapid and the Fall on the west. To-morrow we row across the little basin, and portage to the bottom of the Fall.

This Winnipeg surpasses all rivers I have ever seen, being so much more beautiful than the other large rivers and lakes I have been on. We enjoy our days immensely. D. is so industrious about drawing; he has made a quantity of pretty sketches.

WEDNESDAY, 5TH. – Crossing the small bay was very exciting, for we approached the Fall as if we were just going over it, and at the last moment we turned into an eddy, which swept us into a quiet landing-place.

From the bottom, these great rapids are really beautiful; they appear like one great wall of water, stretching the whole width of the river, and divided into four by islands covered with trees.

We had a short way to go before reaching another portage; here the rapid went around two sides of an island, and we got in at the quiet side. The third portage was about three-quarters of a mile long. At the fourth we crossed an island, and came to a place which looked worse to go down than anything I have hitherto seen. Two rapids met, and there was such a bubbling and boiling that the uninstructed eye could not see the way out of the difficulty. We appeared to start straight for a great hole, and then to be borne away from it by a back current. I was glad when I found myself safe at the bottom.

We came down another long, rough rapid, and stopped early to camp, because the place was so beautiful. It is at the mouth of the Birch River, which here flows into the Winnipeg, and the two are flowing in opposite directions round an island.

THURSDAY, 6TH. – We have been going down quite a chain of rapids this morning, and have had five portages. Some of us came down one that really was a precipice. There was a descent of quite four feet, almost perpendicular, so that our canoe slanted head foremost down, and then rose lightly on the waves.

The whole afternoon we had a fair wind, and sails were improvised in each canoe; with them we went very fast through the water, and landed at five much nearer to Fort Alexander than we expected to get. My tent is in a most picturesque spot. I am in an arbour of trees, and look across the lovely little bay, and down the river – summer lightning enabling me to see the view every now and then. Nellie's tent is behind mine, and she rejoices in the noise of the Fall, which she thinks is a delightful lullaby.

FRIDAY, 7TH. – We got up at six, and had only a cup of chocolate and a biscuit, so that we might get off quicker. When we have a more elaborate breakfast we have to wait so long while the dishes are being washed.

The consequence of our frugality was that we got over 'the long portage' by 8.30. And very long it was, more than three-quarters of a mile, hilly and slippery ground, and hard for the men to carry the heavy canoes over. This day we made five portages; at one a canoe fell, and an immense hole was made in it. The men set to work and mended it quickly; they got balsam-root, with which they sewed the birch-bark over and over, and then with rosin they covered the stitches up, and the canoe was ready for the water again.

As we were approaching Fort Alexander in the afternoon it began to rain hard. The sight of their destination set the men a-singing, and we had all sorts of boat-songs, and rowed our four canoes up to the quay to the triumphant tune of 'En roulant ma boule.' Gunshots were fired from various cottages on the banks as we passed them, and when we landed we found arches for us to pass under.

The hostess at this fort is the daughter of Mr. and Mrs. Flett, of the Stone Fort. Her husband is a Mr. Mackenzie, and she has one dear little boy, and a baby. We had expected to meet our steamer here, but it has not arrived, so Mrs. Mackenzie is going to let us camp in her house. As it is raining, it is pleasant to be under a roof, and we enjoyed a cup of tea with 'real' milk.

SATURDAY, 8TH. – A great disappointment awaited us this morning – the unaccountable non-arrival of our steamer. She ought to have been waiting for us days ago, and we are shut up here until she does come.

There is neither telegraph nor other communication with the outer world.

On a neighbouring reserve we found the old chief to whom D. gave a watch at St. Peter's. We wound the chief's watch for him, showed him how to wear it, and conversed with his brother, who is a pagan, painted, and less civilized, but a jolly old gentleman. He is trying to build a house, but finds it much 'more difficult to make than a wig-wam'; and if the truth were told, he would probably consider it less comfortable when finished.

The Chief told His Ex. that he was 'very hungry' (they all say this), and D. said, 'and I am starving, my steamer has not come in, and I have eaten all my provisions!' Upon which the old chief laughed immensely, and was quite satisfied.

We visited a curious grave – a coffin raised far from the ground on four posts. Thus did we spend the day.

We were just going to sit down to dinner when in walked Mr. Campbell, carrying a mail-bag! Of course we thought our steamer had come. But no; he had started in her, but she ran ashore in a fog, and after vainly trying to pull her off, the Captain sent him on to tell us of his misfortune. It is a great disappointment to everyone concerned. The steamer had been done up for us, and in her we hoped to go round Lake Winnipeg, and to get into the Saskatchewan. Now we shall have to hug the shore in canoes.

Mr. Campbell came in a flat-bottomed boat with two men, and had an adventurous journey. One day he was blown fifteen miles out of his course, and had great difficulty in landing. He slept under his boat at night, and was several times in danger of being upset. There is just a chance that, as the wind blows in the right direction, the *Colville* may get off her mudbank.

SUNDAY, 9TH. – We were all up and ready for breakfast at seven o'clock, and by nine had said 'good-bye' to the Mackenzies, had packed our canoes, and started afresh to Gimli (the Icelandic settlement). We had made up our minds to 'rough it' in the way of provisions, and looked forward to a diet of pemmican. Ugh! We were bearing our disappointment in the most Christian manner, were cheerfully reading our papers, and paddling along in our four canoes, when a cloud of smoke appeared on the horizon, and a cry of 'the steamer!' rose simul-taneously from all the boats. There she was, off her mudbank, and on her way to meet us.

We soon got on board, and found her most comfortably fitted up.

I must confess, when I first saw her at Winnipeg in her working-dress, that, with every desire to make the best of everything, my heart sunk a little at the idea of spending six days in her. Now she looks very nice; she has been repainted, and the hold has been turned into a beautiful dining-room. It has been entirely lined with green baize, while the companion ladder is clothed in red, and she has a most cheerful and comfortable appearance. The gentlemen sleep in this saloon. On deck we have a sitting-room, and out of it are two cabins, with two berths in each. There is another large cabin for Colonel and Mrs. Littleton.

On board we found a little Icelandic maid-servant on her way to Mrs. Mackenzie. Her principal luggage consisted of a flower-pot, with a geranium growing in it. She went on to Fort Alexander in our canoes. We took a tender leave of all our men, who were greatly delighted with a little extra pay D. gave them. They were a good-natured, friendly shabby lot; each day their clothes got more and more ragged.

I think our own clothes are in the same disreputable condition. For, what with dragging oneself through the bush, sitting by camp-fires, lying or sitting on one's hat, and never having one's boots cleaned, one is conscious of being rather uncivilized-looking when one re-enters society. I have been happy in the knowledge that after this journey my gown need never appear again, and that a misfortune more or less is a matter of no importance. I bought, too, at a Hudson's Bay store, a man's soft grey felt hat, which turns up or down, and accommodates itself to every ray of sunshine; the rain may pour upon it with impunity, and I can lean back in it, so that wearing it I suffer no economical pangs. The old gown is grey, and I have one new navy-blue serge in which to encounter natives; this is all the finery I could pack into the canoe.

Nellie has a dear old frock and hat, and one good one in a box for grand occasions. But she cannot have anything of hers on for two minutes without its meeting some serious accident. The glory of her smart frock has been sadly marred during the two days she has worn it.

Of course we have fresh provisions on the *Colville,* so the pemmican diet is postponed for a time.

MONDAY, 10TH. – The longest day I have spent for some time. Lake Winnipeg is so large we were out of sight of land, and the *Colville* is a terrible ship for rolling. In this fine weather she rolled all day, and even when we anchored at night she went on swaying from side to side.

TUESDAY, 11TH. – We started early in the morning, and landed at eight o'clock on the shores of the Saskatchewan. There is not much to see at this particular spot: trees on each side of the river, two large wooden houses at the wharf, and some groups of Indians sitting about. They had put up decorations, and fired off their guns as usual. Mr. McTavish, one of the Hudson's Bay Company, came to meet us, and took us two miles across the portage on a tramway laid down since July, and the first railway in the North-West.

> The great Saskatchewan River, rising in the Rocky Mountains, flows eastward across the prairies into Manitoba. It was navigable for several hundred miles, but not as it neared Lake Winnipeg. There a special railway was being constructed around the rapids to provide a link with the steamers on that lake.

The car was most gorgeously lined with coloured blankets, and when we got out of it we jumped into spring-carts, in which we did the unfinished part of the railway. During the drive we saw some views of the river, and went to the Hudson's Bay Company's store. We inspected a new steel steamer, and lunched. I put in a rivet in the last bit of the railway, and was presented with the hammer.

We met here Mrs. Bompas, wife of the Bishop of Athabasca [the Reverend William Carpenter Bompas, who had formerly been a missionary in Mackenzie River district], and offered her a passage in our steamer, which she was thankful to accept. She has been travelling a month to get here, and her journey from an opposite direction makes us feel as if we had not penetrated so very far into the country after all.

Then came the event of the day – our descent of the Grand Rapids of the Saskatchewan in a 'York' boat. The 'York' is a very large, heavy, wooden boat, which holds about twenty people; and the rapids we went down are four miles long. They are simply extremely rough water, and we found them more sea-sicky and less exciting than the Winnipeg River rapids.

We started off on our journey home about five o'clock, and looked forward with dread to Lake Winnipeg.

WEDNESDAY, 12TH. – We had a very good night, and still better, a beautiful day, so we enjoyed our voyage. We talked to Mrs. Bompas, and heard her missionary experiences. She lives in a place where she never has milk or butter, bread only three times a week (as flour costs 5£. a bag), and fresh meat very rarely – pork and pemmican being her chief food all the year round. No spirit is allowed to be sold in the

North-West, so 'the pleasures of the bottle' are also denied the inhabitants of those distant regions.

In the middle of the day we went ashore to see some Indians. The Chief was such a funny old man. He gave wonderful expression to his one remark, repeated in a variety of ways while D. was speaking to him; all he ever said being 'Ah!' 'Eh!' 'Ah!' 'Eh!'; but one understood his gratitude, his wonder, his assent, and all his feelings, perfectly well each time he emitted the sound. The receipt of a gun evoked a well-satisfied 'Ah!' but the mention of pork and flour brought forth an enthusiastic 'Eh!' and a shout from his people.

THURSDAY, 13TH. – 4 a.m.: Rolling, rolling, doors banging, jugs upsetting; no more sleep to be had, and the melancholy news that it is impossible to land at Gimli to greet us when we feebly struggle down to breakfast.

Gimli is the Icelandic settlement which D. must see, and the alternative before us is either to roll about at anchor until the wind shifts, which it may do in a day or two, or to go all the way to the Stone Fort to coal, and return to-morrow (always provided the wind changes). D. thought the first alternative was out of the question for me, so we settled to come to the Stone Fort – and here I am.

Once safe in a house, with the memory of the rolling fresh upon me, I could not make up my mind to seven hours more to Gimli and seven back again. So Nellie, Mrs. Littleton, my maid, and I remain here for the night, while D. and the gentleman, having arrived here at two, started back again at five. They will get to the mouth of the river before it is dark, anchor there, and, if they can land, go on to Gimli in the morning. I shall have to give you a second-hand account of Gimli. I am very sorry not to have seen it, but the *Colville* is such a lively little steamer in rough water that I dread fourteen hours more of her!

We have telegraphed for horses, and hope to leave to-morrow. Meantime, Mr. and Mrs. Flett are making us very comfortable. D. left with a very bad headache; he was up and down all night, saving our goods from being flung about the cabin, so I was not surprised that he had one.

We landed Mrs. Bompas at the house of Archdeacon Cowley, where she is going to spend the winter.

FRIDAY, 14TH. – Our carriages arrived very early in the morning, and we were able to start before noon in the ambulance, or, as my maid calls it, the 'rumble-tumble machine.' We had, during the next six hours, a real specimen of Red River mud. Imagine driving twenty-five miles over a field of clay soil which has just been harrowed, and you may acquire some notion of the way in which our wheels were clogged with mud, and the horses' tails weighted down with great balls of it. Happily it was fine overhead, and we got 'home' at five.

We had six mail-bags to open, and were busy till dinner-time reading our letters. The housemaid cooked for us, and we enjoyed the quiet evening after all our travelling.

SATURDAY, 15TH. – Such a pouring morning! We are so glad to be safe at Silver Heights.

His Ex. got to Gimli yesterday. He spoke to the Icelanders, and said in his speech:

The homesteads I have visited seem well-built and commodious, and are certainly superior to any of the farmhouses I remember in Iceland; while the gardens and little clearings which have begun to surround them show that you have already tapped an inexhaustible store of wealth in the rich alluvial soil on which we stand.

He then welcomed them to this country, saying,

It is a country in which you will find yourselves freemen, serving no overlord, and being no man's men but your own; each master of his own farm, like the Udalmen and Bonders of old days.

And concluded with these words:

I trust you will continue to cherish for all time the heart-stirring literature of your nation, and that from generation to generation your little ones will continue to learn in your ancient Sagas that industry, energy, fortitude, perseverance, and stubborn endurance which have ever been the characteristics of the noble Icelandic race.

In 1856, in the schooner yacht *Foam*, Lord Dufferin made a voyage to Iceland, Jan Mayen and Spitzbergen. An account of this trip appeared under the title, *Letters from High Latitudes*. Having seen the Icelandic people in their own country, he was particularly anxious to visit the homes they had established on Canadian soil. Lady Dufferin has quoted a few excerpts from his speech, which began:

When it was my good fortune twenty years ago to visit your island, I never thought that the day would come when I should be called upon, as the representative of the British Crown, to receive you in this country; but the opportunities I have thus had of becoming acquainted with your dramatic history, with your picturesque literature, and the kindness I have experienced at the hands of your countrymen, now enable me with the greater cordiality to bid you welcome.

He further commented:

I have not entered a single hut or cottage in the settlement, which did not contain, no matter how bare its walls, or scanty its furniture, a library of twenty or thirty volumes; and I am informed that there is scarcely a child amongst you who cannot read and write.

Happily, many of these treasured books later found a home in a special Icelandic collection in the library of the University of Manitoba.

The gentlemen arrived this afternoon, but the servants did not get through the mud till late in the evening.

SUNDAY, 16TH. – So cold! We are thankful for a fire, and shiver at the thought of our camp to-morrow.

MONDAY, 17TH. – We did not manage to get off till after two o'clock. We started in the ambulance, and with the usual riding-horses and waggons, the only difference in our procession being that, instead of the portly form of Mr. McKay, we had a clerk of his in our guiding-buggy.

We reached the camping-ground at five, having driven to it across the prairie. But our provisions and our mattresses did not arrive, and at first we thought we had absolutely nothing to eat. On closer investigation, we found that the cook had a few scraps with him, and of them he made us a capital dinner.

Instead of a bell-tent we tried a leather 'lodge' – in other words, a regular Indian tent – the chief merit of which is, that in it you are able to have a good fire. We watched the men putting it up. There are thirteen long, stout poles. Three are tied together at the top, and are lifted up, and spread out at the bottom; eight others are then fitted round these, so as to complete the circle at the bottom, and to form a frame for the leather covering. Two corners of a large sheet of leather are attached to two more poles, and with these it is lifted over the skeleton framework. These two poles also work the chimney apparatus.

The tent is quite open at the top, but the two flaps of leather regulate the draught. We had a good fire to go to bed by, and to dress by in the morning; but we let it go out at night. The provisions arrived late in the evening.

TUESDAY, 18TH. – We got up early, and were breakfasting when Mr. McKay arrived. We cheered his arrival, but I am sorry to say he brought the Littletons a telegram from Dr. Grant to say their baby is very ill, and that they had better return home.

They went back to Winnipeg at once, and will telegraph for further news. They cannot get a boat to leave in till to-morrow, and the child may be better.

We were a long time packing our waggons and catching our horses. But at last we started, and had a cold drive over the prairie. D. had a headache, caused, he thinks, by the extremely bad water we had to drink last night. It required no microscope to show the animals in it. Of course we filtered it, but I don't think it was possible to make it wholesome. When we reached our luncheon-place D. lay down, and with a good fire we got a little warm. The sun is bright, but the wind is bitter.

The afternoon was equally cold, and when we reached our camping-ground I was glad to get the 'lodge' up as quickly as possible, that D. might get to bed. He was very feverish, and had a terrible headache.

WEDNESDAY, 19TH. – I found the fire in my leather house so hot this morning that I had to let it burn down before I could dress at it. D. was better, and able to start in the ambulance with us. We drove past Shoal Lake, where we saw quantities of geese and large crow-ducks standing upon pieces of rock in the water. Our way lay through prairie, oak-coppice, and marsh. After a drive of seventeen miles we began to see farm-houses here and there, then a Hudson's Bay station, and finally a little cottage at which we stopped, and from which we looked out on Lake Manitoba.

The cottage is Mr. McKay's. It consists of two rooms, in one of which our dinner will be cooked, and in the other eaten. We pitched all our tents close to the house, and walked down to the Lake, an enormous sheet of water, like a sea. It is fifty miles wide at this spot. The shore is a beautiful sandy beach, and Nellie amused herself with the shells.

THURSDAY, 20TH. – The gentlemen went off in four canoes this morn-ing, and Nellie and I remained alone. We visited the Hudson's Bay store, where Mr. Clark showed us his bears, his dogs and his garden. The sportsmen got home about seven o'clock. His Ex. 18 head, Fred 16, Captain Smith 17, and Mr. McKay 25.

They had several sorts of duck, plover, bittern, grebe, and coot. They saw over a thousand duck, but they were difficult to approach.

D. says the shooting was pretty and curious. They paddled to a sort of marsh, where there were gigantic rushes forming streets, lanes and squares of water. About these waterways they went, trying to get quietly up to the duck; but the birds were very wild.

After dinner Mr. Clark and an Indian agent came over from the Hudson's Bay store, and sat by our fire. Mr. Clark has lived here nine years, has not a single neighbour or companion, and is unmarried.

Mr. McKay described to us how he shot sixteen swans here last April. He had an enormous tub made for himself, which he sunk into the ice; he had it filled with hay, and surrounded with rushes. As he weighs twenty-eight stone, he must have looked funny in his tub. In front of him he placed a stuffed swan, and there he sat, and shot the live ones which came to look at it. He remained there all day, got frightfully chilled, and was ill for fifty days with rheumatic fever – the first ailment he ever had.

The wind began to rise in the evening, and at night the noise in our tent was dreadful; the wind whistled in at the hole in the top, and the chimney flapped about. We had everything we possessed piled upon the end of the flapping oilcloth door to keep it down. There was so much draught we had to wrap up our heads as if we were out of doors.

FRIDAY, 21ST. – Mr. McKay has a terrible headache, and there is too much wind for the canoes. Fred and Captain Smith have walked out to see if they can get anything in the marsh close by.

The wind fell, Mr. McKay lost his headache, and the gentlemen went off for the afternoon's 'hunting,' as shooting is called here. They did not bring back a great deal – the birds were so wild; twenty-six the total bag.

SATURDAY, 22ND. – After luncheon Mr. McKay, D. and Captain Smith went out shooting again. D. got nineteen birds, and Fred shot seven duck, four of which he brought home.

SUNDAY, 23RD. – We lunched close to the house of a German surveyor, who brought us some excellent bread-and-butter, and we visited his wife and daughters. He has established himself upon 1,000 acres of good land. We camped about four o'clock, and soon had the pleasure of seeing Colonel Littleton riding towards us. Mrs. Littleton has gone home, but the child is better. Our letters also arrived, and were very welcome.

MONDAY, 24TH. – Started about half-past eight, and drove along a good road and through five farms to Portage La Prairie. There were arches and an address, bands of painted Indians, and a long procession of 'buggies.' We drove to one farm to inspect it, and as we did not see much chance of any lunch, we asked the old lady for some, and soon filled her house, eat up her bread, tasted her home-made cheese, and drank her rich milk. Her husband and son seemed to take great interest and pride in their farm, and if they had a market they would be well off; the market and the railway will come in time. They have magnificent crops.

Food and presents were given to the Indians, and we drove back to our camp, which is on the way to Winnipeg, and on the way home! Indians came and inspected us, and one very tall man, looking grand in his blanket and red leggings, embroidered with beads, sold us first his garters, and then the stripes off his trousers, while an old friend of his, with a green wreath on his head, and wrapped in a toga (blanket, Nero fashion), nudged him, and egged him on to add dollars to his original prices. The man had a beautiful pipe, which he would not sell.

TUESDAY, 25TH. – We drove till lunch-time through beautiful farming-country. A farmer told me that they built no barns here, because it would be impossible to have them large enough to hold their grain. The only 'ifs' the agriculturists have here are, 'if' the 'hoppers' don't return, and 'if' the railway does come, – then they will be millionaires.

WEDNESDAY, 26TH. – At twelve o'clock to-day we reached Silver Heights, and our journey is virtually over. We have all enjoyed it, and are well and much sunburnt after six weeks of almost constant open air. Our good luck in weather has been extraordinary; there was only one single night that we were driven from our camp-fire by rain. The bad weather always seemed to come the days that we had a roof to shelter us, and this morning's drive was cold enough to make us glad that our camping out is over. Our leather lodge was very comfortable, though a little smoky. But a stove in the hall and an open fire in the drawing-room of Silver Heights are not unwelcome luxuries.

Mr. Mills and Mr. Pelletier (two of the Ministers who have been travelling here) came to see us. [Honourable David Mills was Superintendent General of Indian Affairs, and Honourable Charles Alphonse Pelletier the Minister of Agriculture, in the Dominion Cabinet.]

THURSDAY, 27TH. – Most of us went into town to pay bills and arrange various matters connected with our departure. I called upon the Morrises.

There are such swarms of beautiful birds about the fields and roads. There are orange breasts and crimson breasts, red-brown heads, two or three coloured feathers in a wing, and all the rest black. They must do a great deal of harm to the grain, one would think.

FRIDAY, 28TH. – D. and the other gentlemen went out shooting. The bag was seventeen plover, four prairie-chicken, one snipe, one duck, one goose (shot by Fred), one musk-rat, and one skunk! There is variety for you!

Mr. McKay and Mr. Donald Smith dined with us. The former gave Nellie and me two buffalo robes, and he has presented D. with the most magnificent horns I ever saw.

SATURDAY, 29TH. – Last day in Winnipeg. We said good-bye to Silver Heights soon after breakfast, and drove through Fort Garry and across the Red River to a place where D. and I each drove a spike in the Canada Pacific Railway, the first line in this part of the world. The chief engineer had gone to try and get the locomotive there in time for us to start it, but unfortunately it could not be managed. Mr. Whitehead (the engineer) was a stoker on the first line of railway opened in England, and now he is about to open the first line in the North-West.

> This railway, being built by the Canadian Government from Selkirk to the United States border at Emerson, was known as the Canada Pacific Railway. Later, when transferred to a private company, the name was changed to the Canadian Pacific Railway.
>
> The first passenger train in England ran, over the Stockton and Darlington Railway, on September 27, 1825. It was pulled by *Locomotion,* No. 1 — an engine built, and operated that day, by George Stephenson. It has been preserved and is now exhibited on the station platform at Darlington, Yorkshire, England.

When this ceremony was over we visited the Roman Catholic Schools on this side of the water, and there were addresses both from the boys and girls. We crossed the river again, and drove to the City Hall, where a déjeuner was given to the Governor-General.

His speech was very good, and the company present were much pleased with it. He spoke for about three-quarters of an hour, and people seemed to listen with all their ears, and laughed a great deal at the amusing parts. He tried to give some idea of the great size of the Dominion, and, speaking of this Province, said: –

From its geographical position, and its peculiar characteristics, Manitoba may be regarded as the keystone of that mighty arch of sister provinces which spans the continent from the Atlantic to the Pacific. It was here that Canada, emerging from her woods and forests, first gazed upon the rolling prairies and unexplored North-West, and learned, as by an unexpected revelation, that her historical territories of the Canadas, her eastern seaboards of New Brunswick, Labrador, and Nova Scotia, her Laurentian lakes and valleys, corn lands and pastures, though themselves more extensive than half-a-dozen European kingdoms, were but the vestibules and ante-chambers to that till then undreamed-of dominion, whose illimitable dimensions alike confound the arithmetic of the surveyor and the verification of the explorer. It was hence that, counting her past achievements as but the preface and prelude to her future exertions and expanding destinies, she took a fresh departure, received the afflatus of a more imperial inspiration, and felt herself no longer a mere settler along the banks of a single river, but the owner of half a continent; and in the amplitude of her possession, in the wealth of her resources, in the sinews of her material might, the peer of any power on the earth.

D. had two addresses after lunch, and about four o'clock we got to the hotel, and received till five, saying 'good-bye' to all who came. Then we went over to the Morrises', and had a cup of tea; after which we got on board the *Minnesota,* and started on our return journey amidst much firing and shouting and waving of adieux.

One dear old member of Parliament (who came as Falstaff to our fancy ball) was quite overcome by the grief of parting with us, and almost fell into the water because he would continue his parting speeches until the gangway was partially removed.

We were very sorry to say farewell to Mr. McKay, whose substantial figure, in his well-known buggy, was one of the last things we saw as we steamed away. We felt tired in the evening, for this had been a hard day.

SUNDAY, 30TH. – The *Minnesota's* screw shakes so much that I find great difficulty in writing at all. But as we travel straight through to Ottawa, I think it better to defy it, rather than wait till I arrive there.

There is a cinnamon bear on board; a tame pig, which answers to the name of Dick, and a dog. The bear sometimes hugs the pig, and the dog rushes to the rescue. Someone tied a bun to the pig's tail to-day, which the bear perceived, and seized; but while he was leisurely arranging himself to enjoy it, the pig seized it, and ate it up.

MONDAY, OCTOBER 1ST. – Steaming up the monotonous Red River, we reached Grand Forks at two o'clock, and arrived at Fisher's Landing in the night.

TUESDAY, 2ND. – We went ashore, and saw the engine No. 2 of the Canada Pacific Railway; it is going to Winnipeg, with a train of railway-trucks, and it is to be called the 'Lady Dufferin.'

> The engine, indeed, was to bear her name, but in another form. It was called the 'Countess of Dufferin.' When retired, after long years of service, it too was preserved. This engine, which heralded prosperity in western Canada, is still on exhibition on a special track outside the Canadian Pacific Railway station in Winnipeg, where thousands have viewed it and read the plaque telling something of its story.

We started at three o'clock, and slept in the train.

WEDNESDAY, 3RD. – We reached St. Paul, and had time to go and dine at the hotel, which made a nice break in the journey. The Milwaukee Railway Company gave us an additional car here, and sent us off on their line, free of expense, to Chicago. We came this way in order to see the banks of the Mississippi, but unfortunately we had left the river when we got up in the morning.

THURSDAY, 4TH. – We arrived at Chicago in the afternoon, and went to see an exhibition going on there, dined at the Palmer House, and left at nine in the evening.

FRIDAY, 5TH. – We crossed the St. Clair at Detroit, and arrived that evening at Toronto. The Macdonalds and a number of other people met us there, and sat with us while we had our tea.

SATURDAY, 6TH. – During the night we reached Kingston, and slept quietly in our car till the morning, when, directly after breakfast, we were met by Colonel and Mrs. Hewitt, Sir E. Selby Smyth, and a guard of honour, and went off at once to inspect the new Military College [the Royal Military College]. It is beautifully situated, and is a very flourishing young institution, and D. saw the drill, etc. He then visited the Fort [Fort Henry], but I went straight to the Hewitts' house, as the wind was bitter, and I had caught a cold.

The Hewitts gave us a lunch, and sent us off at two o'clock on our way to Ottawa, where we found the children well and in great spirits.

CHAPTER 20

Our Last Season at Ottawa and Montreal
OCTOBER 1877-JUNE 1878

OTTAWA: SUNDAY, NOVEMBER 4TH. – There was a bad shock of earthquake in the night. I am sorry to say it did not awaken me; but several people in the house got up to see what was the matter, and there are accounts of it in all the newspapers.

A year earlier Lord Dufferin had suggested to Colonel Fred Cumberland, his talented aide-de-camp, that he wished to recommend him to Her Majesty for the honour of knighthood. This Cumberland had declined. Now, on November 17, 1877, he wrote:

Pendarves

My Lord:
   I beg to be permitted to request that your Excellency will graciously be pleased to accept my resignation of the appointment of Dominion Aide de Camp. Originally appointed to that position by Lord Monck, I have, under the favour of three Governors General, continued to hold it for so lengthened a period that I now desire with your Excellency's sanction to retire. I shall always remember with pride and pleasure the happiness of having been attached to your service.
   I am my Lord,
   Your Excellency's most obedient and faithful Servant,
   Fred Cumberland

Taken by surprise, Lord Dufferin replied asking that the subject be not mentioned until further communication. Early in December, while in Toronto, he attempted to see Mr. Cumberland personally.

The latter was in Hamilton on business, but had left some verses, marking the end of their lengthy association and their common interest in poetry. The following note was received at the Cumberland home:

My dear Cumberland:

I cannot tell you how pleased I am. They are excellent, and I want to show them to Lady Dufferin. Won't you let me take them with me, or at all events you will send them after me to Ottawa?

I am so vexed at missing you. I heard you had been away, or I should have asked myself last night to dinner. Tonight, I dine at the Lieutenant Governor's. I wonder whether he will have the happy inspiration to have asked you.

I will not say goodbye, as I trust we may meet yet.

Yours Ever,

D.

In her diary on December 10th, Mrs. Cumberland notes: "Fred dined at Government House to meet Lord Dufferin." While there more poetry was personally presented and the matter of Cumberland's resignation agreed upon.

MONDAY, DECEMBER 24TH. – We went into town, and did a quantity of Christmas shopping, and on our return found that Fred Ward, John Petty Ward and Price Blackwood had arrived. I was busy most of the day getting the Christmas tree ready; it is always a long business. I have it in the middle of the ball-room, with a little red-baize platform round it, and then a green carpet, forming a square, on the floor round that. On the platform and carpet all the heavy things are put, and the display this year is gorgeous.

CHRISTMAS DAY, 1877. – We had such a 'Merry' Christmas. I must tell you about it. In the morning we finished the tree, and then went to church. The children were anxious to kill time, so after lunch we skated on the river till past four o'clock. Then we had tea, and at half-past five I gave the order to light up. Mr. Dixon, the governesses, all the Littletons, and our guests were present. The display of presents was grand. Victoria was hoarse with screaming over hers, and every-one was pleased. Archie (who is home from Eton for the holidays) was delighted, and in a great state of excitement all day. We were twenty-one at dinner, and had some delightful music in the evening.

NEW YEAR'S DAY, 1878. – At five I began to dress my chicks for their play. But before that, I went down to the servants' hall, where all the children were having their tea. The servants had decorated it beautifully. Then I proceeded to the putting of finishing touches to the actors. The piece, 'Fifine, the Fisher Maid,' went off admirably, and everyone was delighted.

At the close of the play, Terence, who was almost twelve years of age, delivered an epilogue, which concluded with the following lines:

The years have slipped away so very fast,
This fairy tale is, sad to say, our last.
Before another merry Christmas Day
The 'company' will all have gone away;
An ocean will divide our little band
From all but memory of your kindly land;
And when we meet again in after years,
Some may be Generals and some Premiers;
Some Nobodies — for some you know must be.
There'll be no ogres, though, I clearly see.
One thing is certain; we shall all have grown,
And some, perhaps, have 'fairies' of our own;
But still we'll not forget, though old and tall,
'The Children's Christmas Play' at Rideau Hall.

WEDNESDAY, 2ND JANUARY. – Skating on our Rink for the first time this winter.

THURSDAY, 3RD. – We went into Ottawa and skated. Some gentlemen had provided a band, and we danced the lancers and other figures. We are still driving on wheels; but the Ottawa is at last frozen over.

This the day of the children's party. I had tea for grown-up people in the recess off the corridor, and for the children in the dining-room. The guests were quite delighted with the play, and, as it lasted from five till seven, were hungry enough to enjoy their tea. Afterwards they had a great romp in the ball-room.

MONDAY, 7TH. – In the morning we skated in town, and danced our lancers and other figures. At lunch the gentlemen were full of tobogganing, although the slide was not quite ready. They soon went out, and at once decided to go down four on one toboggan. There was so much loose snow that the person steering was blinded, and they came up against a tree, and J. P. Ward was seriously hurt. Fred rushed up to the house for brandy and assistance, and in a short time they carried him up. The doctor got here in half an hour, and found his leg broken and his side bruised. He suffered greatly. It is so unfortunate; he was enjoying everything so much; now his whole winter is spoilt.

MONDAY, 28TH. – Archie and Terence left us on their way to school in England. Mr. Higginson went with them to New York. We all miss them, and spent a miserable day. In the evening we got letters from them written in the train.

THURSDAY, 31ST. – Katie and I went into town and had a delightful skate. Mr. Haycock had had a pole put up in the Rink, from which depended a number of ribbons. The dancers stood round it, and each held a ribbon in her hand. Then we went round and round to music, as in the last figure of the lancers, the ribbons being lifted over and under, so that gradually they got plaited round the pole. Then we stopped, turned round, and going in the opposite direction unplaited them again.

Because of his experience and knowledge, gleaned while travelling in Arctic regions, Lord Dufferin was invited to attend a meeting of the American Geographical Society, called to discuss a plan for exploration in the Arctic Ocean. This took place in Chickering Hall in New York on January 31.

After a pleasant speech of welcome by the eminent editor and poet, William Cullen Bryant, Lord Dufferin was proposed by the well-known traveller and writer, Bayard Taylor, as an honorary member of the Society. Unanimously elected and asked to address the meeting, he said:

You are aware that when the great sea-captain, Christopher Columbus, returned to the Court of Ferdinand, he brought with him in chains several captive Indian chiefs as proofs of the reality of his achievements.

When presented to the Court of Spain, the gentle Isabella commanded their manacles to be struck from off their limbs. But the chains I wear are those which have been forged around my heart by the courtesy, kindness and consideration I have received at the hands of the people of the United States, and such fetters even your Imperial mandate would be powerless to loose.

FRIDAY, FEBRUARY 8TH. – The day of the opening of Parliament. It was fine weather, but we had to go in carriages, not in sleighs. The Senate

Chamber was full, and looked very handsome: the ladies well got-up, the judges very splendid, etc. Having dressed in our finery so early, we were somewhat tired on our return, but after tea had to dress again for dinner and the Drawing-room. A thousand people passed – a steady stream for an hour and a quarter – so many curtseys were exhausting.

MONDAY, 11TH. – We left Ottawa, a great party, to stay at Montreal as guests of the City. The only two left behind were Cis (my sister-in-law, Mrs. Rowan Hamilton), who is ill and Mr. J. P. Ward, who was to get up for the first time to-day. Mr. Bierstadt and Mr. Hayes go with us. The latter is the son of the President of the United States. [Rutherford Birchard Hayes had the previous year been sworn in as the nineteenth president.]

We reached Montreal at six, and met with a splendid reception. The place was crowded, there was much cheering, a lovely bouquet for me, an address to D., and a drive with four horses to the Windsor Hotel, the bells of the town ringing out a welcome.

We are by way of opening this new hotel – the Windsor. It is a very fine one, and the Reception Committee were awaiting us in the gorgeous drawing-room. In reply to their words of introduction, D. told them that the humble rooms at Government House would not be able to contain him on his return.

Our dinner was very good, but a long time being allowed for diges-tion between each course, we retired before the pudding, and found Gwen waiting to take the gentlemen on to a ball.

TUESDAY, 12TH. – D., I, and a certain proportion of our party, lunched with Mr. [Joseph] McKay, a dear old gentleman who has spent his hard-earned wealth in building a great deaf-and-dumb institution, which he to-day presents to the City through the Governor-General. After lunch we drove to the institution, our sleigh being escorted by a troop of cavalry. The building was ornamented with flags and full of people.

Afterwards we went to the Villa Maria Convent, where a very strik-ing scene was presented. Turning in from the cold and the daylight (it was a snow-stormy day), we found ourselves in a brilliantly-lighted room, full of young ladies, saw a gorgeous display of flowers, and heard sounds of music – 'God save the Queen' played upon harps and pianos, and sung by numerous voices. All the girls wore black dresses for the Pope's death (Pius IX), but they had white lace bibs and cuffs, broad sashes of coloured ribbon over the shoulder, and in their hands long sprays of artificial flowers. The hall is a very large one, and all along the walls were rows of girls; at the end of the room a rising bank of pupils, and in the centre three platforms: on one the pianos, on the second five harps, and on the third D. and I. We had a good deal of music and six addresses – two in French, two in English, and two from little girls, who presented bouquets.

When we got home we had to dress for dinner and a ball. The latter was given for us in a very fine dining-room in this hotel. There were 2,000 people at it, and it was in every way a success. We entered the room in a procession, and D. danced everything, while I 'did' a few squares, and was introduced to numbers of ladies. Everything went merrily till 4.30 a.m., when we retired to bed. Katie (my sister, later Lady Nicholson) enjoyed this, her first ball, very much, and danced everything.

WEDNESDAY, 13TH. – We went to M'Gill College, and at the gates the students met us and dragged us up to the door. Happily, no one was hurt, though these volunteer horses were constantly falling, being dragged by the rope, and half driven over.

I was taken up to the Hall, where I waited the arrival of the new LL.D., for D. was down in the library being clothed in cap and gown. The students soon filled the hall completely, so that it was impossible for His Ex. to get through it, and he had to be brought up by a back stair, and appeared through a trap-door on the platform, where the learned sat.

The address and reply were in Greek, and I was listening in a vacant manner, when I saw the Greek scholars smiling at me, and I found that the word Countess had been introduced into the harangue. I came in for a share of glory also when the students presented me with a very handsome silver bouquet-holder, made on purpose for me, with Canadian and English symbols, the arms of the College, and an inscription engraved upon it. After a speech from the president, the new graduate signed the register, was handed his diploma, and was called upon for an address.

I suppose a learned and serious speech was expected; but D. surprised his audience by a few light and airy sentences, and I don't think I ever heard him speak more effectively. He had not thought of anything particular to say, and did not wish to enter into a serious speech about nothing; and, as it turned out, his impromptu jokes were much better. I had one or two people to tea on my return, and after dinner we went to the theatre.

The house was crammed, and presented a most brilliant spectacle.

The piece was, in its way, unique, for it was made the excuse for a grand military display. There were at least 160 artillery men and officers, and a number of soldiers in red, exhibited on the stage as about to embark for India. The steamer with its funnel was in the background, the bands played, the regiments marched on board; five horses at a time came on, one ridden, the others dragging the gun-carriage. All was done in regular military fashion, and it made a splendid scene. This was got up for us by the Volunteers, and was most successful. We did not leave the theatre till midnight, and then were dragged by the snow-shoers of Montreal to the hotel. Our two-legged steeds wore a very picturesque costume, and were lively horses and most cheery companions. 'To bed, to bed, said Sleepy Head.'

THURSDAY, 14TH. – We had to leave early to drive out a long way to the Sacred Heart Convent. The children were assembled in a long, narrow room, the walls covered with white-and-gold. At the far end was a stage with rustic arbours on it and quantities of flowers. On it was performed an original musical operetta, in which all the flowers took part, and which ended in the 'Rose' carrying a magnificent basket of flowers to His Ex., each of her attendants holding a ribbon attached to it.

We were shown the house and the fine chapel where the girls, with white veils thrown over their heads, knelt, filling all the centre part of the church, the colours of the painted windows lighting up their white figures, and colouring them with a rainbow light. After, we went straight to lunch, and the nuns did the honours, and talked to us so pleasantly.

Driving home, we went up the mountain – through Mount Royal Park. It is only just made. The road winds to a great height, and the views from it are lovely. It will be a beautiful drive to have so near a city.

This evening there was a banquet, and I am sure no Governor of any kind ever received a more magnificent ovation than this at the end of his term of office. The dinner was in the great ball-room. There was one long table down the side of the room, and ten others across, holding in all 350 people. The first thing I can tell you from personal experience was my own entrance. I went in with my sisters and a few other ladies to hear the speeches. When I came in, everyone stood up, most of them on their chairs, and cheered me for so long that, after acknowledging their greeting repeatedly, I sat down before silence was restored.

Sir Francis Hincks was the chairman, and of course the Queen's health came first, and was enthusiastically received. As a special compliment, D. next proposed the health of the President of the United States (Mr. Hayes), his son being present.

The toast of the evening was the signal for tremendous cheering – the gentlemen stood on their chairs, and waved handkerchiefs; and when D. spoke, almost every sentence was followed by the greatest applause, and all the amusing parts by roars of laughter. Nothing could have gone off better or more brilliantly than this banquet did, and I wish I had time to give you a better account of it.

FRIDAY, 15TH. – We had to be at the Curling Rink at 10.30 to play a great match – the Viceregal Club against the Three Rivers – for the Caledonian medal. The game was an exceedingly close one, but alas! we lost by one point. The Rink was beautifully decorated, even the ice being covered with designs; and our side played well, though it was beaten.

I skated for an hour, hurried home to lunch, and to dress for a reception we had at three. That over, I had the Chief Justice to tea, then got ready for a dinner. In the evening we opened an exhibition of pictures of the Art Association of Montreal, and D. announced that Mr. Bierstadt was going to present the Society with a picture. The hall of the hotel, in which the exhibition was held, is an immense place with a marble floor, and looked very splendid, filled as it was with gaily-dressed company. Some of the principal people came to our room afterwards.

SATURDAY, 16TH. – Our week of ovation is over, and this morning we started for home. Gwen and her dear little baby came to breakfast, and at ten we were off, first of all to visit an indiarubber manufactory and a cotton manufactory, then to the station, where there was an address.

On the way to Ottawa, by a new line of railway, D. had at least one address at every station, sometimes three – and I generally got a lovely bouquet. [They were travelling on a newly-built railway, the Quebec, Montreal, Ottawa and Occidental, on the north side of the Ottawa River, passing through Calumet, Papineauville and Buckingham.] We were very kindly, indeed affectionately, received everywhere, and the whole country seemed to turn out to greet us. A number of gentlemen came part of the way home with us. Lady Sykes and her brother are staying here.

I thought it best to finish the happy part of my Journal first; but there has been a drawback to my pleasure in the week. While D. was dining on Friday and just before I went in to hear the speeches, I received a telegram to say that Basil had scarlet fever. He is going on extremely well, but of course I shall be anxious until I know whether this horrid disease spreads. The other children are separated, but they were with him when he first fell ill. His room is in the centre of the house, and the isolation is not as perfect as I could wish. Here we are, with Cis in bed, Mr. Ward laid up with a broken leg, scarlet fever in the house, and visitors on top of all this who 'are not in the least afraid.' Katie remained at Montreal with Gwen. [Katie at that time was about eighteen years of age.]

But for these domestic misfortunes our week at Montreal would have been an unqualified pleasure. We found everywhere so much personal affection and kindness, and were in every way so magnificently received, that nothing could have been more delightful than it was.

MONDAY, MARCH 4TH. – Mr. Harvey, of Ickwellbury, dined with us, and we had music in the evening. Russell and he played the violin, and Mr. J. P. Ward sang the 'Lost Chord' to us. He has a most beautiful tenor voice. He has only just recovered from the tobogganing accident.

SUNDAY, 10TH. – Mr. Ward fell ill to-day, but we were not at all alarmed about him till the evening, when the doctor told us his illness was most serious, and that there was no hope. He was told so, too, and immediately settled all his affairs and wrote a letter. I went to see him in the evening. He was perfectly calm and happy.

TUESDAY, 12TH. – Mr. Ward passed away this afternoon, having lingered all Monday, exhibiting always the most wonderful patience, resignation and thoughtfulness for others. I was with him when he died; Fred Ward seldom left him. The anxiety was terrible, for on Monday afternoon we were given a ray of hope, soon to be destroyed again.

THURSDAY, 14TH. – He was buried early in the morning; none went to the funeral but those who knew him, and had been with him here. He was a great favourite with us all, and this has been a great sorrow to us.

TUESDAY, APRIL 2ND. – We put off our farewell gaieties as long as we could, but to-day we resume our social duties. I spent the day nursing my voice, driving out, and looking over my parts; at six we dined, and our plays began at a quarter to eight.

'Sweethearts' came first; then 'New Men and Old Acres'; and at the end an epilogue – a farewell D. had written for me to speak. No one knew anything about it, not even my fellow-actors, so that it was a great surprise. The worst of it was that it made the audience so melancholy that the evening ended tearfully.

Excerpts from the EPILOGUE:

Kind friends! for such indeed you've proved to us —
Kinder than just, I fear — and is it thus
That we must quit you? Shall the curtain fall
O'er this bright pageant like a funeral pall,
And blot forever from your friendly sight
The well-known forms and faces that to-night
For the last time have used their mimic arts
To tempt your laughter, and to touch your hearts,
Without one word of thanks to let you know
How irredeemable's the debt we owe
For that warm welcome, which, year after year,
Has waited on our poor attempts to cheer,
With the gay humour of these trivial plays,
Some few hours stolen from your busy days?
Despite ourselves, the grateful words WILL come
For love could teach a language to the dumb.

. . . .

And now one last Farewell — a few months more,
And we depart your loved Canadian shore,
Never again to hear your plaudits rise,
Nor watch the ready laughter in your eyes
Gleam out responsive to our author's wit,
However poorly we interpret it,
Nor see with artist pride your tears o'erflow,
In homage to our simulated woe.

Yet scenes like these can never wholly fade
Into oblivion's melancholy shade,
And oft at home when Christmas fire-logs burn
Our pensive thoughts instinctively will turn
To this fair city with her crown of towers
And all the joys and friends that once were ours.

THURSDAY, 4TH. – Gwen, Russell, the Baby, and Miss Abbott arrived. Muriel is very pretty, and a dear little thing in every way.

FRIDAY, 5TH. – Our last play here. We had an enormous audience, and both 'Sweethearts' and 'New Men' and the epilogue were greatly appreciated. They certainly went off well, and everyone was delighted. But all were sad to think we were having our last party here, and I know I feel miserable about it.

MONDAY, 8TH. – Fred Ward left for England – a signal of our approaching departure, for we shall have left when he returns to Canada. I hate these symptoms of our waning existence here; I have enjoyed it all so much. His departure makes also the first break in what has been a very happy family party.

SATURDAY, 13TH. – In the morning we drove into Ottawa to see an enormous map of Canada, prepared for the Paris Exhibition. We also looked at models of the Welland Canal.

Hearing that the House had been sitting all night, and was likely to sit all day, we determined to come in again in the afternoon to hear what was going on.

The Opposition were talking against time, to prevent a division being taken about some Quebec affairs (the Governor having dismissed his Ministers) until Monday, as the political meetings amongst the French are generally after Mass on Sunday, and they did not wish to have the defeat of their motion announced to the congregations.

Last night there was singing and cock-crowing and all sorts of noises, and when Mr. Plumb [Josiah Burr Plumb, member for Niagara] was speaking another member got up and said he was interrupting the music. When we went – Gwen and I, Mrs. Littleton, and the Colonel – a Member was speaking, merely to fill up the time. He read out of a book, and gave us the title in full several times, and said it belonged to 'his hon. friend the Member for Niagara'; and then, when noise was made, he said he feared hon. members had not heard, and so he would repeat what he had been saying or reading. Singing began – 'Auld Lang Syne.' 'En roulant ma boule' – cock-crowing, and all sorts of noises and fun, while the entertainment – as far as I heard it – ended with the Marsellaise, beautifully sung by a musical M.P.

When I got up to go, what do you think happened? – the whole house, both sides, stood up and sang 'God save the Queen,' and then cheered. Of course I got out as quickly as I could. We were told afterwards that we had been as 'sugar' to the House; that they were just getting very cross when we came in, and that our presence put them in good humour – very good humour, as you may perceive. They were expecting to sit all night, but at six Mr. Mackenzie consented to adjourn, on condition that the division should be taken early on Monday.

We had a Parliamentary dinner that night, so when I was in the House I instituted inquiries as to who would be able to come. On my return a telegram followed me, 'Thirty will not be able to dine'; so I had the dinner moved into the small dining-room, and cut down from forty to sixteen. Soon after another message came to say the House had adjourned, which was agitating. But only thirteen guests arrived, so our table was all right. We had a pleasant little dinner – Mr. Macpherson, Mr. Campbell, Mr. Bunster, Mr. Odell, and the old Mr. Glasier, who went away from our theatricals 'because he did not come all the way down here to see a lot of love-making.' Mr. Ryan and the Deputy Sergeant-at-Arms, Major Smith, were also there.

Among her dinner guests that evening were some Lady Dufferin has mentioned before. While in Toronto, in January of 1877, the Dufferins had tea at the home of Senator David L. Macpherson. Hon. Arthur Bunster, the Member for Vancouver Island, with his wife, had been dinner guests when the Dufferins entertained at Government House while in Victoria.

Hon. William Odell, after seventeen years as Member of the Legislative Council of his native New Brunswick, had been summoned to the Senate in 1867. Also a Senator was the Honourable Alexander Campbell, a sixty-six-year-old Yorkshireman, who had settled in Kingston, Ontario. Previously, for some years he had been a Minister in Sir John A. Macdonald's Cabinet.

'Old Mr. Glasier' — John B. Glasier, at that time sixty-nine years of age — was a lumber merchant from New Brunswick. After serving that province in its House of Assembly, he had been called to the Senate in 1868.

Joseph O'Connell Ryan, a thirty-seven-year-old lawyer, whose home was in Portage la Prairie, was a Member for Marquette, Manitoba.

TUESDAY, 16TH. – D. received the address presented to him by both Houses of Parliament. We – Gwen, Nellie and I – went to the Senate Chamber, where our seats were just in front of the Throne, Ministers' wives, etc. behind. I found it a very melancholy ceremony, and it gave me a nervous headache.

MONDAY, 22ND. – We began our last fortnight of gaieties. Gwen and Russell [Stephenson] are already here, and Miss Abbott and Miss Scott arrived to take part in two concerts. They both live in Montreal.

We also began to say 'farewell.' D. and I went to the Supreme Court and spent an hour and a half, saying good-bye to members and senators. Mr. Kimber and Mr. Fleming dined with us, and we had music in the evening.

WEDNESDAY, 24TH. – We had our last big dinner; the table formed three sides of a square, and we had over seventy people. After the ladies left the room a senator (Mr. Vidal) got up and proposed my health. He sent round to ask D. if he might, and he did not like to refuse. Fred told us, when he saw the party off, they were delighted with their evening. They said they had left a man in the House to talk against time, and had promised to be back at nine; but they did not leave till 10.30.

FRIDAY, 26TH. – In the evening we went to see Charlotte Thompson in 'Jane Eyre.' She is not a handsome woman, but so good an actress that she makes you quite forget her face.

SATURDAY, 27TH. – Our concert took place this afternoon, and was most successful; people seemed delighted. In the evening we went to see Miss Multon ('East Lynne').

TUESDAY, 30TH. – I have organized a bazaar in our tennis-court to pay off the debt on our little church, and we began to arrange it. The carpenters put up the shields on the walls of the tennis-court and set the tables. Some ladies from New Edinburgh came to help; when we locked up for the evening everything was ready, and extremely pretty it all looked.

WEDNESDAY, MAY 1ST. – Will the weather be fine? That is what we are anxious about; it pours all the morning. D. is arranging a Picture-Gallery in the ball-room, to which the public will be admitted upon payment of 25 cents. Every painting, water-colour, engraving or photograph we possess, whether in a book, a portfolio, or a frame, is exhibited here, and in addition we have borrowed two very fine paintings of Mr. Gilmour's. An orange ticket, 25 cents, admits the juveniles, and many of the old people too, to the mysteries of 'Punch and Judy.'

We were putting finishing touches to ourselves and to the tables till the last moment; happily the rain cleared off, and the afternoon was lovely. In the garden we had the Guards' band and a large tin full of small parcels tied up with string. Near this stood two lovely ladies with fishing-rods; for ten cents you were allowed to try your luck – that is, take the rod and fish for a parcel. This became so popular an amusement, both for old and young, that it went on all three afternoons, and made much money.

The buying and selling, the music, the raffles, the tea, the fishpond, all go on merrily.

FRIDAY, 3RD. – The weather was bad yesterday, and we had to keep in-doors, which was a great loss to our pockets. I don't think I was ever so busy in my life, for I found it impossible, from morning till night to take my attention off bazaar business for one moment. At the end we had an auction for about an hour, which amused people much.

The thing was a great success. Instead of my modest anticipations of making 600 dollars, I think we shall clear more than 2,000. Every-one said they had never been to so honest or so pleasant a bazaar, and they proved their sincerity by coming every day. I am going to pay off the debt on our church (for which I got up the Bazaar), and shall give the surplus, and the things left, to the Protestant Orphan Asylum in Ottawa, which is badly off.

THURSDAY, 9TH. – Parliament was prorogued to-day.

FRDAY, 17TH. – This morning we had an exhibition of the phono-graph. Two men brought this wonderful invention for us to see. It is quite a small thing, a cylinder which you turn with a handle, and which you place on a common table.

We were so amazed when we first heard this bit of iron speak that it was hard to believe there was no trick! But we all tried it. Fred sang 'Old Obadiah,' D. made it talk Greek, the Colonel sang a French song, and all our vocal efforts were repeated. As long as the same piece of tinfoil is kept on the instrument you can hear all you have said over and over again. You may imagine how susceptible the needle is when I tell you that the first time D. spoke into the machine he spoke too loud, and tore the tinfoil. The last performance was for D. to say something which should be repeated by the machine to a public exhibition in Ottawa in the evening.

We are scattering for a few days. Nellie goes to Niagara with the Littletons. To-morrow morning D. goes to Toronto for an exhibition of pictures, and I am to spend a week with Gwen at Montreal. Then we all meet at Montreal for a Review on the Queen's Birthday.

The house is full of packing-cases, and everything bare and miser-able-looking, and I am very glad of a rest and a holiday.

MONTREAL: MONDAY 20TH. – In the afternoon Gwen and I walked to the General Hospital, where the Grey Nuns have old people, orphans, and foundlings. We went over the whole institution. The superior gave me a handsome book, a biography of the foundress.

THURSDAY, 23RD. – D., Fred, Colonel Littleton and Dr. Grant reached Montreal this evening, and came up to tea at Gwen's house.

FRIDAY, 24TH. – The Queen's birthday; weather suited to the occasion, bright and sunshiny. The roads were full of carriages and people walking, the effect quite Derby-like. I never saw such a crowd in Canada, the field, the trees, the side of the mountain covered with spectators.

There were about 3,000 troops, and the Governor-General and his 'brilliant Staff' rode down the ranks, stopping opposite a company of United States Volunteers, who had come to take part in the proceedings, to make a speech welcoming them to Canada. The *feu de joie*, the march-past, and a sham battle followed. Everybody was delighted with everything, and what could you wish for more?

We hurried through lunch, and proceeded to the Lacrosse ground. D. was there presented with an address and a 'crosse,' and we saw two games. [These were between the Caughnawagas and Montreal Clubs, with the Indians victorious.] Then we rushed back to the hotel to drop D. for a great military banquet, which began at 5.30. I dined at Gwen's house, and returned to the hotel to pick up the gentlemen on our way to the theatre. The dinner not being over, we went up and peeped in. It was a pretty sight, all the guests in uniform.

SATURDAY, 25TH. – D. and I left Montreal at 9 a.m. and with Colonel Littleton and Dr. Grant returned to Ottawa.

OTTAWA: SATURDAY, JUNE 1ST. – I was 'at home' to say 'Good-bye'; and as the day was lovely we sat out on the grass. It was hard to say 'Good-bye' to so many kind friends. I have two more of these farewells to go through.

SUNDAY, 2ND. – We went to our little church for the last time, and in the afternoon D. and I drove with Nellie, Freddie, and Victoria to the Cemetery, to see the stone put up to J. P. Ward's memory. It is a small Irish cross. On our return we found Dr. Grant. He can't bear to say 'Good-bye,' and comes here nearly every day.

THURSDAY, 6TH. – We went into town, where an address was presented at the Town Hall. The building is a new one, with a fine hall. We shook hands with all the people, then went out on the balcony; an alarm of fire was sounded, that we might see the engines at work.

D. addressed the guard of honour (Governor-General's Foot Guards), and we drove away amidst loud cheers. We were shown a full-length picture of D., an excellent likeness painted by order of the Government for the Parliament Buildings.

I am sure I have told you before how much Fred is liked here, and what a popular A.D.C. he has been. Well, as a proof of their appreciation of his unfailing kindness and courtesy during the last six years, his Canadian friends have presented him with a handsome silver tray, teapot, urn, cream jug, etc. – quite an unprecedented honour.

FRIDAY, 7TH. – Left Ottawa. We had to get up early and be at the boat by seven. It was trying; first we had to say good-bye to all the people about our house, and then at the wharf we found many friends. The large guard of honour was drawn up on the top of the cliff, and at the water's edge were the friends.

A number of young men – the bachelors – were waiting for me on board with a bouquet and silver holder. Then the ship [the *Peerless*] began slowly to move away, and there were long cheers and waving of handkerchiefs till we were out of sight. Ottawa looked lovely as we left, and never shall we forget our happy six years here and our innumerable friends.

We had to change at Grenville into a train, and there say a few more good-byes. After half an hour we got into another steamer, which took us to Montreal. At several of the small places we passed, crowds had collected to give us a parting cheer. At Montreal the steamer was full of people, all come to say good-bye, and to see an address presented. This was from the Curlers, and with it was given a beautiful coloured photograph, with a view of Montreal, and portraits of ourselves and many other people we know. It is an oil picture and is a most charming remembrance. In the middle of the ceremony the galleries began to creak, and the crowd had to get out of them quickly.

SATURDAY, 8TH. – Up very early to see the children off to England. We breakfasted on board the Quebec steamer, and went in a tender to the Allan s.s. *Scandinavian*. The Bishop and Mrs. Dobell are on board, and it was a lovely day for starting. But it was sad seeing all our flock go – and now we have half left Canada.

Dufferin and I, Mr. Reynolds and Mrs. Littleton, went on board the *Druid*, and are now on our way to Gaspé. But we shall not be ourselves till we have slept upon all the partings of the last two days. It has been so delightful in Canada, and never again, I fear, can we hope to be surrounded by so many true and kind friends.

CHAPTER 21

The Eastern Townships, and Last Days in Canada
JUNE-AUGUST 1878

TUESDAY, JUNE 11TH. – Everything we do now seems to be impressed with that horrid word 'last.' Here we are at Gaspé, for the *last* time, enjoying our *last* fishing, cruising for the *last* time in the old *Druid*, and mentally saying 'good-bye' to many a pleasant thing which has become a habit during the past six years.

I elected to remain at home, but Mrs. Littleton went to join her husband on the York. Fred and D. went to the lower pools, where they can fish from the *Druid*.

WEDNESDAY, 12TH. – Rain all night, the river rising. I hope to answer my letters, to braid Victoria an elaborate frock and to be well read in history before I go to Boston. The afternoon was fine, and D. sketched; some important telegrams came. There is a riot at Quebec, the soldiers out, the ringleader shot, and many people wounded.

THURSDAY, 13TH. – D. and Fred went out fishing and brought home only one salmon each; Fred's was a beauty, weighing 29 lbs. D. got a telegram from Quebec asking him to have a British regiment sent there, so thinks he better return at once. The fires are lighted, coal taken on board, and by two o'clock in the night we are off. Before starting we sent off numbers of telegrams; the clerk at the office seldom has so much work to do at quiet Gaspé.

FRIDAY, 14TH. – Such lovely weather, the sea like a glass, and covered with fishing boats.

SATURDAY, 15TH. – At Father Point we received a telegram to say all our rooms were filled with soldiers, beds on the floor, etc. We made up our minds to stay on the *Druid*.

SUNDAY, 16TH. – We found on arrival at Quebec that most of the soldiers had left. Dent [the personal maid, who had become housekeeper after their return from the visit home in 1875] had to provide for sixty officers – give them blankets, towels, etc. She kept them in great order, and insisted upon their replacing a pillow which had come to grief in a bolstering match. Everything seems quiet for the present.

We had an escort of cavalry to come up to the Citadel with. Colonel Strange came to see us, and told us all about the riot. The day was muggy and wet, and in the night there was a severe thunderstorm.

MONDAY, 17TH. – D. was very busy all day, and in the evening we dined at the Lieutenant-Governor's [Honourable Luc Letellier de Saint-Just]. I sat between him and M. Joly, the Prime Minister; on the other side of him was a very pleasant man. They talked a great deal and were very amusing. It was a large dinner.

We had the military chiefs who distinguished themselves in the riot, Sir Narcisse Belleau, Mr. Irvine, and several more of the political celebrities here.

WEDNESDAY, 19TH. – There was a review of the 8th Royals this morning on the Esplanade. It was fine and sunny, and the regiment gave great satisfaction to the military lookers-on. D. complimented them, and on their return to barracks they were disbanded.

THURSDAY, 20TH. – We had a very pleasant expedition to-day. Starting in the *Druid* about lunch-time, we went over to the Island of Orleans, where we drove in a carriage lent to us by a 'Habitan.' The views from the island are lovely.

FRIDAY, 21ST. – We slept on board and started in the morning, reaching St. John, a town at the other end of the island, by breakfast-time. We were not expected there, but the *Druid* was seen in the distance, and by the time we landed every cottage had hoisted a flag or a table-cloth, and people were at every door bowing and smiling.

After our drive around this end of this pretty island, we found more preparations had been made; two men had got themselves into red tunics, and seven or eight young ladies had guns, and fired an impromptu and amateur *feu de joie*. They also had bouquets for us, tied with white ribbon. Mine had written upon it 'For Lady Dufferin, in remembrance of her visit to St. John.' The curé said if he had only known before we should have had all the country-people in to greet us.

QUEBEC: SATURDAY, 22ND. – At three o'clock we went to the House of Parliament, where addresses were presented to D. on his approaching departure; he replied, and both addresses were read in French and English. The room was full, everyone having come to see the ceremony. The speeches in Parliament upon the address were extremely flattering, and, coming from both sides of the House, are very gratifying.

SUNDAY, 23RD. – We had some difficulty in arranging our journey to Boston – to which city D. has been invited in order to receive a Doctor's degree from the University of Harvard – so as to arrive there on Monday. It would take twenty-four hours, and there were no trains on Sunday. We talked of going up to Montreal in the *Druid*, but as that would have cost the Government 100£., we gave up the idea. And virtue was rewarded, for the mail steamer arriving, an express train had immediately to be sent off. So we finished our packing and went in that. D. and I had an excellent night in the train, and reached Montreal at six in the morning.

We started again at nine on our way to Boston. The railway passes through a lovely country – rivers and mountains and fertile valleys – and we arrived at Boston late in the evening. We were met at the station by Mr. Winthrop, who had just been assisting at rather a melancholy dinner – a gathering of the survivors of his class at college fifty years ago. The heavy hand of Time had of course committed fearful ravages in the half-century, and I only wonder anybody was able to dine at all.

He drove us out to Uplands, which is about a quarter of an hour from Boston, in a suburb called Brookline. Our host's family consists of Mrs. Winthrop, his daughter, and an invalid daughter of Mrs. Winthrop's. We had tea and were then glad to go to bed.

> Hon. Robert Charles Winthrop was a descendant of the John
> Winthrop who, in 1629, founded the State of Massachusetts and became
> its first Governor. Like his ancestor, the Dufferin's host was a politician,
> having been Speaker of the House of Representatives and later a
> Senator.

TUESDAY, 25TH. – Immediately after breakfast there were prayers in the hall, which is long and narrow, going right through the house, with a door at each end into the grounds. The walls are wooden, and covered with pictures there are tables, books, busts, and bronzes about, and it makes a very nice sitting-room. On one side is the dining-room, and on the other the drawing-room and another small room.

At eleven we went for a drive in the very pretty neighborhood – villa after villa, surrounded by plots of grass and gardens open to the road. Then we lunched, and then came what I call the American part of the day. I had had an idea of sitting out in the garden and of walking in the grounds; but as I came out of the dining-room I was told that I must rest, and that dinner was at six. I was led therefore up to my room, again reminded of the dinner-hour, and shut up there for the remainder of the day. Having a nice book, I reconciled myself to this un-English way of spending the afternoon. [Lady Dufferin was young; the Winthrops were elderly.]

At dinner I sat between Mr. Winthrop and Mr. Longfellow, with Mr. Dana on the other side of him; Wendell Holmes and Mr. Parkman opposite; the Governor of the State [Governor Rice], the Chief Justice, Mrs. Amory, Mrs. Mason (formerly Sumner's wife), Mrs. Perkins, ourselves, and young Mrs. Winthrop, formed the party.

> The Dufferins had met several of the guests on a previous visit to Boston. Francis Parkman, the eminent writer on historical themes, already had many books to his credit, and more were to follow before his death in 1893, when he was seventy years of age. He was elected to the American Hall of Fame in 1915.

In the evening there was a reception, and we saw a number of distinguished people.

WEDNESDAY, 26TH. – This morning D. drove with an officer in a carriage-and-four to the State House, where he met the Governor, and at ten went with him, escorted by lancers, to the College (Harvard).

We ladies did not leave the house till ten, and then went to Harvard, and took our seats in a handsome theatre, immediately opposite to the platform, where all the University celebrities sat.

There were nine orations; after which the classes came up one by one, listened to some words in Latin from the President [Charles W. Eliot], and were handed a bundle of degrees, which were re-distributed afterwards.

When D. received his he was greatly cheered. We were allowed to peep into the fine hall, where the party (800) lunched. D. was there, and had to make a little speech; he did not get back till six. We went to Mrs. Eliot's (the wife of the President of Harvard), and had a ladies' lunch. She is very pretty and nice, and I enjoyed it very much. I drove home with Mrs. Winthrop through a fine cemetery filled with beautiful plants.

> Harvard University had been sparing of honours granted to men outside the United States. Lord Dufferin was only the thirteenth non-American, in thirty years, to receive her LL.D. award. Previous recipients had included the Earl of Elgin, the Earl of Ellesmere, John Stuart Mill, and Thomas Carlyle.

THURSDAY, 27TH. – I spent a very quiet day, taking a drive with Mrs. Winthrop in the afternoon. D. went to another lunch, with an 'oration' before it. The speeches were not reported, but I hear his was very amusing and good.

> This luncheon followed the annual meeting of the Phi Beta Kappa Society, at which Lord Dufferin, Principal Dawson of McGill College, and Richard Henry Stoddard, the American poet, were elected honorary members.
>
> According to a time-honoured custom, the proceedings were not reported. But in his book about Lord Dufferin, George Stewart Jr. quotes from a private letter from one of the members: "Lord Dufferin was delightful. His speech was most felicitous, natural, spontaneous, cordial, playful and graceful."

FRIDAY, 28TH. – D. and I went to breakfast with Longfellow. He and his daughter, a Mr. Green, and ourselves were the party. Longfellow was very pleasant and kind, and gave me at leaving a copy of 'Keramos,' in which he wrote my name.

He told us of a letter he received from a lady, asking for his autograph, and suggesting that he should copy her one verse of that lovely poem of his beginning 'Break, break, break.' [That poem was written by Alfred, Lord Tennyson.]

We got back to Uplands at eleven, and soon after started on a long drive to see Mr. Adams [Charles Francis Adams, son of John Quincy Adams, sixth president of the United States]. He was Minister in London at the time of the [Civil] War, and made many friends there.

He lives in a charming old-fashioned house, which has been added to in every direction. A few years ago he built a library in the garden

– a fine room, with something quaint about it. There are box borders in the garden, and everything is English-looking.

Mr. Adams has five sons, all doing well. But the New Englanders seem to think that the money of the West will prevent the Eastern men from ever taking a prominent part in politics again. Mrs. Adams is a very nice person, and there was a pretty daughter-in-law there too. We had luncheon with them. The drive is a beautiful one, and the day was warm and sunny.

Mr. Parkman dined with the Winthrops, and had a long talk with D. Miss Motley is staying here.

> John Lothrop Motley, an eminent American historian, who had died the previous year, had been United States Minister to Great Britain, 1869-70. In his speech at Harvard Lord Dufferin had said: "At home I have sometimes had the privilege of welcoming to my roof Prescott, Hawthorne, and Motley."

SATURDAY, 29TH. – We were up early as the train started at eight, and we had a long drive to Boston. The Winthrops and Miss Motley saw us off. They have been most kind, and our visit has been very pleasant.

Indeed I must say that wherever we have been in the States we have been most kindly received. Nothing can exceed the hospitality of Americans; they seem as if they never could do enough for the comfort and entertainment of those who visit them in their own homes. And D. and I have now had many opportunities of appreciating their kindness to strangers.

The day was hot, and it seemed very long in the train – from 8 a.m. till 9 p.m. Then a rush up to the hotel for tea, and then all night in the 'cars.'

SUNDAY, 30TH. – We reached Quebec early in the morning, and came over to the Citadel.

MONDAY, JULY 1ST. – A very hot day. In the evening we started in the *Druid* – Fred, D. and I – for Bic, where we take the train for Causapscal, on the Matapedia [an Indian word meaning 'branching river'].

TUESDAY, 2ND. – This morning we heard that the wind was very strong, and we were going to anchor on account of the fog. When that lifted we found ourselves near Rivière du Loup. When we reached the train at Cacouna, Mr. [C. J.] Brydges, the chief of the line, came into our carriage; he had his wife and family on board his own private car. He and his friends walked about with hats upon which was written 'Great Caesar's Ghost.' We found out that is the name of a barge on which he lives in his river. He fishes in the Restigouche, a magnificent river which branches off from the Matapedia at a place called the Forks. Up this he is drawn in his barge, anchors it at the top and makes excursions in boats, returning to his yacht at night.

We got to our destination [Causapscal, Indian for 'rapid water'] about half-past eight. This is much more civilised fishing than our river affords. A railway runs along the banks of the river; the station is close to the house; there is a telegraph and nothing lonely about the life.

WEDNESDAY, 3RD. – We got up at seven and went out fishing. But eleven o'clock came and not a rise had we had, so we went home to breakfast, and found everyone else had been unlucky. It was too hot, or had been too hot (salmon are wonderful creatures for finding out reasons for not rising) .

THURSDAY, 4TH. – We have Mr. Brydges's private car and an engine whenever we want to move about, so settled to make an expedition to see the river. We started at 7.30, servants and baggage in our car, and D. and I in one canoe, Sir Frederick [Graham, of Netherby] in the other. We had a charming morning going down the river. At eleven we reached Assmaquaghan, where our car was 'anchored,' and in it we found a breakfast laid.

Then we ordered the engine to start and had a lovely 'drive' to Campbellton. The junction of the Matapedia and the Restigouche is quite beautiful. We enjoyed the views and the sea air till our engine had turned round, when we got 'on board' again. We have most comfortable bedrooms, where we slept after we had sat over a splendid camp fire outside.

FRIDAY, 5TH. – We returned to Causapscal in time for eleven o'clock breakfast. In the afternoon D. caught one 28-pound salmon, and Fred one 26. After dinner no less than seven bonfires were lighted in our honour – six on the opposite bank, and one nearer to us. They looked very bright in the dark night.

SATURDAY, 6TH. – Fishing unlucky. At three we left in our special train; in about two hours we got to Rimouski. The next station was Bic, and there we walked through the village and down to the quay, where we found our own boat waiting. Then we set off for Tadousac.

MONDAY, 8TH. – We started up the Saguenay. At one we began to fish for trout, and by three had caught about seven dozen. In the evening we got a boat's crew to row round us, singing Canadian boat-songs.

TUESDAY, 9TH. – Sir Frederick Graham and Fred left us at Chicoutimi (where we arrived early in the morning), and went on an expedition after land-locked salmon. They will camp out for three or four days. D., Gwen and I went by steamer to Ha-Ha Bay, and there, getting into a buggy, drove to A-Mas River. D. had capital sport there with two good salmon, and we enjoyed watching him, and looking at the salmon jumping up the leap.

We returned to the *Druid,* dined, and sat on deck. In the night we started again, and arrived at Tadousac in the morning.

WEDNESDAY, 10TH. – Went over our empty house, took away our blankets, but left all our nice furniture, and shut it up – the last time, I suppose we shall ever see the place. I hate these good-byes.

Russell Stephenson came on board, and we started for Quebec. The day was wet and disagreeable; but the rain will put out the bush fires, which are very bad just now at Three Rivers. The Montreal boat actually had to turn back on account of the smoke.

THURSDAY, 11TH. – Got to Quebec early, and came up to breakfast at the Citadel. I suppose we shall not again spend a night in the dear old *Druid.* In the evening we got a telegram from Sir E. Thornton (Washington), to say that two thousand roughs had left Buffalo, and gone to Montreal to 'help' on the 12th. [They planned to help break up the usual twelfth of July parade of the Orangemen.]

FRIDAY, 12TH. – Great anxiety felt in the morning as to what would happen in Montreal. Three thousand troops are there, and the Mayor has two hundred special constables.

At eleven the General telegraphed, 'There will be no procession.' The end of the whole thing was that the Mayor found an old Act which declared the procession illegal; he seized the marshals as they came out of the Hall, and the rest of the people remained shut up the whole day, and in the evening were conveyed home in cabs. We hope this is the end of it.

SUNDAY, 14TH. – Sir Frederick and Fred returned from a pleasant expedition, but unsuccessful fishing. They came back in a boat full of Americans – forty-seven of the Maine Press Association – and had great fun, as these people sang, and recited, and acted, and made speeches.

They were all in church this morning, and we asked them to come up to see the Citadel and have tea.

We walked about the platform, and they were much pleased when they found they were admitted into the 'inner circle,' and that it was a private spot. We gave them tea and claret-cup, showed the Plains of Abraham, then returned to the Citadel to say 'Good-bye.'

Forty-seven people shaking hands quickly, and all saying the same thing in a different form: 'Thank you for delightful entertainment;' 'Most happy to have seen you;' 'Such a lovely time;' 'Your hospitality;' 'The honour;' 'Hope to see you in the States;' 'Will never forget;' 'Never expected;' 'The feature of our tour,' etc. I smiled almost too pleasantly over this ceremony.

In the morning paper I see that 'their Excellencies received the parties most graciously, and were quite as free from restraint as themselves.' One man told Fred to give his love to his mother, and tell her she had a good son.

SATURDAY, 20TH. – Directly after breakfast we went down to see Sir F. Graham off to England. Colonel and Mrs. Littleton came from Ottawa, and their children sail to-day. I was sorry to say good-bye to them, as it is another break-up of our life here.

The Littletons and Mr. Adams (son of the American Minister in London during the War), with a friend and a young Mr. Potter (son of an English M.P.) dined with us. Mrs. Littleton and I were left till 11.30 upstairs alone, the gentlemen having got into politics downstairs.

TUESDAY, 23RD. – Mrs. Littleton, Gwen, Baby and I drove out to Sillery, where the nuns received us most graciously. Then we went on to the Price's. They have a lovely place on the St. Lawrence, with some fine trees on the lawn and a good view of the river. There is a nice old-fashioned house and flower-garden, and we had tea, with strawberries and cream, and flowers to take home. D. rode there, and found a game of tennis going on when he arrived.

TUESDAY, 30TH. – D. remains another month, at the request of the Secretary of State [the Honourable Richard William Scott, a member of the Senate].

WEDNESDAY, 31ST. – We made up our minds to go out for tea, so drove off to Spencer Wood [the residence of the Lieutenant-Governor], where we sat on the grass and admired the view, and on leaving were presented by the gardener with three bouquets, one for each lady.

The papers are full of 'Our New Governor-General,' and all are delighted at the idea of having a Royal Princess here. [It had been announced that the Marquis of Lorne would succeed Lord Dufferin. His wife was Princess Louise, the fourth daughter of Queen Victoria.]

MONDAY, AUGUST 5TH. – The Roman Catholic Bishops of the Province of Quebec, who had been assisting at the consecration of the Bishop, called. There were seven or eight of them, gorgeous in purple and gold. The new Bishop of Chicoutimi (Racine) was one of the nicest. We heard of the death of the Apostolic Delegate, Dr. Conroy, Bishop of Ardagh. He died in Newfoundland.

TUESDAY, 6TH. – Sir Edward Thornton came to stay with us. At six we went on board the *Druid,* and dined there, as we were engaged to attend an amateur theatrical performance on the Island of Orleans. We landed at eight o'clock and drove to what had been a carpenter's shop, but was now converted into a 'Theatre Royal.' The 'green-room' was a tent.

In front of the stage there were banks of flowers, two little arbours in the corners, and seven figures dressed in powder and Dolly Varden costumes. You can't think how pretty they looked. There were tables spread with refreshments, and behind stood these Dresden figures ready to serve us.

When we had seated ourselves in the armchairs prepared, a little powdered, china-looking girl came and handed me a beautiful bouquet; another came with a painted programme; and between the scenes the grown-up China brought us ices, cake, and claret-cup.

The play was 'She Stoops to Conquer,' and it went off very well. The Tony Lumpkin was admirable, and the prima donna handsome. She is a Mrs. Watson, and had arranged the whole thing. The small figures got very sleepy and tired before the end; but they added greatly to the general effect, and amused us a good deal by the natural way in which they admired their own finery, and examined even the soles of their feet and their coloured heels.

We went to the hotel afterwards, where we were given supper; so that by the time we got to the Citadel it was nearly two.

WEDNESDAY, 7TH. – At eleven we went on the *Druid,* a party of fourteen, and sailed for Montmorency Falls. We landed in boats, and divided when we got ashore. Some went one side of the Fall, some the other, and some sat down and sketched. About three o'clock, having thoroughly enjoyed the sight, we went on board again, where luncheon was spread. Our party consisted of ourselves and A.D.C.'s, the Littletons, Stephensons, Herveys, Judge and Miss Johnston, Colonel Montizambert, the Spanish Consul, and Sir E. Thornton.

THURSDAY, 8TH. – Mrs. Littleton was offered the use of a steam-launch, and invited us all to go and see the Chaudière Falls. We puffed along quickly and had just one little fright when the funnel tumbled. However it was soon put up again.

We had to cross the Chaudière river in a scow. Then D. drove me in a buggy, followed by the others in various machines. We had a great climb to reach the best point of view, but were able to admire thoroughly the volumes of water and of spray and the rainbows which shone through them. D. made a sketch, and we sat idle and enjoyed ourselves till M. Chauveau [who at one time had been Speaker of the Senate] called us to have the champagne with which he had replaced my tea.

MONDAY, 12TH. – We started at one o'clock upon our tour in the Eastern Townships. After crossing the river in a steam-launch, steered by His Ex., we landed at Port Levi, and were presented with bouquets on the way to our car. It is a Grand Trunk private car, and very comfortable.

Our first stop was at Danville, where we had a drive through the town, and saw thousands of people who had come in from the country. We proceeded to Richmond, where we visited a college, and saw the town. Sherbrooke was the station we reached next, and a magnificent reception it gave us. It was dark when we stepped on to a platform, and saw before us a great crowd, brilliantly lighted buildings, and torch-bearers in red uniforms.

I must trust to the newspaper to describe the arches, the lights, the procession shooting up rockets in every direction. But I must mention one arch dedicated to me, and made by ladies. It had an enormous coronet of flowers, surmounting it, with 'Welcome to our Countess' on one side, and 'Kind hearts better than coronets' on the other. We are staying with Mr. and Mrs. Brooks; he is an M.P.

TUESDAY, 13TH. – We drove into Sherbrooke early, and visited a fine new bank, just built. We admired especially the burglar-proof safe, with a lock which, when set to a particular hour, can be opened by neither friend not foe until that hour arrives.

Next we visited the Fire Station, saw the stable-doors opened by machinery, and the horses step out, and fall into their own places in the various fire engines. After this we went to a convent, then to a great wool manufactory, where we saw everything, from wool in its filthiest state to the same article converted into fine cloth. D. was presented with the material for a pair of trousers, and Mrs. Littleton and I were each given beautiful rugs.

D. made a speech to the operatives and we proceeded to Lennox-ville. In the village there was an address, a platform and the usual etceteras, and at the College [Bishop's] and School the same. It is one of the best English schools in Canada, but the boys were away for the holidays. Two rivers pass by it, and the country round is real country.

We had about four miles to drive back to the house of Mr. Heniker [Chancellor of Bishop's], in Sherbrooke. It is situated on the banks of the Magog, and has a magnificent rapid and splendid rocks, and scenery many a great English landholder would give his fortune to possess in his park. Mr. and Mrs. Heniker gave us lunch.

On our return to the Brooks's we had to change quickly for a recep-tion. D. and the Colonel have to spend the night in the train. They meet Mr. Mackenzie [the Prime Minister] at Richmond, do business between the hours of twelve and two, and return here to breakfast in the morning.

WEDNESDAY, 14TH. – We began the morning by being photographed in groups at the door of Mr. Brooks's house. Then I planted a tree. We set off to drive to Compton, fifteen miles through such lovely country. The townships are so rich-looking, so undulating, and so well-wooded.

At the village of Compton Mr. Cochrane [Honourable Matthew Henry Cochrane, a member of the Senate] met us with a drag [a long uncovered carriage with seats around the sides] and four horses. He lives two miles from the village and has a wonderful farm ['Hillhurst Farm']. He is one of those people who get a thousand pounds for a calf, a hundred for a pig, etc.

The house and farm-buildings look so comfortable, and there is a conservatory, flower-garden, and tennis-court in front of the house. Mr. Cochrane has taken in our whole party. There were eighteen people at dinner, and we sat on the verandah afterwards, the grounds being illuminated with Chinese lanterns. Mr. and Mrs. Brooks dined here, and we said good-bye to them afterwards. They were extremely kind, and have entertained us most hospitably.

THURSDAY, 15TH. – We have been out all the morning examining prize cattle. First we inspected calves, bulls and pigs, and then we left the farm-yard and drove about the fields, looking at cows and Shetland ponies. There is a cow here called Tenth Duchess of Airdrie, which has made great sums of money. The views over the country are quite magnificent. I am glad we did not leave Canada without seeing this district.

After lunch we drove fifteen miles in the drag to Coaticook, a prettily situated village, and very flourishing before the hard times. After addresses, we walked to the Mayor's [Mr. L. Sleeper's] house, where we had a cup of tea before driving home. In the evening the neighbours drove over to be introduced, and we walked in the garden, which was lighted up.

FRIDAY, 16TH. – Having said 'Good-bye' to Mrs. Cochrane, her children, and her married daughter (Mrs. Baines), we took our places behind the gallant four, drove through beautiful country, stopping at Hatley, to Stanstead. We sat under the shade of some trees just before we got there, and had lunch.

Mr. Colby, the member for Stanstead, met us, and drove before us into the town. At its entrance we found a large corps of firemen, and the foremost presented D. with a harp made of water-lillies, from the ladies of the place. Suddenly we came upon a fine villa, where marching down the lawn with sprightly step came four or five ladies dressed in the extreme of the fashion – splendid in silks of blue and olive-green, red and pink, etc., waving in each hand a pocket-handkerchief. They were Americans, and came into the landscape of a quiet Canadian village most unexpectedly.

Stanstead is just on the border, and these Americans live half the year in Canada, and half in the States. We lunched with Mr. and Mrs. C. Pierce, and the beautiful ladies came over to his house, and the Governor of Vermont (Mr. Fairbank) met us. They were five widows, all sisters or daughters of his. Mrs. Fairbank sent me a bouquet.

We hurried over lunch to go to a school [Stanstead Wesleyan College], where there were two addresses. D. replied, and having had a little joke, which was highly appreciated, over the American Protection laws, made the people cheer the President of the United States and the Governor of Vermont.

In three buggies we drove twelve more miles to Georgeville, up and down mountains, to Lake Memphremagog, where Sir Hugh Allan's steamer met us. In her we spent an hour and a half going to Magog, where I now am, and where we arrived about ten o'clock. We were drawn a mile up to the hotel by boys and soldiers, replied to two addresses, admired the illuminations of every window, and were much too tired to eat the good food provided for us.

MAGOG: SATURDAY, 17TH. – Sir Hugh Allan came for us at ten, and we steamed up the lake in his yacht. There is a fine mountain in the centre, called the Owl's Head. Sir Hugh's own place [Belmere] is perfect; it is almost on an island. The house is on the top of a high hill, and the smooth grass slope up to it is planted with single trees. The forests of wood on either side, the boathouse and bathing-house, the tennis-lawn, the billiard-room, the bowling-alley, the large verandah, all combine to make it look beautiful and pleasant, while the views from it are splendid.

SUNDAY, 18TH. – Very showery and thundery, and a wretched day to spend in a country inn [the Park House]. We went to church, and were preached to by the Bishop of New Hampshire. He came to see us at lunch-time, and in the afternoon Mr. and Mrs. Brooks brought us the photographs taken of the group at their door, and of the arches at Sherbrooke – all very successful. He also gave me some beautiful specimens of minerals for my Canadian collection. After dinner we spoke to some of the people staying in the hotel who had helped to decorate it for us.

MONDAY, 19TH. – We left Magog by train for Bolton, where Mr. Huntington has a country place. [The Honourable Lucius Seth Huntington was at that time Postmaster General in the Mackenzie Administration.] The view from his house is lovely – a panorama of mountain scenery. It perhaps lacks water, for, although he has five lakes within three miles, one does not catch a glimpse of them from the windows.

An address was presented by the neighbours, while a very smartly dressed band played to us. In the drawing-room was a handsome decoration – the arms of England made in flowers. We had a pleasant lunch, and soon after continued our journey to Waterloo.

It is wonderful what these small towns do to welcome us. We come to a place of 4,000 inhabitants, and find regiments turned out, bands, arch after arch, platforms erected, flags, and all the country collected to meet us. Waterloo really gave us a very fine reception. The platform was well-made and convenient, and not only D. and I, but the whole Staff, were presented with bouquets by little girls dressed in white. Then there were speeches, and such cheers! The village has an English inhabitant, who prides himself upon his 'Hurrah,' and who led the applause.

We drove round the town in a procession, and I am sure D. ought to have blushed as he read the mottoes on the arches! Here are some of them: 'Votre séjour en Canada fournira une belle page dans notre

histoire.' 'Bienvenue la compagne de celui qui a conquis notre affection.' 'To Canada's favourite Ruler.' 'Farewell to him who has won
the hearts of all Canadians.' 'Favourite of the people.' 'Canada's Pride.'
'Il est la gloire du Canada.' 'Prudence, Energy, Charity.' 'Eternal sunshine settle on his head.' 'He is a right good Fellah.' Some of these
come from other places.

We dined and slept in our palatial car, and after sunset went out to
see the illuminations. D. drove round the town, but I sat on the
platform and watched an enormous bonfire burning in the middle of
the Square.

TUESDAY, 20TH. – We started for Granby, another small place, where a
wonderfully pretty reception was prepared. In front of the stage was a
large harp of flowers, which we afterwards put up on the end of our
train as we travelled about.

At West Farnham we merely got out at the station – address, flags,
cheers – and proceeded to Swestsborough, where we drove through
another village called Cowansville. D. generally has two replies to
make, and always one. He speaks extempore, and people like that.

St. Johns was our next point, and it was the end of our official tour.
It gave us a splendid reception; its one handsome street was beautifully decorated. When D. had answered the address both in French
and English (it was read in both languages), we drove to a handsome Roman Catholic church, and a china manufactory, where we
were given specimens of the work. We also saw the English Church,
and then got into our train, and started on a little holiday trip.

We stopped at Plattsburgh, which is in the States, and slept on
board the *Vermont*, a magnificent steamer, on Lake Champlain.

WEDNESDAY, 21ST. – We awoke 'at sea' on Lake Champlain, and sat on
deck and enjoyed the scenery. Ticonderoga is reached at one, and we
immediately got into a train, which in twenty minutes disgorged its
passengers on Lake George.

This is a smaller, very lovely lake. But I prefer Lake Champlain,
as the mountains are more distant. All along the Lake are little hotels,
where we stopped and exchanged travellers. At the end of the Lake
we came to our destination, Fort Henry. We took a quiet drive, and
dined at the hotel.

Such dresses! and such hats to be seen! But we were most amused –
in a melancholy way – by the children. They were dressed out with
the shortest of petticoats, the most magnificent silk and muslin and

lace dresses, the best of coloured silk stockings, and boots with large bows to match; such curls, and fans, and bracelets! And, above all, such airs, and such consciousness of deserving admiration! The way they came into the large dining-room by themselves, and often sat alone at a table, the girls looking twenty, and the boys rather naughty and undisciplined. This young generation living its hotel-life, with no duties, and no object but dressing itself and being admired, is a startling phenomenon.

We came in for a very good concert which Marie Roze, of the Italian Opera, happened to be giving to-night.

THURSDAY, 22ND. – Left the hotel early, and came down Lake George again and on to Ticonderoga, where we visited the old Fort before going on board the *Vermont* again.

We had another pleasant journey down Lake Champlain, and got into our car, in which we proceeded on our way to Montreal. There I found my English letters, for which I have been pining all the week. So ended our last Canadian 'official' tour.

SATURDAY, 24TH. – I received letters which oblige me to return home at once. It is a great disappointment to me to have to leave D. and Gwen, and it made us all very miserable.

FRIDAY, 30TH. – We went down to the *Druid* to say good-bye to the men, and to present the Captain with a telescope.

The improvements which D. suggested should be made at Quebec, with a view to preserving its old walls and gates, its picturesque appearance, and its ancient character, have been begun, and the 'Dufferin Terrace' promises to become one of the loveliest walks in the world.

SATURDAY, 31ST. – A final good-bye to Quebec, and to my happy Canadian life. And good-bye also, for a time, to D. and Gwen. The B Battery turned out to accompany me, and to fire a salute for me, and after the ship [the *Sardinian*] left the wharf they all cheered from the Citadel. Numbers of people came down to the steamer, though it was early in the morning that I left.

In one of his farewell speeches in Canada D. said: 'During a period of six years I have mingled with your society, taken part in your sports and pastimes, interested myself in your affairs and business, become one of you in thought and feeling, and never have I received at your hands, whether in my public or in my private capacity, anything but the kindest consideration, the most indulgent sympathy, and the warmest welcome.' This being so truly the case, no wonder that although the day itself was lovely, it was one of the most miserable I ever spent.

Lord Dufferin's Last Days in Canada

SEPTEMBER-OCTOBER 1878

After I left, D. received a deputation, consisting of the chief officers of all the municipalities of Ontario, who came to Quebec to present him with a joint address. The ceremony took place on the platform at the Citadel, and the deputations arrived, preceded by three Highland pipers dressed in the tartans of their respective clans. In his reply to them he spoke much of the Princess Louise and Lord Lorne, and said that, with regard to the latter, he only knew of one fault – 'of one congenital defect which attached to his appointment as Governor-General of Canada – he was not an Irishman.' Several other addresses were presented to D., and he was made a Doctor of Laval University.

Later he went to Toronto to open a provincial exhibition, and whilst there he visited institutions and made a number of speeches. It was at this time that he suggested in a letter to the Governor of New York State that the Governments of Canada and of the United States should join together to create an International Park at Niagara; that the troublesome touts and squatters, with their hideous shanties and wooden huts, should be got rid of; and that 'the locality should be restored to its pristine condition of wild and secluded beauty.' This project has since been carried out, and the islands in the Niagara River have been called after him.

Before D. finally left Canada there was a change of Ministry, and Mr. Mackenzie, who had been in power for over four years, having resigned, the departing Governor-General swore in Sir John Macdonald on October 17 at Montreal.

The last public act D. performed in Canada was to lay the foundation-stone of the Dufferin Terrace, and on October 19 he sailed from Quebec, receiving at the wharf a final Address from the citizens and residents of Quebec.

Despite their affection for the country and the people they had found so friendly, the Dufferins were never to visit Canada again. Diplomatic assignments took Lord Dufferin to Russia, to Turkey, and then to Egypt. In 1884 he was appointed Governor-General of India and remained there four years.

Their indefatigable travels and unceasing efforts to understand the problems of its myriad races did much to strengthen British rule in that far-eastern country. Communication was made easier by the promotion of railways. One of Lady Dufferin's great interests was to provide better medical care for the women of India. The Countess of Dufferin Fund solicited, and received, contributions from all parts of the country. Hospitals were established and women doctors were trained. It became a national organization, although administered locally by its various branches.

On October 23, 1887, the Dufferins celebrated their twenty-fifth wedding anniversary. Lady Dufferin wrote home:

The termination of a quarter of a century of life, almost unclouded by great sorrows and filled with many blessings, is a real epoch in one's history.

In 1886, Britain annexed Upper Burma, and the Dufferins travelled to Mandalay, and thence on to Ava, the ancient capital. There, Lord Dufferin was fascinated by the myriad towers and shrines, hills crowned with snow-white monuments, and spires rising from the jungle. Such an impression did this scene make that, when honoured by the Queen on his return from India, he chose as his new title, Marquess of Dufferin and Ava.

Further diplomatic appointments were received — two years in Rome, followed by five in Paris. Everywhere the story was the same. Their many journeys and deep personal concern in the interests of the people made them ambassadors of goodwill for Britain.

Tragedy struck in 1900, when Archie, their handsome son and heir to the title, was wounded in battle in South Africa, and died three days later. Thereafter their life was centred in London and around their home at Clandeboye. On February 12, 1902, just a few months before he and Lady Dufferin would have observed their fortieth wedding anniversary, Lord Dufferin died. Lady Dufferin survived her husband for thirty-four years. Her death came on the twenty-fifth of October, 1936.

Terence became his father's heir, second Marquess of Dufferin and Ava. Basil, the next younger son, the baby Lady Dufferin mentions in the first letter in this journal, was killed in action on July 3, 1917, while serving in the European war. When Terence died without an heir in 1918, Frederick, the youngest son, became the third marquess. The present peer, the fifth Marquess of Dufferin and Ava, is a direct descendant of this Frederick, who was born at Rideau Hall in Ottawa.

There are many reminders of the Dufferins' travels among Canadian people. There are Dufferin trophies, Dufferin bridges and Dufferin schools. But perhaps the one best known is Dufferin Terrace in Quebec City. There, from Lord Dufferin's design, was built a promenade which preserved much early Canadian history, while it provided a magnificent view over the majestic St. Lawrence River. And it was while gazing over that breath-taking panorama, brilliant with autumn colours, that Lady Dufferin wrote on September 21, 1872, the words which became historic — "this Canada of ours."

INDEX